D1143793

Sport Policy and Development

- Who makes sport policy and why do we need it?
- What is the purpose of sports development programmes?

Sport Policy and Development answers these questions and more by closely examining the complex relationships between modern sport, sport policy and development and other aspects of the wider society. These important issues are explored via detailed case studies of key aspects of sport policy and sports development activity, including:

- school sport and physical education
- social inclusion
- health
- elite sport
- sporting mega-events.

Each case study demonstrates the ways in which the sport policy and development fields have changed, and are continually changing in response to the increasing political, social and cultural significance of sport. The book helps the reader to understand the complexities of the sport policy-making process, the increasing intervention of government in the sport policy and development fields, and how the short-term, ever-changing and frequently contradictory political priorities of government come to impact on the practice of sport policy and development.

Accessible and engaging, this textbook is an invaluable introduction to sport policy and sports development for students, practitioners and policy-makers alike.

Daniel Bloyce is Senior Lecturer in the Sociology of Sport and Exercise and Co-Director of the Chester Centre for Research into Sport and Society at the University of Chester, UK. He is co-editor of the *International Journal of Sport Policy*.

Andy Smith is a Senior Lecturer in the Sociology of Sport and Exercise and Co-Director of the Chester Centre for Research into Sport and Society at the University of Chester, UK. He is co-editor of the *International Journal of Sport Policy*, and co-author of *Disability, Sport and Society* and *An Introduction to Drugs in Sport*. Both books are published by Routledge (2009).

Sport Policy and Development

An introduction

Daniel Bloyce and Andy Smith

LONDON AND NEW YORK

First published 2010
by Routledge
2 Park Square, Milton Park, Abingdon, Oxon, OX14 4RN

Simultaneously published in the USA and Canada
by Routledge
270 Madison Avenue, New York, NY 10016

Reprinted 2009

Routledge is an imprint of the Taylor & Francis Group, an informa business

© 2010 Daniel Bloyce and Andy Smith

Typeset in Sabon by Taylor & Francis Books
Printed and bound in Great Britain by CPI Antony Rowe, Chippenham, Wiltshire

British Library Cataloguing in Publication Data
A catalogue record for this book is available from the British Library

Library of Congress Cataloging in Publication Data
A catalog record for this book has been requested

ISBN10: 0-415-40406-1 (hbk)
ISBN10: 0-415-40407-X (pbk)
ISBN10: 0-203-89068-X (ebk)

ISBN13: 978-0-415-40406-8 (hbk)
ISBN13: 978-0-415-40407-5 (pbk)
ISBN13: 978-0-203-89068-4 (ebk)

For Ken Green – a mentor and friend, and also the person to be blamed for us writing this book!

Contents

Acknowledgements

We would like to thank the many people who, over many years, have encouraged us and contributed, directly or indirectly, to our development as sociologists and to the development of our thought in relation to sport policy and development. Particular mention should be made in the first instance to the students whom we have had the pleasure of teaching on our sport policy and development modules over the past few years. Discussion stimulated in lectures and seminars has helped strengthen our understanding and appreciation of the many issues involved. Several colleagues took the time to provide us with constructive criticism and insightful commentary on earlier drafts of various chapters of the book. For this we are extremely grateful and our special thanks go to: Fred Coalter, Ken Green, Patrick Murphy, Ken Roberts, Miranda Thurston, Ivan Waddington and, finally, the late Mick Green, whom we were unable to thank personally before his untimely passing.

We would also like to express our gratitude to Barrie Houlihan, with whom we have had the pleasure of working in our capacity as co-editors of the *International Journal of Sport Policy* (Routledge), for his ongoing professional support. We would also like to pay particular thanks to Brian Guerin and Simon Whitmore at Routledge for their continuous support and patience as we completed this book.

Finally, we would each like to pay tribute to our friends and family. Andy would like to pay special thanks to his parents and sister Jenny, for their ongoing support. I would also like to dedicate this book to Nan (the self-proclaimed 'boss'!) and to the memory of my other grandparents. Daniel would like to pay particular thanks to his Mum for her ongoing love and support. I would also like to thank Terry and Margaret Jameson, without the support of whom my house would not be in the pleasant state of décor that it currently enjoys! I would also like to thank Karen, for her love, support, understanding and commitment to the cause – and for being a critical friend in reading numerous chapters. Finally, I would like to dedicate this book to the memory of my dad, Michael Bloyce (1938–2008), who was a diligent and exceptional university lecturer who inspired me in all that I do.

Abbreviations

AAU	Amateur Athletics Union
AfPE	Association for Physical Education
AIHW	Australian Institute for Health and Welfare
AIS	Australian Institute of Sport
ASB	anti-social behaviour
ASC	Advisory Sports Council; Australian Sports Commission
BALPPE	British Association of Advisers and Lecturers in Physical Education
BISp	Bundesinstitut für Sportwissenschaft (Federal Institute of Sports Science)
BMA	British Medical Association
BMI	body mass index
BOA	British Olympic Association
BREEAM	Building Research Establishment Environmental Assessment Method
CAA	Comprehensive Area Agreement
CASM	Canadian Academy of Sport Medicine
CCPR	Central Council for Physical Recreation
CCRPT	Central Council for Recreative and Physical Training
CCT	compulsory competitive tendering
CDC	Centers for Disease Control and Prevention
CHD	coronary heart disease
CPA	comprehensive performance assessment
CSP	County Sports Partnership
CSL 2012	Commission for a Sustainable London 2012
DCMS	Department for Culture, Media and Sport
DCSF	Department for Children, Schools and Families
DETR	Department of the Environment, Transport and the Regions
DfES	Department for Education and Skills
DH	Department of Health
DHfK	Deutsche Hochschule für Körperkultur (German University for Physical Culture)
DIUS	Department for Innovation, Universities and Skills
DNH	Department of National Heritage
DPT	drugs prevention team
DSO	direct service organization
DVS	Deutsche Vereinigung für Sportwissenschaft (German Union of Sport Science)
EC	European Commission

EIS	English Institute for Sport
ESC	English Sports Council
ESD	elite sports development
EU	European Union
FA	Football Association
FKS	Forschungsinstitut für Körperkultur und Sport (Research Institute for Physical Culture and Sport)
FRG	Federal Republic of Germany
GDR	German Democratic Republic
GLA	Greater London Authority
GOE	Government Olympic Executive
HEPA	health-enhancing physical activity
IMD	Index of Multiple Deprivation
IOC	International Olympic Committee
IYS	Institute of Youth Sport
KKP	Knight Kavanagh and Page
LDA	London Development Agency
LEAP	Local Exercise Action Pilot
LOCOG	London Organizing Committee of the Olympic and Paralympic Games
LSC	Learning and Skills Council
LTAD	long-term athlete development
NAO	National Audit Office
NCAA	National Collegiate Athletic Association
NCF	National Coaching Foundation
NCPE	National Curriculum for Physical Education
NDP	National Demonstration Project
NDPB	non-departmental public body
NFPA	National Playing Fields Association
NGB	national governing body
NHS	National Health Service
NOF	New Opportunities Fund
NRG	Nations and Regions Group
NSO	national sports organization
NTSP	National Talent Search Program
NWDA	North West Development Agency
OCOG	Organizing Committee of the Olympic Games
ODA	Olympic Delivery Authority
Ofsted	Office for Standards in Education
PAT10	Policy Action Team 10
PCPFS	President's Council on Physical Fitness and Sports
PCT	Primary Care Trust
PDM	partnership development manager
PE	physical education
PEAUK	Physical Education Association of the United Kingdom
PED	performance-enhancing drugs
PESS	physical education and school sport
PESSCL	Physical Education, School Sport and Club Links strategy
PESSYP	Physical Education and Sport Strategy for Young People

PHAC	Public Health Agency of Canada
PI	performance indicator
PLT	primary link teacher
PSA	public service agreement
PVP	Pre-Volunteering Programme
SCW	Sports Council for Wales
SDC	Sports Development Council
SDOs	sports development officers
SEU	Social Exclusion Unit
SHA	Strategic Health Authority
SOCOG	Sydney Organizing Committee of the Olympic Games
SSC	specialist sports colleges
SSCo	school sports coordinator
SSP	School Sport Partnership
TASS	Talented Athlete Scholarship Scheme
TID	talent identification and development
UKSC	United Kingdom Sports Council
UKSI	United Kingdom Sports Institute
USOC	United States Olympic Committee
WHO	World Health Organization
WSP	Whole Sport Plan
WWF	World Wide Fund for Nature
YOT	youth offending team
YST	Youth Sport Trust

Introduction

In recent years the promotion and development of sport have become increasingly common features of government sport policy and sports-development-related activity in many countries (Bergsgard *et al.*, 2007; Coalter, 2007a; Houlihan and Green, 2008). This tendency has been strongly associated with the parallel tendency for government and other state agencies to become increasingly interventionist in setting the sport policy agenda and, hence, the sports development work that emerges from it. In this respect, there has been a growing willingness to use sport and physical activities as vehicles of social policy designed to achieve a range of other non-sport objectives. As Bergsgard *et al.* (2007) have noted, the increasing salience of sport to governments and their various policy agendas is an expression of the growing social and cultural significance of sport; the malleability of sport as a resource to help achieve non-sport policy goals (e.g. reducing youth crime and drug use, enhancing social inclusion, the promotion of health, and community regeneration); and the multidimensional character of sport where it is seen not only as 'a distinctive public service and, in many countries, an important aspect of overall welfare provision, but is also an important element of the economy in terms of job creation, capital investment and balance of payments' (Bergsgard *et al.*, 2007: 3–4).

The steady increase in government and state involvement in sport has not, however, been accompanied by a comparable growth in analyses of that involvement. This omission has been in marked contrast to other areas of public policy, especially the costly areas of national policy such as education, defence, health and welfare, but also in newer and more modestly funded policy fields such as environment and culture (Houlihan *et al.*, 2009). As Houlihan (2005: 164) noted in his survey of nine major English language journals from January 2001 to September 2003, 'only 3% of the articles utilised the extensive array of concepts, analytical frameworks and theories developed in mainstream policy analysis to aid … understanding of sport policy making and the role of government'. Between September 2003 and mid 2008 that proportion had increased slightly to 18 per cent, with the vast majority of articles providing perceptive analyses informed by theory and concepts drawn from other social sciences, especially sociology and cultural studies, and from the humanities, particularly history (Houlihan *et al.*, 2009). What was notable, however, was that too few of these articles acknowledged, and fewer still investigated, the role and increasing intervention of representatives of the state, other government agencies and the private sector, for example, in helping to set the sport policy agenda and influencing the development of modern sport more broadly (Houlihan *et al.*, 2009). We may begin to develop more adequate explanations of the complex relationships that exist between modern sport, sport policy and development and other aspects of the wider society, by enhancing the insights derived from these perspectives and complementing them with 'a more explicit and theoretically informed understanding of the process of sport policy-making and the role and significance of government and state agencies' (Houlihan *et al.*, 2009: 1). This is, then, a book that we hope begins to fill this gap in the existing literature. Our intention here is to make a modest contribution to our understanding of sport policy and development. Set in this context, it is worth making clear to the reader what this book is about and, equally importantly, what it is not about.

The purpose of this introductory text is to examine some of the complex relationships between modern sport, sport policy and development and other aspects of the wider society. It is also primarily intended for those either studying sport policy and sports development or who work in both these fields. In this regard, it is hoped that the content of the book will appeal to those who are following courses in a diverse range of subjects, including sport policy and development, sports studies, sport and exercise sciences, physical education (PE), as well as sociology, political science and policy analysis. In particular, it is hoped that our preference for focusing on detailed case studies of some key aspects of sport policy and sports-development-like work will help to broaden the appeal and readership of the book. The case studies are also intended to help demonstrate something about the ways and extent to which the sport policy and development fields have changed, and are continually changing. Although many of the case studies and examples provided in subsequent chapters come from Britain and, in some cases, primarily England, we have, wherever possible, sought to incorporate international research in order to demonstrate the cross-cultural and international relevance of the various topics to an understanding of sport policy and development.

In light of our preference for focusing on some of the major issues that characterize current sport policy and development activity via a case study approach, the book is not intended to be a comprehensive survey of all the possible issues that may have been explored. Indeed, such are the often short-term, ever-changing and frequently conflicting and contradictory political priorities of government that it is impossible – indeed, fool-hardy – to attempt to examine all of the various sport policy initiatives and sports development programmes that are currently in operation in Britain and elsewhere. It is perhaps almost inevitable, therefore, that we have left many stones unturned. There will be some readers who would have liked us to have included chapters on many other sub-jects than we have been able to here and some of which have appeared in other intro-ductory texts on sports development (e.g. Hylton and Bramham, 2008). Other readers may feel – quite rightly – that much more could have been said about each of the various topics that are covered in the book. Themes such as elite sports development, sport and social inclusion and sporting mega-events, among others, are deserving of books in themselves. Indeed, in many cases, several existing texts have begun to examine the complexities involved in studying these areas of sport policy and development. Amongst the many and more recent examples that could be cited in this regard include the work of De Bosscher *et al.* (2008), Green and Houlihan (2005) and Houlihan and Green (2008) on the extent of state investment in, and direction of, elite sports development systems. Together with Nicholson and Hoye's edited collection of essays that explore the complex relationships between sport and the development of social capital (Nicholson and Hoye, 2008), Fred Coalter's excellent book *A Wider Social Role for Sport: Who's Keeping the Score?* (Coalter, 2007a) provides an important and invaluable survey of the many and complex explanations for increasing governmental interest in sport, in particular the growing emphasis that has come to be placed on the use of sport to alleviate a variety of social problems. In relation to the complexities that surround the increasing social significance and importance of hosting sporting mega-events (e.g. the Olympic and Paralympic Games and soccer World Cup), Preuss (2004), Roche (2000) and Cashman (2006), for example, have all made valuable contributions to our understanding of this aspect of contemporary sport policy and development. Finally, mention should also be made of the substantial contribution by Barrie Houlihan to our understanding of the politics associated with various aspects of sport policy and development (e.g. Houlihan, 1991; 1997; 2005; Houlihan and White, 2002), especially youth sport (e.g. Houlihan, 2000; Houlihan and Green, 2006) and elite sports development (e.g. Green and Houlihan, 2004; 2005; 2006; Houlihan and Green, 2008). For these and many other reasons, this book is intended to complement the important, though at times competing, explanations that have been advanced in the field thus far. We hope that this will help us develop our understanding of the relationships that exist between sport policy and development and aspects of the wider society. We also hope to show, throughout this book, something of the ways in which a distinctly *sociological* approach to understanding these issues may hold out the promise of developing relatively adequate explanations of sport policy processes and the variety of sports development activity that emerges from them. It is now appropriate, therefore, to say something about the theoretical perspective that underlies this book.

The theoretical perspective of the book: figurational sociology

The general theoretical approach on which we have drawn in this book is that of figurational or process sociology, which has grown out of the work of Norbert Elias (1897–1990). As Houlihan *et al.* (2009) have noted, the writings and ideas of Elias and his figurational approach to sociology are coming increasingly to be used in analyses of policy processes both within sport (e.g. Bloyce *et al.* 2008; K. Green, 2008; Hanstad *et al.*, 2008; Murphy *et al.*, 1990; Waddington, 2000; Waddington and Smith, 2009; Williams *et al.*, 1984) and in policy contexts such as health service management (e.g. Dopson, 2005; Dopson and Waddington, 1996). However, until now it has not been consistently applied to the study of sport policy and development in the manner that we have attempted in this book. For the most part, the figurational perspective has been used here implicitly in order to limit the more explicitly theoretical aspects of the book and thus make it as accessible as possible to those who have an interest in sport but who do not have a grounding in sociological theory. The one exception to this is to be found in Chapter 1, where we have found it necessary to make more explicit reference to several of the key concepts and ideas that underpin Elias's approach in order to try to understand the realities of the sport policy-making process.

Figurational sociology is one among a number of competing paradigms within sociology but, over the past three or four decades, it has become a particularly well established theoretical framework within the sociology of sport. As Waddington and Malcolm (2008: 3) have noted, the work of Eric Dunning, together of course with Elias's own writings on sport, 'have helped to establish figurational sociology as a particularly influential theoretical framework within the sociological study of sport'. The prominence of figurational sociology within the study of sport leads us to accept Malcolm's view that 'the maturity of figurational sociology is now such that we can move away from extended theoretical re-statements and assume that such information is readily available elsewhere' (Malcolm, 2008: 261) (e.g. Bloyce, 2004; Dunning, 1999; Mennell, 1992; Murphy *et al.*, 2000; van Krieken, 1998). As a consequence we do not feel it necessary to provide a detailed outline of the principles of figurational sociology. Nonetheless, it is worth offering a brief overview of the figurational approach, and the manner in which it might be employed to help explain aspects of the sport policy process and the sports development work that emerges from it.

The central organizing concept of figurational sociology is, unsurprisingly, the concept of 'figuration' itself. Elias described a figuration as 'a structure of mutually oriented and dependent people' (Elias, 2000: 316). A central dimension of figurations or dynamic interdependency ties is power, conceptualized not as a substance or property possessed by particular individuals or groups but as a characteristic of all human relationships (Elias, 1978). Elias developed the concept of 'figuration' as a means of trying to overcome some of the difficulties associated with more conventional sociological terms and theories; in particular, he was critical of what he regarded as misleading and unhelpful dualisms such as that between the 'individual' and 'society'. The way in which Elias's approach helps to overcome such dualisms is perhaps best seen in his game models (Elias, 1978). His approach recognizes that human action is, to a greater or lesser extent, consciously directed towards achieving certain goals and that all human action necessarily involves both cognition and emotion. In this sense it fully takes into account the fact that humans are thinking and feeling animals and that, in the individualized societies of the West, we each have our own more or less individual pattern of intentions and preferences. However, Elias also emphasized that the outcomes of complex processes involving the interweaving of the actions of large numbers of people cannot be explained simply in terms of the intentions of individuals. Indeed, he suggests that the normal result of complex processes involving the interweaving of the more or less goal-directed actions of large numbers of people includes outcomes that no one has planned (Elias, 1978). As we explain in Chapter 1, in relation to the study of an area such as sport policy and development, Elias's approach indicates how policy processes and their outcomes can be seen as an expression of unequal power relations and differential relational constraints between groups of people whose interests and perceptions are likely to diverge. In subsequent chapters we also argue that many of the case studies on which we draw to illustrate aspects of sport policy and development activity are particularly useful ways of identifying and analyzing the figurations, or networks of relationships, of which sports development officers (SDOs) and others (e.g. policy-makers, government ministers and school teachers) involved in the organization and provision of sport are a part. This reveals the ways in which these figurations have both enabling and constraining effects on the actions of the groups involved. As we shall see throughout the book, the sheer complexity of the patterns of interaction, involving large numbers of people all of whom have an interest in sport policy and development, has had some important unintended outcomes. The unintended outcomes of the kind identified in this book are, we shall argue, not unusual aspects of social life. Indeed, it is important to recognize that, as Elias pointed out, the *normal* result of complex processes involving the interweaving of the goal-directed actions of large numbers of people includes outcomes that no one has chosen and no one has designed. As Mennell (1992: 258) has noted, for Elias, 'unanticipated consequences are not a curious footnote to sociology but nearly universal in social life'. It is hoped that this book, by drawing on Elias's work, may help to draw attention to this generally neglected aspect of policy-making within the world of sport generally and in sports organizations more particularly. One other key aspect of Elias's work on which we have drawn explicitly and which provides a central integrating theme for the book as a whole relates to Elias's writing on involvement and detachment.

As Murphy *et al.* (2000) have noted, one particularly distinctive characteristic of the figurational approach also worthy of consideration is Elias's position on the relationship between human understanding and values. This is an issue that has traditionally been discussed in abstract terms in which proponents have argued for 'objectivity' and 'subjectivity', for 'value-neutrality' or 'value-bias'. Elias (1987) explicitly rejected 'all or nothing' polarities such as these. It was his recognition of the relational complexities involved in all human relationships that led him to claim that 'researchers can realistically only aspire to develop explanations that have a greater degree of adequacy than preceding explanations' (Murphy *et al.*, 2000: 94). Elias argued, therefore, that we require 'a more adequate conceptualization of our ways of thinking about the world, and of the processes as a result of which our present, more scientific, ways of thinking about the world have developed' (Waddington and Smith, 2009: 4) beyond the all too prevalent tendency to think in terms of a mutually exclusive and radical dichotomy between objectivity and subjectivity.

Elias conceptualized the relationship between human knowledge and values in terms of degrees of involvement and detachment – a relational and processual conceptualization that helps us to examine the development, over time, of more object-adequate or reality-congruent from less object-adequate or reality-congruent knowledge (Elias, 1987; Murphy *et al.*, 2000). He did so on the premise that it is neither possible nor, for that matter, desirable to attain complete detachment or involvement. In that respect, Elias did not conceptualize the relationship between involvement and detachment in dichotomous terms, or as a simple equivalent of that between objectivity and subjectivity. He instead considered it as a continuum along which blends of involvement (that is, conducive to more fantasy-laden and mythical thinking) and detachment (that is, conducive to the production of more reality-congruent or object-adequate knowledge) are located (Elias, 1987; Murphy *et al.*, 2000). Elias summarized the challenges faced by sociologists in combining an effective balance between their involvement with and detachment from the processes and phenomena they study in the following way:

> The problem confronting [sociologists] is not simply to discard (their more involved, political) role in favour of … [a more detached, scientific one]. They cannot cease to take part in, and to be affected by, the social and political affairs of their group and time. Their known participation and involvement, moreover, is itself one of the conditions for comprehending the problems they try to solve as scientists. For while one need not know, to understand the structure of molecules, what it feels like to be one of its atoms – in order to understand the functioning of human groups one needs to know, as it were, from the inside how human beings experience their own and other groups, and one cannot know without active participation and involvement.
>
> The problem confronting those who study one or the other aspects of human groups is how to keep their two roles as participant and enquirer clearly and consistently apart and, as a professional group to establish in their work the undisputed dominance of the latter.
>
> (Elias, 1956: 237)

Thus, in order to understand more adequately the reality of the sport policy process and sports-development-like activity, it is imperative that we seek to achieve in our work greater degrees of detachment in the hope that this will help to maximize the development of knowledge that is more reality-oriented and that is less mythical and fantasy based. Attempts to examine problems of this kind are best achieved, Elias (1987) argued, not directly, but by means of a 'detour *via* detachment' in which those who are able to hold their ideological orientations 'in check', as it were, throughout the course of their research are more likely to generate explanations that have a higher degree of reality-congruence than preceding explanations (Dunning, 1999; Elias, 1987; Murphy *et al.*, 2000). That is, assuming we do not get lost along the way, if we as sociologists are able to successfully undertake a detour via detachment it should help us to produce knowledge about the sport policy-making process and related sports development work that complements existing knowledge, or, when compared against existing explanations, knowledge that has a greater degree of adequacy and that is more reality-congruent than previously (Elias, 1987).

It is a leitmotif of the figurational approach, like many other sociological and disciplinary approaches, that scientific work rests upon an indivisible interdependence between, and interpretation and observation of, theoretical and empirical work that contributes to the development of funds of social-scientific knowledge that 'becomes *more extensive, more correct, and more adequate*' (Elias, 1978: 53; emphasis in the original) continuously and cumulatively over time. In other words, at the heart of the analysis we attempt to offer of the various case studies in this book is the need to ensure that there is a constant dynamic interplay between our theoretical assumptions and empirical observations. This, we contend, is important because it is just one means by which it is necessary to move 'in the direction of that blend between involvement and detachment which is most conducive to [developing more] reality-congruent knowledge' (Dunning, 1992: 253). It is also impor-tant for, as we shall discuss in Chapter 1, analyses of the nature of sport policy-making and sports development work are characterized by a relative lack of detachment, by a high commitment to ideological or extra-scientific concerns and by a high level of emo-tional involvement. It is more likely that the resulting explanation will end up allocating praise or blame rather than enhancing our level of understanding of the reality of sport policy processes and of the relational constraints that come to impact upon the day-to-day work of sports development officers (SDOs). It is therefore a central and necessary task for any researcher, and not just figurational sociologists, motivated by a desire to advance knowledge and understanding to subject to critical scrutiny the ideologies and mythologies surrounding social phenomena (including sport) that they are studying. Indeed, such is the strength of the prevailing ideologies that surround what Coalter calls the 'mythopoeic nature of sport' (Coalter, 2007a: 22), there is a real 'need to think more clearly, analytically and less emotionally about "sport" and its potential' (Coalter, 2007a: 7). In doing this we need to examine many of the assumptions and premises upon which sport policy and development work rests.

The search for a relatively detached understanding of the complex relationships between sport policy and development and of the realities of sports development activity constitutes the central objective of this book. Our perspective, it should be noted, almost inevitably leads us to be critical of much existing policy and the development work on which it is based. Such policies frequently bear the hallmark of ideology and are based on a one-sided and uncritically accepted view of sport rather than a relatively detached analysis of the processes involved. In this respect, we have sought in this book to develop a more realistic and adequate understanding of sport policy and development and, where relevant, to question some of the taken for granted assumptions that surround many of the issues that we examine. Despite the criticisms that we make in this regard, it should be stressed that our objective in this book is *not* to engage in easy expressions of moral indignation about the nature of sport policy and work of sport policy-makers and SDOs but, rather, to enhance our understanding of these issues. Our primary objective is therefore an academic one – to enhance our sociological understanding of sport policy-making and sports development activity. However, it should be noted that a better understanding of aspects of sport policy and development is a precondition for more effective policy formation and implementation, whatever our policy goals may be. In this sense, it may be argued that, as Waddington and Smith (2009: 8) have noted, 'there is nothing as practical as good theory'. It is hoped, therefore, that this book will have some value not merely in academic but also in policy formation terms. This is important, for, as Elias noted, 'sociology, in particular, is failing in its task if its research cannot be made fruitful for other disciplines' (Goudsblom and Mennell, 1998: 172). In our case, such disciplines that may stand to benefit from the insights that may be derived from a sociological analysis include the fields of sport policy and development. More particularly, we hope that the analysis provided in the book will have some policy relevance for those working in these disciplines, for, as Keech has rightly noted:

> Applied policy analysis is often seen to be of little relevance to practitioners, whether they are teachers or sports development professionals. What counts, apparently, is whether or not the individual is able to do 'their job'. Agreed – but only in part! Many of those who work in Physical Education, physical activity or sport development often became involved through their enjoyment of sport and/or activity, but now fail to realise that they work within a highly politicised environment. Within ongoing debates about professional development, it is proposed that until practitioners develop a greater strategic awareness of the complex policy context within which they operate, they will not be fully able to realise why policy doesn't always work in practice and therefore lobby more effectively for the resources required to fulfil their responsibilities and do 'their job'.
>
> (Keech, 2003: 211)

It is hoped that this book may contribute in some small way to making the relevance of such a sociologically informed approach clear to practitioners. In this regard, we consider this introductory text as nothing more than a symptom of a beginning in the pursuit of developing a more adequate sociological explanation of the reality of sport policy-making and of sports development activity. We would stress, however, that in doing so we have not attempted to provide *the* definitive sociological account of the subject matter but *an* interpretation of it. We hope that, if nothing else, the book provides a starting point on which others can build and that it may encourage others to undertake greater systematic study of sport policy and development. We do not for one moment labour under the misconception that this book is in any way a definitive account of the sport policy and development figuration. In our view there is, and can be, no such animal. It is, of course, for the reader to form her/his own view on the extent to which we achieve what we take to be our modest objectives.

Terminology: what is sport policy and development?

Perhaps the first point worthy of note is that it is especially difficult to define and demarcate the scope of sport policy from other policy areas (Bergsgard *et al.*, 2007), such is the increasing willingness of government and policy-makers to draw upon the perceived malleability of sport to help achieve a wide range of different policy objectives to which it is expected to contribute. In this regard, Houlihan and White (2002: 80) argue that 'sports development is at best a series of overlapping policy objectives and associated processes'. It is not our intention here, then, to provide an overview of the various 'models' of sports development (see Hylton and Bramham, 2008). This is because, useful though the literature that examines the various models of sports development is, most of it is prescriptive: it describes not how sports development exists in practice in the real world but how, in an ideal world, it ought to be organized and structured, and, in this respect, most of the literature is not empirically grounded. What is arguably more important is not a description of what should happen in the name of sports development, or what sports development should look like in theory. Rather, what are required are more empirically based explanations of how sport policy and development exist and are delivered in practice, and, in that respect, it is intended that this book will begin to provide explanations of this kind.

It is also important to note that the term 'sports development' and the profession to which it refers are more widely known – in name at least – in the United Kingdom than elsewhere in Europe and beyond. It is, however, difficult to identify precisely what the day-to-day role of an SDO, in both local authorities and national governing bodies (NGBs) of sport, entails. At first sight, their main priorities are to develop sport and provide sporting opportunities for local residents and other identified target groups (Bloyce *et al.*, 2008; Eady, 1993; Houlihan and White, 2002). However, as Houlihan and White (2002: 2) have noted, the 'title of sports development officer is by no means universally adopted by those who are clearly involved in similar work'. Their roles and responsibilities are typically ambiguous and difficult to define, and these can often vary considerably within and between local authorities and NGBs. In a not dissimilar way, Nesti (2001: 196) has pointed out that 'it remains a difficult, and some would argue impossible task, to identify the exact point at which it is legitimate to talk about the beginning of sports development work'. To this he adds that, given the difficulties associated with delineating clearly the boundaries of sports development work and the precise roles and responsibilities of SDOs, it can properly be said that 'sports development is the concern of a much broader group than SDOs' (Nesti, 2001: 197). This is a point that, as we explain in subsequent chapters, is increasingly apposite at a time of rapidly changing social and political policy in many countries. Such are the frequent organizational changes that typically result from the dynamic political and social policy climate, the nature of sports development work and the job of an SDO are almost terminally unstable. This is largely because sport policy initiatives and programmes shift with what has been perceived by some within the profession as monotonous regularity, and as some initiatives and development workers increasingly pass through what amounts to an ever-revolving-door policy as SDOs are increasingly expected to contribute to a range of competing policy agendas (Bloyce *et al.*, 2008; Collins *et al.*, 1999). Despite the uncertainty that surrounds the jobs of sports development professionals and the often vague, contentious definitions of sports development and the roles and responsibilities of SDOs, it may nevertheless be said that a more or less key aspect of sports development is getting more people involved in sport. It also appears to be the case that, as we shall attempt to demonstrate in Chapters 3–7, those working in sports development in the current social and political policy climate are expected to try to use a range of sports and physical activities in order to achieve this objective (Bloyce *et al.*, 2008; Houlihan and White, 2002).

The structure of the book

Given that until now few texts have attempted to bring together in one volume a range of topics that begin to examine some of the key issues that surround sport policy and development, we have deliberately sought to ensure that each chapter provides the reader with an introductory guide to a number of key issues that begin to help us make socio-logical sense of the relationship between sport policy, sports development work and aspects of the wider society. Whilst we hope that some readers would be interested in reading the book from cover to cover, to try to make the book as accessible as possible to the reader, we have deliberately set out to provide a text that contains chapters on discrete topics that can be read in any order. Indeed, they could be used as part of a broader area of study than sport policy and development. The one exception to this is Chapter 1 – entitled 'The sport policy process: a sociological perspective' – which should be read in conjunction with each of the other chapters. It is our contention that in order to understand something about the other key issues that are explored in the book it is helpful for the readers to have some appreciation of the various phases and components of the sport policy process and to explore how these can come to impact on the day-to-day activities of sports development work. In all cases, however, each chapter begins with a series of objectives that indicate the content to be explored and concludes with a list of further reading, useful websites and a series of revision questions that may be used as part of further discussions on the issues raised.

In Chapter 1 we outline the beginnings of a figurational approach to the study of policy processes that, we believe, can help to explain these processes more adequately on a theoretical level. We also attempt to convey something of the ways in which our sociological approach can be of some practical relevance for policy-makers and SDOs who are faced in the course of their day-to-day activities with constraints that come to limit the extent to which they are able to achieve their own personal and/or group interests and objectives. Throughout the chapter we stress the need to focus upon iden-tifying and analyzing the figurations, or networks of relationships, of which SDOs and policy-makers involved in the organization and provision of sport are a part. This, we hope, helps to reveal the ways in which these figurations have both enabling and con-straining effects on the actions of the participating groups. A consideration of these and related issues, we argue, is a vital prerequisite for understanding adequately the realities of sport policy-making processes and the impacts these have on the operations and practice of sports development work. Chapter 2 then examines the emergence and development of sport policy in Britain, and particularly England, since the 1960s. It also considers some of the major changes to the organization and administration of sport over the last half-century or so before focusing, in particular, on the recent policy agendas of government where an increasingly explicit emphasis has come to be placed on the achievement of non-sport policy goals alongside other sports-related objectives. Chapter 3 focuses on youth sports development policy and the adequacy of the assumptions that underpin those policies. In particular, the chapter explores the growing political importance of PE and school sport (PESS) and the emergence of the Youth Sport Trust (YST) as the insti-tutional focus for PESS in England. The chapter also draws on a case study of one of the most significant youth sports development policies to have been introduced in schools in England in recent years, namely, the Physical Education, School Sport and Club Links (PESSCL) strategy, which has since been retitled the Physical Education, School Sport and Young People (PESSYP) strategy. It does so in order to show how the development of the School Sport Partnership (SSP) programme, as one component of the PESSCL strategy, has become one of the most important overarching infrastructures through which government has attempted to achieve its sports-specific goals and non-sport objectives related to PESS and youth sports development in schools.

A case study approach also forms the basis of the analysis presented in Chapter 4. We explore how one consequence of the increasing intervention of government in sport policy-making has been that sport policy priorities have shifted away from the development of sport and the achievement of sport-related goals towards the use of sport to achieve other desired social objectives such as the promotion of social inclusion. To convey something of the ways in which the social inclusion agenda has impacted upon aspects of community sports development, the chapter draws on several high-profile sports-based social inclusion initiatives. These include the Barclays Spaces for Sports programme, the Kickz – Goals Thru Football programme, and anti-crime and drug-reduction schemes such as the various Positive Futures projects currently in operation in the UK. In doing so, we conclude that, perhaps with the exception of some Positive Futures projects and despite the strong and increasing political policy commitment to the social inclusion agenda, there is currently little hard evidence of the effectiveness of sports-based schemes in reducing the complex causes of social exclusion, particularly levels of crime, drug use or anti-social behaviour among identified target groups. Chapter 5 continues with the theme of how sport has been used as a driver for non-sport objectives. Health is seen to be something that is synonymous with sporting participation, and it is perhaps no surprise that governments have consistently subscribed to the notion that sport can be used as a tool to develop good health. In this chapter we analyse the ways in which sport and physical activity have been identified in policies around the world as a tool with which to deal with growing levels of obesity. In doing so, the distinction between sport and physical activity has become increasingly blurred. However, we argue that it is important to distinguish between sport and other forms of physical activity, since competitive sport carries with it potential health risks, often ignored by policy-makers. Furthermore, we highlight in this chapter, through a case study of the development of health policies in the UK, how sports professionals have been increasingly constrained to become involved in health promotion activities. The 'role' of the SDO has, in this sense, become ever more fluid.

In the final two chapters we turn our attention to elite sports development. In Chapter 6 we examine the ways in which elite sports development (ESD) systems have become increasingly prevalent in many developed nations around the world. In the main, although we argue that the American collegiate system developed many of the characteristics of such systems earlier than was the case elsewhere, as far as government-sponsored and government-led ESD systems are concerned, the countries of the former Eastern bloc were key to their development. After the Second World War, East Germany and the Soviet Union developed ESD systems that clearly made no small contribution to the Olympic success experienced by these two countries. So successful were they that the ESD systems quickly came to be emulated in several Western countries. Once again, we use a case study of the development of the key characteristics of such ESD systems in the UK, a relative latecomer to such clinical focus on ESD. We conclude the chapter by arguing that the inter-state rivalry that is central to our understanding of the spread of ESD systems around the world has contributed to diminishing contrasts between the ways in which athletes in these countries are prepared for international sporting competitions. At the same time, however, there are prevailing national characteristics within each ESD system that, it might argued, have contributed to increasing variety in the adopted approaches to ESD. In the final chapter, Chapter 7, we examine how sports mega-events have influenced domestic and international sport policy and development. By focusing primarily on the Olympic Games, we examine how and why competition to bid for the Games has become so intense. Over the last twenty years or so there has been a significant focus on the legacies that are said to emerge from hosting the Games, most notably after the widely heralded Summer Olympics in Barcelona in 1992. As the intensity to compete with other bids increases and the apparent desire to better all previous Games plays heavily on the mind, we argue that the people behind the bids, and, most especially, their government backers, are increasingly constrained to play up the apparent legacy benefits of hosting the Games. Amongst these are economic growth, urban regeneration, and even social inclusion and sustainable development. We focus our attention in the second half of the chapter on the bid and the build-up to the 2012 Games to be held in London. It is clear that legacies are central to the bid process, and the fact that the 2012 Games are to be hosted in the UK has had, unsurprisingly, a significant impact on sport policy in broader terms.

1 The sport policy process
A sociological perspective

Objectives

This chapter will:

- examine a figurational approach to the study of the policy-making process;
- outline the key interdependent features of the policy-making process; and
- identify the practical relevance of a sociological understanding of the policy process for sports development practitioners.

Introduction

As we explained in the Introduction, the general theoretical perspective that underlies this book is that of figurational or process sociology. We also noted that although there is a large and expanding literature on the nature of sports development and the sport policy process generally, very little has been written about these issues from a distinctly *sociological* perspective. The objective of this chapter is to begin to lay the foundations for a specifically figurational understanding of the sport policy process. In doing so, it attempts to outline how these concepts and assumptions can be of practical relevance for policy-makers and SDOs who are charged with the formulation and implementation of effective sport policy 'on the ground'. In this regard, by focusing on the dynamic networks of relationships or human figurations in which policy-makers and SDOs are embroiled, the chapter examines the various stages in the policy process (such as how a policy issue comes to be defined as such, the objectives and priorities of policy-makers, and monitoring and evaluation processes) and, in particular, the unplanned outcomes that result from the complex interweaving of the intended actions of those involved.

Conceptualizing the policy process

Perhaps the first question that we need to ask ourselves before explaining the dynamics involved in the policy process is: what actually constitutes policy? The answer may seem fairly obvious, but, as we will see throughout the rest of this book, the formulation and implementation of certain sport 'policies' can be criticized on the basis that the 'policy' does not constitute a policy whatsoever, and is more a 'statement' of intent or description of a 'problem'. Due to its rather ambiguous and contested nature it is difficult to conceptualize adequately what is meant by the term 'policy' (Houlihan and White, 2002). It seems reasonable to suppose, however, that all policies can be viewed as involving the following overlapping and interrelated features: human action aimed at achieving certain objectives; human action aimed at resolving, or at least ameliorating, an identified 'problem'; and human action aimed at maintaining or modifying relationships within an existing organization, between different organizations, or a human figuration of some other kind (Murphy, 1998; Smith and Platts, 2008). In addition, as the British Medical Association (BMA) (2002) has noted, the search for effective responses to a range of social problems – such as the use of performance enhancing drugs in sport and the improvement of the nation's health – is also fundamental to any public policy, even though this will, inevitably, involve value judgements by those concerned. In this regard, they add that 'in an ideal world' problems of these kinds would 'be self-evident, solutions would be based on a detailed understanding of the issues, objectives would be clear and progress toward them measurable, and there would be lasting commitment from policy makers' (BMA, 2002: 89).

However, we do not live in an ideal world and it is clear that the policy process rarely follows the neat, rational models of change set out in some of the literature, and many sport and other public policies are rarely based upon a detailed, evidence-based and relatively detached understanding of the problems that they purport to tackle (BMA, 2002; Coalter, 2007a; Dopson and Waddington, 1996; Waddington and Smith, 2009). In light of such problems, then, how can we begin to conceptualize the policy process in reality? How is it possible to begin to advance our *sociological* understanding of the complexities involved? How are the actions of policy-makers and other groups involved enabled and constrained by the wider relational networks of which they are a part?

Before we examine these issues, it is important to remind ourselves that any study of the complexities involved in the policy process is fraught with several difficulties, the most important of which is that we are always dealing with the study of dynamic, complex social processes or human figurations. Indeed, we are ourselves in process, and part of broader social processes. It is for these reasons that we can only realistically aspire to explain the relational complexities involved in the sport policy process more adequately (Murphy, 1998; Smith and Platts, 2008). As with our knowledge of broader social processes more generally, it would be foolhardy to suggest that it is possible to have a complete understanding – or, indeed, anything approaching it – of the processes involved. In this regard, what follows is an attempt to begin to conceptualize and come to some understanding of the policy process in reality. While this process has, for analytical reasons, been conceptualized in terms of a series of phases and constituent elements, as falling into a particular sequence, we are acutely aware of the shortcomings of this approach. The reality is that, like colours in the colour spectrum, these aspects of the policy process shade into each other; they frequently overlap, fuse and merge in complex ways and often occur simultaneously. In the following analysis, we have, therefore, attempted to offset the limitations of this approach and to convey something of the dynamic interdependence between the component parts involved in the various phases that make up the policy process. The analysis represents a particular stage in our understanding of the policy process and is, of course, constructed on the basis of our theoretical insights and empirical observations, many of which derive from the figurational framework employed in this book. At the very least we hope that it will help the reader to think and ask important questions about the nature of the problems that policy-makers face and the situations they wish to change, the adequacy of their objectives, the problems they are likely to encounter, and the outcomes that may result from the various strategies that might be pursued to tackle such problems.

The definition of policy 'issues'

As Dopson and Waddington (1996: 546) have noted, the policy process involves 'many people at different levels within and outside the organisation, and the extent to which different groups are committed to or opposed to the prevailing policy, and the strategies which they adopt in relation to that policy, play an important part in determining its outcome'. Indeed, within particularly complex organizations and other human figurations, different groups are differentially constrained to pursue their own perceived interests, which may or may not coincide, or only very partially coincide, with those of other groups, and which may also be at distinct variance with those of others (Dopson and Waddington, 1996; Smith and Platts, 2008). It is a vital prerequisite in any study of the policy process, therefore, that we focus on the differential patterns of interdependencies that characterize the relational networks within which policies are formulated and implemented, for it is not adequate to focus exclusively on the values, priorities and intentions of the groups involved. More particularly, for figurational sociologists it is only possible to understand adequately the likely effectiveness of sport policies by recognizing the wider human figurations within which sport policy-makers, SDOs and other interested groups are embroiled, and the tensions, conflicts and degrees of consensual elements that characterize these dynamic power relationships. Such an approach also helps us to begin to anticipate some of the unintended, unplanned outcomes – to be examined in more detail later – that inevitably result from the combined actions of the groups involved, and the associated power struggles that accompany the implementation of any proposed policy reforms. This is not only important on a theoretical level, but is also of practical relevance for policy-makers, who, like all human beings, are never able to understand fully 'the constraints within which either they or other key players work and, as a consequence, they frequently misunderstand, or at best only very partially understand, the actions and intentions of other players' (Dopson and Waddington, 1996: 545).

When conceptualized in this way it becomes clear that all policies begin life as issues that develop and change over time and out of existing human relationships. They also vary over time and from one society to another, as some groups are more able to take up interests in some developments whilst simultaneously ignoring others in order to sustain, protect and advance their own interests (Murphy, 1998). In this regard, the foregoing problems have come to be defined as such by groups who, because of the particular relational constraints that they experience, are better able to pursue, to a greater extent than are other groups, their own priorities. They are also more likely to be able to develop more effective and coordinated action in relation to policy formation. Such groups are also often better able to define what constitute social problems or 'issues' for which some kind of remedial action, in the form of policy, is warranted and can come to determine the policy objectives and priorities to be pursued. By contrast, those who are less enabled by their particular relational constraints are often less likely to develop policy and tend to be those groups who are less integrated and who lack sufficient requisite coordination to bring about desired change through the formulation and implementation of policy. In this regard, the policy-making process involves the selection of actions and strategies to move from one unsatisfactory position to an alternative, more satisfactory position (Murphy, 1998; Smith and Platts, 2008). The construction of sport policy, like all other areas of policy, presupposes a commitment among those individuals and groups involved who are better able to develop various activities that enable them to bring about desirable change in ways that other individuals and groups may not.

Placing human figurations at the heart of our analysis of the policy process helps, therefore, to reveal the ways in which these figurations that enable and constrain action consist of different groups of people often seeking to maintain, protect and advance their individual and/or group interests. It also helps to point towards how policy processes and their outcomes can be seen as an expression of the differential constraints and unequal power relations between groups of people whose interests and perceptions are likely to diverge (Elias, 1978; 1987). These dynamic power relational networks involve several groups with differing perceptions and interests: those who are enthusiastic about change; those who are willing to go along with the proposed policy changes with some misgivings; those who are against the proposed changes; and those who are completely opposed to the policies being proposed (Dopson and Waddington, 1996; Elias, 1978; 1987). As we shall see in the remaining chapters of this book, the sheer complexity of the patterns of interaction, involving large numbers of people all of whom have an interest in sport policy and development, often has some important unplanned outcomes. Those involved in the planning and implementation of policy, however, rarely reflect upon the possible side-effects (both more immediate and longer term) of pursuing a particular policy. Of course, this is not altogether surprising given the external constraints that policy-makers and SDOs are frequently under 'to do something' about the problems with which they are faced. But what are the likely outcomes that arise out of the tendency for sport policies to be based upon claims that have a high fantasy content that is 'emotionally much more attractive for people than knowledge which is more reality-oriented' (Elias, 1987: 67)? In other words, what are the issues and likely outcomes facing policy-makers and SDOs whose activities are premised upon policies that frequently offer 'fantasy laden solutions to social problems' (Elias, 1978: 27)? What are the benefits of having an appreciation of some of the possible side-effects of pursing a particular policy?

Perhaps the first point to note in this regard is that for some groups (in particular increasingly interventionist government ministers and policy-makers) the primary objective of their work is to try to stimulate change designed to reduce or eliminate particular perceived social problems, or to claim for sport things that help to protect their own vested interests. Such an approach, however, tells us rather more about the particular values and prejudices of those groups and tends to reinforce, rather than challenge, the widely held beliefs and myths surrounding the policy issues under examination. Indeed, much of the heavily value-laden character of many existing sport policies has the effect of obscuring, rather than clarifying, the development of a more adequate understanding of the problems they are designed to tackle, and constitutes a poor basis for future policy formation (Coalter, 2007a; Dopson and Waddington, 1996; Smith and Platts, 2008; Waddington and Smith, 2009). One consequence of the tendency for much policy to be 'saturated' with ideology and premised upon a lack of evidence is that many policy problems 'are often poorly defined and constantly evolving; policy solutions are frequently selected on the basis of a poor understanding of the problem, or because they fulfil some other need, such as that for a quick, cheap and visible response; objectives are frequently poorly specified and sometimes not specified at all; and evaluation of implementation is rarely budgeted for' (BMA, 2002: 89).

A further problem of conceptualizing the likely outcomes that emerge from pursuing particular policy options is that of the deep-rooted tendency among policy-makers and government ministers towards thinking about social phenomena such as sport and the issues surrounding sport in 'present-centred' terms (Elias, 1978; Goudsblom, 1977). This deep-rooted tendency to understand various sport policy issues, like many other social policy issues, from an all too-limiting and present-centred view usually means that, among other things, many sport policy-makers and development officers rarely attempt to understand how perceived problems have come to be the way they are. Still less are such groups constrained to think about the whole range of implications this poses for the formulation of future policy. As Elias (1978) has noted, this is not altogether surprising for there has been a long-term and increasing tendency among those involved in planning and implementing policy to make deliberate and conscious attempts at managing social change. This is a process that, it should be noted, is part of broader unplanned developments that have provided the basis for the kinds of planned programmes in which policy-makers and SDOs are now themselves involved (Dopson and Waddington, 1996).

The tendency for policy-makers and SDOs to ignore the significance of the long-term interweaving of planned and unplanned processes arises out of the fact that they 'are all too often involved in networks of relationships which constrain them to deliver results in the short-term' (Dopson and Waddington, 1996: 535). In particular, these groups are increasingly involved in policy planning and change that is concerned with the here and now and, in that respect, they frequently emphasize the benefits of a present-oriented and practically led approach to policy planning over one that is more theoretically informed and developmental in character (Coalter, 2007a; Dopson and Waddington, 1996). This tendency has become further exacerbated since the late 1990s by the vulnerability of sport as a policy area in which the participating groups, especially policy-makers and SDOs, are under increasing 'pressure to deliver short-term outcomes in a relatively short window of opportunity' (Coalter, 2007a: 44) and because the policy status of sport increasingly depends on the ability of such groups to 'prove its cross-cutting value' (Coalter, 2007a: 44).

There are several problems with adopting such a present-centred approach to policy planning. The need to engage in a longer-term developmental analysis of the structural roots of the perceived social problems with which policy-makers are faced and to detach themselves, insofar as it is possible, from their own entrenched ideological preconceptions is vital to the process of policy formation. This is because

> it is only through striving to understand long-term processes that we can move towards obtaining an orientation that is sufficiently wide-ranging and reality-congruent to enable us to decide whether short-term practical measures designed to overcome difficulties and disadvantages will not, in the longer term, produce difficulties and disadvantages that are even greater.
>
> (Dopson and Waddington, 1996: 535)

It is our contention, then, that if policy-makers and SDOs wish to improve the effectiveness of their programmes, and to appreciate what realistically their strategies are likely to achieve, then it is important that they examine policy problems, not from an overly involved position, but from a relatively detached and longer-term developmental per-spective. Of course, we appreciate that it is very difficult within the heat of the struggle for sport policy-makers and development officers to stand back and try to develop such a relatively detached view. We are also aware that it is difficult for these groups to begin to translate into practice – should they be inclined to do so – the insights that could be derived from engaging in the foregoing type of abstract sociological reflection. However, we are of the view that 'those who are able to do so will almost certainly encounter fewer problems and will also enhance their chances of achieving rather more of their stated goals' (Dopson and Waddington, 1996: 545).

Establishing policy objectives and priorities

It should be clear from our foregoing discussion that the initial phase of the policy process – that of defining the problems to be targeted and the likely outcomes that result from doing so – can be fraught with several difficulties. These complexities also characterize the processes surrounding the setting of desired policy objectives and priorities, that will, of course, be constrained by the particular circumstances and resources (such as appropriately trained staff, equipment, facilities and so on) available for the programmes in hand. Ideally, before pursuing their agendas, policy-makers would engage in a systematic review of the effectiveness of existing policies and then seek to form a realistic view of the obstacles that are in the way of achieving their desired objectives (Coalter, 2007a; Dopson and Waddington, 1996; Murphy, 1998; Pawson, 2006). They would then seek to ensure that these objectives are clear and the achievement of one or more of their stated goals does not undermine the achievement of other goals and existing valued arrangements. These objectives may vary greatly and can be very specific, and can be broad or narrow and involve longer or shorter time spans. They can also vary in their complexity and the degree to which they are categorically achievable or ongoing, whilst the criteria by which the relative success and relative failure of policy objectives can be assessed should be clear and easy to determine (Coalter, 2007a; Dopson and Waddington, 1996; Pawson, 2006). As Coalter (2002) has noted, the desired outcomes from sports development programmes and policies typically range from being more sport-specific in orientation (e.g. increasing levels and frequency of sports participation) to more intermediate outcomes that relate to the impact upon the behaviour of participants (e.g. reduced drug use and increased levels of fitness and health) and those that are related to wider social or community-wide outcomes (e.g. reductions in overall levels of crime and drug use).

As subsequent chapters will make clear, a longstanding problem in many policies that seek to promote sport for sport's sake and those that use sport and physical activities as vehicles for achieving other wider social objectives is the lack of consistency and clarity regarding the objectives of those policies. When 'objectives' of one kind or another are identified, they tend to be overly ambitious, unclear, non-specific and internally inconsistent. They are also all too often based on an uncritical and one-sided perception of sport that amounts almost to a statement of faith in its effectiveness to achieve desired social outcomes. In this respect, it is not uncommon for sport policy objectives to be premised on poorly developed and vague rationales. The absence of such clearly developed rationales and the prevailing tendency for many policies and sports development programmes to be characterized by largely ideological thinking limits the extent to which policy-makers and SDOs are likely to achieve their formally stated objectives (Coalter, 2007a; Dopson and Waddington, 1996; Smith and Platts, 2008). This failure may be traced to three principal and interrelated sources:

> (i) their objectives may be impracticable, unrealizable, (ii) even when they are realizable, their attempts to achieve them may be undermined by their limited perspective and knowledge and an important aspect of this restricted vision stems from the prevailing

tendency to view the world through eyes which are preoccupied with ideological concerns, (iii) perhaps, above all, their pursuit of their goals is undermined or at least mediated by the sheer complexity of the relational network that, ideally, their strategies should have taken into account. But in truth, the depth of this complexity is such that even the most sophisticated of thinkers can only aspire to develop strategies which prove, in the event, to have a degree of adequacy.

(Murphy and Sheard, 2006: 556)

An additional, and particularly salient, problem with which policy-makers and SDOs are faced is that, like all social phenomena, their policy objectives and the reforms they may wish to implement exist in a wider social context (Audit Commission, 2009; Coalter, 2007a). It is important, therefore, that they do not see one objective or policy to the exclusion of other objectives and policies. They are but one element in other human figurations and this is bound to have other, as yet unforeseen and unintended, consequences. Such consequences are the normal outcomes of the complex, dynamic relational networks in which policy-makers and SDOs are embroiled, and it is within these networks that such groups also face the possibility that their interests and objectives may be at variance with those of other groups since the resources available to meet those interests and objectives are likely to be scarce. Nevertheless, one of the ways in which policy-makers and SDOs may seek to anticipate some of these unplanned consequences is by continually monitoring and evaluating their strategies, and by making modest predictions or forecasts about the future.

Information gathering and forecasting

A third difficulty with developing and implementing effective sport policy is the ability of policy-makers and SDOs to gather appropriate and relevant information on the problem to be tackled, and to make predictions regarding the future. These are notoriously complex processes since our ability to predict the future is particularly limited by the power struggles and accompanying planned and unplanned outcomes associated with the figurational complexity that characterizes the relational networks in which policy-makers and SDOs find themselves. Such groups are also limited by their knowledge of and ability to control wider social processes and, as we noted earlier, their capacity for examining all aspects of the policy process from a relatively detached perspective. Despite these potential pitfalls, it is important that policy-makers seek to develop among themselves a realistic appreciation about what is feasible and to recognize the need to be both modest and sceptical in their predictions. Their assessment of future developments related to the achievement of their desired ends should also be based on systematically collected, appropriate evidence that can be gathered within funding constraints and which can be interpreted by an effective conceptual theoretical framework. In our view, it is an appreciation of the figurational perspective that would appear to have greater explanatory and practical relevance for policy-makers and SDOs. In particular, it is our contention that if information gathering and forecasting are to be of practical relevance then they have to be conducted in as relatively detached a manner as possible. Without doing so it would be self-defeating for policy-makers to set out to establish what they want to achieve by selecting only the evidence that supports their own ideological commitments (Coalter, 2007a; Murphy, 1998; Smith and Platts, 2008).

Although it may be that policy-makers and other groups may feel constrained to use selected evidence for a range of personal and political reasons, and to justify particular courses of action, maximizing the effectiveness of any policy can only be achieved by an ability to combine one's capacity for relatively detached thinking with the selection of appropriate policy tools. But what methods could policy-makers use to gather evidence on the problems with which they are faced and the likely outcomes of their actions? There are, of course, a range of ways in which policy-makers and SDOs can generate relevant data to inform their proposed policy solutions. These include observation, surveys, interviews, attendance registers and analyses of the available literature. However, the selection of which method or, as is most frequently the case, which combination of methods is used should be determined by the nature of the problem to be tackled (Bloyce, 2004). The extent to which these can inform processes of monitoring and evaluation, which should be inbuilt in all sport policies, will be discussed at greater length later, but it is enough here to note that these will, of course, be constrained by the resources (including time) available and also by the research capacities of those charged with performing the research.

Policy implementation

In this section we will focus on the implementation phase of the policy process, a stage that is also characterized by several difficulties that place policy-makers under considerable constraints, and that come to threaten, even undermine, the extent to which policy can be implemented as intended. Before examining these issues, it is worth noting that in an ideal world policy-makers would wish for themselves 'complete control' over the circumstances in which they find themselves, including the resources and staffing they have at their disposal, their ability to understand policy problems perfectly, and to implement their strategies as intended without opposition from other groups within and outside the organization (Dopson and Waddington, 1996; Murphy, 1998; Smith and Platts, 2008). In the real world, however, such luxuries are impossible and there are many processes that are beyond the direct control of policy-makers and limit the extent to which they can achieve their formally stated goals (Coalter, 2007a; Smith and Platts, 2008). The allocation of desirable resources – to be discussed in more detail later – that are required to implement policies effectively, and which should be built into all aspects of the process, are almost always particularly limited and subject to a variety of competing demands from different groups.

The outcomes that accrue from the struggles over the distribution of appropriate resources, and which come to limit the extent to which the proposed policies are designed and implemented effectively, are exacerbated further if the proposed policies are not cost effective and are unrealistic or impractical. If sport policies contain any one or a combination of these elements, then it becomes increasingly problematic to identify whether any difficulties that are encountered result from the way the policy was designed or from the processes involved during its implementation. However, even if a policy is realistic and the requisite resources have been secured and distributed appropriately, its effectiveness is still dependent upon the understanding, skills and abilities of those who administer it as well as those charged with implementation. Indeed, as Dopson and Waddington (1996: 533) have noted, it is hugely misleading to assume that even if policy-makers were armed with 'proper' information and 'sound' management it would still be very difficult for them to 'implement change in such a way that the outcome, within closely defined limits, [was] more or less what was intended'. Among the reasons for this is that while some groups may have a greater capacity to make crucial decisions over things such as the content and priorities of policy, they are nevertheless 'constrained by the nature and complexity of the human figurations in which they are located and their aspirations and their strategies are more or less continuously mediated and even thwarted' (Murphy and Sheard, 2006: 555) by the other groups involved, such as the implementers themselves, intentionally and otherwise. Consequently, it is important for policy-makers and other key decision-makers to have some appreciation of the power structure of both the organization and external context within which policy is administered, for it is the power struggles that accompany policy implementation processes that help to limit significantly the extent to which they achieve their formally stated goals. The 'policy–implementation' or 'policy–practice' gap, as it is often referred to, is something that should therefore be regarded as the norm rather than as something unexpected, for, as we noted above, the policy implementation process is always accompanied by the unintended, unplanned outcomes of the interactions of the dynamic, differentially interdependent human beings involved (Dopson and Waddington, 1996; Murphy and Sheard, 2006; Smith and Platts, 2008).

Monitoring and evaluation

If policy-makers want to know what is 'going on out there', so to speak, then they need to consistently monitor and evaluate the effectiveness of their programmes. Although it could be argued this is not a particularly profound statement, in Britain the importance of demonstrating evidence of effectiveness has been further enhanced by the increasing emphasis that the Labour government has come to place on the need to provide evidence of policy effectiveness in all areas of social policy, not just sport (Coalter, 2007a). The importance that has come to be placed on 'evidence-based policy-making', demonstrating value for money and the need to undertake outcome evaluation of all areas of public investment, is also an expression of the 'increased emphasis on outcomes and effectiveness and an aspiration to base policy and practice on robust evidence to ensure the delivery of the government's policy goals' (Coalter, 2007a: 1). However, despite this general, alleged concern amongst government with basing policy and practice on outcomes and effectiveness (Coalter, 2007a; Pawson, 2006), Coalter (2002: 11) has noted that, in the world of sport, the 'systematic monitoring and evaluation of sports development programmes (especially those concerned with social inclusion) are in their infancy'. The frequent failure to integrate these processes throughout all phases of the policy process can be related to the general absence of a culture of monitoring and evaluation within the sports development profession, and the tendency for some policy-makers and SDOs to be resistant to such processes (Coalter, 2007a; Collins *et al.*, 1999). This may be due to a general lack of awareness of the processes involved in monitoring and evaluating programmes and because if, and when, such tasks are undertaken they may come to indicate something about a lack of clarity concerning the aims and objectives of sports development programmes and strategies. The general lack and poor quality of monitoring and evaluation can, moreover, be related to the ways and extent to which both processes come to be strongly associated with accountability and assigning blame should the programme, or elements of the programme, be perceived to be failing according to the agreed criteria and objectives (Bloyce *et al.*, 2008; Coalter, 2007a; Pawson, 2006). It can also be attributed to the tendency by key decision-makers, when faced with dealing with the consequences of mounting financial constraints, to cut back on the resources allocated to the monitoring process in the belief that this will not impact negatively upon the project (Coalter, 2007a; Collins *et al.*, 1999).

We clearly recognize that policy-makers frequently operate under a myriad of constraints that may result in them relinquishing their attempts to monitor the effectiveness of their programmes. It is naïve to assume, however, that a policy designed to achieve particular objectives actually achieves those objectives and that it does not have consequences that, in the event, may well be the very reverse of what was intended. The failure to monitor and evaluate adequately and continuously the effectiveness of sport policies is, then, a serious matter of concern, not least because without such inbuilt processes it becomes increasingly difficult to monitor the intended and unintended outcomes of those policies, and so their efficacy is difficult to determine. Thus, insofar as the development and implementation of sport policies is a complex process that inevitably has unplanned consequences, it is imperative that such policies are systematically monitored and evaluated with a view to asking whether or not those policies are achieving the desired ends. It is just as important to monitor and evaluate policy reforms consistently if we are to minimize what may be held to be potentially undesirable consequences – for some groups at least – that may arise during their implementation (Coalter, 2007a; Dopson and Waddington, 1996; Waddington and Smith, 2009).

On the assumption that monitoring and evaluation should be built into all policies from the outset, and not considered as afterthoughts, 'add-ons' or something that can easily be dispensed with (Coalter, 2007a; Collins *et al.*, 1999; Pawson, 2006), there are a number of methods that policy-makers can utilize to 'provide evidence of the extent to which the programme is being delivered as intended, meeting its targets and making progress towards the achievement of its objectives' (Coalter, 2006: 9). The chosen methods will, of course, be dependent upon the complexity of the processes to be monitored, but if we are to come to some understanding of the effectiveness of sports development programmes it is of particular importance that theory-based evaluations of such programmes are undertaken (Coalter, 2007a; Pawson, 2006). In this regard, Coalter, drawing heavily upon the work of Pawson and Weiss, has noted that if we wish to better understand why particular sport policies and programmes produce, or are assumed to produce, particular impacts and outcomes, then, 'rather than simply measuring outcomes (itself a very difficult task), what is required is a better understanding of process – which sports work for which subjects in which conditions' (Coalter, 2007a: 29). More particularly, if we are to understand better why programmes achieve desired and unwanted outcomes, there is a need to move away from more summative approaches to monitoring and evaluation that frequently involve simple outcome-based evaluations of the effectiveness of sports development programmes, towards utilizing more formative approaches that are participatory, process-led and which are centrally concerned with examining ways of enhancing the implementation and management of interventions (Coalter, 2007a; Pawson, 2006). As we shall see in subsequent chapters, the alleged need for more *process* monitoring and evaluation, rather than simple outcome-oriented policy and practice, is said to require theory-driven evaluations of sports development programmes that involve asking questions about 'what type of participation is presumed to lead to what type of outcomes for what type of participant in what circumstances' (Coalter, 2007a: 45).

The generation of baseline data – some of which are more quantitative in kind, others of which can be more qualitatively oriented – is an additional method that is often encouraged if policy-makers and SDOs are inclined to demonstrate the efficacy of their programmes (Coalter, 2007a; Collins *et al.*, 1999; Nichols, 2007). Although it is not uncommon for policies to be implemented without first gathering baseline data, in order to help make some judgement of the effectiveness of sport-focused interventions it is often important that baseline data are collected at the outset of the programme to help clarify the size and nature of the problem before committing time and resources towards its achievement. Whilst there are numerous methodological difficulties involved in trying to arrive at a precise estimate of the extent of perceived social problems (e.g. levels of youth crime and the prevalence of drug use in modern sport) and the seriousness with which they are viewed, it is important that we strive, insofar as it is possible, to estimate as accurately as we can the extent of these phenomena among the target groups of the programme (see Chapter 4). It is important that we begin to address such questions, because until they are answered it is difficult to know what criteria should be used in monitoring and assessing, for example, the success of youth crime and drug reduction and prevention policies. In this regard, there is a pressing need to define clearly the objectives of any policy, as well as the groups for whom they are intended, and to specify exactly the criteria for monitoring the success of that policy. The clarity of these criteria and the need for baseline data will, of course, be dependent upon the clarity of the policy objectives and aims of the programme, as well as the available resources (Coalter, 2007a; Collins *et al.*, 1999; Nichols, 2007).

Ideally, monitoring and evaluation should also be continuous processes, for a more secure and reliable basis from which we can judge policy effectiveness and the outcomes of its implementation would be to concern ourselves with producing systematically generated data that are collected over time, and that can be compared to similar programmes or interventions should they exist (Coalter, 2007a; Crabbe, 2008; Murphy, 1998). While this is often perceived as a somewhat onerous task, the production of such comparative data that are collected over the duration of the programme is one worth making and has the advantage of sensitizing us to the need for learning from the relative success and failure of such policies as they develop. Longitudinal monitoring techniques such as these can be impractical, however, and it may be that phased appraisals, or point-in-time assessments of various kinds, may be more appropriate, though less adequate, means of identifying the extent to which intermediate objectives and priorities are achieved (Coalter, 2007a; Crabbe, 2008; Nichols, 2007). It may also be the case that the selection of monitoring techniques is constrained, to a greater or lesser degree, by the preference of some policy-makers for 'hard' quantitative data (particularly in the form of statistical data), even when more qualitative methods would prove to be more adequate indicators of a programme's relative success or failure (Coalter, 2007a; Crabbe, 2008; Nichols, 2007). Indeed, although some policy-makers 'are sceptical about the value of qualitative data regarding it as subjective, capable of selective presentation and of limited value to general policy making' (Coalter, 2006: 44), with intelligent and relatively detached interpretation these data can frequently offer invaluable insights into the processes involved (Murphy, 1998). This, of course, is not to deny the possibility that more quantitative data can also be frequently subject to selective presentation and thus be of limited value to policy-makers.

Regardless of which course of action is taken, it would be wrong to rely entirely on any one individual monitoring method, for this will provide only a partial and potentially distorted picture of the processes involved, and of the extent to which any policy or programme is achieving the desired objectives (Coalter, 2007a; Murphy, 1998). If it is possible, therefore, it is often useful to complement the data generated by one method (e.g. through surveys and attendance registers) with those derived from other methods (such as interviews, leader/coach reports and observations), in order to triangulate – and perhaps help bolster the reliability of – the findings of the monitoring process. Policy-makers engaging in the monitoring process can also benefit from engaging in comparative analysis of the relative success or failure of their own and other projects (Coalter, 2007a; Crabbe, 2008; Murphy, 1998). Among other things, this may involve cross-comparisons between different organizations, societies and historical periods. It may also entail – although, as we note in subsequent chapters, this is something that is rarely done – policy-makers seeking to draw upon the knowledge and experiences of those in other social policy areas (for example cultural and educational policy), and to identify both similarities and differences between the situations in which they find themselves and those beyond the immediate context of the project. Finally, ad hoc discussions with the implementers, together with their own observations of direct involvement in the implementation process and experience of the developing policy, may also offer valuable insights and knowledge of its effectiveness and success (Coalter, 2007a; 2008; Murphy, 1998). Of course, this further creates the possibility that policy-makers may bring their own personal commitments about how policy ought to be pursued to bear upon the monitoring process, and how its relative success or failure is interpreted. This also increases the likelihood that policy-makers may seek to claim retrospectively that any of the reported 'positive effects' were part of their original plans or, conversely, to deny the connection between their actions and what are perceived to be the unanticipated 'negative side-effects'. As we noted earlier, neither of these scenarios may be seen by some parties as desirable, yet for other policy-makers the resultant unplanned outcomes that accompany the implementation of a policy may be highly desirable for a variety of reasons. Nevertheless, it is crucial that policy-makers seek, insofar as possible, to combine simultaneously their own level of involvement with a certain critical degree of detachment, especially if the intention is to develop a more realistic assessment of the intended and unplanned consequences that accompany policy implementation.

This having been said, in light of the growing political pressure on policy-makers to develop evidence-based policy and practice, secure additional funding and work with a range of other stakeholders, it is becoming increasingly likely for outside, or so-called 'independent', consultants to be asked to conduct monitoring and evaluation exercises and/or to act as advisers for developing new policy agendas. This is a tendency that is becoming increasingly common in many countries, and in the sporting context there are numerous examples we could cite of the growing involvement of 'independent' bodies in many aspects of the policy process. The publication of the *Independent European Sport Review* (IESR) (Aranut, 2006) is a case in point. The IESR was the outcome of a review of European football initiated by the UK Presidency of the European Union (EU) in 2005, and is said to be 'a report, independent of the Football Authorities, but commissioned by UEFA, on how the European football authorities, EU institutions and member states can best implement the Nice declaration on European and national level(s)' (Aranut, 2006: 139). As is invariably the case, the extent to which strategies such as the IESR were 'independent' was rather questionable, however (Smith and Platts, 2008); indeed, it is even noted in the report that the 'Terms of Reference have been drafted in consultation with UEFA and … led by UEFA' (Aranut, 2006: 139). Accordingly, while the sports ministers of various EU Member States played a central role in the formation of the report, and despite the self-proclaimed public consultation that accompanied this, it might be concluded, as Miettinen (2006: 57) has put it, that the IESR was 'commissioned by UEFA, written by UEFA about UEFA'. In relation to the monitoring and evaluation of sports-related programmes in the UK, it might also be noted that commercial organizations such as Knight, Kavanagh and Page (KKP) have been commissioned to evaluate the effectiveness of County Sports Partnerships (CSPs); the market research company Ipsos

MORI is charged by Sport England with collecting data on sports participation (see Chapter 6; Rowe, 2009); Substance, a social research company led by researchers from several English universities, conducts case study research in the areas of sport, youth inclusion and community regeneration (see Chapter 4); and the Audit Commission, together with a range of other organizations, is responsible for examining the effectiveness of the local provision of public sport and recreation services (Audit Commission, 2009).

The rationale for the involvement of 'external' agencies in monitoring and evaluating the effectiveness of sport-focused interventions usually takes a variety of forms. It might be thought, for example, that insofar as monitoring and evaluation require specialized skills, it is more prudent to utilize agencies with particular expertise in the area (Crabbe, 2008; Murphy, 1998). It could also be, in principle at least, that 'outsiders' have the advantage of lifting the burden from already busy staff, help distance the latter from the appraisal of projects in which they themselves may have been involved and subsequently avoid the possibility that the failure of any policy can be attributed to one particular individual or group within the responsible organization (Murphy, 1998). As we alluded to above, however, in reality outside consultants are not always as 'independent' as they first appear. They may, for example, bring with them their own priorities and preconceptions of how a particular organization ought to be run, how a particular policy ought to be pursued, reappraised or dropped, or what, in their view, constitutes relative policy success and failure (Crabbe, 2008; Murphy, 1998). They may also be under pressure to tailor their findings towards the particular objectives and interests of the host organization. All these scenarios and more are possible, but they each carry with them the possibility that aspects of monitoring and evaluation processes, and the reports on which they are based, become distorted in a variety of ways (Murphy, 1998). It is frequently advisable, therefore, to approach the reports of external consultants with a degree of scepticism, particularly when they are made available for public consumption. It is also important to be alive to the possibility that the conclusions drawn could be based on the extent to which some groups have been successful in ensuring that the findings reflect positively on their actions. By contrast, claims to the effect that a policy has been particularly successful or otherwise may also be an expression of the ways in which other groups have sought to cast unfavourable light on and mediate the actions of others.

It should be clear, then, that none of the available options to monitor and evaluate policy effectively is without its respective pitfalls. As a consequence, a consideration of the techniques for monitoring and evaluating policy, how these processes are to be conducted, and who will be assigned the responsibility of such tasks, should be decided at the outset and form an ongoing part of the policy process. The same might also be said for issues of resource allocation.

Resource allocation and budget planning

All phases and elements of the policy process do, of course, operate within a variety of resource and budgetary constraints. These constraints come to limit significantly the kinds of policies that can be realistically pursued. In that respect, all policies and sports development programmes have to be devised and implemented with these limitations in mind, although the priorities and resources given to different policies are matters of some contention. It is important to note, however, that these constraints are not just aspects of the overall power struggles that accompany the struggle over resources for the immediate policies being devised. As an aspect of the relational networks that characterize the policy process as a whole, they also have implications for other policies and proposals within the same organization and, consequently, can impact on the decision to pursue one policy option over another. For example, the allocation of appropriate resources can be frequently dependent on the relative success or failure of existing policies, as well as the relationships between the budget-holders and other groups within and outside an organization. These relational constraints, and the consequent budgetary and resource implications, are, of course, subject to considerable local variation, and are dependent upon the nature of the problem to be tackled and the objectives of the proposed policies (Coalter, 2007a; Murphy, 1998). The precise nature of this variation can only be determined empirically, but there are several techniques that policy-makers can use to determine the most cost-effective way of achieving their desired goals, namely, cost–benefit analysis and a balance sheet approach (Coalter, 2002; 2006; Gratton and Taylor, 2000; Murphy, 1998).

The first of these, the cost–benefit analysis approach, is perhaps the most commonly used technique in which an attempt is made to calculate and judge the direct and indirect costs and benefits of pursuing a particular policy. This frequently involves assigning a monetary value to various 'factors' and is an approach that underlies most attempts to determine whether particular projects (e.g. staging the Olympic Games or building a new local leisure centre) represent value for money (see Chapter 7). The approach can sensitize us to the fact that not all costs and benefits of policy are incurred immediately. It can also help decision-makers, over time, with budget planning. It is, however, a notoriously difficult task to achieve and it is not always possible for some costs and benefits to be expressed in financial or monetary terms (e.g. the 'feel good' factor of hosting the Olympics) (Coalter, 2002; 2006; Gratton and Taylor, 2000; Murphy, 1998). More particularly, cost–benefit analysis is not always an appropriate technique to determine the allocation of resources and can, in some cases, even come to determine the particular direction of policy and structure the activities of the implementers. It is also an approach during the course of which key selective and subjective decisions are made, but which nevertheless remain hidden behind the presentation of seemingly 'hard' and reliable statistical data.

As Murphy (1998) has noted, a more promising method that helps decision-makers come to some judgement about the implications of pursing a particular policy is the balance sheet approach. Pursuing this approach, he contends, helps policy-makers to resist the tendency to reduce everything to a common (financial) denominator and involves assessing the range of costs and benefits in terms of a number of criteria (Murphy, 1998). These criteria can be largely quantitative, economic and numerically based, but the balance sheet approach also permits the use of more qualitative means of assessment where this is applicable. Such an approach is, of course, no less subjective than pursuing the cost–benefit method, but it can be a more adequate means by which to clarify the most realistic and appropriate policy option to pursue if it is conducted systematically and in an upfront way (Gratton and Taylor, 2000; Murphy, 1998). In our view, the balance sheet approach represents the most appropriate means of helping policy-makers to come to deal with the unavoidable budgetary constraints under which they work, and of addressing their often overwhelming priority, namely, how to achieve their desired goals and deliver the most efficient service at the lowest possible cost (Coalter, 2007a; Collins *et al.*, 1999; Murphy, 1998).

Policy succession and policy closure

The final phase of the policy process that we shall consider here is that of policy succession and closure. Before briefly examining the processes involved, it should be stressed that we use the word 'final' in a cautionary way, for, as we noted at the beginning of this chapter, all policies emerge out of existing relationships and policies that are in a constant state of flux. Like all complex social processes, policy and organizational change are unavoidable features of the policy process given the consensual and conflicting elements that accompany the dynamic power struggles between the various groups involved. As we shall see in Chapter 2, however, a strong degree of continuity also exists in the policy agendas of various sporting and non-sporting organizations. But let us return to our central question.

Like policies generally, some sport policies are designed to run over a set period of time, while others are implemented (with modifications along the way in some cases) and then terminated once a particular problem has been resolved, partially alleviated or perhaps even considered to be insurmountable (Coalter, 2007a; Murphy, 1998). In other situations, there may be an open-ended commitment to particular policies that are subject to periodic reviews, and which may or may not be contingent upon continued funding, the availability of staff and other resource constraints. Regardless of which of these scenarios prevails, when there is the possibility of policy change, especially radical policy and structural change, such moves are likely to be met with strong resistance by some parties within an organization. Depending on the nature of the policy to be implemented such resistance may also be met by outsiders as well. This is largely because such moves – which can emanate from within and outside an organization – can be perceived to threaten some, if not all, the interests of policy-makers and other members of that organization (Coalter, 2007a; Murphy, 1998). Even if upon the completion of a project that was established to tackle a specific policy problem that programme is then subsequently threatened with closure, the personnel involved may wish to seek to prolong the length of the prevailing policy to protect, maintain and advance their own vested interests. They may also do so to undermine those of others.

As we noted earlier, because of their differential power chances and divergent interests not all groups are able to or want to adapt to the same degree, or in the same way, to impending structural and policy change. Some groups may be more capable of adapting to such changes because of the significance of their policy remit and/or the skills of their members. Some may do so because of the attitudes of their members and the sufficiently high degree of coordination and consensus among them. Others may have the ability to survive by coping with and accommodating the proposed modifications without undermining their existence and operations (Coalter, 2007a; Murphy, 1998). Finally, it may also be that some organizations and decision-makers have the potential to adapt to changes in the continually changing policy environment but do not recognize this capacity. This limited perspective may stem from a number of sources. These include an unwillingness to contemplate change, and an unswerving belief among members of an organization in their own abilities and experiences to withstand the outcomes that may result from change. This restricted vision may also be traceable to the limited knowledge among key personnel of the merits of monitoring and evaluating the effectiveness of their current policies and the relative strengths and weaknesses of their own organization, which, of course, is itself constituted by complex networks of human figurations (Coalter, 2007a; Murphy, 1998). It is clear, therefore, that if policy-makers and other members of staff are able to internalize the need to monitor and evaluate their activities continuously and systematically, then it is more likely that they will be able to respond better to, and perhaps even withstand, the sometimes dramatic changes that can characterize the dynamic environment in which they work.

Summary

The central objective of this chapter has been to outline the beginnings of a figurational approach to the study of policy processes that, we believe, can help to explain these processes more adequately on a theoretical level. It is also an approach that can be of practical relevance for policy-makers and SDOs who are faced, in the course of their day-to-day activities, with constraints that come to limit the extent to which they are able to achieve their own personal and/or group interests and objectives. Throughout the chapter we have stressed the need to focus upon the following interdependent features of a figurational analysis of the policy process: the composite unit in which policy-makers and SDOs find themselves; the planned and unplanned processes that result from the more or less goal-directed actions of the various groups involved; the importance of power as an aspect of interdependency ties; the importance of approaching the policy problem in a relatively detached frame of mind; and the need to locate the policy problem being addressed in its wider social context.

We are acutely aware that the foregoing analysis may be interpreted as a sceptical view of the policy process but, if that is a view which prevails, we would stress that it should not be dismissed as sceptical, but as a realistic view of the difficulties associated with formulating and implementing effective sport policy and sports development programmes. As we noted earlier, it is an analysis that is predicated on the premise that our understanding of and our ability to control social processes are, in reality, particularly limited because of the constraints imposed upon us as people and our knowledge of those processes. This recognition of our limited ability to control social processes generally, and policy processes specifically, is not to argue that we have no control, and nor does it imply that we should abandon our attempts to pursue formally stated policy goals and agendas that may have hitherto proved to be particularly limited. On the contrary, we would argue that it should be the goal of policy-makers to strive to make their strategies more effective. This is a task that, in our view, would benefit fruitfully from the insights that can be derived from a figurational perspective on the policy process and sports development more specifically, even though the perceived interests of other groups may be damaged as a consequence. Finally, and this is a point that cannot be emphasized too strongly, we would stress that our foregoing analysis cannot capture all of the complexities involved, particularly in relation to local variations in the policy formation and implementation process. It is, however, presented with a view to enhancing the adequacy of our understanding of the policy process. In Chapter 2, we seek to develop a related feature of our figurational analysis of sports development and policy by examining the emergence and development of sport policy and the sports development profession in Britain since the 1960s.

Revision questions

1 Provide a sociological examination of a sports development strategy of either a local authority or NGB of your choice.
2 To what extent can the sport policy process be explained adequately from a figurational sociological perspective?
3 What practical insights may be developed from the analysis presented in this chapter for either sport policy-makers or SDOs?

Key readings

Coalter, F. (2007a) *A Wider Social Role for Sport: Who's Keeping the Score?*, London: Routledge.
Elias, N. (1978) *What is Sociology?*, London: Hutchinson.
Pawson, R. (2006) *Evidence-Based Policy: A Realist Perspective*, London: Sage.

Recommended websites

Coalition for Evidence-Based Policy: www.evidencebasedpolicy.org
Demos: www.demos.co.uk
Institute for Public Policy Research: www.ippr.org.uk

2 The emergence and development of sport policy

Objectives

This chapter will:

- examine the changing organization and administration of sport in the UK since the 1960s;
- explore increasing government involvement in sport policy; and
- examine how key government policy changes are currently impacting on sport policy priorities.

Introduction

The organization and administration of sport in many countries, including Britain, have undergone considerable change over the past fifty years or so and these changes have had a significant impact on the ways in which SDOs have sought to develop and implement a variety of sport policy and development strategies. While it is impossible to trace here all of the complexities involved in this regard, the central objective of this chapter is to examine some of the major organizational changes that have impacted on sport policy through the shifting priorities of government. This is important, it is argued, for in order to adequately understand something of the ways and extent to which government sport policy and development priorities are currently being implemented, it is necessary to examine how the present situation of sport policy-making and sports development activity has developed. It is equally necessary to examine something about the changing political and policy priorities given not only to the role of local authorities and NGBs of sport in implementing national sport policy, but also to the emphasis given to sport as an aspect of local authority sport policy and development provision more generally.

The 1960s to mid-1970s: growing systematic government involvement in sport

Although we clearly recognize that the roots of the organization and administration of modern sport can be traced back to England, in particular, during the eighteenth and nineteenth centuries (Dunning *et al.*, 2004; Holt, 1989; Houlihan and White, 2002), it was the period between the 1960s and mid-1970s that was characterized by a growing willingness by the British government to accept sport and leisure as a legitimate area of public policy, not least because of the commitment towards developing and sustaining the welfare state ideology and the recognition of the growing social significance of sport. Indeed, in the period before the 1960s and 1970s, there was little, if any, 'systematic central government interest in sport' (Coalter, 2007a: 9). The prevailing political preference was for non-intervention in either setting the sport policy agenda or organizing and administrating sport, especially because the then established view of sport as an amateur pursuit meant that many politicians came to see sport as something with which government should not be concerned. On those occasions when government did become more involved in the provision of sport, it was 'reluctant intervention, justified only by the ... need to achieve urgent social goals, such as the combating of potential social disorder [with unemployment very high], or of preparations for war' (Henry and Bramham, 1993: 113). In other words, while there was initially a strong degree of reluctance to intervene in the provision of sport, the growing receptivity of government to sport and the potential benefits of sport as a malleable policy tool that could be used to help achieve particular social objectives related to the welfare state (Coalter, 2007a; Henry and Bramham, 1993; Houlihan and White, 2002) meant that sport began increasingly to gain 'support from those who saw it as a vehicle for social cohesion and integration' (Keech, 2003: 15). This view of the potential use of sport as a tool for social cohesion and promoting national prestige amongst members of the British government was further encouraged by the more explicit ways in which governments in Europe, in particular, were beginning to view the social role of sport. As Coghlan (1990: 7–8) has noted, 'the belief that sport had a larger role to play in society was debated, and underlying it all the thoughts that Government should be in some way more involved were entering the minds of sports administrators', particularly because of the financial gains that could be made from political support for sport during this period.

Despite the initial government antipathy towards sport in the early decades of the twentieth century, one of the key organizations that came to play a central role in sport policy and sports development activity in Britain was the Central Council for Physical Recreation (CCPR), the inauguration of which, in 1935, was primarily a response to growing concerns over the health of the nation (CCPR, 1960). The CCPR was, and still is, an independent voluntary body representing a wide range of governing bodies in the promotion, improvement and development of sport. In 1957, the CCPR commissioned Sir John Wolfenden to serve as Chair of a Committee to examine the status of sport in the UK, and the subsequent 'Wolfenden Report', published in 1960, not only raised the profile of sport among government, but also helped provide 'the context within which public involvement in sport was to be considered for the next generation' (Houlihan and White, 2002: 18). In view of the perceived interest that government was taking in sport and the sport policy and development policy agendas, Coghlan (1990: 11) has claimed that the Wolfenden Report was published against what he referred to as a 'somewhat euphoric background'. For the most part, this was because the Report was published within the context of growing public, media and even political support for greater funds to be directed at sport, and especially following the perceived success of the British Olympic team at the Summer Olympics that took place in Rome during the same year. The Report and the implications of its contents were not met with universal acclaim, however, for some within the British Olympic Association (BOA), for example, expressed particularly strong reservations about the Committee that was to produce the Wolfenden Report, since no BOA members were to be represented on it. In particular, there were said to be concerns by bodies such as the BOA that 'the CCPR might attempt to use it to increase its own power and influence at the expense of other bodies' (Evans, 1974: 146). Similar concerns over the lack of representation on the Committee were also expressed by the

Scottish and Welsh arms of the CCPR, who felt that they, too, were not sufficiently represented on the Committee (Evans, 1974).

When the Wolfenden Report was eventually published in September 1960, it was the most comprehensive policy document concerning the organization and administration of sport that had been seen in Britain until that time. The Report focused, in particular, on young people and was concerned with, amongst other things, the opportunities available for developing better and more readily available sports facilities and coaching, and argued that there was a need to improve the broader organization and administration of sport in the country (CCPR, 1960). It is also important to note, however, that while the Report extolled many taken for granted assumptions about the apparent contribution that sport could make to alleviating a variety of social problems, such as those related to criminal behaviour, health and education (see Chapters 3–5), the claims that were made about the alleged social impacts of sport were accompanied by a degree of circumspection that has rarely been seen in sport policy documents published in Britain since. In relation to the supposed character-building qualities that are often thought to be developed through sports participation, the Report acknowledged that while these qualities may be an outcome of participation, 'it is easy to exaggerate (and to react from) this kind of claim' (CCPR, 1960: 5). A similarly appropriate and cautious conclusion was also arrived at in relation to the use of sport as a vehicle of social policy designed to prevent youth crime. In this regard, the CCPR (1960: 4) claimed, once again, that while sport could be expected to make a contribution to reducing crime and anti-social behaviour among young people, it was recognized that 'the causes of criminal behaviour are complex, and we are not suggesting that it would disappear if there were more tennis courts or running tracks'.

Beyond the reference that was made to the alleged contribution that sport could make to addressing particular social problems, the majority of the Report focused very much on the promotion of sport for sport's sake and especially the need to raise participation levels in sport and reduce the numbers of young people who drop out of sport upon the end of compulsory schooling. This policy focus came to be expressed on the basis of what the Report identified as a

> manifest break between, on the one hand, the participation in recreational physical activities which is normal for boys and girls at school, and, on the other hand, their participation in similar (though not necessarily identical) activities some years later when they are more adult.
>
> (CCPR, 1960: 25)

Concern with this so-called 'Wolfenden Gap' became a key policy priority that has remained a more or less central feature of sport policy over the last thirty years or so, and for many groups it is still seen as a key area for sports development work (see Chapter 3). At the time when the Report was published, it was claimed that to help reduce the dropout rate from sport and physical activity 'young people, particularly at the stage of adolescents [need to be] given the opportunity for tasting a wide range of physical activities' (CCPR, 1960: 7). It was also alleged that to support the encouragement of young people towards participating in a wider range of sports and physical activities more sports facilities needed to be developed, and, in that respect, the Report encouraged the Conservative government at the time to make the £5 million funding available annually that had been promised in its pre-election campaigns for facility development and the enhancement of sport provision (CCPR, 1960).

It was not altogether surprising, therefore, that a second main recommendation of the Report was that a new body, a Sports Development Council (SDC), be created, with responsibilities for the distribution of government grants to sporting organizations (such as the CCPR and governing bodies of sport) and the promotion of sport generally. In particular, the Report concluded that while 'no fundamental change is suggested in the general pattern of our sports organisation', there was a need for 'greater co-operation and integration' (CCPR, 1960: 109) between the numerous NGBs, other national organizations with responsibility for sport, including the National Playing Fields Association (NFPA), the BOA and the CCPR, and the various local authorities who had some responsibility for sport and leisure provision as well. To this end, it was proposed that the SDC could help to encourage greater cooperation between the diverse groups whose interests and motivations for the provision of sport within their own organizations were, to a greater or lesser degree, likely to be similar and/or at distinct variance to those of other groups. The Report recognized, however, some of the problems that would inevitably be encountered by trying to bring about greater cooperation between the various competing groups who comprised the complex networks of relationships within which sport and sports development were organized and provided. The significance of these figurational complexities for enhancing the organization of sport found particular expression in the Report when it was stated that:

> In a field where progress and development must manifestly depend in the main upon voluntary service and personal, and often very specialised, enthusiasms, it would be illusory to hope for the elimination of all overlapping, 'empire-building' or self-centredness ... Therefore, occasional signs that a few bodies of people take a somewhat narrow view of their responsibilities or attach a rather disproportionate importance to their own activities have not worried us unduly. Such things are inseparable from volunteers and pioneers alike, whether in sport or in other spheres.
>
> (CCPR, 1960: 53)

In addition to the important role that the Council could potentially adopt in relation to enhancing the organizational efficiency of sport, it was recommended that the Council should remain 'independent' from government to preserve the so-called 'non-political' nature of sport. In this regard, the Report concluded that the inauguration of the SDC, unlike the distinctly political Ministry of Sport that existed in France, for example, would help preserve the alleged apolitical nature of sport and offset any public criticism that could be expressed over the perceived 'incongruous juxtaposition of departmental control and private leisure-time activity' (CCPR, 1960: 97). Despite the fact that the Report was 'supported by powerful personalities in both the House of Commons and the House of Lords' (Coghlan, 1990: 11), the then Conservative government failed to respond to the proposal by Wolfenden that a new umbrella organization, the SDC, be formed to develop sport. In December 1962, they did, however, make Lord Hailsham, an existing Cabinet minister, a 'Minister with special responsibility for Sport'. Although the appointment of Lord Hailsham was one indication of the growing political recognition of, and interest in, sport at the time, for the most part the Conservative Party retained the view that sport should be dealt with at arms length by the government. This was a view that was shared by Lord Hailsham, who suggested that 'whilst he agreed with the substance of the Wolfenden Report, he did not agree with the establishment of a Sports Development Council' (Coghlan, 1990: 12).

Whilst the then Conservative government failed to respond to the proposal by Wolfenden that a new umbrella organization be formed to develop sport, this body – established in 1965 – became known as the Advisory Sports Council (ASC) following the election of a Labour government in 1964. Having supported the proposal of an SDC in opposition, the newly elected Prime Minister, Harold Wilson, stated that sport was one of those subjects (like the arts) 'essential to Britain's economic and social development which had not been given priority in the past' (Wilson; quoted in Polley, 1998: 21). Denis Howell was appointed to a new junior ministerial position within government, the Sports Minister, and he subsequently became the first Chair of the ASC and was supported by various staff from the CCPR who were seconded to help run the ASC, including the General Secretary, Walter Winterbottom, who became Director of the ASC. Although the ASC was not the 'independent' body sought after in the Wolfenden Report, the new Labour government considered that the Council should be run *for* government and it was expected that the Council would advise the government on sport in terms of the standard of facilities available, the use of the available resources and priorities for the coaching of sport, as well as 'to foster cooperation among the statutory [local] authorities and voluntary organizations concerned' with sport (ASC, 1965).

The main policy priorities that characterized sport policy during the 1960s related to maintaining and enhancing social order and increasing international sporting success, as well as meeting the demand for wider opportunities for people to participate in sport and physical activity (Henry and Bramham, 1993; Green and Houlihan 2005; Houlihan, 1997). This was related to 'increasing electoral pressure for an expansion of sport and recreation facilities' (Green and Houlihan, 2005: 52) in light of the significant degree of publicity that had been attracted by the Wolfenden Report (Coghlan, 1990). This was also a period in which the competing policy emphases of promoting elite sport and mass participation began to emerge as the various groups involved in the organization of sport in Britain were, in essence, involved in either the promotion of elite-level sport or 'Sport For All'. Indeed, one more or less consistent feature of government policy for sport in Britain ever since has been set around the increasing tensions amongst those involved in the sport policy community regarding the promotion of elite or mass sport participation. At this relatively early stage in the debate over which of these dual sport policy objectives should be prioritized in policy terms, however, there was said to be a large measure of consensus among the various groups involved. This, ostensibly, was because 'an increase in facilities was the first priority' (Houlihan, 1991: 99) for all those involved in the development of sport regardless of particular allegiances and interests.

The emphasis that came to be placed on the enhancement of facility provision as one of the first priorities for the ASC is not altogether surprising, for, as Coghlan (1990) has noted, in 1964 it was estimated that there were no more than four indoor sports centres in the UK. The perceived need to embark upon a programme of facility building was limited by the prevailing lack of government and public funds that were available for sport. Accordingly, to help meet the expectation that more facilities would be built to enhance the provision for sport for members of the population, members of the ASC were increasingly constrained to generate monies to help meet this obligation. In this regard, 'as the main providers would increasingly be the municipal authorities the Council agreed that a partnership between local authorities and sports people should be established regionally' (Coghlan, 1990: 24). To this end, the ASC established numerous Regional Sports Councils in England, and Councils for Scotland and Wales, that were also to be advisory councils to the ASC. With increased public funding becoming available for distribution through the ASC, there was a perceived need to employ professional staff within many of the NGBs, which were all still largely staffed by honorary officers and officials, and volunteers. The appointment of development officers within many of the NGBs was seen to be 'crucial for many governing bodies ... particularly as these appointments were grant-aided from public funds' (Coghlan, 1990: 35–36).

Following the election of a new Conservative government in 1970, it was intended that a 'Sports Council' with executive powers be developed as a body 'independent' of government, since many members of the Conservative Party still claimed that sport should operate at arms length from the government and considered Denis Howell's position as both MP and Chair of the ASC inappropriate. Given this situation, in 1971 the Conservative government proposed that the ASC be given executive powers by way of granting a 'Royal Charter'. In this regard, the Scottish Sports Council and the Sports Council for Wales were established with 'Royal Charter' statutes in December 1971 and February 1972, respectively. A Great Britain Sports Council, that would have specific responsibility for England, was also finally established by Royal Charter in the summer of 1972 (a Sports Council for Northern Ireland was established in January 1974), at a time when sport was becoming increasingly recognized as an accepted area of government policy. The decision to establish the various Councils as 'executive' bodies was, initially, expected to result in the break-up of the CCPR since it was to be subsumed into the new executive Sports Councils. However, after much deliberation at various CCPR meetings, it was decided that, although most of the paid staff of the CCPR were to transfer to work for the Sports Council, the CCPR would remain as an organization that would serve as the consultative body to the Sports Councils and act as a general voice for the NGBs that constituted its membership (Coghlan, 1990; Evans, 1974). The assets of the CCPR, such as the National Centres that had been set up with charitable status under their auspices, were transferred to a charitable trust, with the Sports Council as trustee. This 'arrangement', Houlihan (1991: 91) notes, 'reflected the CCPR's misgivings at losing control over major sports resources'. Houlihan adds in this connection that although the creation of the executive Sports Council was 'warmly welcomed' by many within the sports community, especially as there remained a desire to establish more sports facilities around the country, 'it posed serious problems for the relationship with the CCPR' (Houlihan, 1991: 91).

It is perhaps unsurprising, therefore, that since the Sports Council was to be funded by Exchequer funds, various tensions and conflicts accompanied the prevailing pattern of relationships that existed between the two organizations at the time (Jackson, 2008). Indeed, as the emergent network of relationships that came to characterize the organization and administration of sport at the national, regional and local levels lengthened and became more complex, 'the question of which organization did what and which was more important in British sport continued to dog development' (Coghlan, 1990: 32) and helped undermine the extent to which the government could realize its sport policy goals.

Notwithstanding the relational complexities that were coming to impact on the operations of the various organizations involved in the administration of sport during this period, the granting of Royal Charter status meant that the Councils were defined as executive bodies and nominally free from ministerial control. This effectively meant that the Sports Council became a non-departmental public body (NDPB) – that is, a body that

> has a role in the processes of national government, but is not a government department, or part of one, and which accordingly operates to a greater or lesser extent at

arm's length from ministers ... Ministers are however ultimately responsible to Parliament for a NDPB's independence, its effectiveness and efficiency.

(Cabinet Office, 2006: 2)

More specifically, Haywood *et al.* (1995) have claimed that while Royal Charter status was granted to the Sports Council to ensure sport remained at arms length from the government, its 'insulation from governmental influence has been eroded' (Haywood *et al.*, 1995: 191) gradually over time. Despite the claimed independence that the government would have from the Sports Council, it is, of course, highly unlikely to find that a large degree of formal independence could exist between the two groups (see Chapter 1). As Polley has noted, the extent to which the Council could operate 'independently' of the government is minimal, given that the Council

> was to be chaired and constituted by government appointees, funded by government, and should, in the words of the Royal Charter, 'have regard to any general statements on the policy of Our Government that may from time to time be issued to it by Our Secretary of State'.
>
> (Polley, 1998: 22)

The inability of the Sports Council to retain a significant measure of independence from the political influence and policy priorities of increasingly interventionist government ministers during this, and subsequent, periods is not altogether surprising, as the differential networks of interdependencies of which these groups were a part were becoming increasingly complex and characterized by power struggles of many kinds. Indeed, one consequence of the increasing figurational complexity and the interweaving of the more or less goal-directed actions of large numbers of people who constituted the Sports Council and government was the emergence of a series of outcomes that no one planned. A good example of this is the ensuing tension that developed between the Sports Council and the CCPR. The CCPR, when it commissioned the Wolfenden Report, did not intend for its organizational status to be threatened or refined in some way. And nor, for that matter, did the Sports Council intend for the CCPR, which remained as a separate organization, to develop as a rival organization with a more effective means of lobbying. As we noted in Chapter 1, these outcomes can be seen as an expression of unequal power relations and differential relational constraints between the various groups involved whose interests and perceptions are likely to diverge.

The mid-1970s to the early 1980s: facility development and target group identification

One of the main priorities of the Sports Council was to increase the facilities for public participation in sport and physical activity and, while there had been some development of leisure centres and swimming pools in the 1960s, it was during the period from the early 1970s to the early 1980s that a transformation of 'the opportunities for participating in sport' (Houlihan and White, 2002: 21) became an increasing policy priority for SDOs. This was also a period during the course of which the emphasis in sport policy came to be characterized by a rapid expansion in the development of sport and leisure centres in local authorities funded primarily by the Sports Council and other public organizations. As a consequence, through the grant aid that they received from the Sports Council, local authorities came increasingly to be seen as significant providers of opportunities and facilities to participate in sport and physical activity. Indeed, between 1971 and 1981 the Sports Council helped local authorities within the public sector to 'achieve the construction of over 500 new swimming pools and almost 450 new indoor sports centres' (Houlihan and White, 2002: 21). The increased expenditure within local authorities was also, in large measure, associated with the reorganization of local government during the early 1970s, one consequence of which was the establishment of larger units of authority, with considerably greater budgets (Houlihan, 1991). In this regard, during this period those working in the sports development field became locked increasingly into wider networks of relationships that began to comprise many local councillors within some local authorities who regarded the development of state of the art leisure centres as a means of securing votes from local residents, and who often competed with neighbouring authorities to provide the best available sports facilities (Jackson, 2008). The increasing level of investment in sports facilities in local authorities was, in turn, strongly associated with the perceived lack of appropriate facilities available for both participation and performance sport, despite the lack of obvious strategic direction for the funding to be spent (Coalter, 2007a; Houlihan and White, 2002; Jackson, 2008).

Facility development remained a key aspect of sport policy even following the further change in the British government that saw the Labour Party elected to office in 1974. Denis Howell was once again appointed to the junior position of Minster for Sport within the new government, even though he had initially 'been opposed to the establishment of the executive Sports Council' (Coghlan, 1990: 57) during a short tenure as Chair of the CCPR whilst he served as a Member of Parliament in opposition. As Coghlan (1990: 57) has noted, the election of Howell as the Chair of the CCPR had been controversial and added further to the 'conflict with the Sports Council which has continued to a greater or lesser extent to the present day'. However, under the terms of the Royal Charter the Labour government was not in a position to repeal the executive powers of the Sports Council. The poor economic climate within Britain, as elsewhere, at this time also meant that the organization of sport was said to require better coordination and management. This was to be funded largely by using existing resources given the considerable financial constraints that the previous desire to develop new sports halls, swimming pools and other sports facilities had brought to bear upon those working in local authorities.

In an attempt to provide a more cohesive sport policy strategy, in 1975, the British government published, for the first time, a White Paper on sport, entitled *Sport and Recreation*. Among many other things, the government distinguished between 'sport' and 'recreation', with the former being regarded as the performance and excellence dimension of sports development work, and the latter said to be more concerned with mass participation (Department of the Environment [DoE], 1975). By distinguishing between these features of sports development, Houlihan and White (2002: 25) argue that this made it 'more difficult to conceptualise sports development as an integrated set of activities and objectives'. To this they add that while the Sports Council may have adopted the slogan 'Sport For All' as their policy mantra, they also 'stressed that elite competitive sport was as much a part of Sport For All as the provision of community opportunities for participation' (Houlihan and White, 2002: 25). The White Paper also expressed the government's view that there was a need for 'a tightening-up of organisational arrangements (to ensure against duplication and overlapping), for the fuller use of existing facilities, and for the establishment of a clear order of priorities for such limited new provision as may be possible' (DoE, 1975: 2). In addition, it was stated that 'the role of government is to co-ordinate and give a lead to the planning and use of resources within the community' and not 'to adopt a paternalistic attitude to the many different providers of recreation in this country' (DoE, 1975: 4). It was not altogether surprising, therefore, to find that while local authorities, in the view of government, had 'become the main providers of new sports facilities and of parks and open spaces for informal outdoor recreation in the towns' (DoE, 1975: 8), there was no government support for the idea 'that a statutory duty should be placed on certain local authorities to provide adequate recreational facilities' (DoE, 1975: 9). This was, in large measure, because of the evident concerns that came to be expressed in the prevailing economic climate, where constraining local authorities to make 'adequate recreational facilities' available to members of the community would place even greater financial pressure upon the budgets of local authorities. In relation to sport and recreation this was particularly significant, for since both were not statutory services that local authorities would provide to their residents, the budgets of sport and recreation services were often the first to be reduced, often substantially so, to help manage the mounting financial pressures with which local authorities were faced (Coalter, 2007a; Houlihan and White, 2002).

As well as concentrating on the perceived need to enhance the organization and administration of sport, additional emphasis came to be placed on the increasing desire of the government for the Sports Council to use sport as a vehicle for 'community develop-ment' and for achieving a range of non-sport government objectives. As Polley (1998: 22) has noted, the White Paper 'was particularly blunt on this, with its claim that "by redu-cing boredom and urban frustration, participation in active recreation contributes to the reduction of hooliganism and delinquency among young people"'. Against this growing emphasis that came to be placed on the role of sport in the achievement of wider social objectives, the government accepted that 'recreation [including sport] should be regarded as ... part of the general fabric of the social services' (DoE, 1975: 1). This was a clear departure from the more circumspect announcements that were to be found within the Wolfenden Report published fifteen years earlier, and by this time there was a very clear, openly declared interest from the government in viewing 'sport as an instrument of social policy' (Houlihan and White, 2002: 28) that began to be more narrowly focused upon the needs of particular target groups. To this end, *Sport and Recreation* focused, in particular, upon the needs of young people, but also disabled people, retired people and women, especially mothers, and provided the context within which, during the early 1980s, 'there were clear signs of a shift away from facility provision ... to a strategy of concentrating resources on particular sports or sections of the community' (Houlihan and White, 2002: 33). The reorientation of policy towards focusing upon identified target groups did contribute to the Sports Council's focus on 'Sport For All', although it could be argued that this 'was simply an articulation of a movement that had been underway in Britain for some time' (Coghlan, 1990: 35). Arguably the relatively poor economic climate of the day had contributed to the clearer articulation of such thinking, such that existing facilities might be used as part of 'new' and more overarching policies more efficiently and economically. As Coalter has argued:

> Against the background of economic decline, rising unemployment and problems of inner-city decay, there was a quickening of the pace of governmental use of sport in urban policy ... the apparent political neutrality of sport, and its presumed ability to provide 'an economy of remedies' ... made it a more attractive option than addressing fundamental structural change.
>
> (Coalter, 2007a: 10)

Thus, notwithstanding the supposed 'independent' status of the Sports Council, the government provided 'substantial dedicated funds ... for specific "social" programmes' (Coalter, 2007a: 11). For example, perhaps because of the fact that the government did not expect sport and recreation to be a statutory requirement within local authorities, the 'inner urban areas in which recreational deprivation is associated with a conjuncture of other forms of social and environmental deprivation' were going to receive from the government more directly 'the highest priority for grant-aid' (DoE, 1975: 16).

The 1980s: sport as a tool for achieving social goals

Alongside the growth in publicly funded facility provision there was a correlative development of policies that focused more fully upon addressing the symptoms of urban riots and unrest in inner cities (such as in Liverpool, Bradford and Bristol), as well as focusing resources on particular sports, sections of the population (such as football hooligans) and under-participating groups (such as women, disabled people and people from various ethnic minority groups) (Green, 2006; Haywood *et al.*, 1995; Houlihan, 1997; Houlihan and White, 2002; Hylton and Totten, 2008). These changing policy priorities, particularly in relation to the use of sport as a means of alleviating the symptoms of various social problems, developed within the context of the so-called 'winter of discontent' and as Margaret Thatcher led the Conservative Party into office in 1979. Houlihan and White (2002: 27) argue that the broadly consistent view of 'welfare policy', and the place of 'recreational sport' within that policy paradigm, was 'subject to an abrupt and sustained challenge' from the Thatcher government. Thatcher did not particularly like sport, and in terms of her political position her view was bolstered by the perceived problem that football hooliganism posed for her government and, of particular significance, members of the wider society. Despite her evident dislike, and even distrust, of those involved in the organization and development of sport, Thatcher and her government still perceived sport as a potential solution to the problems of social unrest in various inner-city areas. The role that sport was perceived to play in this regard was made clear in two major innovations in the early 1980s. The first innovation was brought about through the Manpower Services Commission – which was established by the government in 1974 to help coordinate and manage the country's employment and training services – and the Sports Council, both of whom established the Action Sport programme in 1982. The Action Sport programme, which is widely regarded as 'the forerunner of many subsequent sports development projects' (Coalter, 2007a: 11), began to provide local authorities in various inner-city areas with £1 million per year between 1982 and 1985. A central objective of the 15 Action Sport programmes – which were run in Birmingham and London in response to the inner-city riots of 1981 – was to develop, in partnership with other interested agencies, sustainable, consumer-driven opportunities for low-participant groups (particularly the unemployed). The significant diversity in the populations of each authority was expressed in the diversity and type of programmes offered by groups of SDOs who were recruited by local authorities to implement them. Many local authorities recognized the contribution that sports development could make to their local communities and subsequently provided further funding for the programmes that they then sought to tailor towards the needs of groups within their region. In this respect, the scheme was significant in helping to 'promote sports development as a legitimate local authority activity' (Houlihan and White, 2002: 37), especially because each of the fifteen participating authorities were required to employ sports leaders (ninety were employed overall).

The implementation of the Action Sport programme constrained the newly recruited sports leaders who were working in local authorities to begin developing partnerships with other non-sports organizations. Some of the early examples of partnership working, particularly with those that were developed with other groups in the broader welfare (especially health) policy fields, found particular expression in the various National Demonstration Projects (NDPs) that were launched during the 1980s. The purpose of the NDPs was to identify strategies to remove the barriers to participation for a range of underrepresented groups. In particular, the formally stated purposes of the NDPs was: (1) to improve participation through outreach development in the community; (2) to enhance opportunities for particular target groups such as women and disabled people to partici- pate in sport; and (3) to develop school sport, in partnership with the education autho- rities (Sports Council Research Unit, 1991). What is of particular significance here, however, was that despite the emphasis that came to be placed upon partnership working the Sports Council reported that 'managing the wide range of partners necessary for project implementation and the challenge of reconciling sports development objectives with those of non-sport partner bodies' (Houlihan and Lindsey, 2008: 227) was of parti- cular concern for many working within sports development. This perceived threat to the status of sports development work stood in marked contrast to the generally positive perception of the increasing relationship between government and many sports organi- zations that existed under the previous Labour government. Under the Thatcher admin- istration, however, the position of sports development within the activities of local authorities came increasingly under threat given the prevailing antipathy that the gov- ernment expressed towards sport more generally. It is not unsurprising, therefore, that the Sports Council and sports development workers became increasingly concerned with working in partnership with organizations whose policy goals and priorities lay beyond sport. While this enabled them to continue pursuing their sporting priorities, it simulta- neously constrained them to meet the non-sporting objectives of their partners whose main objectives were not commensurate with those of the Sports Council. One con- sequence of this closer collaboration with non-sporting bodies was that it was not uncommon that 'the sport development objectives of the partnership were often margin- alised or even undermined by the core activities of the other partner organisations' (Houlihan and Lindsey, 2008: 228). Rigg (1986: 3), in his evaluation of the Action Sport programme on behalf of the Sports Council in 1986, also argued that because the pro- gramme was largely a response to the urban riots that took place in the inner cities during 1981 'it was set up with a great deal of haste and rather less detailed planning than we [the Sports Council] believe was necessary for such a large scheme'. Houlihan and White have also drawn attention to some of the problems that were associated with the poor policy planning that accompanied the implementation of the programme. In particular, they suggested that 'the alacrity with which the Sports Council adopted Action Sport was due as much, if not more, to financial opportunism than to conscious policy reorientation' (Houlihan and White, 2002: 35).

The perceived inadequacies that were said to have accompanied the implementation of the Action Sport programme, and the growing tendency for sports development workers to emphasize the social benefits of sport, are perhaps understandable. This was because, under the Thatcher government, there was growing suspicion over the way in which public money was being spent and the Sports Council, as we explained above, began to extol widely the broader social goals that could be achieved through the provision of sports development programmes in an attempt to protect their funding. Equally, it was also not surprising that the government 'started taking a much closer eye on the performance of the many Non-Departmental Public Bodies under their aegis' (Collins, 2008: 63), which, of course, included the Sports Councils. To this end, Coghlan (1990: 57) argues that the Sports Minister appointed by Thatcher in 1981, Neil Macfarlane, 'increasingly wished to control sports affairs, either directly or through the Sports Council where weak leadership failed to stand up to the pressure and ceded power and influence point by point'. The growing accountability and suspicion of the way in which many NDPBs were spending public money was further expressed when Macfarlane himself stated that 'if public funds are used to finance sporting activities, isn't it proper that politicians should make political decisions affecting these funds? After all they are accountable' (Macfarlane; quoted in Coghlan, 1990: 57–58). This emphasis that was coming to be placed on the accountability of NDPBs such as the Sports Council was not, it should be noted, something that was unique to the Thatcher government, for – such is the nature of all social relationships – it was also the case that the Sports Council was never able to act completely independently of the previous Labour government priorities either.

As we noted earlier, the second major policy innovation that emerged during the early 1980s was the tendency for the Sports Council to move 'beyond simply advocating and subsidising more facilities to cater for all-comers, and [to set] targets for increased participation in specific age and sex groups, and urging local authorities to do likewise' (Roberts and Brodie, 1992: 10). The focus of the Sports Council on these under-participating groups was further bolstered in their 1982 publication *Sport in the Community: The Next Ten Years* (Sports Council, 1982). In this document it was argued that 'not to tackle the needs of these groups would put the Council in breach of its Royal Charter' (Sports Council, 1982: 7). The central role that local authorities were also perceived to play in enhancing participation was clearly recognized when it suggested that

> most sport is played locally, and so the development of mass participation depends critically on local initiatives. This will require local authorities and education authorities, local sports clubs, other local voluntary groups and local commercial interests to work both separately and in partnership.
>
> (Sports Council, 1982: 35)

Of particular significance to *Sport in the Community* was the expectation that was placed upon sports development workers to engage in partnership working, for it was suggested that 'action by the Sports Council will be at best palliative, and at worst futile, unless its actions relate to the social policies of other agencies, and the Council looks forward to a working partnership with statutory and voluntary agencies' (Sports Council, 1982: 36). It is not surprising, once again, that, with NDPBs being held to greater account under Thatcher's government, 'for the first time a target for increasing participation was set' (Collins, 2008: 63) as a central objective of the proposals set out in *Sport in the Community*. In a similar manner to the Action Sport project, in *Sport in the Community* the government also focused on particular 'targeted groups' – the so-called under-participating groups (especially the unemployed) – and this policy focus was related to the perception that 'sport could be seen as fulfilling an ameliorative function' (Houlihan and White, 2002: 34). However, as Coalter (2007a: 11) argues, 'although the rhetoric of recreation as welfare was ideologically potent, it remained politically weak and relatively marginal to core public policy developments, and the Sports Council's largest single financial commitment (45 percent of the total) was to elite sport'. This, it seems reasonable to suppose, was related to the fact that the Council was still dominated by former CCPR staff, whose prior engagement in sport had been primarily 'deferential towards the needs of the elite athlete' (Houlihan and White, 2002: 36). It was not altogether surprising, therefore, that the Sports Council's focus on community sport during the 1980s, alongside the competing interests of those who prioritized the development of elite sport objectives, helped to divide those working within the organization and development of sport. Let us examine these issues a little further.

The facility development that had characterized much of the first decade of the Sports Council's existence had contributed significantly to the promotion of elite-level sport and the development of mass participation. Tensions had been largely suppressed, at least publicly, with supporters of both of these particular agendas being able to pursue their own vested interests through the support that was provided by government, and especially local authorities, for the development of sports facilities. However, the relatively new focus on the experience of the participant (whether for elite or leisure sport), as opposed to simply providing facilities for the whole range of participants, saw 'tensions between those whose primary concern was elite achievement and those concerned with increased participation [begin] to surface' (Houlihan and White, 2002: 38). Indeed, the network of relationships that comprised the organization and development of sport in Britain during the 1980s was already very much characterized by 'petty feuding and personal rivalries' (MacFarlane; quoted in Coghlan, 1990: 151), with particular divisions and tensions said to have been particularly prominent between the CCPR and the Sports Council. This found particular expression through the ways in which the CCPR was still regarded as the forum for the collective voice of the NGBs of sport, and yet most NGBs all but ignored the Sports Council's request that they discuss with them the 'role they wish to play' over the 'next ten years' (Sports Council, 1982: 34).

In 1988, the Sports Council, seemingly undeterred by the lack of evident interest from the government, or even the NGBs, regarding the proposals that they outlined in their *Sport in the Community* strategy, published a follow-up strategy: *Sport in the Community – Into the 90's*. Building on the target group approach that it took in *Sport in the Community* and the NDPs, in this strategy the Sports Council once again focused on specific under-participating groups, particularly women and young people, together with a broad focus on promoting performance and excellence, which, it was argued, 'has to be closely linked to developing mass participation' (Sports Council, 1988: 71). According to Coghlan (1990: 154), the Sports Council's strategy document once again failed to gain significant 'attention from government and national governing bodies of sport', despite the fact that 'the House of Commons and the Government [had] recently concluded that the Sports Council produces good returns for public money' (Sports Council, 1988: 6–7). Nonetheless, in 1989 the structure of the Council was altered in response to criticism from the government over the confusion that was said to exist surrounding the number of different people and bodies responsible for the organization and administration of sport (Houlihan, 1991), an issue that had been raised in the recent past. A related aspect of this criticism of the prevailing organizational infrastructure and administration of British sport was the fact that the 'NGBs in general were extremely conservative organisations and were slow to generate momentum in sports development' (Houlihan and White, 2002: 45). Considerable tension also existed, as in earlier periods, between the CCPR, the BOA and the Sports Council, which seemed to have further 'coloured the attitude of the NGBs towards the Sports Council' (Houlihan and White, 2002: 49). Consequently, the Conservative government proposed that there should be a reduction in what it saw as the excessive bureaucracy of the Sports Council and the CCPR with a view to making them more effective organizations. This was one of a number of 'threatened reorganisations', which Houlihan and White (2002: 52) point out 'were hardly conducive to policy stability', and which help to explain why 'the organisation and administration of sport policy in the UK has been bedevilled by the lack of a coherent "voice" for sport' (Green and Houlihan, 2005: 54) for some considerable time. It is perhaps unrealistic, however, to expect that a single, coherent 'voice' for sport could, indeed, exist in this manner. This is clear not least because, as in many other areas of social life, the sheer complexity of the differential interdependency ties that characterize the particular power relationships of which the groups involved in the promotion of sport are a part can come to limit significantly the extent to which those groups can agree on some kind of desired action in relation to the future organization of sport. In this respect, it is likely that the specific organizations themselves could not be regarded as a 'single' voice for sport, given the internal rivalries that are a characteristic of all such figurations.

Around the same time that these concerns were being raised about the perceived lack of organization for sport within the UK, Houlihan and White (2002: 40–41) have argued that the well-known pyramid model of the sports development continuum, 'first used in a report authored by Derek Casey in 1988 (Scottish Sports Council, 1988)', was becoming 'widely used by sports organisations throughout the UK'. The sports development continuum focused on the notion that developing a wide participation base would, by extension, help widen the apex of the 'pyramid' of sporting excellence. Arguably, the promotion of the continuum model by the Sports Council represented its attempt to reconcile the evident tensions between those promoting elite sport and those promoting grassroots participation, for this conceptualization of sports development work suggested that these dual policy goals were inextricably interdependent. It could also be argued that the promotion of this view of sports development was also a way in which the Sports Council hoped to convey something of the interdependence that was said to exist between the variety of organizations involved in the administration of sport from the foundation level to the higher levels of participation, performance and excellence (Houlihan and White, 2002).

In addition to the lack of policy stability for sport that existed during the 1980s, the perceived need to streamline the organizational structure of sport in Britain, reduce levels of bureaucracy and increase the efficiency of those bodies responsible for the organization and delivery of sport helped generate considerable structural change at the local authority level in particular. The Conservative government was concerned that many local authorities at the time were particularly inefficient financially and that there was, as a consequence, a need to control local government spending more closely (Coalter, 2007a; Houlihan and White, 2002). One of ways the Conservative government attempted to do this was through the introduction of compulsory competitive tendering (CCT). CCT was originally introduced in the Local Government Planning and Land Act in 1980 and was extended in the Local Government Act of 1988 to include a wider variety of service provision, including the management of sport and leisure facilities such as pools, leisure centres, golf courses and tennis courts (Henry, 2001). The Act meant that local government services could be put out to 'tender' for private administration, and whilst the tendering of sport and leisure services through CCT eventually began in the early 1990s, 'sports development was still peripheral to most strategies' (Houlihan and White, 2002: 44) when they were put out to tender.

Even though many contracts for the right to deliver local services were won in-house by local authorities, it was recognized that the introduction of CCT and the considerable structural change this would bring about at the local authority level would have a direct 'impact on sport' (Sports Council, 1988: 7). This was almost inevitable, especially when the Audit Commission reported that 'many authorities do not have a clear idea of what their role in sport and recreation should be' (Audit Commission; quoted in Coalter, 2007a: 12). This was because, in essence, the Audit Commission (1989) considered there to be a lack of monitoring and evaluation, and accountability, of the use of leisure services in local authorities by the local population. Since sport, recreation, leisure services and facilities were still not statutory local authority services it is unsurprising that there was little, if any, systematic monitoring of participation and use of facilities, or even a clear understanding of what such services might provide to the local population – beyond, that is, the simple use of the facility. However, for reasons we explained earlier, the prevailing political climate during Thatcher's time in office meant that while local authorities were supported considerably by central government monies, this was associated with greater accountability. As part of this overall concern with demonstrating the extent to which sport and leisure services were providing 'value for money', analyses such as those undertaken by the Audit Commission (1989) 'led to the more general policy of Compulsory Competitive Tendering (CCT) being applied to local authority sport and recreation services' (Coalter, 2007a: 12).

Despite the attempts by the Sports Council over the previous decade to work more closely with local authorities in order to develop more coherent sports development policy and practice, in terms of promoting 'Sport For All', sports development was still peripheral to most strategies when they were put out to tender (Houlihan and White, 2002). A clear implication of the introduction of CCT was that services should be economical, and, in this regard, it has been frequently suggested that this contributed to a growing focus, even in the contracts that were won by the in-house work forces, or direct service organizations (DSOs), on the commercial viability of sport and recreation targets (Coalter, 2007a; Houlihan and White, 2002; Jackson, 2008). As Jackson (2008) has noted, those working in the emerging sports development arena, whose primary purpose was said to be targeting previously neglected sporting communities (those who the Sports Council had, over the previous decade or more, specifically targeted for sports development intervention), were 'a clear casualty of this focus on bottom-line financial calculations' (Jackson, 2008: 33). Indeed, the introduction of CCT was strongly associated with 'a decade of price increases above inflation' (Collins 2008: 65) in local authority sport and leisure centres; so much so that the 'reaction to the extension of CCT to sport and recreation services was almost uniformly negative' (Coalter, 2007a: 12). Despite the hostility that accompanied the introduction of CCT to sport and leisure services, this policy reform nevertheless contributed to a sea-change in the way in which such services were, and still are, run. As Coalter argues, the 'need to produce detailed contract specifications to provide the basis for monitoring performance' within the CCT process 'marked a broad shift from the rather vague approach of management by objectives ... to objective-led management' (Coalter, 2007a: 13). Such an objective-led management approach, in terms of setting stated targets and providing specific monitoring and evaluation of those targets, has remained a significant feature in sports provision at the local level. Indeed, this emphasis was retained throughout much of the 1990s under John Major, who succeeded Margaret Thatcher in 1990. Major's arrival as Prime Minister, and subsequent success at the 1992 General Election, did not lead to a substantial change in the broader neoliberal policies, such as CCT, of the previous administration (Coalter, 2007a). Indeed, under the Major government the continued support of CCT contributed, albeit indirectly, to the greater state involvement that was coming to characterize sport policy-making and the delivery of sports development in local authorities and NGBs of sport. It is important to note, however, that while Major's government retained this commitment to implementing the CCT programme in sport and leisure services, it did nevertheless lead, as we shall see below, 'to a more proactive approach to sport' (Coalter, 2007a: 14).

The early 1990s to 1997: from addressing inequity to school and elite sport

As we explained above, the period between the 1960s and 1980s was characterized by a significant growth in the contribution of local authorities to the organization and administration of sport, even though this was curtailed somewhat by the introduction of CCT and 'a marked lack of sustained political interest and direction in sport' (Houlihan and White, 2002: 52) that continued in the early 1990s. It was also around this time when, building on the work of the Action Sport Programmes and NDPs that were developed during the 1980s, the Sports Council published a series of policy 'Frameworks for Action' for young people, women, black and ethnic minorities, and disabled people in which it was developing the concept of sports equity. The Sports Council defined the concept of sports equity as being

> about fairness in sport, equality of access, recognizing inequalities and taking steps to address them. It is about changing the structure and culture of sport to ensure that it becomes equally accessible to everyone in society, whatever their age, race, gender or level of ability.
>
> (Sports Council, 1993: 4)

As Houlihan and White (2002: 63) have noted, the introduction of sports equity as a central feature of each of the Frameworks for Action 'represented a shift in thinking from the target group approach that had been popular in sports development work in the 1980s'. For the first time it also placed responsibility for addressing inequity on governing bodies, local authorities and other traditional providers of sport. In this context, the Sports Council began to place considerably more emphasis on the ways in which the principles of equity should be embedded across all levels of the sports development continuum. It also focused particular attention on the need to break down not only the individual and social constraints to sports participation but, significantly, those aspects of the structure and culture of sport that also came to limit the involvement of under-participating groups that included young people, women, and disabled people. These various position statements helped draw attention to issues of equity, particularly gender equity and specifically the rights and experiences of women, which had a significant impact on international sport policy following the publication of the Brighton Declaration (1994). The general principle of sports equity that underpinned the Sports Council's series of policy statements 'stimulated little comment at the time' (Houlihan and White, 2002: 63) by government, however, and 'had limited impact on the sports development community' (Houlihan and White, 2002: 64). According to Houlihan and White the marginal impact that these equity policies had on those working in sports development, particularly in some local authorities, can be related to

> the weak influence of the [Sports] Council at the time, and partly because the ideas they contained did not fit with the immediate priorities and concerns of governing bodies or Conservative-controlled local authorities. Those local authorities that were

Labour-controlled considered themselves well ahead of the Sports Council on equity issues, regarding the Council as a conservative and somewhat inequitable institution itself in both its membership and operations.

(Houlihan and White, 2002: 64)

It was also clear that whilst the principles underpinning the notion of equity would 'prove significant over the medium term to longer term' (Houlihan and White, 2002: 63), the marginal impact that the Sports Council's recommendations on equity initially had at government level can be related to the general lack of interest in sport by the Thatcher government. Following Thatcher's replacement by John Major, however, the political salience of sport increased substantially such that sport policy and sports development policy, in particular, 'was about to enter a period of sustained increase in public investment in sport, but also one of sustained governmental interest and debate about the role of sport in society' (Houlihan and White, 2002: 52–53). Upon victory at the 1992 General Election, Major's government established the Department of National Heritage (DNH), in which sport was included, and in 1994 a National Lottery was introduced and this has since provided substantial additional funds to sport and helped change the landscape of sport policy in the UK. Let us examine these issues in some detail.

The election of the Major government and the establishment of both the DNH and National Lottery helped contribute to the growing state involvement in sport policy and development. Following the establishment of the DNH in 1992, the Sports Council was subject to further structural and policy changes. In the early part of 1993, it was proposed that the structure of the Sports Council be radically changed to incorporate a new UK Sports Commission, which would oversee performance and excellence, and an English Sports Council, which would have a similar participation-oriented remit to the other 'home councils' in Scotland, Wales and Northern Ireland. However, by August of the same year, these proposals were scrapped by the DNH, on the basis that this would simply increase further the bureaucratic nature of an already bureaucracy ridden organization. The government also considered that the recent passing of the National Lottery Bill through parliament justified a rethink over exactly how, and even if, it was necessary to restructure the organization and administration of sport at this time. This was because it was widely hoped that when the National Lottery was to be introduced in 1994 significant sums of money would be made available to sport, for distribution by the Sports' Council. David Pickup (1996), the Director-General of the Sports Council at the time, was particularly scathing of the decision to scrap the plans to reorganize the Sports Council on the 'whim' of the newly appointed Sports Minister, Iain Sproat. The intervention of the new Sports Minister in this manner was not altogether surprising for, as Houlihan and White (2002: ix) have noted, it has often been the case that 'incoming ministers for sport … have a capacity to translate their particular enthusiasms into policy priorities in a way that is inconceivable in other government departments'. This tendency was further compounded by the relatively low policy status afforded to sport by the government, even under a largely enthusiastic Prime Minister in John Major. Indeed, sport is an area of policy that was, and still is, susceptible to more ephemeral change than other policy areas because it often has less well-established and coordinated lobby groups than those that are to be found in other areas of governance, such as education, health and policing. It is also the case that many ministers of sport have seen the job as a way to gain 'promotion' to another ministerial position by seeking to make an immediate impression upon their appointment to the post (Pickup, 1996).

In July 1994, just one year after Sproat had announced his decision to reconsider the restructuring of the Sports Council, he announced that there would, indeed, be a restructuring. This was to involve a separation of the Sports Council into a UK Sports Council and an English Sports Council, while the other home nation Councils would remain intact. This was not a significantly different proposal to the one that he delayed one year previously. It was also announced by the government that more support would be given to professional sport and greater effort was to be made to bring key sporting events (such as the Olympic Games and soccer World Cup) to Britain. These proposals were to be compensated for in the abandonment of work in a number of previously key areas to the Sports Council, the most significant of which was the decision by Sproat to

> withdraw from the promotion of mass participation, informal recreation and leisure pursuits and from health promotion, [which are] laudable aims, but they are secondary to the pursuit of high standards of sporting achievement. In due course, those changes will allow us to give much greater help to our most important national sports.
>
> (Sproat; quoted in Pickup, 1996: 205)

The introduction of the National Lottery in November 1994 contributed even more substantially to the state's steady involvement in setting the sport policy and development agenda. This found particular expression in the 'increasingly contractual relationship between the Sports Councils and NGBs ... and the agreements that were entered into prior to the release of National Lottery funding' (Houlihan and White, 2002: 57). Initially, the National Lottery was incredibly successful and 'the early years of the Lottery produced income well above expectations' (Collins, 2008: 67), with the policy area of sport, as one of a number of identified 'good causes', benefiting greatly from the substantial increase in funding. In view of the steady flow of Lottery monies that were made available by the government, the existing duties and roles of the Sports Council were extended and its members were given the responsibility of distributing 83 per cent of Lottery proceeds allocated to 'sport'. The increasing political salience of sport policy to the government, and the larger sums of money available to the Sports Council, NGBs of sport and local sports providers, was both enabling and constraining for each of the groups involved. On the one hand, the various organizations involved in running, developing and promoting sports now had greater access to money that was previously unavailable. But, on the other hand, this simultaneously helped to constrain their activities through the growing accountability that was associated with the increasing autonomy that the National Lottery monies helped give them.

Insofar as the introduction of the National Lottery helped sustain increases in public investment in sport during the 1990s, the publication of a second government White Paper on sport, *Sport: Raising the Game*, by the DNH in 1995, was an important landmark in the growing involvement of the state and governmental interest in sport. Within the context of local authority sports development, the publication of *Sport: Raising the Game* (DNH, 1995) was of particular significance, for it marginalized considerably the role of local government and made little reference to mass participation ('Sport For All') or to local authorities who are the key vehicles of its promotion. The explicit policy emphasis was not on mass participation or enhancing the involvement of specific target groups, as had been the case previously, but on school sport and elite performance, with a more efficient and streamlined structure for the organization of sport in the UK also being emphasized as a key priority (DNH, 1995; M. Green, 2008; Houlihan and White,

2002). That local authorities and the concept of 'Sport For All' were largely ignored in *Sport: Raising the Game* was particularly important, for as we noted earlier it is in the context of local authority leisure provision (such as leisure centres, private health clubs and gyms) that many members of local communities participate in sport and physical activity. As Houlihan (2002) has noted, the lack of attention that was paid to local authorities and mass participation in *Sport: Raising the Game* can be interpreted as an expression of the government's view that the facility infrastructure for mass participation and, hence, the achievement of 'Sport For All' objectives were not in place and that responsibility for these was a matter that could be left to local government. In addition, and of equal importance, was that the little attention that was paid to 'the contribution of local government, which spends over £800 million each year on sport, was a reflection of the Conservative government's longstanding antipathy towards local authorities' (Houlihan, 2002: 196). The focus of much of the funds that were made available to sport through the National Lottery was also disproportionately skewed towards the achievement of the dual policy objectives of elite and school sport. As Houlihan and White (2002) have noted, although local authorities were heavily constrained to develop funding strategies to access approximately 40 per cent of Lottery money allocated to them and were encouraged by the Sports Council to think more strategically about sport and recreation, 'there was little incentive for local authorities to respond as bids for Lottery funding based on analysis of need and levels of participation, or on goals such as the reduction of deprivation or community regeneration, were explicitly prohibited' (Houlihan and White, 2002: 73). It is not unsurprising, therefore, that during the mid-1990s the sports development needs of community members in local authorities were, at best, pushed to the margins of the sports development policy as state involvement in setting the national sport policy agenda began to increase quite substantially.

As we noted earlier, insofar as the role of local authorities in sports development work was ignored in *Sport: Raising the Game*, school and elite sport were very much seen to form the centrepiece of the prevailing sport policy priorities of the Conservative government. In particular, in *Sport: Raising the Game* the government reaffirmed its belief in 'the intrinsic benefits of team sports and introduced a raft of policy initiatives ... to strengthen sporting opportunities within the PE curriculum and within extra-curricular activities' (Bramham, 2008: 21). For reasons we explain in Chapter 3, the emphasis that came to be placed on the need to promote school sport and the increasing availability of Lottery monies together helped provide the context within which the YST was established, which is now based at Loughborough University. The YST was established in 1994 and during the 1990s it became a very influential body in the organization and provision of school sport and PE for young people. As Chapter 3 makes clear, the YST has since been able to make a significant impact in setting the youth sport policy agenda in a variety of ways, and its increasing salience to government has ensured that it continues to receive a steady stream of external funding from government and other sports agencies, such as the various Sports Councils (M. Green, 2008; Houlihan and Green, 2006).

The other important organizational changes that were proposed by the government in *Sport: Raising the Game* included the establishment of a British Academy of Sport, for the pursuit of sporting excellence and the encouragement of NGBs to develop closer links with schools to meet their elite sport objectives by integrating school sport 'into a process of talent identification and a ladder of competition designed to meet the needs of governing bodies' (Houlihan and White, 2002: 67). The increased funding that was becoming available to the Sports Council, almost exclusively from the initial success of the Lottery, unsurprisingly encouraged the Council to develop a very compliant 'new' strategy in 1996. Titled *England: The Sporting Nation* (ESC, 1996), the strategy was a close 'reflection of government policy' (Collins, 2008: 68) and was effectively a more or less direct elaboration 'on themes in *Raising the Game*' (Collins, 2008: 68). The UK Sports Council (UKSC) and the English Sports Council (ESC) were eventually established by Royal Charter in January 1997. One of the key reasons for this restructuring was to 'eradicate the anomaly of the former Sports Council having both British and English functions', but the overall, unintended, 'outcome was the bifurcation of sports development' (Houlihan and White, 2002: 70). The UKSC was to oversee developing excellence, particularly in international competitions where representative teams of the UK were participating, such as at the Olympic Games, and also to administer doping control. The ESC, by contrast, 'was charged with the development of sport in England, from foundation through to excellence' (Houlihan and White, 2002: 70), which involved the concentration of its resources on a select group of sports in order to develop their services and promote, amongst other things, participation in sport and physical activity. The various Sports Councils for Northern Ireland, Scotland and Wales remained in place.

Sport policy and development since 1997

The impact of *Raising the Game* was limited somewhat by the election, in May 1997, of a Labour government that upon entering office immediately replaced the DNH with a new Department for Culture, Media and Sport (DCMS). The inauguration of the DCMS meant that sport now featured for the first time in the title of a British government department, even though the position of Minister for Sport was still a junior ministerial post. Blair gave the job to Tony Banks. This was something of a surprise move, given that Tom Pendry had been the opposition spokesperson for sport before Labour were elected to office. Banks would report to the new Cabinet position of the Minister for Culture, who at the time was Chris Smith. Aside from these developments, as Houlihan (2002: 197) has noted, the newly elected Labour government 'was surprisingly hesitant and faltering in its initial attempts to impose a "New Labour" stamp on sport policy', especially given that Labour had taken the unusual step of producing a 'Manifesto for Sport' whilst in opposition in 1996 (Houlihan, 2002). However, that the new Labour government did not immediately impose itself on sport policy is no major surprise, for sport policy had always been, and still remained, low on the government's agenda in comparison to other areas of policy such as education, crime, health and defence.

In the absence of a clear governmental steer, in 1998, the ESC developed the slogan 'More People, More Places, More Medals'. It organized its work around this slogan when developing the Active Programmes a year later in a move in which the ESC was, on the surface, appearing to anticipate the likely policy priorities that the Labour government was going to pursue on the basis of what was contained in the Labour Manifesto for Sport. In the publication *Sports Development Planning* (ESC, 1999: 5), the ESC suggested that sports development should provide 'opportunities for people, regardless of age, gender, race, or ability to participate in sport and achieve their potential' (ESC, 1999: 5). The central policy plank derived from *Sports Development Planning* was the creation of the Active Programmes. This alleged 'new' model of sports development focused on four areas of work: 'Active Schools', 'Active Communities', 'Active Sports' and 'World Class'. According to Houlihan and White (2002: 87), 'the Active Programmes were not designed to supplant the model of the sports development continuum, but were a part of the rebranding of the English Sports Council that included the adoption of the title Sport England as its marketing name'.

The New Labour government had been elected with the so-called 'Third Way' at the heart of its political and policy philosophy. The Third Way, it is argued, 'is said to be simultaneously a modernised version of social democracy and beyond the old left–right dimension of politics' (Roberts, 2009: 111). In this respect, New Labour had tried to distance themselves from the previous conception of the Labour Party – in opposition and in government – as being a party that would set income taxes high and spend public money in large sums. Instead, they were keen to integrate, insofar as possible, private enterprise and supposed accountability with public spending, and considered that many public services required 'modernizing'. In order to do this, it was claimed that a process of 'joined-up thinking' was needed to permeate all such organizations as well as between government departments. As Pollitt has observed, this process of 'joined-up thinking' relates to

> the aspiration to achieve horizontally and vertically co-ordinated thinking and action. Through this co-ordination it is hoped that a number of benefits can be achieved. First, situations in which different policies undermine each other can be eliminated. Second, better use can be made of scarce resources. Third, synergies may be created through the bringing together of different key stakeholders in a particular policy field or network. Fourth, it becomes possible to offer citizens seamless rather than fragmented access to a set of related services.
>
> (Pollitt, 2003: 35)

Furthermore, because of the prevailing desire among members of the government to find a 'new or "Third Way" to address social and economic problems, sport was to achieve a new, more clearly articulated, prominence in social policy' (Coalter, 2007a: 14). This policy commitment was emphasized through the alterations that were made to CCT and the policy focus of *A Sporting Future for All* (DCMS, 2000), which was the first sport policy to be released by the current Labour government in 2000. Although the Labour government acknowledged the 'role of CCT in improving cost management and widening service provision, the Labour Party strongly criticised the CCT legislation for promoting a universal focus on costs to the exclusion of social objectives and quality' (Robinson, 2004: 11). After considerable debate between members of the government, in 1999 Labour finally published the Local Government Act, which meant that CCT was to be abolished on 2 January 2000, and 'Best Value' services were to be provided from 1 April 2000. In this respect, Collins (2008: 70–72) argues that CCT 'was made voluntary' and Best Value was to be a 'broader and more demanding regime … in which local authorities had to justify their modes of provision (direct, contracted or trusts), demonstrate efficiency through Performance Indicators (PIs) and consult with and report to their residents' (Collins, 2008: 70–72). According to the former Department of the Environment, Transport and the Regions (DETR):

> We all rely on local services. They are essential to our quality of life. We all have an interest in seeing them improved and in ensuring that the best use is made of public funds in providing them. Best value is designed to deliver those better quality services and real value for money. It places a duty on local authorities to secure continuous improvement in local services.
>
> (DETR, 1999: 7)

Not surprisingly, this broader policy development had a significant impact on sport and leisure provision at local government level, and especially on local authority sports development units. The underlying rationale for Best Value, it was alleged, was 'a concern with quality, effectiveness, performance measurement and customer focus' (Robinson, 2004: 11), with the two key principals behind Best Value being the service reviews and an annual Best Value Performance Plan. In particular, the introduction of Best Value meant that local authorities had to complete service reviews over a five-year period that incorporated the following '4 Cs':

- *challenge* why and how the service is being provided;
- *compare* performance with that of others across a range of relevant indicators, taking into account the views of both service users and potential suppliers;
- *consult* local tax payers, service users, partners and the wider business community in the setting of new performance targets;
- consider fair *competition* as a means of securing efficient and effective services.

(Sport England, 2001: 35)

The second key principal, the annual Best Value Performance Plan, effectively established the principle of performance measurement as a central aspect of the work of local authorities. In many respects, it is this performance measurement component that has had the greatest impact on the delivery of sports development within local authorities. When Best Value was being introduced, Sport England (1999: 16) suggested that it marked 'a crossroads for sports development from which the service will either grow or retrench'. As a result of the inconsistencies that had faced sports development work within local authorities over the previous decade or so, especially because of the introduction of CCT, Sport England went as far to say that 'given this context, the temptation to reduce sports development activities within any Best Value Review is clear' (Sport England, 1999: 16). This is because sport and leisure was still not a service that local authorities were obliged to provide and, in this regard, Sport England (1999: 16) feared that a 'threat [to] ... the future of sports development is evident'. Sport England responded to the potential threat by pledging its support to local authorities. It suggested that, in promoting Active Communities, it 'will be working closely with local authorities, enabling them to respond in a positive way to the shift in the role of local authorities in the light of the Government's "Best Value" and "Modernising" initiatives' (Sport England, cited in Carlisle City Council, 2002: 11).

Despite the evident concern from Sport England, amongst others, that Best Value could be considered a threat to sports provision within local authorities, these fears were assuaged, to some extent, by the publication of *A Sporting Future for All* (DCMS, 2000). In contrast to *Raising the Game*, in *A Sporting Future for All* the Labour government indicated that, amongst other things, local authorities were regarded as a 'catalyst' and central to the effective delivery of sports development work (DCMS, 2000: 13). Local authorities were also considered by the incoming Labour government to play a central role in developing and managing 'inter-agency working and partnerships for the delivery of both sports development objectives and broader community regeneration benefits' (Houlihan and White, 2002: 111). As M. Green (2008: 97) has noted, whilst *A Sporting Future for All* and *Sport: Raising the Game* from the previous Conservative government 'are from different sides of the political spectrum, they demonstrated a striking note of unity on the twin emphases of school (youth) sport and elite development'. Of particular relevance here, however, was that in addition to the retained emphasis on school and elite sport, there was a renewed commitment by the government to the promotion of 'Sport For All' and to the role of local authorities (particularly those in areas of high deprivation) in achieving this objective. In addition, the Labour government also expressed a commitment to developing local authority facilities and working with other private commercial leisure facilities as just one means by which to develop mass participation in sport and physical activity and to ensure that local residents 'have easy access to high quality and affordable facilities' (DCMS, 2000: 36). The renewed emphasis on 'Sport For All' and the parallel emphasis that came to be placed on the role of local authorities as the main agents in delivering mass participation goals and policy implementation clearly distinguished the sports development policies of the Labour government from those of its predecessors. However, while local authorities featured prominently in *A Sporting Future for All*, many of the other policy proposals contained within the document served to harden 'the emerging bifurcation between sports development as participation and sports development as talent identification and elite achievement' (Houlihan and White, 2002: 86).

The most significant sport-related document yet published by the Labour government appeared in 2002. In December of that year, the DCMS and the government's Strategy Unit published the joint paper *Game Plan: A Strategy for Delivering Government's Sport and Physical Activity Objectives* (DCMS/Strategy Unit, 2002). Central within *Game Plan* was a focus on health and community outcomes at a local level, whilst retaining a focus on elite sport for national governing bodies of sport as well as school and youth sport. In order to attempt to achieve the aims set out in *Game Plan*, the government introduced a number of organizational changes, all of which expressed these changing policy priorities for sport in the UK. A particular premise outlined in *Game Plan* was the suggestion that the organizations involved in running sport in the UK had been poorly coordinated, lacked efficiency and focus in their policy objectives, and duplicated a number of services/ roles already performed by other organizations. For example, it held that, 'currently, multiple statements of strategy lead to confusion; complex structures lead to inefficiency; staff do not have the right skills; and many management systems could be improved' (DCMS/Strategy Unit, 2002: 18). It was also claimed that 'if participation is to be increased, it is at the local (not central or regional) level that most activity must be focused' (DCMS/Strategy Unit, 2002: 183). It also acknowledged that

> Sport and physical activity are not always seen as a priority at a local level ... As a result, sport and leisure expenditure is often the first to suffer if resources are reduced. A significant proportion of budgets is spent on the management and maintenance of facilities (rather than the strategic development of sport and recreation).
>
> (DCMS/Strategy Unit, 2002: 183)

One way in which it was proposed that local authorities might be encouraged to place sports provision more centrally within their services was indicated by a similar desire to develop performance indicators at a local level. After eighteen years out of office, 'New Labour' instigated a reinvigorated effort to 'modernize' government organizations and the public sector generally (M. Green, 2008). As Driver and Martell have noted:

> Labour modernizers see New Labour as a 'project' that is taking politics 'beyond Thatcherism' ... The name 'New Labour' itself was one of the first [attempts to modernize], signalling to the electorate a turn away from the unpopular policies of

Labour in the past by the constant distinction of 'new' from 'old' – and indicating a government that wished to create a modernized 'new Britain'.

(Driver and Martell, 2002: 67)

Almost inevitably, this modernizing agenda encompassed sport policy and sports development. As McDonald (2005: 594) argues in relation to the broader 'national' agenda: 'Like other areas of policy, the organizational structure of sport has been "modernised"', with evidence-based policy being an emerging and increasingly significant aspect of this process (Pawson, 2006; Coalter, 2007a). In this regard, sports organizations, and those working within sports development, are now increasingly expected to provide detailed data regarding the monitoring and evaluation of strategies to demonstrate the impact their services are having on the achievement of desired social outcomes. Thus, a particular policy priority of *Game Plan* is that 'there should be a non-directive approach to local provision, with more use of performance framework tools such as public health focused targets and local PSAs (Public Service Agreements)' (DCMS/Strategy Unit, 2002: 162), which are now very much part of the day-to-day reality of the operations of sports development work in local authorities (Bloyce *et al.*, 2008). Such a target driven approach found further expression in 2005 with the development of the Comprehensive Performance Assessment (CPA), as part of the Best Value process with which all local authorities had to comply. The CPA included a 'cultural' component to the strategy as a statutory requirement of all local authority service provision. Included in the culture performance indicators were some sport-related targets, related to local participation figures in sport, volunteering and sports facility provision. This meant that for the first time as part of the broader Best Value policy there were now statutory targets for sport. The CPA is due to be replaced with the Comprehensive Area Agreement (CAA), but, at the time of writing, it is likely that the current sports indicators will continue to be assessed.

One of the policies that was central to many New Labour sport policy documents and distinguished its policy approach from that of the previous Conservative government was the policy emphasis that it came to place on the role that local authorities, amongst other organizations, could play in the achievement of greater social inclusion (see Chapter 4). That local authorities were considered important in contributing to the social inclusion agenda was reinforced further in Sport England's series of publications entitled *Sport Playing Its Part*, in which sport and key agents of its promotion, including local authorities and schools, are seen as important mechanisms by which desired social outcomes such as reduced crime and drug use, greater educational attainment, community and economic regeneration and the promotion of health can be developed among young people (Sport England, 2006a, 2006b, 2006c, 2006d). This view of sport as making a substantial contribution to the enhancement of young people's lives and to the achievement of wider social objectives, particularly though locally based interventions delivered by local authorities and sporting organizations, was further articulated in *Shaping Places through Sport*, published by Sport England in November 2008. These reports once again sought to demonstrate the alleged role that sporting organizations and related projects can play in developing strong, sustainable and cohesive communities (Sport England, 2008b); the improvement of health and reduction of health inequalities (Sport England, 2008c); enhancing the life-chances and experiences of young people (Sport England, 2008d); reducing anti-social behaviour and fear of crime (Sport England, 2008e); and using sport as a vehicle for economic development and the enhancement of personal skills and employability (Sport England, 2008f). As Coalter (2007a) has argued, and for reasons we explain in Chapter 4, despite the proliferation of policy documents in which the promotion of social inclusion is a central objective, those measures that are frequently used to determine the efficacy of sports development programmes in achieving the wider social goals of government, such as social inclusion, are almost virtually impossible to assess. This, Coalter (2007a: 17) argues, remains the case despite the fact that the articulation of sport policy priorities 'with core Third Way concepts provided a much greater degree of legitimation and apparent integration' of sport within the broader policy priorities of government.

Notwithstanding the growing willingness to use sport and physical activities as vehicles of social policy designed to achieve a range of non-sport objectives, the government and other state agencies have recently reiterated the desire to achieve a range of sport policy goals. Amongst the most prominent and recent sport policy documents to have been released almost simultaneously in England was the *Sport England Strategy 2008–2011* (Rowe, 2009; Sport England, 2008a), and the DCMS publication *Playing to Win* (DCMS, 2008a). Following the award of the 2012 Olympic and Paralympic Games to London (see Chapter 7), in December 2007 the DCMS asked Sport England to conduct a review of community sport in England. The review resulted in the publication of Sport England's new strategy for community sport in England, for the period 2008–11. The strategy is said to contain several features that represent 'a significant shift in focus and direction' (Sport England, 2008a: 1) and that help Sport England to meet its objectives related to its 'Sustain, Excel and Grow' programmes (Rowe, 2009; Sport England, 2008a). Although, at the time of writing, it is too early to undertake some assessment of the extent to which Sport England has been able to achieve its objectives in this regard, it was nevertheless clear that Sport England intends to work with a range of partner organizations to focus on a range of community sport policy priority areas. In particular, the Strategy makes explicit Sport England's present policy focus in the following way:

> Sport England focus on ensuring quality opportunities exist beyond the school gates and enabling children and young people to migrate seamlessly from the school environment to community sport. Sport England's work with the Youth Sport Trust on the Five Hour Offer, its focus on reducing drop-off in participation at the age of 16 and its ambitions to develop a modern sports club network in partnership with National Governing Bodies, will be key components of this transition.
>
> (Sport England, 2008a: 2)

In addition to these policy priorities, Sport England's Strategy is said to reflect 'a shift in emphasis and role for National Governing Bodies' (Sport England, 2008a: 2), who are intended to be 'the primary drivers to deliver this new strategy for community sport' (Sport England, 2008a: 13). In return for the significant degree of autonomy that NGBs of sport would be given by Sport England over the investment of public funds within their sport, NGBs would be expected to take 'greater responsibility for the delivery of the outcomes' (Sport England, 2008a: 2) and reinforce the need to develop Whole Sport Plans (WSPs) – already a requirement in place following *Game Plan* – to indicate how they will meet the relevant objectives of the Strategy.

The prevailing policy emphasis towards the development of community sport that was expressed in Sport England's latest Strategy was reinforced in *Playing to Win* (DCMS, 2008a), which is the latest major sport policy to be published by the Labour government. *Playing to Win* was described by Andy Burnham, who was appointed as Secretary of State for Culture, Media and Sport in January 2008, as 'a plan to get more people taking up sport simply for the love of sport; to expand the pool of talented English sportsmen and women; and to break records, win medals and win tournaments for this country' (DCMS, 2008a: Preface). By focusing on the three policy areas of PE and sport for young people, community sport and elite sport, the plan also sets out the government's 'vision for sport to 2012 and beyond. It suggests a shared goal to unite around – maximising English sporting success by expanding the pool of talent in all sports. In short, more coaching and more competitive sport for all young people' (DCMS, 2008a: Preface). In this regard, a central objective of *Playing to Win* is 'to give more people of all ages the opportunity to participate in high quality competitive sport' (DCMS, 2008a: 3) and to 'engage a million more people in regular sport participation' (DCMS, 2008a: 8) by 2012–13. In relation to elite sport, it is made clear that the role of UK Sport is:

> to lead on the development of world class sporting talent, focused on winning medals at international championships, and creating a world leading high performance sporting system that will support that success into the future. UK Sport is responsible for investment in UK level programmes and therefore works in partnership with the three other Home Nation Sports Councils and Institutes alongside Sport England and the English Institute of Sport.
>
> (DCMS, 2008a: 9)

We shall return to the ways and extent to which both the Sport England Strategy and *Playing to Win* have come to impact on the changing political and policy priorities for youth sport and elite sport in Chapters 3 and 6, respectively.

Summary

In this chapter we have been centrally concerned with establishing the emerging policy context within which current sport policy and development work have emerged. In particular, we have suggested that since the 1960s sport has come to be seen increasingly as a policy tool for government to achieve wider social goals. In addition, greater importance has come to be placed by governments on achieving international success, a process that is examined in greater detail in Chapter 6. The impact of these more recent policy frameworks, and the associated changes to which we drew attention above, helps provide the context within which the various contemporary issues are examined in the remaining chapters of this book. In Chapter 3, we shall begin to examine some key aspects of the prevailing youth sports development priorities that have come to inform much contemporary policy related to school sport and PE in schools.

Revision questions

1   Examine the processes associated with increasing government involvement in sport.
2   To what extent has a national governing body or local authority of your choice been impacted by national government policy?
3   Compare and contrast how the policies of Conservative and Labour governments since 1990 have come to impact on sport policy and development.

Key readings

Henry, I. (2001) *The Politics of Leisure Policy*, 2nd edn, Basingstoke: Palgrave Macmillan.
Houlihan, B. and White, A. (2002) *The Politics of Sports Development: Development of Sport of Development through Sport?*, London: Routledge.
Hylton, K. and Bramham, P. (2008) *Sports Development: Policy, Process and Practice*, 2nd edn, London: Routledge.

Recommended websites

Central Council for Physical Recreation: www.ccpr.org.uk
Institute for Sport, Parks and Leisure: www.ispal.org.uk
www.sportdevelopment.info

3 Youth sports development

Physical education, school sport and community club links

Objectives

This chapter will:

- examine the levels and patterns of young people's participation in sport and physical activity;
- examine some of the most significant youth sports development policies to have been introduced in schools in recent years; and
- reflect upon some of the opportunities and challenges associated with the future of youth sports development in schools.

Introduction

There has been growing concern over the past three decades or more with what is said to be a trend towards sport and physical activity becoming increasingly rare features of contemporary lifestyles, and especially those of young people. Indeed, one of the most striking characteristics of British government policy towards youth sport in recent years has been the assumption that PE, school sport (especially competitive team sport) and physical activity are in rapid decline. More specifically, the apparent failure of many schools to provide youngsters with what has been ambiguously described as 'two or more hours of high quality PE' (Department for Education and Skills [DfES]/DCMS, 2003), as well as the purported 'privileging' of sport and team games over physical activity in PE curricula (Kirk, 2004; Penney and Chandler, 2000; Penney and Evans, 1999), is believed to be among the central reasons for young people's supposed declining levels of participation and the perceived failure of physical educationalists in ensuring that young people remain actively involved in leisure-sport and physical activity both in the short and long term (Green *et al.*, 2005a; Kirk, 2004; Smith *et al.*, 2004). What is particularly striking about this concern over aspects of young people's lives is its near-universal acceptance across a range of societies in the Western world and beyond for, in both more and less developed societies, there is now a broad consensus that declining participation in sport and physical activity – alongside the growing prevalence of 'unhealthy' diets and an increasing preference for engaging in sedentary leisure activities – is the main 'cause' of a 'health crisis' said to be emerging among children and youth (see Chapter 5).

Set in the context of this concern, the central objective of this chapter is to examine those policies that are designed to address these perceived problems by promoting the development of youth sport through PE and school sport (PESS) and the enhancement of school and community sports club links. The chapter begins with a brief discussion of what the available empirical evidence suggests about the levels and patterns of young people's participation in sport and physical activity in Europe and elsewhere. In doing so, it questions the adequacy of many of the existing assumptions about these aspects of young people's lives. This is then followed by a more detailed examination of what might be regarded as one of the most significant youth sports development policies to have been introduced in schools in England in recent years: the Physical Education, School Sport and Club Links (PESSCL) strategy. In particular, we shall discuss how the implementation of the School Sport Partnership (SSP) programme, as part of the PESSCL strategy, has come to impact on the activities of teachers, and hence the experiences of PESS among their pupils, in rather differential ways and in a manner that may, in the event, have a number of outcomes that no one has planned and which no one has intended. The chapter concludes by reviewing some of the salient issues raised by the implementation of PESSCL and SSPs and briefly reflects upon the future of youth sports development in schools.

Young people's participation in sport and physical activity

Studies of sports participation among young people tend to be somewhat conservative and cannot by their very nature reveal much about the intensity and seasonality of participation, the significance of sport and physical activity to young people's lives, or the quality of their experiences (K. Green, 2008; Smith, 2006). The available data indicate, however, that in many countries current levels of participation in sport and physical activity among young people are higher than those reported in the 1960s and 1970s. Indeed, whilst there has been a plateauing in overall participation in the twenty-first century, and even a slight decline amongst some groups (K. Green, 2008), there has been a clear trend towards increased participation among young people in very many countries, and especially those in Western Europe. In Britain, Roberts (1996a; 1996b) has noted how, contrary to received wisdom, between the 1970s and mid-1990s there has been an empirically observable increase in young people's participation in sport and physical activity. More specifically, from his analysis of the government's own surveys of participation in the mid-1990s, Roberts concluded that

> young people were playing more sports in and out of school than in the past ... the drop-out rate on completion of statutory schooling had fallen dramatically ... social class and gender differences had narrowed [and] ... sports had higher youth participation and retention than any other structured forms of leisure
>
> (Roberts 1996b: 105)

Indeed, such was the increase in young people's involvement Roberts suggested that, contrary to the alleged 'golden age' of sports participation (said to have existed around the 1960s), the level of sport and physical activity participation for young people had grown to be 'well above the levels [of] ... the 1950s and 1960s' (Roberts, 1996a: 52), with fewer dropping out of sport and physical activity at the end of their compulsory full-time education.

Data from government-funded surveys conducted by NDPBs such as Sport England and the Sports Council for Wales (SCW) have also indicated that the demonstrable

tendency among young people towards increased and then stabilized levels of involvement in sport and physical activity – both inside and outside schools – has continued. In
2002, for example, almost all young people in England and Wales were participating
'occasionally' (at least once in the past year) in sport and physical activity via National
Curriculum Physical Education (NCPE) and over three-quarters were involved on a 'regular' (at least ten times in the past year) basis in both countries (SCW, 2003; Sport England, 2003). It was also apparent that while there has been a 'small, but notable, increase
in the numbers of young people who are *not* taking part in at least one sport regularly'
(Sport England, 2003: 5; original emphasis), 'there are now fewer young people spending
less than one hour, or no time, in a week doing sports and exercise than was the case in
1994' (Sport England, 2003: 58).

It is not only the frequency with which young people participate and the time spent
doing so that has allegedly increased, however, for alongside these trends there has been
an increase in the number of sports and physical activities in which they frequently participate in school (SCW, 2003; Sport England, 2003). These increases are particularly
worthy of note, not least because they point to the ways in which many PE teachers in
England appear to have, over the last eight years, focused more upon '*increasing the
range* of sports that young people take part in' and less upon 'the frequency in which they
participate in individual sports' (Sport England, 2003: 19; emphases added). These trends
towards increased participation and the provision of a wider range of sports and physical
activities in NCPE have also been observed in the 2006/07 *School Sport Survey* (TNS,
2007). The Survey indicated that, in relation to the proportion of young people who
undertook at least two hours or more PE and out-of-hours school sport in a typical week,
there 'have been very marked improvements in levels of participation in Years 1–6 (5–11-
year-olds)' (TNS, 2007: 2) since 2003/04, with 'smaller improvements' (TNS, 2007: 3)
being reported for those aged 11–16 years old. It was also reported that the range of
activities provided for young people by their teachers had continued to increase during the
period surveyed: those 11–16-year-olds who attended secondary schools typically received
21 sports (on average) as part of curricular and extra-curricular PE, whilst primary-aged
school children (5–11-year-olds) were provided 16 sports on average (TNS, 2007).

Overall, it is clear that on the basis of the available evidence, there has been an
increase in young people's involvement in sport and physical activity through NCPE in
England and Wales. Since the mid-1990s, in particular, there also appears to have been an
even more substantial increase in young people's out-of-school involvement in sport and
physical activity. Data from the most recent Sport England (2003) survey of youth participation 'out-of-lessons', for example, indicated that over three-quarters of all young
people were regular participants in some sport and physical activity, while just over half
of all youngsters surveyed by the SCW (2003) were involved 'regularly' during extra-
curricular PE. In England, it is also clear that whilst 14 per cent participated in no sport
or physical activity 'out-of-lessons' (compared with 17 per cent in 1999), the proportion
of young people who played seven or more sports frequently outside school lessons in 2002
(26 per cent) has steadily increased since 1994, with most young people involved in five
sports and physical activities on average (Sport England, 2003).

As we noted earlier, the upward trend in participation among young people in recent
decades is not restricted solely to Britain, for studies conducted in Australia (e.g. Dollman *et
al.*, 2006) and in a number of European countries (e.g. Samdal *et al.*, 2006) have also indicated
that whilst sport and physical activity participation among young people has increased
rapidly over the past three decades, this has stabilized somewhat since the late 1990s. In

particular, studies of participation in sport and physical activity among young people in several Scandinavian countries have consistently pointed towards relatively continuous increases in participation in recent decades. In Finland, for example, Laakso *et al.* (2008: 151) have noted that 'Leisure time physical activity among young people in Finland increased ... from 1977 to 2007', especially among young women. They also noted that whilst 'the frequency of unorganized spontaneous leisure time physical activity had remained at the same level or increased slightly' (Laakso *et al.*, 2008: 149), the biggest increases in youth sports participation had been observed in sports clubs. Similar conclusions can be drawn from studies of youth sports participation in Norway (Mamen and Aaberge, 2006; Sisjord and Skirstad, 1996), where since the 1970s there is said to have been a 'tremendous increase in the number of young people taking part in organized sport' (Sisjord and Skirstad, 1996: 173), which remains 'the most popular [leisure] activity among youths' (Sisjord and Skirstad, 1996: 175). In Sweden, Kristèn *et al.* (2003: 25) have also pointed towards the alleged 'dominance' of sport in the lives of young people and described the 'sports movement' as being the country's 'largest and most vigorous popular movement' (Kristèn *et al.*, 2003: 24), whilst in 2007 in Iceland more 14–15-year-olds reported participating in sport and physical activity overall and in sports clubs since 1992 (Eiðsdóttir *et al.*, 2008).

In other reviews of participation, De Knop and De Martelaer (2001: 41) have explained that available data in the Netherlands continue to indicate that 'young people participate in large numbers' in leisure-sport and physical activity, whilst in Flanders 'more and more teenage boys and girls' are said to be increasingly 'involved in leisure-time sports participation' (Scheerder *et al.*, 2005: 325) in the twenty-first century. These findings are consistent with those of a cross-sectional study of youth sports participation in Belgium, Estonia, Finland, Germany, Hungary and the Czech Republic, which concluded that 'physical activities and sports [continue to] belong to the most popular [leisure] activities of young people' (Telama *et al.*, 2002: 140). A more recent study of 10–18-year-olds in Portugal concluded that the tendency for participation to increase among young people as they get older helps indicate the increasing 'importance of sport [participation] among youth' (Seabra *et al.*, 2007: 379) in the country. All in all, it seems that the vast majority of young people *are* taking part in sport and physical activity reasonably regularly both in and out of school in many countries, and particularly so in northern Western European countries.

A related and notable feature of the trend towards increasing levels of participation among young people has been the broadening and increasing diversification in the kinds of activities undertaken by young men and women, especially in their leisure time. Of particular significance in this regard has been the increasing preference among young people – particularly during the 1980s and 1990s – to participate in what have been described as 'lifestyle activities' (Coalter, 1999). The growing popularity of these 'lifestyle activities' has been strongly associated 'not only in Britain but in other countries, too, with the emergence of commercialized, consumption-based, body-image-oriented and highly individualized fashions such as jogging, aerobics and the use of mechanized fitness clubs' (Dunning and Waddington, 2003: 355–56). The increasing involvement of young people in these kinds of activities, which tend to be characterized as individual or small-group activities that are more flexible in nature, usually less competitive and tend to be pursued more recreationally than competitive team-based sports (Coalter, 1999), has also been strongly associated with the rapid expansion of public and private sports leisure centres and the adoption of 'Sport For All' policies both inside and outside schools. As Roberts (2004: 91) observes, these kinds of activities have become increasingly popular not least because 'public facilities that are available for general public use, on a pay-as-you-go basis, seem more congruent with present-day young people's and adults' lifestyle preferences than the stronger commitment involved in club membership'.

In this regard, the increasing desire among young people (and adults) in many countries to engage in more commercialized, individualized and flexible sports and physical activities rather than regular, more structured, forms of involvement such as that required by a strong commitment to club-based sport, would appear consistent with the broader changes in the increasingly individualized lifestyles of participants (Coalter, 1999; Roberts, 2004; Smith, 2006). It is perhaps not altogether surprising, therefore, that in several European countries, including Britain, 'there is believed to be a problem of young people failing to join sports clubs' (Roberts, 2004: 91) during their leisure time. Indeed, whilst it is clear that 'in recent years some European countries' sports clubs have experienced a loss of members' (Roberts, 2004: 32) and 'that today's young people seem to be less "clubbable" than their predecessors' (Roberts, 2004: 91), this is not to say that young people are abandoning sport and physical activity. Rather, as Roberts has noted in relation to elsewhere in Europe (though the general point may apply equally well to Britain):

> It is more a case of them engaging in recreational swimming, surfing, skiing, sailing and so on without joining clubs and teams, and participating in competitions. This does not mean that competitive sport is threatened with extinction. It is more a shift in the constantly moving boundary between club sport and self-organised recreation.
>
> (Roberts 2004: 32)

These points notwithstanding, it might with equal validity be noted that while there has been a gradual move away from young people participating in club-based sport in leisure and schools since the 1980s, this has not meant that the numbers playing competitive sports have been eliminated or even reduced (Roberts, 2004). It is more the case that although involvement in club sport declines with age – during the secondary school years and especially upon the end of full-time compulsory education – and is not necessarily a long-term pursuit for many young people who first take it up, for a minority of youngsters (especially males) competitive club sport is an important aspect of their sporting lives (De Knop *et al.*, 1998; Roberts, 2004; Telama *et al.*, 2002; TNS, 2008).

With the shift away from competitive sports towards more recreational 'lifestyle activities' among some young people, there are several caveats regarding trends in levels and types of participation in sport and physical activity. First, and notwithstanding the evident popularity of 'lifestyle activities' among young people, this does not preclude team sports (which are, by their very nature, especially competitive) from being pursued more recreationally. Nor, for that matter, does the popularity of recreational versions of sports preclude involvement in activities where the primary motive for participating might be 'competition'. Second, while these kinds of 'lifestyle activities' have, as Coalter (1999) observes, experienced substantial increases in participation by young people and are frequently among those with the most regular participants, nevertheless it seems that sport and team games as well as 'lifestyle activities' have become an integral feature of young people's participation both inside and outside school in many countries (Green *et al.*, 2005a; Smith *et al.*, 2004; Telama *et al.*, 2005). The third point is that the evident shift towards 'lifestyle activities' should not be taken to indicate that young people are turning their back on competitive sport, and team games in particular, for this is to oversimplify what is, in reality, the rather complex nature of young people's leisure-time participatory repertoires. As Green *et al.* (2005a) have noted, while over half of young people in the secondary age group in England in 2002 participated in team games frequently in their leisure time, it is not only football and other 'traditional' games – such as cricket – that remain popular among a minority of secondary-age youngsters. Rather, other team sports (such as basketball) as well as partner sports (such as tennis, badminton and table tennis) also feature alongside more potentially recreational, less competitive 'lifestyle activities' (such as swimming, cycling, roller-skating/blading and skateboarding, running and tenpin bowling) (Sport England, 2003). Indeed, it seems that young people's levels of participation in football has remained roughly the same since the 1990s – though some other team games like cricket continue to lose appeal among boys – and many games remain as popular now as previously, with netball, hockey, tennis and badminton, for example, becoming more popular among secondary-aged youngsters (Sport England, 2003). Similarly, in Wales those activities in which marked increases in curricular participation were observed in 1999 compared to 2002 included, for example, sports such as football, basketball, cricket and gymnastics, alongside more individual 'lifestyle activities' such as circuit training, aerobics and weight training (SCW, 2003).

In short, as Telama and colleagues have pointed out with regard to Finland – although the point might equally be applied to many youngsters across Europe, including in Britain – 'the most popular types of sports [or, rather, physical activities] among adolescents are … cycling, swimming, walking and running' (Telama *et al.*, 1994: 68), alongside other more potentially competitive, performance-oriented team sports such as football and basketball. This having been said, it is important to keep in mind the point that while for many young people sport makes a relatively limited contribution, it is clear that more individualistic and flexible activities dominate their leisure-sport and physical activity lifestyles (Coalter, 1999; Smith, 2006). Indeed, these are the kinds of activities in which they are more likely to continue participating 'indoors' at their local sport and leisure centres, gymnasium or health clubs where they can 'play their preferred sports, with their own friends [and] at times of their own choice' (Roberts, 1996b: 113).

Despite the existence of a romanticized view of young people's supposedly higher participation levels in sport and physical activity at some unspecified point in the past, the available data indicate an increase and a gradual stabilizing during the early twenty-first century in Britain and elsewhere since the 1970s, alongside a broadening and diversification of participation. Indeed, while there is a significant minority of youngsters doing relatively little or absolutely nothing, and while they may not be doing as much as some (such as government, PE teachers and NGBs of sport) might want – nor, for that matter, as much or at the level deemed desirable for the improvement of health – they appear, according to empirical studies, to be doing far more than is commonly claimed (Green *et al.*, 2005a; Roberts, 1996a; Smith *et al.*, 2004).

This having been said, it would be wrong to assume that all young people participate as regularly, to the same extent or even, for that matter, in the same kinds of activities. Such a clear-cut formulation cannot capture all of the complexities involved. In fact, there appears to be a polarization of young people's sport and physical activity participation levels into those who participate on an almost daily basis and those who participate rarely, if at all, with most young people somewhere in the middle (Roberts, 1996a, 1996b; Smith, 2006; Telama *et al.*, 2002). Participation levels, as Roberts (1996a: 51) observed, continue to be distributed along a bell-shaped curve: 'Most are towards the middle. At one extreme a minority are highly active relative to the norm. At the other extreme another minority is inactive both relatively and absolutely.'

Although young people as a whole are experiencing a broader diet of sports and physical activities in PE and in their leisure time than previous generations, their participation continues to vary differentially over time and from one society to another. As has been made abundantly clear elsewhere, the evidence also indicates quite clearly that young people's participation in sport and physical activity continues to be structured by many forms of social division, particularly gender, social class (including highest level of education obtained) and age (Coalter *et al.*, 1995; Green *et al.*, 2005b; Roberts, 1996a).

Having said something about what the available empirical evidence tells us about the participatory patterns and tendencies of young people, the rest of this chapter will examine some key aspects of youth sports development in England. In particular, the chapter will examine the establishment of the YST and two policy developments that have come to generate some of the most profound impacts on the practice of PESS and that have been strongly associated with the increasing involvement of SDOs in PESS in recent years: the introduction of the PESSCL strategy and the creation of SSPs.

Youth Sport Trust: the institutional focus for physical education and school sport

As Houlihan and Green (2006) have noted, prior to the early 1990s political interest in PESS was, in policy terms at least, marginal. There was also said to be a general 'lack of philosophical and conceptual coherence among organizations representing PE and school sport interests regarding the contribution that PE might make to the development of pupils' (Houlihan and Green, 2006: 75), particularly during the debates in the 1980s over whether PE should be included in a new National Curriculum. Following the appointment of John Major as Prime Minister in 1990, and the subsequent re-election of the Conservative Party two years later, there was a 'dramatic change in the political salience of school sport and PE' (Houlihan and Green, 2006: 74). As explained in greater detail elsewhere (e.g. K. Green, 2008; Houlihan and Green, 2006; Penney and Evans, 1999), particularly significant was the increasing intervention of government in educational policy, as expressed, for example, in the development of a new NCPE. Introduced in 1992, the NCPE was intended to enhance the position of 'traditional', competitive team games (such as football, cricket, rugby and hockey) to the school curriculum. The emphasis that came to be placed on the importance of competitive team sport as being the focal point of PE, together with the emphasis on elite sport and the perceived role PE was believed to play in helping to raise standards of international success, was strengthened substantially in the revision of the NCPE and the publication of the government's policy document *Sport: Raising the Game* in 1995 (DNH, 1995; see Chapter 2). In this regard, both publications revealed quite clearly how government was becoming increasingly interventionist in setting the PESS policy agenda during the 1990s. They also illustrate how some groups (such as government and the elite sports lobby) had a greater capacity to privilege some values and priorities (e.g. elite and school sport, competition and international success) over others (e.g. mass participation and more recreational forms of physical activity), and to develop alliances with other groups to achieve their desired objectives. One alliance that the government developed to help achieve its elite and PESS objectives during the mid-1990s was with the YST.

The YST is a registered charity that was established by Sir John Beckwith in 1994 and is located at Loughborough University. The central objective of the YST is to develop and implement a series of educational and sporting programmes for young people aged

4–19 in schools and their local communities (YST, 2007). These programmes are variously designed to help, among other things, enhance levels of participation and enjoyment in PESS, as well as provide young people with what are considered the best teaching, coaching and resources possible to enable them to develop to the best level they can in their chosen sport. They are delivered through schools and are supported by a complex network of corporate partners (e.g. Nike, BSkyB and Sainsburys), trusts and foundations and government departments (e.g. DCMS and Department of Children, Schools and Families [DCSF]) (YST, 2007). Among the many programmes that could be cited in this regard are the TOPs programmes (including TOP Play for 4–9-year-olds and TOP Link for those aged 14–16) that were first developed in the 1990s and are designed to provide young people, regardless of their ability, with opportunities to participate in sport and physical activity within school-based PE. The TOPs programmes are also said to provide teachers, particularly those in primary schools, with a range of child-friendly equipment and resources as well as additional training and support to enhance the quality and quantity of PESS provision young people receive in schools (YST, 2007). Step into Sport is another initiative organized by the YST, Sport England and Sports Leaders UK and funded by the DCMS. This sports development programme – as part of the PESSCL strategy to be discussed later – began in 2002 and is designed to establish a framework of coordinated opportunities to enable 14–19-year-olds to begin and sustain participation in volunteering and leadership training in sport. Step into Sport is particularly intended to enable pupils to gain leadership qualifications (such as the Junior Sports Leader Award), coach children in primary schools and help them organize their own sports festivals, and take up sports volunteering placements in their local communities (YST, 2007).

A similar programme to Step into Sport is the Sky Living for Sport initiative that was introduced in 2003 and is currently delivered by the YST in conjunction with BSkyB and supported by the DCSF. The three-year programme targets 11–16-year-olds who are considered by their teachers to be 'at risk' of being excluded from the perceived benefits of school life, whether through poor attendance, lack of confidence or poor behaviour. In this regard, the scheme is designed to enhance pupils' behaviour, attitude and communication skills by encouraging them to set their own personal targets and goals by working with their teachers, sometimes outside normal school PE lessons. As part of the programme pupils are given the opportunity to participate in a range of activities – particularly non-traditional ones – including archery, canoeing, martial arts, sailing and skateboarding, and are then required to organize a sporting event (such as inter-school competitions and dance performances) for a local school or community group. By 2007 Sky Living For Sport is said to have been delivered to more than 14,000 young people in over 600 secondary schools in England, Northern Ireland and Scotland and is now being offered to all schools in these countries (YST, 2007). In addition, the YST and BSkyB have now developed a range of downloadable resources and Continued Professional Development tools to encourage teachers in all schools to develop and run the programme themselves and to tailor it towards the particular needs of pupils in their school.

The aforementioned programmes represent some of the more recent developments that are expressive of the ways and extent to which the YST has gradually begun to adopt an increasingly central role in the delivery of PESS as well as youth sports development activity more broadly. Indeed, the inauguration of the YST helped provide the kind of institutional focus for PESS that was said to be lacking prior to the mid-1990s. This lack of institutional and policy focus and the absence of any real consensus among professional

PE bodies such as the Association for Physical Education (AfPE) (formerly British Association of Advisers and Lecturers in Physical Education [BALPPE] and Physical Education Association of the United Kingdom [PEAUK]), together with the institutional weakness of the DCMS when compared to other more politically influential and powerful central government departments (such as those related to health and education), has meant the YST has come increasingly to be seen as the institutional focus for PESS and has been able to obtain a greater capacity to define policy priorities in the area (Houlihan and Green, 2006).

Such was the growing influence and power of the YST and the increasing tendency for government to fund many of its activities during the late 1990s, the Trust was charged by the current Labour government to implement aspects of its first sport policy document, *A Sporting Future for All* (DCMS, 2000). As we noted in Chapter 2, *A Sporting Future for All* was premised, amongst other things, on the perceived need to reverse a supposed decline in young people's participation in sport and physical activity through school-based PE and its alleged relationship with such things as lack of international sporting success, declining standards of health and educational attainment. In light of these presumed tendencies, the government focused particular attention on extending the range of sporting opportunities available to young people in curricular and especially extra-curricular PE, the creation of 110 Specialist Sports Colleges (SSCs) that were to have an explicit focus on elite sport and be located in communities of greatest need, the appointment of 600 School Sport Coordinators, and the enhancement of school links with community sports clubs. The policy commitment (in *A Sporting Future for All*) to creating SSCs formed part of the specialist schools programme that was ostensibly launched by the previous Conservative government in 1994 'to help secondary schools to develop strengths and raise standards in a chosen specialism' (Office for Standards in Education [Ofsted], 2005: 5); in effect, to act as centres of excellence for particular subjects such as sport, technology or science. The first SSC was designated in 1997 and since then the phased implementation of SSCs meant that by August 2008 578 schools had been designated SSCs. By seeking to establish a more efficient national infrastructure for PESS, the main objectives of the SSC policy included: improving participation and achievement in PESS amongst students of all abilities; raising standards of teaching in schools; providing a structure through which students can progress to careers in sport and PE; and promoting the development of young talented athletes through the SSCs' links with other schools, sporting agencies, clubs and the regional centres of the UK Sports Institute with whom they are involved (DfES/DCMS, 2003; Ofsted, 2005).

As the body responsible for supporting the implementation and organization of SSCs, the YST has been able to exert quite considerable influence over how this aspect of contemporary policy towards PESS has come to impact on the activities of teachers and the experiences of pupils. As Flintoff (2008a: 151) has noted, the extent to which the Trust has been able to achieve some degree of control and influence has been through, for example, its 'application, evaluation and redesignation procedures; its annual conference, and other continuing professional development opportunities for those teachers working in the colleges'. Given the relatively greater position of power of the YST in implementing policy related to the SSC programme, many schools and teachers have been 'only marginally involved in innovations emanating from the programme as it has progressively developed' (Flintoff, 2008a: 151). This is not to say, of course, that teachers and the schools in which they teach have no power to control policy outcomes or to constrain the actions of seemingly more powerful groups such as the YST. Indeed, while there is, at the time of writing, little available evidence regarding the ways in which teachers working in SSCs have sought to manage the implementation of government's SSC policy through the YST, the findings of studies conducted in the North and North West of England indicate that there exists differential practice between teachers and schools in relation to the ways in which aspects of the SSP and SSC programmes have been embedded in the practice of PE and sport in schools (Flintoff, 2003; 2008b; Smith, Odhams, Platts and Green, 2009). The data from these studies suggest that part of the explanation for the existence of such differential practice in SSCs is that, despite the extent to which the YST attempts to control, within closely defined limits, the implementation of policy towards SSCs, this is often very dependent on the characteristic features and complex networks of relationships that comprise individual schools. Of significance in this regard are the particular enthusiasms, habitus and life-experiences of teachers, senior management and head teachers towards PESS; the 'kinds' of pupils who attend particular schools; the sporting traditions of schools; available facilities and other resources (e.g. access to sports coaches and SDOs); pre-existing links between schools, local sports clubs and the wider community; and the extent to which drawing on the specialist schools programme can bring specific advantages to schools (e.g. purchasing additional equipment, employing extra staff and extending the provision of activities and opportunities, especially outside curriculum time) (Flintoff, 2003; 2008b; Smith, Odhams, Platts and Green, 2009). The findings of these studies suggest that while groups such as the YST, because of the particular relational constraints under which members of the organization work, have a greater capacity to make crucial decisions over things such as the content and implementation of the SSC programme, they are nevertheless constrained by the nature and complexity of the network of relations in which they are located. The aspirations and strategies of such groups are also more or less continuously mediated (and sometimes thwarted) by other groups such as PE teachers, sports coaches and SDOs. One consequence of this is that those groups are able, to a greater or lesser degree, to reinterpret policy and to implement the activities of SSCs, and the SSP of which they are a part, in ways that they feel are most appropriate to the local context of schooling and that may, therefore, not have been intended by government and the YST (Flintoff, 2003; 2008b; Smith, Odhams, Platts and Green, 2009). We shall return to the significance of some of those unintended outcomes that have been associated with the implementation of SSPs later.

Although a principle objective of the SSC initiative was to help government (and, hence, the YST) to meet its objectives related to the enhancement of participation and desirable experiences of PESS, a related aim of the SSC initiative, and the SSP programme of which it is a part, is the achievement of other social objectives. As Houlihan and Green (2006) have noted, the policy goals and priorities of *A Sporting Future for All*, such as those related to the creation of SSCs, were indicative of the way in which under the Labour government the political salience of PESS has not only been maintained, 'but also emerged as a significant cross-departmental vehicle for the administration's broader social objectives' (Houlihan and Green, 2006: 77). Of particular significance in the present context is that one central aspect of the YST's increasing power to influence the policy priorities for PESS is 'the strength and clarity of the institutional message and values conveyed by the organization, namely that school sport and PE initiatives have a significant role to play in helping government achieve policy goals that extend beyond a narrow focus on school sport and PE' (Houlihan and Green, 2006: 85). It should be noted, however, that the growing influence of the YST over the content and policy priorities of school-based youth sports development policies cannot be comprehended in isolation from the increasing willingness of its Chief Executive, Sue Campbell, to present PESS as a solution to many of the government's wider policy concerns regarding, for example, social inclusion, educational attainment, community cohesion and crime reduction (see Chapter 4).

The increasing political profile and prominence given to PESS in recent years have been repeatedly emphasized by Sue Campbell. Perhaps because of her governmental advisory role on these policy areas, Campbell has been able to persuade civil servants and government ministers that PESS can have a prominent role in 'achieving broader educational objectives such as whole school improvement, community development and affecting personal behavioural and attitudinal change among pupils' (Houlihan and Green, 2006: 82). Given the apparent success that Campbell and others appear to have had over the last decade in convincing government and civil servants of the alleged benefits that investing in PESS might have for the achievement of other government objectives, it is perhaps not surprising that such views were strengthened further in the PESSCL strategy, outlined in the cross-departmental document *Learning through PE and Sport* (DfES/DCMS, 2003), published in 2003. Before examining the policy priorities and goals of the PESSCL strategy, however, it is perhaps of some significance that, as we briefly noted in Chapter 2, such has been the growing power and influence of the YST in setting and implementing the PESS policy agenda since the mid-1990s, the DCMS and Sport England announced recently that the YST is now to be the sole organization with direct responsibility for PESS (DCMS, 2008a; Sport England, 2008a). The activities of the YST are, in turn, expected to be integrated into the broader sports development work undertaken by County Sports Partnerships (CSPs) that is expected, amongst other things, to contribute to the delivery of PESSCL, develop links between school, community and performance sport, and help ensure that school and community sport is enhanced by, and focused on, the various Whole Sport Plans of the NGBs of sport (for a review, see Houlihan and Lindsey, 2008; McDonald, 2005; YST, 2007).

Physical Education, School Sport and Club Links strategy

As we noted earlier, the PESSCL strategy – which started in 2003 – can properly be seen as one of the most significant youth sport policy initiatives to have been introduced in schools in England in recent years. The original overarching aims of the strategy were to:

a. establish a national infrastructure for PE and school sport by creating
    i.   400 Specialist Sports Colleges, subject to sufficient high quality applications, by 2005; and
    ii. 400 School Sport Coordinator partnerships by 2006; with
    iii. 3,200 School Sport Coordinators in secondary schools and 18,000 Primary or Special School Link Teachers by 2006. There will be 2,400 School Sport Coordinators and 13,500 Primary or Special School Link Teachers by 2005;
b. improve the quality of teaching, coaching and learning in PE and school sport; and
c. increase the proportion of children guided into clubs from School Sport Coordinator partnerships.

(DfES/DCMS, 2003: 2)

To achieve these aims the PESSCL strategy was intended to bring together a range of already existing programmes to provide a more coordinated, efficient and effective way of enhancing the provision and experiences of PESS among young people. This would appear to have been the case even though the PESSCL strategy was supported by considerable resources that are funded largely by the Exchequer, with additional monies being supplied from the National Lottery's New Opportunities Fund (NOF). The level of investment that was allocated to the implementation of the eight programmes that constitute the basis of PESSCL was made clear in the strategy, which stated that

> the Government is investing £459 million to transform PE and school sport. This funding is on top of £686 million being invested to improve school sport facilities across England. Together, this means that over £1 billion is being made available for PE and school sport, and all schools in England will benefit in some way.
>
> (DfES/DCMS, 2003: 1)

The YST, together with the DCSF and DCMS, is responsible for implementing the PESSCL strategy, which had a joint DfES (now DCSF) and DCMS Public Service Agreement (PSA) target to 'increase the percentage of school children in England who spend a minimum of two hours each week on high quality PE and school sport within and beyond the curriculum to 75% by 2006' (DfES/DCMS, 2003: 2). This figure was later revised to a target of 85 per cent by 2008. On the basis of the findings generated by the 2006/07 *School Sport Survey* referred to earlier, this was said to be achieved a year early, with 86 per cent of 5–16-year-olds said to have hit the target (TNS, 2007). Data from the later 2007/08 *School Sport Survey* indicated that the proportion of young people who spent a minimum of two hours each week on high-quality PESS had increased to 90 per cent (TNS, 2008). It is important to note, however, that the proportion of pupils who are said to have achieved the desired two hours of activity per week varied substantially between those in the primary (5–11-year-olds) and secondary (11–16-year-olds) years. In general, the proportion of pupils who reported participating in two hours of PESS each week initially increased across the early primary school years, and ranged from 95 per cent amongst those in Year 1 (5–6 years old) to 97 per cent in Year 6 (10–11-year-olds) (TNS, 2008). In secondary schools, however, the opposite pattern was observed, with the proportion of pupils who claimed to spend two or more hours engaged in PESS each week declining from a peak of 95 per cent reported by those in Year 7 (11–12-year-olds) to 71 per cent for Year 10 pupils (14–15-year-olds) and 63 per cent for those in Year 11 (aged 15–16) (TNS, 2008).

It is clear that achieving the PSA target of increasing the proportion of school children in England who spend a minimum of two hours each week on high-quality PESS within and beyond the curriculum to 85 per cent by 2008 was a, if not the, key policy priority of the government's PESSCL strategy during the first five years of implementation. Given that this was evidently the case, it is also not surprising that the attention of much of the YST's activities – and the evaluation of its work – since the strategy was implemented revolved, in particular, around assessing the extent to which schools achieved this policy goal. What is particularly noteworthy, however, is that there is very little credible scientific evidence for why this is regarded as an important policy goal by government and other interested parties. Indeed, whilst there has always been a perceived need and desirability for young people to receive a minimum of two hours of compulsory PE as part of the National Curriculum amongst government and others within the profession, this taken for granted, heavily ideological assumption has rarely been subject to any serious critical examination and yet it continues to form a bedrock on which much school-based youth sports development policy is based (Roberts, 1996a; Smith *et al.*, 2004). As we shall see next, one of the eight programmes of the PESSCL strategy that is considered to be 'the central component in fulfilling the Government's strategy to help all young people access at least two hours of high quality PE and school sport a week' (YST, 2007: 7) is SSPs.

School Sport Partnerships

The SSP programme – formerly the School Sports Coordinator Programme – is a central component of the PESSCL strategy. From 2006 SSPs were introduced in phases and by 2007 all state-maintained schools and some independent schools had become members of the programme. These schools now constitute the complex network of 450 SSPs that currently exist in England. Partnerships are groups or 'families' of schools that receive an additional £270,000 funding per year and are required to help enhance opportunities for young people to participate in PESS. Each Partnership is led by a full-time partnership development manager (PDM), who is usually located at a local SSC, which acts as the central hub for the SSP. The PDM is responsible for the strategic development of the Partnership, liaises with other agencies (e.g. the YST, local sports clubs and local authorities) and is partly accountable to a local management group that is typically comprised of primary and secondary school head teachers, a director of specialism (sport) and local authority SDOs (Houlihan and Lindsey, 2008). Typically, an SSP also consists of between four and eight secondary schools each of which employ a school sports coordinator (SSCo) – an existing teacher who is usually released from the teaching timetable for two or two and a half days per week. The SSCo is responsible for the coordination and development of school sport (especially intra- and inter-school sport, physical activity and competition) in his or her own school and its family of between four and eight primary and special schools. Each of these schools, in turn, has a nominated link teacher (primary link teacher [PLT]), a teacher who is released from teaching for twelve days per year, and who is responsible for improving the quantity and quality of PE and sport provision in his or her own school.

The key policy outcomes of the SSP programme can be summarized as increased participation and standards of performance by young people across a range of sports, improved motivation, attitude and self-esteem resulting in increased personal and social development on the part of young people, and an increase in the number of qualified and active coaches, leaders and officials working in local primary, secondary and special schools and in local sports clubs and facilities (Flintoff, 2003; Houlihan and Lindsey, 2008). To these policy outcomes can be added seven more outcomes, including: 'improved attitude, behaviour and attendance in PE and the whole school' (Institute of Youth Sport [IYS], 2008a: 5) and 'increased attainment and achievement in and through PE, OSHL [out-of-school-hours learning] and sport' (IYS, 2008b: 5).

That the policy outcomes of the SSP programme and the PESSCL strategy of which it is a part contain sports development and non-sport objectives is not altogether surprising for, as we noted earlier, one consequence of the increasing political salience of PESS among civil servants and government ministers over the last decade or so has been the extent to which key organizations such as the YST and its constituent members (e.g. Sue Campbell) have been effective in claiming for PESS a range of perceived benefits. The assumed benefits that participation in PESS is said to have for young people were neatly captured in the PESSCL strategy, in which it is claimed that PESS, both within and beyond the curriculum, can improve:

- pupil concentration, commitment and self-esteem; leading to higher attendance and better behaviour and attainment;
- fitness levels; active children are less likely to be obese and more likely to pursue sporting activities as adults, thereby reducing the likelihood of coronary heart disease, diabetes and some forms of cancer; and

- success in international competition by ensuring talented young sports people have a clear pathway to elite sport and competition whatever their circumstances.

(DfES/DCMS, 2003: 1)

These uncritically accepted views of the supposed worth of PESS to the enhancement of young people's lives are not, of course, confined to the policy area of PESS, for they also underpin much government policy related to young people. Among the more recent policy initiatives that focus on young people's lives and which, to some extent, overlap with the priorities of the SSP programme and PESSCL strategy are the *Every Child Matters* initiative launched in 2003 (The Stationery Office [TSO], 2003), and *The Children's Plan: Building Brighter Futures*, published by the DCSF (TSO, 2007). As with the PEESCL strategy and SSP programme, both documents clearly indicate the extent to which the various 'needs' of young people are becoming increasingly central to the cross-cutting policy priorities of government. Both emphasize the alleged role played by education (including PESS) in meeting those needs (particularly in relation to physical and mental health, emotional well-being, safety and future educational attainment). It is not altogether surprising, therefore, that as a consequence of responding to the changing policy priorities of, and conflicting pressures from, government, aspects of the provision of PESS have come increasingly to be characterized by a move towards a slight downgrading of delivering sport and physical activity programmes through PE to achieve sports-related outcomes, in favour of implementing strategies designed to achieve other non-sport government objectives. But to what extent can government hope to achieve its objectives related to the promotion of PESS if teachers are being constrained to focus on the delivery of non-sporting goals? Has the shifting emphasis in government policy towards using PESS to achieve broader social and welfare policy goals made it more difficult for government to meet its targets in relation to the development of PE and sport in schools? In effect, have these policies resulted in unplanned consequences that may well be the very reverse of what was intended? The next section examines what the limited available evidence has to say about the impact of both the PESSCL strategy and SSP programme.

The impact of PESSCL and SSPs: sport policy goals

In an evaluation of the specialist schools programme, Ofsted (2005: 15) claimed that 'the majority of sports colleges have improved the curriculum in PE and are offering a wide range of accreditation opportunities ... suited to the needs of a wide range of pupils'. They also noted that since 1998 'pupils aged 16 in specialist schools have performed significantly better in external examinations than those in other schools' (Ofsted, 2005: 6). Moreover, all SSCs were said to have 'effective links with other schools, sports clubs and national sports bodies in their communities' (Ofsted, 2005: 28), and some 'use specialist coaches to support activities, sometimes in less accessible activities, such as ice-skating, horse-riding, martial arts and golf, both in lessons and out of school' (Ofsted, 2005: 29). Similar findings were also reported in a more specific evaluation of the impact of the SSP programme undertaken by Ofsted a year later. In particular, it was suggested that since their implementation SSPs have helped to 'improve the quality of provision in physical education and school sport, particularly in primary schools' (Ofsted, 2006: 2), in terms of both curricular and extra-curricular time. As a consequence of attending schools linked to an SSP, young people were also said to have 'greater opportunities to play sport outside school through schools' strong links with local sports clubs and sports coaches in the community' (Ofsted, 2006: 2). It is important to note, however, that whilst the impact of the SSP programme varied differentially between primary and secondary schools, in general terms it was observed that 'support for the programme, and its impact, were not as strong in secondary schools as in primary schools' (Ofsted, 2006: 2).

Given that the provision of PE and sport in primary schools has historically been considered largely underdeveloped by comparison to secondary schools, it is not surprising to find that those in the primary sector were said to have 'benefited substantially from the opportunity to focus specifically on improving provision for PE and on involving pupils in sport' (Ofsted, 2006: 10). Amongst the other alleged benefits that primary schools are believed to have obtained from being part of a Partnership is the ability of teachers to provide pupils with a wider range of activities (including non-traditional ones and multi-skills clubs) in which to participate inside and outside lessons; the allocation of two hours per week to PE; the provision of additional resources (especially equipment) to support the delivery of PESS; and enhanced training in PE for many primary school staff (Ofsted, 2006). The greater use of specialist community coaches to develop links between schools and community clubs, to help deliver sports clubs outside school time, and, in some cases, to lead curriculum lessons whilst enabling some primary teachers to use this time to engage in planning, preparation and assessment for other areas of the curriculum, was also cited as a perceived benefit of the SSP programme (Ofsted, 2006).

Evidence cited in support of the impact of the SSP programme on the provision and quality of young people's experiences in secondary schools was also related to ways in which more schools claimed to be providing pupils with at least two hours of PESS since being involved in the programme; the continued broadening and diversification of activities available to pupils within and outside the curriculum; and the growth of accredited leadership opportunities (e.g. the Junior Sport Leader Award) and examination courses available to young people in PE and sports studies (Ofsted, 2006). The growing involvement of specialist coaches, particularly in the provision of extra-curricular activities and clubs, together with the increasing number and range of community links teachers are developing with local clubs, sports development units and other schools (especially primary schools) to enhance the opportunities available for young people to participate in PE and sport, is also considered to be among the other positive impacts brought about by the SSP programme (Flintoff, 2003; 2008b; Ofsted, 2006; Smith, Leech and Green, 2009). These presumed benefits notwithstanding, the implementation of SSPs has not appeared to increase the amount of time available for PESS at Key Stage 4 (14–16-year-olds) to the same extent that has been seen elsewhere across the primary and secondary years. It has also been claimed that in some secondary schools 'involvement in the programme was judged to have had little impact on the leadership and management of PE ... because the [PE] department had a tradition of independence and was unreceptive to new ways of working' (Ofsted, 2006: 17). Accordingly, Ofsted (2006: 3) has claimed that there is a need for teachers working in secondary schools to 'work more closely with partnership managers and school sport co-ordinators to maximize the impact of the programme for all pupils'. Indeed, for reasons we shall explain later, Ofsted, and hence the government, are now increasingly encouraging teachers and other members of SSPs to work with a range of partners in schools, including SDOs and coaches, to deliver their policy goals related to the SSP programme and especially those linked to the provision of PESS outside of normal curriculum time.

More recent national evaluations of the SSP programme have been undertaken by the IYS on behalf of the DCSF (IYS, 2008c; 2008d; 2008e; 2008f). The overall findings of these studies indicate that since 2004 the range of sports and activities available to young people has expanded substantially: in 2007, 87 per cent of Partnerships claimed to offer twenty or more activities to young people and almost all of them (99 per cent) offered multi-skills clubs to pupils (IYS, 2008d). In the majority of SSPs, the most widely available activities were those that have been traditionally present in many PE curricula such as football, cricket, gymnastics, athletics and netball (IYS, 2008e; 2008f). Although the implementation of SSPs has strengthened the place of these kinds of activities at the heart of PE provision in schools, other sports such as boxing, golf, rugby union and swimming are being made available to pupils as part of curriculum PE but, increasingly, as part of extra-curricular time too. This growth in the availability of a wider range of sports is also said to have been supplemented by increases in the provision of activities such as archery, cycling, martial arts and orienteering (IYS, 2008e; 2008f). Confirming the findings of the 2007/08 *School Sport Survey* (TNS, 2008) and smaller-scale studies of teachers involved in the implementation of the SSP programme (Flintoff, 2003; 2008b; Smith, Leech and Green, 2009), the IYS has also reported that since their inception SSPs have been effective in enhancing both the amount of time available for pupils to engage in PESS and the links between schools, community sports clubs, sports development units and specialist sports coaches. The latter, in particular, are said to have been effective in helping to increase the number and diversity of intra- and inter-school sports competitions and events among young people across all school years, even though participation remains clearly differentiated by sex and age. More specifically, the available data indicate that whilst 'participation levels in inter-school competition for both girls and boys have steadily increased' (IYS, 2008e: 13) since SSPs were established, they have so far failed to break down the long-established gap in participation levels between girls and boys in inter-school competition. In fact, the gap in participation between school-aged young people 'has remained broadly the same with girls' participation equating to around three-quarters that of boys' (IYS, 2008e: 13), and age-related declines in participation in inter-school competition remain across the school years, with a marked drop-off in participation continuing to exist for both boys and girls in the later secondary school years (IYS, 2008e; TNS, 2007).

In terms of the impact that SSPs have had on the complex relationships that exist between the various partners involved in the programme, Houlihan and Lindsey have noted that

> the strongest partnership links are between secondary schools (via the SSCo) and their cluster of primary schools. In general the relationship is perceived as being mutually beneficial insofar as primary schools, who often do not have a specialist PE teacher, receive training from the Coordinator while the secondary school receives new entrants to year seven who have a higher standard of sports skills.
>
> (Houlihan and Lindsey 2008: 230)

Furthermore, according to Houlihan and Lindsey (2008), while the SSPs may have the advantage of enhancing the sporting skills of primary-aged young people, equally important are the perceived benefits to the secondary school that are not associated with the formally stated outcomes of the SSP programme. Of particular importance, they argue, is that 'secondary schools, who are often in intense competition with each other for primary pupils, see the work of their Coordinator as a way of promoting and marketing the school to primary pupils (and their parents)' (Houlihan and Lindsey, 2008: 230). It is this increasing marketization of education and the associated relational constraints and pressures that help explain the apparent differential engagement of primary and secondary schools within SSPs, and especially why the cooperation between secondary schools is thought to be much weaker than that which characterizes the relationships between secondary schools and the clusters of primary and special schools with whom they are linked (Flintoff, 2003; 2008b; Houlihan and Lindsey, 2008; Smith, Leech and Green, 2009). Writing of the impact that the marketization of education appears to have on the operations of SSPs, Houlihan and Lindsey (2008: 230) have rightly noted that whereas there is 'no market competition between secondary and primary schools, there is frequently fierce competition between secondary schools for new pupils which is often a disincentive to cooperate'. To this they add that 'a number of secondary schools consider that they have little to gain from active involvement in the SSP as they have good facilities and sufficient qualified PE staff and fear that they might lose by allowing pupils from other secondary schools access to their resources' (Houlihan and Lindsey, 2008: 230). Although it is unlikely that all secondary schools will react in such a way, it is clear that the particular network of power relationships that characterize the operations of SSPs, and that constitute the increasing marketization of education, will come to impact upon the ways and extent to which SSPs within the particular kinds of local education markets that exist in England can achieve desired policy outcomes in the future (Flintoff, 2003; Penney and Evans, 1999). It also appears to be the case that one unintended consequence of the development of partnerships between secondary and primary schools, in particular, is that those working in secondary schools see the SSP programme as one further way in which they are able to identify, and subsequently recruit, desirable pupils from the local primary feeder schools with whom they are linked (Smith, Leech and Green, 2009). In this regard, one of the principal motivations of partnership workers from secondary schools, often after being encouraged by their head teachers and senior management team, is to develop partnerships with primary schools and to develop links between them, SDOs and coaches, precisely because it may enable secondary school teachers to recruit a better standard (especially in sporting terms) of pupils than may otherwise be the case (Smith, Leech and Green, 2009).

The impact of PESSCL and SSPs: non-sport policy goals

Despite the generally positive evaluations of SSPs undertaken by Ofsted in particular, evidence of the extent to which those who deliver the programme are successful in achieving other policy outcomes has been considerably more variable and limited. This is particularly the case in relation to those policy outcomes of the PESSCL strategy and the SSP programme in which PESS are seen as important vehicles of social policy designed to achieve government's non-sports objectives. As we noted earlier, in addition to using PESS to help achieve sports-specific policy goals, the SSP programme is also expected to help contribute towards the achievement of non-sports objectives related, among other things, to young people's health, behaviour, attainment and attendance, not just in PESS but across the whole school. This uncritically accepted view that PESS can bring about effective behavioural and attitudinal change and develop among young people perceived desirable qualities can, of course, be traced back over the century-long history of the subject (Kirk, 1992). Of particular significance in this regard were the various PE syllabi that were published since around the turn of the twentieth century, the ideologies and practices that surrounded the use of games in the public schools of nineteenth-century Britain, and the publication of various sport policies since the launch of the Wolfenden Report in 1960 in particular (see Chapter 2). All of these and many other developments expressed, to a greater or lesser degree, the many presumed health and physical benefits, as well as the social (e.g. character development, discipline and leadership skills), affective (e.g. personal and social well-being, self-esteem and self-efficacy) and cognitive (e.g. academic performance) benefits that have been widely extolled on behalf of PESS (Bailey *et al.*, 2009; Coalter, 2007a; Sandford *et al.*, 2006). As we make clear in Chapter 4, these ideologies about the supposed worth of PESS to the enhancement of young people's lives currently find expression in the government's social inclusion agenda, in which sport is believed to contribute to the development of people and their communities by generating improvements in health, crime, employment and education. But what does the available evidence suggest about the extent to which these policy outcomes have been, and perhaps more importantly can be, achieved through the use of PE and sport in schools?

Having reviewed much of the published literature that explores the links between sports participation and educational performance, Coalter (2007a: 108) concluded that there currently exists 'mixed, inconsistent and largely non-cumulative evidence about the positive educational impacts of physical education and sport'. A similarly balanced and appropriately cautious conclusion was also reached by Sandford *et al.* (2006), who reviewed the use of school-based physical activity interventions to re-engage young people with school life and promote their educational prospects. In particular, they suggested that whilst 'sport and physical activities are able, to *some* degree, to facilitate personal and social development in *some* disaffected young people under *some* circumstances' (Sandford *et al.*, 2006: 261; original emphasis) it is misleading to argue that simply participating in 'PESS' leads to improved educational performance among young people (see also Bailey *et al.*, 2009; Coalter, 2007a). Data from three more recent studies of the impact of SSPs on pupil attendance (IYS, 2008a), attainment (IYS, 2008b) and behaviour (IYS, 2008c) also reveal similar findings. In relation to attendance, 42 per cent of head teachers and 52 per cent of Heads of PE surveyed felt – somewhat impressionistically – that attendance had improved 'slightly' or 'markedly' since their school had become involved in the SSP, with over half (53 per cent) of head teachers reporting no change (IYS, 2008a). Of those who felt attendance had improved, just over two-fifths of head teachers (43 per cent) and one-half of Heads of PE (52 per cent) felt that observed changes in attendance were attributable 'slightly' or 'substantially' to the SSP programme, and 38 per cent of head teachers claimed that the Partnership of which their school was a part had no impact on attendance (IYS, 2008a).

In terms of the impact that SSPs were thought to have on pupil attainment, similar proportions of head teachers (45 per cent) and Heads of PE (46 per cent) felt that attainment had 'improved a little' since their school had been part of the Partnership, 21 per cent of head teachers and 14 per cent of Heads of PE claimed that it had 'improved markedly', and approximately one-third (32 per cent) of head teachers and just under two-fifths (38 per cent) of Heads of PE thought that there had been 'no change' in pupil attainment since their school had been part of the Partnership (IYS, 2008b). One half (50 per cent) of head teachers who claimed that attainment had improved felt that this was 'slightly due' to membership of the SSP programme, a further 25 per cent said that the Partnership had had 'no impact' on pupil attainment and just under one-fifth (18 per cent) of head teachers did not feel it was possible to identify the impact of the SSP programme on the attainment of pupils in their school (IYS, 2008b). National attainment data from the DCSF also indicated that those schools who were part of the first and second phase of Partnership designation performed better in attainment tests for 6–16-year-olds. There was, however, no significant relationship between a school's membership of an SSP and higher attainment scores, except for those pupils aged 6–7 years old (IYS, 2008b). In addition, whilst many respondents to the IYS study felt that there were notable improvements in other perceived aspects of attainment (e.g. the 'ability to learn', development of communication and motivation skills, confidence and coordination), 'these improvements were rarely backed up with robust evidence and were largely anecdotal' (IYS, 2008b: 26).

Finally, in relation to pupil behaviour, similar proportions of head teachers and Heads of PE felt that there had been 'no change' (46 per cent and 44 per cent, respectively) in pupils' behaviour or that 'behaviour had improved a little' (42 per cent and 43 per cent, respectively) since their school had been part of the Partnership. Of those who thought that being part of an SSP impacted positively on pupil behaviour, approximately half of head teachers (50 per cent) and Heads of PE (47 per cent) reported that there had been a 'slight improvement' in pupil behaviour, whilst 17 per cent of head teachers and one-quarter of Heads of PE felt that being part of the Partnership had 'no impact' on the behaviour of pupils (IYS, 2008c). What is particularly noteworthy, however, was that the PDMs and head teachers involved in the study did not feel 'tackling behavioural issues was the central concern of the SSP programme' and for some 'the establishment of causal links between the SSP programme and behavioural change [was] an "impossible" task' (IYS, 2008c: 5). Indeed, a frequent, substantial methodological challenge facing both researchers and those involved with SSPs relates to the impossibility of establishing a simple cause and effect relationship between increases or changes in the relations that characterize PESS as a result of the implementation of the Partnership programme and enhanced attendance, attainment and behaviour within the wider school context. For many of the participants in the three impact studies conducted by the IYS – though this applies to many other studies too (for reviews, see Bailey *et al.*, 2009; Coalter, 2007a; Sandford *et al.*, 2006) – it was difficult to isolate the specific impact that SSP membership had on any observed changes in pupils' educational performance from the outcomes of other programmes that were being delivered simultaneously by colleagues in schools. In fact, if the experiences pupils derived from PESS did have an impact in affecting desired behavioural and attitudinal change among pupils (particularly in small targeted groups with pre-existing poor attendance rates, behaviour and low levels of attainment), then this was most likely to occur indirectly, when PESS and the other activities of SSPs were used as part of a broader complex package of interventions aimed at improving and managing whole school change (IYS, 2008a; 2008b; 2008c).

This is not the only methodological difficulty that serves to limit the extent to which the impact of participation in PESS through SSPs can be identified, for there exists some significant variability in how different schools define and record: appropriate forms of behaviour; the types of attainment tests provided for pupils; and authorized and unauthorized absences (IYS, 2008a; 2008b; 2008c). In addition, as we noted above, many of the comments from head teachers and other Partnership staff (e.g. PDMs, SSCos and Heads of PE) involved in these and other studies tend to be based on the impressions they formed during the context of their day-to-day teaching, rather than on the basis of any hard, reliable and systematically collected data regarding the effectiveness of the impact of the SSP on pupils' behaviour, attendance and educational performance.

Notwithstanding the lack of robust evidence for the effectiveness of SSPs in generating desired impacts on young people's educational performance, there is some preliminary evidence – beyond the more quantitatively based analyses undertaken by the IYS – that indicates that those working within SSPs have nevertheless been making a range of inevitably ideological claims about their ability to use PESS as a tool for achieving a range of desired social outcomes (Flintoff, 2003; 2008b; Smith, Leech and Green, 2009). In one recent study of a SSP in the North West of England, for example, the presumed benefits of the SSP programme to young people's educational experiences were often accepted uncritically and perceived as almost inevitable outcomes of participation in the programme by Partnership workers (Smith, Leech and Green, 2009). It was not uncommon to find, therefore, that often few attempts were made by Partnership workers to systematically monitor and evaluate SSPs for their desired impacts on young people. This is not especially surprising since monitoring observed changes in pupil behaviour and attainment is further compounded by the difficulties of identifying the presumed impacts on these complex aspects of young people's educational experiences. Indeed, it was not uncommon for many of the teachers in this study to claim that while they and other partnership workers sought to improve attendance and pupil behaviour and attainment, measuring the precise impact of their efforts, beyond the generation of basic quantitative outcome data, was especially difficult.

The roots of the claims that are frequently made on behalf of PESS by those involved within the SSPs in this study and other studies (e.g. Flintoff, 2003; 2008b) were, in part, traceable to the particular individual and group ideologies of PESS that characterized the thoughts and practices of those working within SSPs. It was also clear, however, that such groups have nevertheless been constrained, by virtue of the broader network of relationships or figurations of which they are a part, in championing enthusiastically the perceived value or 'power' of PESS. This tendency has, in turn, been reinforced by the prevailing ideological tendency of government, the YST and other professional bodies to exhort in policy and practice the alleged benefits that are thought to be accrued by young people from regular engagement in PESS (Smith, Leech and Green, 2009).

Despite the willingness with which teachers and others involved in SSPs often claim for PESS a variety of positive benefits for which there is, at best, very limited empirical evidence, it was nevertheless possible to understand why they did so. There are, as we noted earlier, a variety of widespread and longstanding ideologies linking sport and sports development with a range of perceived positive social outcomes and these have been largely uncritically accepted and continue to inform many of the programmes that teachers, SDOs and coaches are required to implement by government and other groups such as the YST as part of the SSP initiative. It is also the case that in the battle for public funding PE teachers and other school staff, like SDOs (see Chapters 4 and 5), have to compete with representatives of many other public services that might generally be perceived to have a more pressing claim for a greater share of public funds (e.g. health) (Bloyce *et al.*, 2008; Coalter, 2007a). In this regard, PE teachers and other Partnership workers (e.g. SDOs and coaches) especially are being constrained to move beyond simply extolling the intrinsic benefits of sports participation towards providing a more persuasive justification for using more public funds to develop sport. That is, by virtue of the particular network of power relationships of which they are a part, and within the context of the continued struggle to justify their own professional status, PE teachers are being required to draw on broader government policy agendas in order to bolster both their own professional standing and the position of PESS within the strategies of government. This is a point of considerable importance for, as Coalter (2007a: 44) has noted, PESS, like many other areas of sport policy, is 'a vulnerable policy area, under pressure to deliver short-term outcomes in a relatively short window of opportunity' and it is, therefore, becoming necessary for those working in SSPs to be addressing – or, at least, to be seen to be addressing – the policy desire by government to use the programme as a relatively cheap and apparently convincing solution to a myriad of complex social problems (Bloyce *et al.*, 2008; Coalter, 2007a). In this regard, it is clear that the ever-lengthening and increasing complexity of the networks of relations of which PE teachers are a part can be seen to have both constraining and enabling elements. They are constraining insofar as PE teachers are being expected by government, Sport England, the YST and others to tailor their activities towards the achievement of desired policy goals, even if those goals may be unrealistic. Simultaneously, however, these relational constraints also enable PE teachers to meet the agendas of their schools and, more importantly, their personal priorities. In this regard, the growing tendency for PE teachers to make many of the claimed contributions for PESS cannot therefore be adequately seen in isolation from broader professionalization processes, and from the ways in which PE teachers seek to advance their own interests by responding to the conflicting pressures under which they work.

But to what extent has the emphasis that has come to be placed on the promotion of 'educational attainment, learning and development *through* school sport and PE' (Houlihan and Green, 2006: 88; original emphasis) resulted in outcomes that may not have been intended or expected by government? Perhaps the first point worthy of note is that whilst the priorities of the PESSCL strategy and SSP programme have increasingly constrained those charged with their implementation to work with a wide variety of other organizations in order to achieve the government's non-sport policy goals, the outcomes of this increasingly complex interweaving of the actions of the many different groups may well have made it more difficult for the implementers to achieve the government's goals in relation to school-based youth sports development proper, an outcome which it is fair to assume was neither intended nor desired by government (Bloyce *et al.*, 2008; Dopson and Waddington, 1996; Elias, 1978). Equally, as the complexity of the relational networks surrounding youth sports development increases, so it becomes more difficult for any one group – even a group as powerful as the government – to retain control over the implementation of the PESSCL strategy and SSP programme. It also becomes difficult for such a powerful group as the government to retain control over the outcomes that emerge from the implementation of the PESSCL and SSP initiatives so that it is able, within closely defined limits, to pursue effectively its sporting and non-sporting objectives. In this regard, it might be argued that the use of PESS as a means to pursue the government's non-sporting goals has had the effect of undermining the extent to which the government is able to achieve its sporting priorities. It is also clear that whilst the government has a greater capacity to make crucial decisions over the policy priorities to be pursued in the PESSCL and SSP strategies, the nature and complexity of the human figurations in which they are involved means that the extent to which the government is able to achieve its objectives is very dependent on the actions of other groups such as those who work within SSPs as they, too, attempt to protect, maintain and advance their own individual and/or collective interests. Finally, it should be emphasized that unplanned outcomes of this kind are not unusual aspects of social life; indeed, it is important to recognize that, as we explained in Chapter 1, the *normal* results of complex processes involving the interweaving of the goal-directed actions of large numbers of people include outcomes that no one has chosen and no one has designed.

Summary

In this chapter we have attempted to examine one of the most significant youth sports development policies to have been introduced in schools in England in recent years, namely, the PESSCL strategy. We have also sought to examine the SSP programme as one aspect of PESSCL that arguably became one of the most important overarching infrastructures through which government has attempted to achieve its sports-specific goals and non-sport objectives related to PESS and youth sports development in schools. Indeed, on the basis of the analysis presented here, it is clear that PESS in particular, and sport for young people more generally, remains an integral part of the current Labour government's conceptualization of sports development. Increasing significance has also been placed on the government's initiatives that prioritize the achievement of a range of other social objectives using sport and physical activity as key vehicles of social policy.

In relation to the policy and practice of PESSCL and the SSP programme, it seems reasonable to conclude that much recent school-based youth sports development policy is predicated on the assumption that there is a need to provide young people with four 'Cs', namely: more *chances* to participate in sport and physical activity; more *coaches* to facilitate opportunities to participate and to improve the quality of young people's experiences of sport and physical activity; a wider range of *competitions* in which young people can participate; and a more extensive *club* infrastructure designed to develop and enhance links between participation in PESS and local community clubs.

Such an approach to youth sports development was hardened even further when the PESSCL strategy was replaced – at least in name – by the PE and Sport Strategy for Young People (PESSYP). This began to be delivered in schools and colleges in England from September 2008. Overall responsibility for PESSYP lies with the DCSF and DCMS in conjunction with the Department for Innovation, Universities and Skills (DIUS), with the YST once again playing a central role in its implementation in primary and secondary schools (DCMS, 2008a; Sport England, 2008a). The PESSYP, which builds on the work of the PESSCL strategy, is supported by an investment of £783 million to improve the quality and quantity of PE and sport undertaken by young people aged 5–19. This commitment to enhance the take-up of sporting opportunities by 5–19-year-olds is now set out in PSA target 22, the objectives of which are, as we explain in Chapter 7, explicitly related to the delivery of a successful London 2012 Olympic Games and Paralympic Games and to enhance the proportion of young people engaging in PESS. In relation to increasing the take-up of sporting opportunities among young people, the PSA target states that:

> in addition to at least 2 hours per week of high quality PE and Sport in school for all 5–16 year olds, all children and young people aged 5–19 will be offered opportunities to participate in a further 3 hours per week of sporting activities provided through schools, Further Education (FE) colleges, clubs and community providers.
>
> (HMSO, 2007: 3)

Collectively, this commitment is now commonly referred to as the 'Five Hour Offer', the responsibility for which belongs to the YST, with support from the DCMS and Sport England (DCMS, 2008a; Sport England, 2008a; Rowe, 2009). The implementation of PESSYP and the introduction of the 'Five Hour Offer' coincided with the publication of two recent English sport policy documents, namely, *Playing to Win* (DCMS, 2008a), and the *Sport England Strategy 2008–2011* (Rowe, 2009; Sport England, 2008a). As we noted in Chapter 2, both policies reinforce the currently prevailing policy priorities associated with reducing drop-off in participation at the age of 16 by enhancing school sport and community club links (Rowe, 2009; Sport England, 2008a) and providing 'more coaching and more competitive sport for all young people' (DCMS, 2008a: Preface) as part of an overall plan to develop 'an integrated and sustainable sporting system which will nurture and develop sporting talent, underpinned by a high quality club and competition structure' (DCMS, 2008a: 3).

While at the time of writing PESSYP had only began to be implemented in practice, it seems reasonable to suppose that the policy objectives and priorities that underpin PESSYP are one more expression of the way in which SSPs, SSCs and other schools will remain at the heart of the government's future innovations related to youth sports development in England. However, it might with equal validity be noted that, as Coalter (2007a) observes of sport policy more generally and as we make clear elsewhere in this book (see Chapters 4 and 5), the future policy status of PESS is likely to continue to depend – perhaps increasingly so – on the ability of those working in these fields to demonstrate its cross-cutting value and to help with the achievement of the government's wider social goals. It is also likely, therefore, that this continued policy emphasis on the use of PESS to help achieve government's non-sport objectives will encourage those working within school-based youth sports development schemes such as SSPs to continue championing enthusiastically the benefits that participation in PESS is thought to have for other aspects of young people's lives. As we noted earlier, however, this could be viewed as less of an opportunity and more of a threat to the future of PE and sport in schools and may help undermine the position of some of those involved in delivering the SSP and PESSYP programmes, an outcome which it is fair to assume may not be intended or desired by those within and outside the youth sports development policy community.

Revision questions

1   Why are young people and school-based youth sports development of particular importance to the government's sport policy agenda?
2   Examine the various policy issues that surround the use of PESS as vehicles of social policy designed to achieve a variety of non-sport policy goals.
3   Given the prevailing direction of government sport policy and development priorities, how and in what ways might school-based youth sport develop in the future?

Key readings

Flintoff, A. (2008a) 'Physical education and youth sport', in K. Hylton and P. Bramham (eds) *Sports Development: Policy, Process and Practice*, 2nd edn, London: Routledge.
Green, K. (2008) *Understanding Physical Education*, London: Sage.
Houlihan, B. and Green, M. (2006) 'The changing status of school sport and physical education: explaining policy change', *Sport, Education and Society*, 11: 73–92.

Recommended websites

Sport England: www.sportengland.org
Teachernet: www.teachernet.gov.uk
Youth Sport Trust: www.youthsporttrust.org

4 Community sports development
Promoting social inclusion

Objectives

This chapter will:

- examine some of the policy issues associated with the increasing adoption of sport and physical activities as vehicles of social policy targeted at achieving greater social inclusion;
- examine the various contributions that sport and physical activities are thought to make to the achievement of greater social inclusion; and
- review the evidence for the effectiveness of sports development programmes in which the intention is to prevent crime and drug use among young people.

Introduction

In Britain, as in many other Western societies, there has, over the last two or three decades, been growing concern over a range of perceived social problems that together are seen as stemming from what is currently popularly described as 'social exclusion'. The term 'social exclusion' was first used in French social policy in the 1970s and, from the 1980s, in the European Union (EU) as unemployment was increasing rapidly in several Member States and as immigration was also rising (Levitas, 2004; Roberts, 2009). Together, these processes were associated with growing concern that came to be expressed about the formation of groups who were not only unemployed or just poor, but somehow seen as 'outside' and 'apart from' mainstream society (Roberts, 2009). In Britain, fears regarding the spread of unemployment were accompanied by a debate over whether an emergent underclass could be distinguished from other groups in the wider society. By the time New Labour had won the 1997 general election, however, discussions about the existence of an 'underclass' in society had been replaced by the concept of social exclusion. In the period since 1997, the concept of social exclusion has become the preferred, political and ideologically saturated, label used to refer to the forms of disadvantage that are said to be experienced by those groups who are identified as 'disadvantaged' in one way or another (Roberts, 2009). The concept has also 'been subjected to changes in meaning that are closely related to the political arguments encapsulated in third way debates' (Levitas, 2004: 44) and the associated ideological preoccupations of government (see Chapter 2). More particularly, as part of the somewhat ambiguous and contentious 'Third Way' approach to much British government policy (Levitas, 2004), particular concern has been expressed about what can happen when people and local communities become 'socially excluded' by experiencing a combination of linked 'problems'. These 'problems', that were once referred to as multiple deprivation or multiple disadvantage (Roberts, 2009), include rising levels of crime and drug use, unemployment, low income, family and community breakdown, lack of social integration and participation, and declining standards of employment, education and health (Social Exclusion Unit, 1998). Such a view of social exclusion is 'spectacularly vague' (Levitas, 2004: 45) and fails to explain adequately the wider social processes that are associated with the development and existence of these perceived social problems. Recent policy and political emphasis on social exclusion has been underpinned by a concern with inadequate social participation, lack of social integration and power amongst local communities. A parallel emphasis has also come to be placed on personal responsibility and accountability (Coalter, 2007a; Levitas, 2004). More specifically, as Coalter has observed,

> the emphasis on community and social inclusion is accompanied by an emphasis on personal responsibility – to work or to seek work, to provide for family, to behave responsibly, to take responsibility for personal health, to contribute to the solution of community problems and so on.
>
> (Coalter 2007a: 47)

This concern with community renewal, social inclusion and personal responsibility has been expressed in a variety of ways, not least in the emergence of a plethora of policy initiatives designed to combat the outcomes of those processes that are strongly associated with experiences of social exclusion amongst people and the communities that they form. Among these initiatives have been policies based on an amalgam of usually untested assumptions about the important contribution that sport and physical activities are thought to make to the achievement of greater social inclusion. This is a view that has been articulated in several policy statements since the early 1960s (CCPR, 1960; DCMS, 2000; Sports Council, 1982; Sport England, 2008b; 2008c; 2008d; 2008e; 2008f).

As we noted in the Introduction to this book, over the past two decades or so, in particular, one consequence of the increasing intervention of government in sport policy-making has been that sport policy priorities have shifted away from the development of sport and achievement of sport-related goals towards the use of sport to achieve other desired social objectives. Indeed, those currently working in sports development in a variety of capacities and in a range of diverse organizations and settings are becoming increasingly, though differentially, constrained to maintain their sports development priorities within the context of 'conflicting pressures through being expected to contribute to the government's social inclusion objectives' (Houlihan and White, 2002: 107). These conflicting pressures are, in turn, being generated within a rapidly changing social and political policy climate where, in the battle for public funding, those working in sports development have to compete with representatives of many other public services that might generally be perceived to have a more pressing claim on a greater share of public funds (for example health and education). As a consequence, many SDOs are now being constrained increasingly to move beyond simply extolling the intrinsic benefits of sports participation towards providing a more persuasive justification to develop sport for broader social objectives (Bloyce *et al.*, 2008; Coalter, 2007a; Houlihan and White, 2002). This tendency has been hardened further by the fact that some SDOs themselves believe in the intrinsic value and potential of sport in bringing about desired social outcomes

(Bloyce *et al.*, 2008). In light of this situation, we are now faced with what Coalter (2007a: 70) describes as 'widely ambitious, extremely difficult to define and measure claims for the social impacts of sport', particularly in relation to the ability of sports development workers to use sport as a means of providing solutions to the government's social inclusion agenda. Set in this context, the central objectives of this chapter are: (1) to examine some of the policy issues surrounding, and the outcomes of, the increasing adoption of sport and physical activities as vehicles of social policy targeted at achieving greater social inclusion, particularly among young people; and (2) to examine a point of fundamental importance in policy terms: do such sport-based schemes work?

Sport and social inclusion: the policy context

As we noted earlier, since the 1980s social exclusion, and, by extension, social inclusion, has come increasingly to dominate the policy agenda of many Western governments, and especially those in Europe, the US and Australia. Within the EU, for example, Articles 136 and 137 of the Amsterdam Treaty, which, among other things, helped place greater emphasis on citizenship, democracy and the rights of individuals through an expansion of the powers of the European Parliament, recommended that social exclusion should be one of the social policy goals of Member States. In one of the declarations annexed to the Treaty, the role sport is perceived to play as a tool of social integration was emphasized. A similar view was also articulated in the Lisbon Strategy, launched in 2000, and emerged out of discussions amongst EU leaders of Member States about how best to 'modernize' Europe. In particular, in the Lisbon Strategy the creation of more jobs, more competition and greater social cohesion were identified as three key policy goals that were expected to lie at the centre of the government policy agendas of Member States, who were each expected to contribute to a coordinated approach towards tackling social exclusion within the EU (Daly, 2007). The Lisbon Review 2005 (known as the Kok Report) was heavily critical of the Lisbon Strategy, however. The Review identified a clear implementation gap in the ways and extent to which Member States had adopted social inclusion policy objectives, and pointed towards a lack of determined and weakly coordinated action in relation to the prevalence of social exclusion in the EU (Daly, 2007). Consequently, the Kok Report recommended that a reinvigoration of the Lisbon Strategy was needed and that social exclusion should be downgraded as a policy objective, with a much sharper focus being placed on the achievement of social inclusion through economic growth and the creation of jobs (Daly, 2007). Within the sporting context, the role that sport was believed to play in the achievement of greater social inclusion (and particularly as a tool for social and economic development) at the EU level was expressed recently in the White Paper on Sport that was adopted by the European Commission (EC) in July 2007. The EC, which was formerly the Commission of the European Communities, is said to be independent of national governments and constitutes the executive arm of the EU, which is an economic and political union of 27 Member States located in Europe. That the EC represents the executive arm of the EU means that it is responsible for implementing the decisions of the European Parliament and Council. The EC is also charged with implementing the policies and programmes of the EU, as well as spending its funds. In some of the more recent policies that have emanated from the EC, it was suggested, somewhat uncritically, that sport 'makes an important contribution to economic and social cohesion and more integrated societies' (EC, 2007: 7) and can help with 'job creation and … economic growth and revitalisation, particularly in disadvantaged areas' (EC, 2007: 7). It was also alleged that the provision of, and support for, 'sport-related activities is important for allowing immigrants and the host society to interact together in a positive way' (EC, 2007: 7). Finally, sport was also perceived to be important for meeting the 'specific needs and situation of underrepresented groups ... [such as] young people, people with disabilities and people from less privileged backgrounds' (EC, 2007: 7).

As we noted earlier, in Britain, following the election of the Labour government in May 1997, social inclusion became a more or less central aspect of many social policies, including those related to sport. More particularly, upon entering office the Social Exclusion Unit (SEU) was established by the Labour Party and then Prime Minister, Tony Blair. It was set up to examine how the government's commitment to enhancing social inclusion and broader welfare policy objectives could be achieved through 'joined-up government' (see Chapter 2), that is, through cross-departmental strategies leading to 'the construction of a comprehensive policy response to a complex and multidimensional problem' (Houlihan and White, 2002: 84). One of the first steps the SEU took to meet this remit in relation to sport was to establish the PAT (Policy Action Team) 10 Working Group, who were asked to report on the potential contribution that sport and the arts make to the promotion of greater social inclusion (Collins *et al.*, 1999). Together with the review of the England National Lottery Strategy in 1998, the findings of the PAT 10 report, which have been outlined in some detail elsewhere (e.g. Collins *et al.*, 1999; Collins and Kay, 2003), provided the foundation for a focus on social inclusion in future sport policy. Significantly, however, despite the recommendations of the PAT 10 report, much of this policy has subsequently failed to recognize that it is poverty and socio-economic status (together with other sources of social division) that lie at the core of social exclusion (e.g. Collins and Kay, 2003). Among the many policies that could be cited in this connection is *A Sporting Future for All*, in which government claimed that:

> Sport can make a unique contribution to tackling social exclusion in our society ... We fully recognise that this is not something that sport can tackle alone but by working with other agencies we believe it can make a significant contribution.
>
> (DCMS, 2000: 39)

It has also been alleged that sport can make a positive contribution not only to the health service (see Chapter 5) but to preventing crime and engaging those who are thought to be alienated from education (DCMS, 2000). In this context, local authorities (in conjunction with schools and local sports clubs) are frequently identified as playing a more or less central role in the development of 'creative and innovative ways of using sport to help re-engage people and to equip them with the skills and confidence to re-join the mainstream of society' (DCMS, 2000: 39). As well as being a core policy priority of *A Sporting Future for All*, social inclusion is also a central theme that runs through aspects of *Game Plan* (DCMS/Strategy Unit, 2002). *Game Plan* featured a list of benefits that participation in sport and physical activities is alleged to have in the promotion of social inclusion of particular social groups, including disabled people and ethnic minority groups, but especially young people. Indeed, whilst a myriad of groups are considered vulnerable to social exclusion in much current government policy, it is young people and school-aged children (particularly those identified as being 'at risk') who are the principal target group of many sport-related interventions where proactive responses to a range of social problems and the achievement of broader social goals are emphasized (Coalter, 2007a; Green, 2006;

Houlihan and Green, 2006). As we noted in Chapter 2, this focus on young people has also found particular expression in a series of recent Sport England publications, especially *Sport Playing Its Part* and *Shaping Places through Sport*.

A central idea underpinning these reports and the policy-led debate about the potential role of sport in social inclusion strategies tends to be that of social capital (and the closely related concepts of cultural, economic and physical capital and 'active citizenship'), which has been most closely associated with the work of Bourdieu, Coleman and Putnam (Coalter, 2007a). Readers who wish to find out more about the extent to which the 'diffuse and contested concept of social capital' (Coalter, 2007a: 49) – and especially Putman's contribution to the debate – has come to impact on the sport and social inclusion policy agenda in Britain might usefully consult the excellent work by Coalter (Coalter, 2007a; 2008; Coalter *et al.*, 2000). For present purposes, however, it is sufficient to note that the concept of social capital is rarely examined in great detail in many sport policy documents and its use 'is consistently vague, with no systematic attempt to articulate clearly its precise meaning and sport's role in its development' (Coalter, 2007a: 49–50). This is unsurprising, for, as we noted earlier, it is not uncommon in policy areas of this kind for the contribution that sport, and those working in sports development, can make to the development of people and their communities to be based on a one-sided perception of sport that amounts almost to a statement of faith in its effectiveness to achieve desired social outcomes associated with the social inclusion agenda. We shall return to the policy problems associated with this tendency for many sport-based social inclusion programmes to be based on a series of largely untested assumptions of sporting culture later. It is clear, however, that, notwithstanding the vagueness and uncritical acceptance of the role that sport and physical activities are believed to play in the promotion of social inclusion and especially social capital, both concepts continue to be attractive to policy-makers inside and outside sport (Coalter, 2007a; Hoye and Nicholson, 2008; Nicholson and Hoye, 2008). As Coalter has noted, there would appear to be at least two reasons for this:

> First, evidence seems to suggest that there is a correlation between communities high in social capital and a number of desired policy outcomes: lower crime rates, better health and lower rates of child abuse ... Second ... the (vague) concept of social capital contributes to New Labour's desire to reform central government by reducing departmentalism and encouraging 'joined-up government' – individual government departments can adopt it as an objective, enabling all to 'sing from the same hymn sheet'. Such policies enable and require sport to claim its contribution.
>
> (Coalter 2007a: 50)

Given the increasing emphasis that has come to be placed on social inclusion in government policy, those working in sports development are now being increasingly constrained – though to considerably varying degrees – to demonstrate the efficacy of sports-based programmes in achieving not only traditional sports development objectives (such as increased participation and provision of sporting and coaching opportunities) (see Chapter 3) but, equally importantly, broader social goals. Indeed, it is now clear that several aspects of sport policy and the development work (especially in local authorities) on which it is based are becoming increasingly characterized by a desire for developing people and their communities *through* sport alongside a correlative decline in the commitment to simply developing sport amongst people *in* their communities (Bloyce *et al.*, 2008; Coalter, 2007a; Houlihan and White, 2002).

Sport-based social inclusion schemes

Such has been the rapid expansion of other sport-based programmes designed to promote social inclusion *through* community sports development and other social inclusion initiatives, there now exists an expanding literature that has begun to examine the effectiveness of these programmes, with a number of evaluations being conducted in various countries, including Britain (e.g. Coalter, 2007a; Coalter *et al.*, 2000; Long and Sanderson, 2001; Nichols, 2007; Taylor *et al.*, 1999), the US (e.g. Hartmann, 2001; Hartmann and Depro, 2006; Witt and Crompton, 1996) and Australia (e.g. Morris *et al.*, 2003). Despite obvious differences in, amongst other things, methodology, available resources (e.g. staffing and cost), the aims and objectives of the programmes and the use (or lack thereof) of monitoring and evaluation to judge effectiveness, these programmes can be divided broadly into two main approaches that can be conceptualized as lying at opposite ends of a continuum, with other schemes located somewhere in between these poles (Coalter, 2007a). Coalter (2007a) refers to these two broad approaches towards sport-based social inclusion programmes as *sport plus* and *plus sport*. The first of these, sport plus, are those programmes 'in which traditional sport development objectives of increased participation and the development of sporting skills are emphasized' (Coalter, 2007a: 71). These objectives are, however, 'rarely the sole rationale and very rarely the basis for external investment and subsequent evaluation' (Coalter, 2007a: 71); indeed, in the majority of cases sport is used in these programmes as a cost-effective tool to address a range of broader social issues (e.g. levels of crime and drug use) (Coalter, 2007a). It is important to note, however, that in sport plus approaches 'sport' is only one among a number of other social activities (e.g. educational programmes and arts and music activities) that are used to achieve the desired outcomes of policy-makers. As we shall see later, such an approach is not uncommon to many of the Positive Futures programmes currently in operation in the UK. The second broad approach described by Coalter is plus sport, 'in which social, educational and health programmes are given primacy; and sport, especially its ability to bring together a large number of young people, is part of a much broader and more complex set of processes' (Coalter, 2007a: 71). In approaches of this kind, short-term outcome measures (e.g. behaviour change) are said to be more important than the long-term sustainable development of sport and the achievement of sport development objectives that are central aspects of sport plus approaches (Coalter, 2007a). There are many schemes – whether sport plus or plus sport – and these vary considerably in terms of both the source of funding and the organizations and personnel involved. They also vary in terms of whether they are open to all members of the community or whether they are targeted at specific groups (for example drug users and ex-offenders). However, the critical question in terms of public policy is: do such schemes work? In other words do such schemes have a significant impact either on the level of criminal activity or on the amount of illegal drug use by young people and therefore contribute to the achievement of greater social inclusion? Given that sport plus is the most widely used approach to sport-based social inclusion programmes, we shall focus on some of these schemes and their effectiveness – especially those designed to tackle crime and drug use among young people – in the rest of this chapter.

Before we examine these issues, however, it is important to remind ourselves of a point of some importance: sport-based social inclusion schemes, like many sports projects, are appealing to government, many policy-makers and SDOs because there is a 'willing industry' for them. That is, such projects can be promoted to, and implemented by, project workers and practitioners who believe in the alleged 'power' and benefits of sport, and many young people (especially young males) can be attracted by the appeal of participating in such projects. It is also the case that governments often present sport as a simple, cost-effective solution to complex social problems since this is one way in which they can be seen to be 'doing something' about those perceived problems (Coalter, 2007a). While governments can always invest in sport and physical activities as vehicles of social policy, they cannot always – indeed, are sometimes unwilling to – provide long-term, sustainable, effective solutions that may help to tackle the complex causes of social disadvantage. We shall return to these issues later, but let us now examine some of those social inclusion schemes that currently use sport as a means of achieving a range of policy outcomes.

Barclays Spaces for Sports: developing people and places through sport

One sport-based social inclusion initiative that has been launched in the UK, with the intention of 'developing sport in the community and developing the community through sport' (Ramwell *et al.*, 2008: 46), is the Barclays Spaces for Sports programme. The Spaces for Sports programme was launched in 2004 as a three-year phased £30 million community investment programme by Barclays, in conjunction with two national charities, the Football Foundation and Groundwork, who provided an additional £29 million to support the initiative. Among the main purposes of the programme was the development of community sports facilities and the creation of opportunities for participation in sport and physical activity in areas of high social and economic deprivation and where there was an identified need for facility development (Ramwell *et al.*, 2008). As part of Barclays' community investment activities and its overall corporate responsibility and sustainability strategies, the Spaces for Sports programme was described as an initiative that 'combines both capital and revenue investment to develop local communities through sport' (Ramwell *et al.*, 2008: 10). The capital investment for the project is being used to build 200 new state-of-the-art sports spaces (including multi-use games areas, skate parks, bike tracks and climbing walls) that are being administered predominately by Groundwork with support from the environmental charity BTCV and Nacro, a crime reduction charity. Of these spaces, 174 were built in the UK as 'local sites' for the provision of over twenty-five community sports (including football, hockey, cricket, tennis, BMXing, dance and skateboarding) that residents can engage in for free, and on an open-access basis. The remaining twenty-six sites – termed 'flagship sites' – are larger sporting spaces that are jointly funded by Barclays and the Football Foundation and administered by the Football Foundation. These sites are designed to develop community sport in disadvantaged areas and are typically located next to Barclays Premier League or Football League clubs in England. The revenue funds that are allocated to the programme are then used to support sports development activity (including the role of volunteers) at each of the 200 sites, whilst additional funds are also available for the provision of over 4,000 coaching packs (comprising equipment and clothing) to teams and organizations to help stimulate and sustain participation in a variety of sports. Local Hero Awards, which are awarded to those who are identified as making a substantial contribution to grassroots sport in the local community, are also funded from these additional monies (Ramwell *et al.*, 2008).

Although the Spaces for Sports programme was particularly concerned with building a sustainable physical infrastructure for sports development activity, an associated objective of the programme was the development of sustainable activities on each of the sites to encourage local residents to continue engaging in sport and physical activity and to ensure that the site remains at the heart of community life (Ramwell *et al.*, 2008). In addition, and of particular importance, was the extent to which local residents were intended to be represented and involved in the development of a site to ensure that it was, indeed, meeting the needs of the local community. It is, of course, often very difficult to obtain consensus among local residents on what local 'needs' are and not all residents are equally able and/or willing to engage in the development of such community engagement projects that are designed to promote social inclusion and social capital (Coalter, 2007a; Nicholson and Hoye, 2008). This was a conclusion that was drawn by one study commissioned by Barclays, and which examines the impact of the programme on the development of people and their local communities during the capital build phase (2004–07) of the programme (Ramwell *et al.*, 2008). The study was published by an independent research group at Manchester Metropolitan University who utilized a range of research methods, including interviews, observations, site visits, field notes and documentary analysis to: 'Measure the impact of the scheme on local communities and individuals; Capture key learning from a groundbreaking public:private partnership to inform future corporate programmes; Provide dynamic feedback enabling Barclays to successfully deliver the programme while minimising risks and maximising successes' (Ramwell *et al.*, 2008: 7). In relation to community engagement, the research group concluded that there exists a 'clear distinction at a significant number of local sites between the individuals involved at the consultation, formation and build stage, and those involved at the development and delivery stage once a site had been launched' (Ramwell *et al.*, 2008: 40). It was also noted that whilst the Spaces for Sports programme is targeted at all members of the local community, in practice it has been school-aged young people who have become the principal target group at many sites since the inception of the programme. As a consequence, it was claimed that there is a need to engage other members of the community, including those of pre-school age (0–4 years) and older people aged 50 and above, who may wish to use the site. This was important, it was claimed, because unless such groups were integrated into the activities of the programme '[m]any sites will stand idle during the day in term times. Targeting these other groups would see the space being utilized by groups who may not at first glance recognise an opportunity for themselves to use the site' (Ramwell *et al.*, 2008: 40). Given the variable community engagement that has accompanied the introduction of Spaces for Sports, it was also recommended that project workers should seek to develop 'an understanding of how they are engaging within their respective communities' and report back on 'what elements of the community they engage with' (Ramwell *et al.*, 2008: 40) in future evaluations of the programme. Although it may be easier and desirable to identify, often using more quantitative measures, which groups of the local community engage in social inclusion schemes such as the Spaces for Sports programme, determining the extent of community engagement or cohesion in sport-based programmes, as in other areas of social and welfare policy, is altogether a different matter. As Long *et al.* (2002) have noted, these kinds of outcomes are not always amenable to simple forms of quantitative measurement. In that respect, the challenge for policy-makers and SDOs involved with the Spaces for Sports programme may then revolve around what constitutes 'evidence' for the impact of the programme in enhancing community engagement.

Since the Spaces for Sports initiative is a relatively new project, it is difficult at the time of writing to establish, with a large degree of confidence, the effectiveness of the programme and the extent to which other desired outcomes of the programme have been achieved.

Nevertheless, in addition to the reported experiences of participants and workers that are detailed in each of the in-depth case studies undertaken by the research team at selected flagship sites (for examples, see Ramwell *et al.*, 2008), there are said to have been a 'variety of different legacies [that] have been delivered by the programme' (Ramwell *et al.*, 2008: 12) for local communities and the lives of residents (Ramwell *et al.*, 2008). Of particular relevance in the present context is the claimed effectiveness of the programme in providing lasting legacies – for a more detailed consideration of the concept of legacy, see Chapter 7 – in relation to: the provision of physical sporting infrastructures provided for local residents; the development of knowledge about, and a model for, public–private partnerships to engage in community sport investment programmes; and community legacies that are brought about by greater social participation in the programme and through the development of skills, job opportunities and training for residents. Mention has already been made of the development of physical infrastructures that has been associated with the programme, particularly in relation to the provision of extensive community sport facilities and multi-use games areas for use by local residents on an open access and freely available basis. In this regard, the Spaces for Sports scheme is said to have made a significant contribution to the achievement of objectives associated with the regeneration of sporting facilities and provision of sporting opportunities, as well as the immediate wider regeneration and reinvigoration of local communities (Ramwell *et al.*, 2008). This is perhaps arguably the most significant – or, at least, the most immediate – impact that the programme has had on the lives of some residents since it has been running in local communities. By contrast, many of the 'knowledge legacies' thought to have been produced by workers on the programme would appear to have been developed most strongly amongst those public and private organizations whose interests surround 'targeting, commissioning, building and launching community sports sites' (Ramwell *et al.*, 2008: 40) as well as pursuing other, perhaps hidden, agendas and priorities. More particularly, Spaces for Sports does appear to have had a measure of success in enhancing inter- and intra-organizational learning about the provision of opportunities and facilities for community sports development, whilst encouraging partners such as some local Groundwork Trusts to develop and deliver sport-based projects where previously they had little or no experience in this area (Ramwell *et al.*, 2008). In terms of developing knowledge amongst participants, engagement in the programme is also thought to have benefited volunteers, whose efforts have been recognized by project workers, and through accreditation opportunities associated with their achievement of recognized coaching qualifications and awards (Ramwell *et al.*, 2008).

The final set of impacts thought to have been brought about by the programme are those that relate to the use of sport to develop people and their communities. Central among these perceived community legacies is the estimate that, as a result of the introduction of Spaces for Sports, 'over half a million people in the UK have (had) an opportunity to benefit from the programme' (Ramwell *et al.*, 2008: 13). A related feature of this provision of additional opportunities to participate in sport and physical activity is that, on the basis of monitoring data gathered by the Football Foundation, an average of more than 50,000 people are now thought to be using Barclays Spaces for Sports sites every week (Ramwell *et al.*, 2008). On the basis of the available evidence, however, it is not clear whether those who engage in the programme in this way are 'new' participants who would not otherwise have participated in sport and physical activity without the programme. It is also not clear whether the participants were already engaged in community-led sports development activities and whether their involvement in the programme was in addition to or a replacement for their participation in other sports development contexts. Finally, the extent to which those engaged in the programme are 'occasional' or 'regular' participants or, as is often the nature of sports participation (especially among young people), whether their involvement in the scheme is characterized by sustained participation followed by periods of 'drop-out' remains unknown. We should perhaps be rather more cautious, therefore, about the claimed effectiveness of the programme in bringing about long-term changes in the lives and behaviour of participants and, in particular, of providing sustainable legacies for local communities. It is also clear that given the general absence of systematically collected and reliable data on these and other elements of the programme, the scheme will require careful and consistent process-monitoring and evaluation in the future to provide evidence of the extent to which the programme is being delivered as intended, meeting its targets and making progress towards the achievement of its desired objectives in the long term. In addition, such process-led monitoring and evaluation is, as we noted in Chapter 1, a vital prerequisite for establishing what types of participation at each of the sites generate what types of outcomes for what types of participant in what types of circumstances (Coalter, 2007a). Finally, process-led monitoring and evaluation may also be of some use in establishing the degree to which the public–private partnership model on which the programme is based is sustainable in the long term, an objective that is clearly of particular importance to the funders of the programme (Ramwell *et al.*, 2008).

The Kickz – Goals Thru Football programme

The Spaces for Sports programme is just one amongst many other examples that could be cited of sport-based programmes in which the promotion of social inclusion among key target groups, especially young people, has been associated with a general downgrading of emphasis on the achievement of traditional sports development objectives. Alongside this, as we noted earlier, there has been a correlative increase in the prioritization given to sport, and particularly sports such as football, as a cheap and convenient policy solution to the complex causes of social exclusion (Collins *et al.*, 1999; Tacon, 2007). As Tacon (2007) has noted, in Britain football has, since the emergence of Football in the Community schemes during the mid-1980s (but especially after the election of the current Labour government), increasingly been considered as a particularly useful vehicle of social policy designed to promote social inclusion among 'at risk' groups, particularly young males. They are also thought to make a substantial contribution to community regeneration. These schemes now operate at all Premier League, Football League and some Football Conference clubs, which, together with a range of partners in the local community (including sports development agencies), deliver a variety of schemes that are designed to promote social inclusion among young people who are considered 'at risk' or 'hard to reach'. One such scheme that uses the appeal of professional football to engage young people who are considered vulnerable to crime (as victims or potential offenders) from local estates and neighbourhoods that experience high crime rates, anti-social behaviour and multiple deprivation is the Kickz – Goals Thru Football programme (Football Foundation, 2008). The programme was initially developed out of discussions between the Metropolitan Police, the Football Foundation, the Premier League, the Football Association and the Football League. These discussions focused, in particular, on how to engage more young people from local communities in so-called 'positive activities' (including sport) and how traditional barriers that may exist between young people and local police could be broken down further. The overall concern is to help promote social inclusion (through the reduction of youth anti-social behaviour) and community engagement by providing young people with opportunities to participate in sport and develop a range of other life-skills. The programme is currently managed by the Football Foundation and is delivered locally – using an area-based and young person-centred approach – by football clubs and local steering groups. These include members of Police Safer Neighbourhood teams, various local authority agencies (including youth services), youth offending teams (YOTs), leisure and sports services and social housing providers (Football Foundation, 2008). Kickz is also supported by central government through the Respect Task Force and the DCMS, as well as a range of other partners including the Metropolitan Police, v (the national youth volunteering charity) and the Department of Health. Much of the funding for the programme is provided by the Football Foundation, the Metropolitan Police and the DCMS via the Premier League's Good Causes fund; for the period 2007–10, approximately £11 million of funding was allocated to the delivery of Kickz from these bodies (Football Foundation, 2008).

Following the completion of pilot projects at four football clubs (Brentford United, Fulham, Manchester City and Tottenham Hotspur) the Kickz programme was formally launched in 2006 and rolled out nationally to a further 21 professional football clubs in the 2006/07 football season. By the end of 2008, 38 clubs (including all 20 Premier League clubs) were delivering Kickz to 15,000 young people aged 12–18 (Football Foundation, 2008). The overall aim of the programme is to 'create safer, stronger, more respectful communities through the development of young people's potential' (Football Foundation, 2008: 5), which is complemented by a range of interrelated and overlapping objectives. These are:

- to engage young people in a range of constructive activities which link to the Every Child Matters framework;
- to increase playing, coaching and officiating opportunities for participants;
- to break down barriers between the police and young people;
- to reduce crime and anti-social behaviour in the targeted neighbourhoods;
- to create routes into education, training and employment;
- to encourage volunteering within projects and throughout the target neighbourhoods; and
- to increase young people's interest in and connections with the professional game.

(Football Foundation, 2008: 5)

To help achieve these aims and objectives, the Kickz programme is said to be underpinned by a concern to move away from 'more conventional sport development models which emphasise the simple delivery of activities to large numbers of participants over short periods of time' (Football Foundation, 2008: 11) towards offering football schemes that enable project workers to 'build relationships and trust' with participants. The programme is also intended 'to move beyond the delivery of football coaching and competition, and [to] discuss difficult social and developmental messages with participants' (Football Foundation, 2008: 11). Of particular importance here, it is claimed, is the regularity with which young people can be engaged in the scheme. Unlike traditional sports development schemes that may require participants to attend for relatively short periods of time (e.g. once per week for twelve weeks), activity sessions that are delivered on the Kickz programme are offered on a minimum of three nights per week, for forty-eight weeks per year. These sessions typically include two nights of football and one additional session that can include 'elements such as other sports, music-based sessions and a range of developmental activities such as drug awareness, healthy lifestyles, volunteering, accreditation, career development and anti-weapons workshops' (Football Foundation, 2008: 8). Although football is seen as 'the single most important engagement strategy' (Football Foundation, 2008: 28) of Kickz, the content of the additional, 'flexible' sessions is chosen by the young people themselves. This is because a crucial assumption that informs the Kickz strategy is that if young people are to engage better with the programme it is vital that project staff 'need to build strong relationships with young people with whom they are working' (Football Foundation, 2008: 26). In this regard, given the emphasis that is placed on establishing such cooperative and supportive relationships with young people, project staff are expected to 'create relatively non-authoritarian, non-judgemental and mutually respectful environments' (Football Foundation, 2008: 26) on the scheme. In addition, where appropriate, they are expected 'to meet with young people on their own terms and to avoid heavy-handed punishments' if they are 'to succeed in engaging young people who frequently feel marginalised from more traditional forms of service delivery' (Football Foundation, 2008: 26). As we shall explain in relation to the Positive Futures scheme later, such an approach that places particular emphasis on consulting with young people, engendering amongst them a sense of ownership and inclusiveness in the scheme, and giving them relative freedom to choose which activities they would like to do and with whom they do them, would appear vital prerequisites for enhancing the likely future efficacy of Kickz. Indeed, this is a conclusion that was reached in a study entitled *Tired of Hanging Around*, which was published recently by the Audit Commission (2009). In particular, it was claimed that to help increase the effectiveness of programmes that use sport and leisure activities to prevent anti-social behaviour among young people it is important that project staff consult with young people when designing programmes and ensure that such projects are as accessible, reliable and relevant as possible to the diversity of young people's needs and lifestyles (Audit Commission, 2009).

Since the Kickz programme has only been delivered nationally since the 2006/07 season, it is clearly very difficult and too early to assess adequately the extent to which the various existing Kickz projects are achieving the desired objectives, whether progress towards the achievement of the programme aims are being made and whether the programme is being delivered as intended. Despite the lack of available data that exist in this regard, some preliminary assessment of the evidence of the impact of Kickz has, however, been undertaken in the first monitoring and evaluation report of the programme that consists of both quantitative (e.g. surveys) and qualitative (e.g. testimonies from participants) measures (Football Foundation, 2008). Perhaps the first point to note is that between September 2006 and the end of April 2007, 7,054 young people had engaged in the scheme overall, with approximately 300 participants being engaged, for an average of forty-three hours each, in the first phase of Kickz projects. Of those young people who had participated in the scheme, approximately 59 per cent (4,160) were classified as 'involved' (defined as being in contact with projects for twelve weeks or longer at the time data were collected) in Kickz, and of these 42 per cent (n = 1,728) had completed at least 60 hours or more with the programme. A further one-third (33 per cent; n = 1,406) completed at least 75 hours or more and one-quarter (25 per cent; n = 1,026) had completed 100 hours or more with the programme on average (Football Foundation, 2008). Thus, since projects were usually run, on average, three days per week for forty-eight weeks per year, it may be concluded that the amount of time spent on the programme each week ranged from just over one hour per week for some young people to approximately two and half hours per week for those who reported being engaged for 100 hours or more with the programme. These data suggest, therefore, that if participants did, in fact, engage with the programme three times each week, then the average amount of time spent attending each session was, for some young people, approximately half an hour, and perhaps just under one hour for those most persistently engaged in the programme. Although such modest estimates are almost bound to entail a degree of error and mask considerable variations between the amount of time some groups of young people spent attending the projects, they nevertheless raise questions about the extent to which the limited time spent on the programme by some young people could have contributed significantly to any reported changes in their behaviour, and to the achievement of the various objectives of the programme. These reservations aside, however, it is clear that the scheme has been successful in maintaining contact with large numbers of young people and has retained the engagement of many of those who live in areas identified as socially and economically disadvantaged in one way or another.

In addition to the variable time that young people spent engaged in the programme, engagement with the scheme was also differentially related to the gender and age of participants. As is common with many schemes of this kind, many more males (84 per cent) than females (16 per cent) were involved in Kickz during the 2006/07 census period, whilst just over 45 per cent of participants were aged 15 or over (Football Foundation, 2008). That the Kickz programme has been overwhelmingly male dominated is not altogether surprising, for not only has football been a traditional 'male preserve', but higher rates of offending have consistently been reported amongst some members of the scheme's principal target group, namely, groups of males who are thought to be more likely to drop out from sport as they grow older and whose behaviour (especially those from lower down the social hierarchy) is often controlled and regulated less effectively by adults, and particularly adult males (Nichols, 2007; Skille and Waddington, 2006). This is not to say, however, that Kickz is completely ineffective in targeting young women for, as noted earlier, project staff have enjoyed some limited success in attracting a significant minority of young women to the scheme; indeed, in some cases (e.g. the Arsenal and Charlton Athletic Kickz projects) approximately 25 per cent of young women are reported to have attended Kickz projects (Football Foundation, 2008). It remains to be seen, however, whether project workers will be able to attract similar, if not higher, proportions of young women to other Kickz initiatives. Indeed, it may be that the highly structured organization of the programme and the inclusion of more conventional, formally organized activities such as football, which tends to emphasize a strong degree of competitiveness and which can be particularly physically demanding and intensive, *could* reinforce very traditional patterns of gender power relations that may be antithetical to the involvement of some young women in the scheme and which may serve to reinforce male dominance in this specific context (Skille and Waddington, 2006).

One additional problem worthy of consideration here, and which arises when attempting to arrive at some understanding of the effectiveness of Kickz, relates to the scheme's efficacy in reducing crime and anti-social behaviour using a variety of educational programmes and anti-weapons and crime workshops. To come to some estimate of the impact of the projects on levels of crime and anti-social behaviour in the immediate areas surrounding each of the projects, crime data – based on official Home Office classification codes of crime – from September 2006 to August 2007 (the first full season in which Kickz ran) were compared to data from the previous year (when Kickz schemes had not begun). The findings indicated that in all geographical areas levels of recorded crime fell on each of the days that Kickz was delivered, with data for London and the North West revealing that crime reduction was over five times higher on days when the Kickz programme was running compared to those days without sessions. These reductions in crime, it is claimed, do not appear to have displaced crime to other nights when schemes were not delivered; indeed, of the twenty-five project areas on which data are available, increases in crime on non-Kickz evenings were recorded in just one following a decrease in crime on nights when sessions were delivered (Football Foundation, 2008). It is important to note, however, that these kinds of data do not provide unambiguous support for the effectiveness of Kickz in reducing crime and anti-social behaviour among young people. First, it is important to note that the programme requires prospective youngsters to volunteer their participation. While this is not in itself problematic, it does create a number of problems in terms of evaluation. As Collins and Kay (2003: 170) have noted, one of the major problems with such schemes is that any reported decreases in 'levels of delinquency may arise because the young people who come onto schemes are self-selecting' and are less likely to offend than those who do not volunteer. In this regard, it becomes difficult to attribute any decline in the incidence of delinquent behaviour to the programme itself. At the very least, this emphasizes the need to ensure that the aims and objectives of any such programmes are clear and that the potential consequences of voluntary participation are carefully considered in the final analysis. The second point to note is that, as with many schemes such as Kickz, 'it is impossible to show a direct connection between any scheme and its impact on local crime and ASB [anti-social behaviour]' (Football Foundation, 2008: 41). Notably, where there is said to be a connection between attendance on the programme and reductions in crime and anti-social behaviour, those involved in the delivery of the projects claim that this is most typically observed when Kickz is offered in conjunction with a variety of other local crime reduction strategies; in such cases, reductions of up to 50 per cent in crime and delinquency have been reported in some areas where the projects are delivered (Football Foundation, 2008).

That it is very difficult – indeed, perhaps impossible – to establish a cause and effect relationship between social inclusion programmes and reductions in crime and anti-social behaviour is not something that is specific to the Kickz programme. As Coalter (2007a) has noted, such difficulties in isolating from other existing crime reduction schemes the precise contribution of individual sport-based programmes to any observed changes (which are frequently indirect impacts of schemes) in participants' behaviour and the wider social contexts of local communities is also a problem that is encountered in the evaluations of very many social inclusion projects. Indeed, if sport is combined with a range of programmes – which often have similar objectives and goals – then it is particularly difficult to establish whether it is the sport-based intervention that results in any change of behaviour, or an intervention of another kind, or a mixture of both. Writing of these problems in relation to the British Summer Splash Schemes that were introduced with the objective of using sport and arts activities to reduce street crime and robbery by 9–17-year-olds in several of the most deprived neighbourhoods and city centres during school holidays, Long et al. (2002) noted that, while there are some evaluative data in support of the effectiveness of the schemes, 'it is not clear precisely what the data relate to' and there is 'real difficulty in distinguishing between and accessing crime data covering the exact project boundaries of such schemes' (Long et al., 2002: 44–45; see also Nichols, 2007). As we shall see next, a similar conclusion may also be reached in relation to other youth-focused anti-crime and drugs schemes.

Sport and social inclusion programmes: reducing crime, delinquency and drug use among young people

Perhaps one of the earliest and most well-known sport-focused interventions designed to promote social inclusion by combating criminal behaviour among young people is the so-called 'Midnight Basketball' programmes introduced in the US during the 1990s. These programmes were designed to reduce crime and prevent violence by young African-American males (aged 16–25) in poor inner-city urban areas with high levels of recorded crime and youth delinquency by engaging them in supervised basketball matches during the so-called 'high crime' hours between 10.00 p.m. and 2.00 a.m. (for a review, see Hartmann, 2001; Hartmann and Depro, 2006). Originally designed as a 'diversionary' programme that focused primarily on the provision of basketball as a means of reducing crime and delinquent behaviour, the concept of 'midnight sport' has subsequently been developed, with programmes using other sports such as soccer, golf and table tennis being introduced not only in the US, but also in countries such as Australia and Hungary and in urban as well as inner-city areas (C. Green, 2008). Despite the rapid growth of, and success claimed for, such schemes as midnight basketball/sport, they have traditionally lacked any kind of coherent and evidence-based theoretical rationale and there is very little evidence for their effectiveness in diverting participants away from committing crime and engaging in other so-called delinquent behaviour (C. Green, 2008; Hartmann, 2001; Hartmann, and Depro, 2006). For example, one study of the impact of midnight basketball programmes on levels of crime amongst young males living in urban areas in the US concluded that whilst lower crime rates were reported in those cities where the programme had been established longer, the relatively small numbers of young people who participated in such schemes meant that any observed changes in behaviour could not, in and of themselves, account for the reported decreases in crime in local areas (Hartmann and Depro, 2006). In those cases where reduced levels of crime were observed in areas where midnight basketball programmes operated, these decreases were most usually reported when these schemes were 'part of a whole package of crime prevention programmes' (C. Green, 2008: 135) in local communities. This is a point that is by no means exclusive to the midnight sport models of sports development, for, as we noted above, sport-based projects rarely exist in isolation from other existing schemes.

In Britain, similar schemes that have sport at their heart have also won support from all of the major political parties as well as the police, the youth probation and educational services, local authority workers and from organizations with an interest in promoting sport, such as Sport England. On this basis, such schemes have attracted large amounts of funding both from the government and from voluntary sector organizations, particularly those concerned with the welfare and lifestyles of young people. One example of these schemes is the Positive Futures initiative, which is the largest national sport- and activity-based social inclusion programme currently in operation in the UK. Positive Futures was launched in 2001 as a joint partnership between the Home Office Crime and Drug Strategy Directorate, Sport England, the Youth Justice Board and the Football Foundation. The initial twenty-four Positive Futures projects were launched in 20 per cent of the most deprived neighbourhoods and were targeted at 10–16-year-olds, with the objective of increasing regular participation in sport and physical activity and using these activities to reduce anti-social behaviour, crime and drug use among participants in the locality of projects (Sport England, 2002). As Nichols (2007) has noted, it was also intended that some of the Positive Futures projects would supplement the operations of other organizations whose existing work already meets the objectives of Positive Futures, and who can apply for extra funding to contribute to government's social inclusion policy priorities. Consequently, some of the Positive Futures projects have tended to be based on a sport plus approach that is characterized by partnership working between sporting and non-sporting organizations that use sport and other developmental activities, including a range of lifestyle, educational and employment activities, to achieve the intended outcomes (Coalter, 2007a).

As the programme has developed, and especially since responsibility for its management passed, in 2006, to the charity Crime Concern, there has been a growing recognition that where evidence exists in support of the effectiveness of the projects this is significantly related to the ongoing personal and social development of participants that accompanies their long-term engagement with the programme (Coalter, 2007a; Crabbe, 2008; Nichols, 2007). More particularly, it is clear that while 'sport' may be particularly helpful in attracting young people considered vulnerable or 'at risk' of committing crime and using illegal drugs, the provision of sport on its own is not sufficient to achieve the desired outcomes of the programme. To increase the efficacy of the projects, therefore, it is now recognized that sport needs to be complemented by a range of other activities that help foster the long-term development of young people, and which are commensurate with their broader lifestyles, where sport is only one among many other leisure priorities that have to be balanced (Coalter, 2007a; Crabbe, 2008; Nichols, 2007). This is one reason why, following the lessons that were learned during the early years of the programme, Positive Futures has since not been designed as 'a conventional "diversionary" or sports development project'; rather, it is said to be 'a relationship strategy' in which these various sport and other activities are 'used to establish relationships with ... socially marginalized young people who are alienated from officialdom and "authority" figures such as teachers, probation officers and even parents' (Home Office, 2003: 6). Consequently, the programme 'is not concerned with the celebration, development or promotion of sport as an end in itself', nor is it concerned with providing sports and physical activities as a diversion from, or alternative to, 'time spent engaging in substance misuse and crime' (Home Office, 2003: 8). Rather, sport, it is said, 'is just a hook, a means of establishing relationships with marginalized groups' (Home Office, 2003: 16) such as some young people. Central to the effectiveness of the scheme is the extent to which they form relationships with others on the scheme, particularly project workers (Crabbe, 2008; Home Office, 2003; Nichols, 2007). In this regard, workers on the Positive Futures scheme are said to be 'concerned to gain a more complete picture of the ways in which *projects* (rather than sport or other activities) influence participants' attitudes, engagement, interests, education, employment, peer groups and relationships' (Crabbe, 2008: 31; original emphasis). Let us examine the emphasis that is placed on building relationships between project workers and young people on such schemes as Positive Futures a little further.

Developing relationships and the importance of peer leaders

It has often been recognized that the quality of relationships that are established between project leaders and participants on programmes is crucial to maintaining and enhancing their effectiveness in achieving desired outcomes (Audit Commission, 2009; Coalter, 2007a; Crabbe, 2008; C. Green, 2008; Smith and Waddington, 2004). This is a point that is reinforced by Crabbe (2008: 32) in his evaluation of Positive Futures, when he suggests that 'for those who remain engaged, Positive Futures can help to build both breadth and depth into project related friendships, networks and opportunities rather than just access to "more" or "different" people'. It is not simply the relationships *per se* that participants form with others on the scheme that appear to be crucial, however. What is arguably more important to the effectiveness of schemes like Positive Futures is the use of volunteer peer leaders to deliver programmes and engage participants, the rationale for which is typically grounded in educational and learning theory (Coalter, 2007a; 2008). As Coalter has observed,

> because young people's attitudes are highly influenced by their peers' values and attitudes, peer educators are less likely to be viewed as 'preaching' authority figures and more likely to be regarded as people who know the experiences and concerns of young people.
>
> (Coalter 2008: 53)

Insofar as youth peer leaders are perceived to be effective role models for participants on sport-based social inclusion schemes, this, it seems, is related both to the characteristics of the peer leader and his or her perceived similarity to the learner (Coalter, 2008). This is crucial, Coalter suggests, because learning in young people

> is most likely to occur when the learners perceive that they are capable of carrying out the behaviour (self-efficacy expectancy), think that there is a high probability that the behaviour will result in a particular outcome (outcome expectancy) and if the outcome is desirable – all of which can be reinforced via peer education.
>
> (Coalter 2008: 53)

The use of peer leaders in bringing about desired changes in the behaviour of participants and the sensitivity they adopt in relation to their needs are thus key components of the effectiveness of sport-based social inclusion programmes. There are, however, a number of additional problems that may need to be resolved before we can hope to measure more accurately the effectiveness of schemes in which the development and maintenance of relationships between participants and project staff are amongst the main objectives. It is not generally clear, for example, how we are to 'measure' – if that were possible – the relationships young people form with others on sport-based social inclusion schemes and within the wider society more generally. What criteria should be applied in this analysis? For how long do the young people involved have to have established a 'relationship' with others for the project to be considered a success? Are these relationships likely to last in the long term? For it is the nature of people's, and especially young people's, networks of relationships that they will frequently change as they grow older; some relations with friends and other groups will remain, while others will become less significant in their lives. This is especially important when one considers that the relationships young people are expected to form with project leaders and others on social inclusion schemes are, in many cases, only temporary. Indeed, despite evidence of their effectiveness, such close one-to-one relationships with project leaders can be particularly difficult to establish on a long-term basis on many large-scale schemes. They are also particularly difficult to achieve on those schemes that are short-term and that have a high turnover of both project staff and volunteers as well as of the young people themselves (Coalter, 2007a; Collins and Kay, 2003; C. Green, 2008; Nichols, 2007). These problems may be further compounded by the tendency for project workers to work under almost constant pressure to secure funding for future projects and to meet the short-term priorities of partners. Not surprisingly, these and many other constraints often mean that rather less emphasis is given to long-term evaluation, project development and, especially, to the development of people, as volunteers and/or participants. These and many other constraints can make it particularly difficult to assess the effectiveness of projects and the likely long-term impact that engagement in them will have on the quality of the relationships that may be established as a consequence (Audit Commission, 2009; Coalter, 2007a; Nichols, 2007).

The significance of some of these issues might usefully be explored by one of the most systematic and careful evaluations of social inclusion schemes that was carried out by Davis and Dawson for the Home Office (1996). They reviewed six projects using diversion to communicate drugs prevention messages to young people. One of these projects was based primarily around physical activities – in this case an outward bound camp – but other forms of diversion included a young people's music project, production of a local newspaper, summer holiday play schemes and the production of a newsletter using computer graphics and text. Davis and Dawson (1996) noted a number of key themes emerging from these projects. First, they noted that there was particular confusion about what is meant by 'diversion'. In this context, they noted that some projects that they observed had been in existence for some time before a drugs component, linked to funding by the local drugs prevention team (DPT), was appended to it. They argued that if these projects had previously been successful in attracting youngsters to the activities that they offered, then they could fairly claim to have been diversionary. If a drugs component was added subsequently, this could more accurately be described, not as diversionary, but in terms of drugs education. This is not merely a matter of semantics; the real question is whether the projects had been properly thought through and, in that regard, Davis and Dawson concluded that

> unfortunately this was not always the case and confusion surrounding the meaning of diversion may in some part be to blame. This is because the bolting on of a drugs education component to an existing venture was often motivated purely by the need to secure DPT funding and was unconvincing in educational terms, no matter that the original project may have been well received.
>
> (Davis and Dawson 1996: 28)

Second, it was suggested that drugs prevention team funding is not an unalloyed blessing. It was noted that pressure to secure funding for youth work leads project managers to cast their net widely. One possibility is to apply for funding to the local DPT. Sometimes, however, this money is applied for without sufficient thought or planning and on occasions, they note, the element of DPT funding created a pressure to address the drugs issue in ways that were perceived to distort the original nature of the project – perhaps because of the element of compulsion involved to meet the requirements of the funding body or, in some cases, because some workers (especially volunteer workers) lacked confidence in their ability to transmit drugs messages effectively (Davis and Dawson, 1996).

Third, there were a number of weaknesses associated with short-term policy initiatives (such as using sport to reduce drug use among young people) and, in this regard, Davis and Dawson (1996) argued that it is extremely difficult to convey drugs messages effectively on a short-term basis. They suggested that attempts to deal with the drugs issue in a concerted fashion in the context of a summer project were not particularly successful.

Fourth, they argued that the only projects that are likely to be effective in terms of 'diversion' are those that offer young people an activity about which they are passionate.

The other key ingredient, they suggest – though they recognize that this is based on very limited observation – is that there needs to be some prospect of the activity in question having some permanent place in the lives of young people, perhaps even offering the prospect of future employment. They cite not just sport but also music and computer technology as three examples of activities that have the capacity to excite passion and to offer the possibility of long-term engagement (Davis and Dawson, 1996).

Finally, it was argued that a key factor in the success or failure of projects was the personalities of the coordinator and the other people drawn to work on the project. Specifically, Davis and Dawson (1996) suggested that it is important that project workers should have 'authority' in the eyes of the young people attending these projects, but it was also important that they should not be seen as authority figures; their authority must lie in relevant knowledge and practice and, as we explained earlier, it is also important that project leaders have a high level of skill in the core activity (see also Audit Commission, 2009; Coalter, 2007a; Smith and Waddington, 2004). They also noted the difficulties in conveying drugs messages to young people and the fact that volunteers often felt that they lacked appropriate knowledge. They concluded that the problem is best tackled not by giving volunteer workers ad hoc drugs education sessions, but rather by utilizing specialists who could more confidently address these topics (Davis and Dawson, 1996). The general conclusion of the report was balanced and cautious and did not go beyond the evidence available. It is worth quoting at length, and we use it to precede our brief discussion of some of the more general policy issues associated with the use of sport-focused schemes designed to contribute to the achievement of greater social inclusion. They argued:

> All the projects which we visited – even the most impressive – were modest in their claim to influence drug related behaviour in the longer term; what is more they all conceded that even if they did have an impact, this would be extremely difficult to demonstrate. But leaving aside this question of the impact upon drug related behaviour, it was evident that projects might be more or less effective in their pursuit of related goals such as the transmission of new skills, improving self confidence, developing good relationships with adults, and gaining an increased understanding of the potentially harmful consequences of drug abuse. Some projects appear to us to be powerful interventions if measured in these terms; others were less impressive. Perhaps all we can say is that it is at least plausible to suppose that some projects may have had an impact on the drug taking behaviour of some of their customers; and that in respect of some other projects it would have been implausible to suppose that they had any such impact. Powerful sustained interventions may influence behaviour; marginal, ephemeral interventions will not.
>
> (Davis and Dawson, 1996: 31)

Are sport-based social inclusion schemes effective?

As we and many others have noted (e.g. Bloyce *et al.*, 2008; Coalter, 2007a; Collins and Kay, 2003; Smith and Waddington, 2004), present-day policy-makers and SDOs hold particular ideological views and assumptions about the supposed worth of sport in conferring upon participants what are regarded as pro-social behaviours and values (e.g. reduced crime and drug use). These views and assumptions, as with those related to the presumed impact that sport and other activities have on the promotion of health (see

Chapter 5) and educational achievement (see Chapter 3), for example, are expressions of the differential ways in which the thoughts and actions of policy-makers and SDOs are unavoidably constrained by the relations they have formed with others in the past, and which they continue to form in the present. Such is the impact that being a part of these historically produced and reproduced networks of interdependence can have on policy-makers' and SDOs' views and practice of sport it is now increasingly common to find them championing enthusiastically the presumed social impacts of sport. Notwithstanding these rhetorical and commonsense claims made on behalf of the effectiveness of sport in social inclusion-based schemes, the consensus among more critical observers is that despite the vast numbers of such schemes currently in operation in the UK and elsewhere, there is a widespread lack of robust research on, and hence very little evidence for, their effectiveness in reducing and preventing crime and drug use among young people (Coalter, 2007a; Collins and Kay, 2003; Dunning and Waddington, 2003; Hartmann, 2001; Long and Sanderson, 2001; Nichols, 2007; Robins, 1990). For example, on the basis of their review of the existing literature, which examined the relationship between sport and social inclusion as part of their PAT 10 report for the DCMS, Collins *et al.* (1999: 4) found that only eleven of the studies that they reviewed examined outcomes 'with any-thing approaching rigorous evaluations' of the effectiveness of sport-based social inclusion programmes. In this regard, they concluded that beyond these eleven studies, many social inclusion schemes involved little, if any, evaluation, and where monitoring of such schemes did take place this typically involved the recording and measurement of rather simplistic outputs (Collins *et al.*, 1999). A similar conclusion was reached by Tacon, who has noted that, despite the increasing policy and political commitment to social inclusion initiatives, 'there is, to date, little evaluation evidence to demonstrate the effectiveness of these types of sports-based projects' (Tacon, 2007: 2) in achieving their desired outcomes. In addition, Tacon (2007: 19) adds that whilst currently 'there are strong theoretical claims, and even stronger political claims that sport, particularly football, can make a positive contribution to social issues ... there is little evidence to support these claims'. Despite the existence of what Tacon sees as the 'strong theoretical claims' for the pre-sumed impact of sport-based schemes in contributing to the achievement of greater social inclusion among key target groups, particularly young people, there are also a number of other theoretical reasons – in addition to the absence of supporting empirical evidence that we discussed above – why one might be sceptical about the claims made on behalf of the effectiveness of such schemes. One frequent justification for the use of sport in schemes where crime and drug reduction or prevention is the main objective is that sport can create enjoyment and excitement, and thus provide an antidote to boredom, for young people (Coalter, 2001; Crabbe, 2000; Nichols, 2007). It is certainly the case, as Elias and Dunning (1986) have argued, that sport can be seen as a 'quest for excitement'. However, as Crabbe (2000: 383) has noted, 'this is often for much the same reason that [young people] might also choose to use illicit drugs, become involved in criminal activity or even sport-related violence'. Indeed, even a cursory examination of some of the most salient aspects of youth cultures should therefore sensitize us to the fact that there are, as Crabbe (2000: 390) has put it, 'very real problems in using an activity such as sport that is seen to replicate the experience or excitement of drugs if it is intended to help young people come to regard drugs as a futile and sterile activity in comparison. The fact that the same emotions of excitement, euphoria, celebration, tension and fear are being used does not suddenly result in drugs no longer being seen as "fun" or worthwhile'. To this we might also add that any scheme designed to combat drug use among young people should also seek to account more adequately for the *context* in which they use illegal drugs as well as the people (especially their friends) with whom they frequently consume them, not least because this might lead to a more secure basis from which to formulate policy that is based upon a greater understanding of the broader dimensions and realities of young people's leisure lives (Smith 2006; Smith and Waddington, 2004).

The need to account for the context in which young people use drugs becomes even more apparent when one examines another commonsense justification for the effectiveness of such schemes (known as the so-called 'displacement thesis'), namely, the claim that simply participating in sport as part of a programme prevents youngsters from simultaneously committing crime or using illegal drugs of one kind or another (Coalter, 2007a; Nichols, 2007). However, to the relatively detached observer – that is, to those who have some appreciation of the other aspects of sporting culture – it is clear that some young people may value playing sport alongside other leisure pursuits that positively promote drug use and other deviant behaviour; a good example would be the heavy drinking culture that has traditionally surrounded a number of sports, including rugby and soccer, in the UK (Coalter, 2007a; Dunning and Waddington, 2003; Smith and Waddington, 2004). Indeed, Crabbe notes that, in contrast to approaches that stress sport's allegedly wholesome and socially cohesive character, it might, with equal validity, be noted that sport provides environments in which 'acts of violence, confrontation and drug use are licensed in ritualized fashion and given meaning through their association with the hegemonic masculine ideals of toughness, heroism and sacrifice' (Crabbe, 2008: 23). Such observations should, therefore, sound a warning against making simplistic assumptions about the effectiveness of sporting participation as a means of combating drug use and other activities popularly regarded as indicative of the anti-social behaviour of target groups.

In addition to the theoretical problems that are associated with sport-based social inclusion programmes, and particularly those designed to reduce crime and anti-social behaviour, there is, as we explained earlier, a lack of systematic evidence of the effectiveness of such schemes. But how might we begin to account for this lack of supporting empirical evidence for sports development programmes and other schemes that are expected to achieve a vast array of desired social outcomes such as the reduction of crime and drug use? Coalter has argued in this connection that the lack of existing evidence of the efficacy of these schemes can be related, in particular, to

> an absence of a culture of monitoring and evaluation, bolstered by a range of factors: a simple belief in the efficacy of such interventions; limited project funding is concentrated on provision rather than evaluation and a general lack of research expertise. However, most fundamentally there has been a widespread lack of clarity about the nature of outcomes and their measurement; substantial methodological difficulties in controlling for intervening variables and assessing cause and effect relationships.
>
> (Coalter 2007a: 117)

We shall briefly consider some of these issues in the remaining pages of this chapter.

Establishing the scale of the problem

A longstanding problem in social policies where sport is used as a vehicle for enhancing social inclusion by, amongst other things, preventing and reducing crime and drug use among young people is the lack of consistency and clarity regarding the objectives of those policies. When 'objectives' of one kind or another are identified, they tend to be overly ambitious, unclear, non-specific and often premised on poorly developed and vague rationales.

At one level the failure to clarify such questions is not altogether surprising since it is frequently the case that government and other interested organizations seek to develop such policies without first gathering baseline data that may be used to help clarify the size and nature of the problem before committing time and resources towards its achievement. While there are numerous methodological difficulties involved in trying to arrive at a precise estimate of the extent of young people's criminal activity and use of illegal drugs, it is important that we strive – insofar as it is possible – to estimate as accurately as we can the extent of criminal behaviour and drug use among the young people for whom the policy is intended. It is important that we begin to address such questions because until they are answered it is difficult to know what criteria should be used in monitoring and measuring the success of drug-reduction and prevention policies intended for young people. In this regard, there is clearly a pressing need to define more clearly the objectives of policies of this kind as well as the groups for whom they are intended, and to specify more exactly the criteria for monitoring the success of that policy.

Monitoring and evaluating sport-based social inclusion schemes

Writing in 1990, Robins (1990: 1) noted that 'research into the relation between sport and delinquency has been virtually non-existent in the UK'. One of the few systematic studies that existed at that time was by Coalter (1989), who, following a review of the literature on the subject, was unable to conclude that there is a correlation between high levels of sports participation and low levels and frequency of delinquency among young people in the UK. Beyond Coalter's review, however, Robins observed that there was a dearth of properly conducted and monitored evaluation of schemes where the reduction of crime via sports participation was a main objective. It was in this context that Robins critically examined all the major programmes that had then been set up with the aim of using sport and recreation as part of a crime prevention strategy. These included a wide variety of schemes – for example community development schemes, police schemes and schemes designed to rehabilitate young offenders – and Robins (1990: 89) concluded that there was 'little evidence of evaluation of the effect of programmes on young people' and that, as a consequence, 'information about outcomes was hard to come by' (Robins, 1990: 92). An additional problem, he added, was that none of the programmes surveyed included a process of follow-up or aftercare in their objectives and, specifically with regard to those schemes that were targeted at convicted offenders, he noted that information about re-offending patterns, where it was available, was generally sketchy. He also noted that 'no clear picture of aims and objectives and their underlying rationales emerge' (Robins, 1990: 88).

Despite the points raised by Robins and Coalter two decades ago, there has been relatively little progress in terms of monitoring the effectiveness of such schemes. For example, Nichols and Taylor (1996) examined the effects of the West Yorkshire Sports Counselling Scheme and concluded that while there was evidence of the effect of the programme on crime, with a significant reduction in reconviction rates for young offenders participating in the programme for eight weeks or more, the sample size of young offenders was too small to provide a statistically reliable estimate of the value of the benefits gained, to set against the cost of the programme. More recently, Coalter (2001: 31) has noted that there is 'an absence of robust intermediate or final outcome data ... for large-scale diversionary projects' as well as other rehabilitative programmes. Such programmes, he adds, also 'tend to have vague rationales, overly ambitious objectives and a relatively unsophisticated understanding of the variety and complexity of the causes of criminality' (Coalter, 2001: 31). In addition, Taylor *et al.* (1999) identified 54 programmes operating in 34 probation service areas; they noted the huge variety of programmes on offer, particularly in terms of their duration, scale and intensity (from one-day sessions to two-week residential programmes), and in terms of the activities offered and the programme rationales. As Gratton and Taylor (2000) have pointed out, this diversity of programmes can be interpreted in one of two ways: either as a reflection of uncertainty about both why the programmes are provided and what is effective or, alternatively, as an indication that with such a complex set of intermediate outcomes there are many possible ways to achieve one or more of those outcomes.

It is also worthy of note that where monitoring and evaluation processes are built in to sport-based schemes they tend to be applied rather inconsistently and the emphasis is often placed upon demonstrating the 'benefits' afforded to individual participants on the programme (e.g. Crabbe, 2000; Long *et al.*, 2002; Nichols, 2004; 2007; Robins, 1990). While those involved in running and analyzing these programmes often, with some justification, point to particular individuals whose involvement led in the short term to changes in interpersonal relations, capacities for self-reflection and social adjustment, 'it should be remembered that whatever short term efficacy the programme may have on individuals … may be rapidly dissipated in the absence of any process of follow up and after care' (Robins, 1990: 93). Robins (1990), for example, has written in this connection of the problems of over-relying on individual data in his review of the Solent Sports Counselling Project in Hampshire, UK. The report included an analysis of the re-offending patterns of a random sample of 48 clients. Of the 13 clients who were involved with the project for less than three weeks, only 2 were not subsequently charged with offences within a year of leaving the project. The re-offending patterns of the remaining 29 (information was not available for 6 of the sample) indicated that almost half the clients had maintained a trouble-free record since being involved with the project and a further half-dozen clients appeared to have reduced their previous rates of offending (Robins, 1990). However, Robins points out that, although the evaluation refers to trouble-free records and reduced rates of re-offending by almost half of the clients, it is not at all clear whether this was causally connected to attendance at the project and there may be other more significant reasons why such changes occurred.

Similar methodological problems of this kind also arise in relation to other studies in which there is an attempt to provide evidence of the effectiveness of sports provision in terms of reductions in, or changing patterns of, recidivism rates. For example, in a study of four British schemes in the mid-1990s, Tsuchiya (1996) reported that the participants in two of the schemes (data were unavailable for the remaining two because no monitoring or evaluation of the schemes was conducted) had a 36 per cent and 50 per cent reconviction rate after one and two years, respectively. At first glance, such figures would appear rather convincing, although a closer examination of the data cited in support of these claims should encourage us to be rather more cautious about the alleged effectiveness of these schemes.

The first scheme for which Tsuchiya (1996) reports data included four types of programme: (1) offending behaviour group work; (2) craft workshops and education; (3) life-skills sessions; and (4) sports and outdoor pursuits. From Tsuchiya's analysis, however, there is no indication of which of these elements of the programme was responsible for its claimed effectiveness and, while the evidence may be less convincing in the case of sports and outdoor pursuits, it would be surprising if the first three of the programmes provided as part of the scheme had no impact at all on reconviction rates. With regard to the second scheme cited by Tsuchiya, 260 (54 per cent) of the 483 youngsters who were referred to the scheme signed up to start the programme, but of these a further 67 (14 per cent) failed to show up for the initial interview, 104 (22 per cent) did not show up for the first session and 52 (11 per cent) were not interested in taking part or were unable to participate for other reasons (Tsuchiya, 1996: 297). In other words, of the 260 young people for whom the scheme was originally intended, only 37 youngsters actually started the programme and only half of these did not re-offend within two years. In light of these considerations, one might justifiably question the likely effective on recidivism rates and the cost-efficiency of such schemes as well as the generally positive analysis Tsuchiya provides of them. Collins and Kay, among others (e.g. Nichols and Taylor, 1996), have suggested that one reason for the lack of evidence for the effectiveness of schemes of this kind is 'because of the difficulty and cost in establishing the true re-offending rate amongst a very mobile population, even when costly access is given to the national computerised crime records' (Collins and Kay 2003: 170).

A further difficulty that is frequently encountered when attempting to establish the effectiveness of sport-focused schemes arises in relation to the frequent overreliance on individual data, or isolated anecdotal stories, in which participation in such schemes is presumed to lead to changes in participants' behaviour. Such problems were particularly clear in a study by Nichols (2004), who outlines a sport-based project delivered by SDOs in West Yorkshire and in which interviews were conducted with just nine young people. In his paper – which provides data on just four of the nine youngsters on the project – Nichols notes that 'the programme has had a limited diversion effect' (Nichols 2004: 191) both during and after participation in the scheme. The limited effect of this project is all the more apparent when one considers that 'there was only evidence that three of the nine case study participants were progressing to independent sports participation and one of these would probably have done so anyway' (Nichols, 2004: 188). Indeed, the lack of evidence for the effectiveness of this project is perhaps unsurprising since 'its main focus was on achieving sport development objectives' (Nichols, 2004: 192) and because it is provided by SDOs whose primary interest is with the development of sport and *not* with a reduction in criminal behaviour by the participants.

Similar problems arise in relation to intervention schemes that use sport as part of a drugs education or drugs rehabilitation programme. For example Crabbe (2000) analyzed the rehabilitative and diversionary elements of the Leyton Orient Community Sports Programme in London, the objective of which was to establish a programme of activity that would provide local ex- and stabilized drug users with a range of sporting and personal development opportunities. Crabbe (2000: 388) concluded, following four months of observation of the project, that the participants 'are benefiting from the alternative focus that the sports activities provide and the need to remain "stable" that participation requires'. He noted that several participants, as a result of their involvement, had obtained qualifications ranging from junior team managers awards to qualifications in photography and places on other courses at local colleges. Two of the participants were subsequently employed on a casual basis in the community sports programme itself. Crabbe's evaluation is, on the whole, a positive one, although his evaluation is, like other more recent studies (e.g. Nichols, 2007), based on the identification of individual participants who have benefited from the scheme rather than on the analysis of a variety of systematically gathered quantitative and qualitative information, which would help provide a more reliable basis for judgements about the effectiveness of such schemes.

The social context of sport-based social inclusion schemes

In addition to the problems of judging the effectiveness of social inclusion schemes in helping to bring about desired change in the behaviour of individual participants, it is often overlooked that, as we noted in Chapter 1, it is not simply the provision of 'sport' that may account for any of the achieved outcomes of such programmes. In addition, of particular importance are the ways in which different kinds of sports and activities are experienced differently by different kinds of participants in particular circumstances. Indeed, it would be misleading to think that just because the provision of particular kinds of sports in particular social contexts may help bring about desired change among some individuals or groups this can be generalized unproblematically to many other participants. Thus, since the experience of programmes varies differentially between individuals and groups of young people, it cannot simply be assumed that they will each derive the intended benefits, if any, of the programme in the same way, or for the same reasons. It might with equal validity be noted that any changes in the observed behaviour may not be attributed directly to the operations of the scheme, but to changes in the wider social context. Accordingly, not only do we need to know something of the context within which the outcomes of sport-based social inclusion schemes are produced, but it is also important to have some appreciation of the broader social context in which the schemes, the participants and those who design and deliver them exist (Audit Commission, 2009; Coalter, 2007a). In short, there is a need to analyze those processes and experiences that are associated with programmes that may or may not be considered successful. No less importantly, if we are to move towards a more adequate means of judging the effectiveness of such schemes, it is important to examine what works, for which participants, in what particular circumstances when designing and delivering sport-based social inclusion schemes (Audit Commission, 2009; Coalter, 2007a).

The importance of recognizing the social context within which sport- and non-sport schemes operate is a conclusion that can almost certainly be arrived at from data generated by the birth cohort studies that are conducted in Britain (Feinstein *et al.*, 2005; Robson and Feinstein, 2007). Data from the 1970 cohort, for example, suggest that participation in unstructured youth clubs that typically attracted higher proportions of more 'disadvantaged' youth and that were less likely to be heavily supervised by adults was associated with adult forms of social exclusion and socio-economic disadvantage. Those young people who attended youth clubs and engaged in youth offending when aged 16, for example, were significantly less likely to have educational qualifications at age 30 and were more likely to be a teen parent than those who did not (Feinstein *et al.*, 2005). Conversely, participation in sports clubs and community activity centres, which had a greater degree of structure than youth clubs, was said to have a positive, marginal long-term impact on later life outcomes by young people from all levels of the social hierarchy. In particular, the participation of 16-year-olds in the more structured social contexts that were to be found within sports clubs and community centres was said to help ameliorate the long-term effects of poor family background and possession of fewer educational qualifications (Feinstein *et al.*, 2005). It is important to note, however, that the perceived negative effects of only attending youth clubs when aged 16 were offset or nullified to some extent by engaging in combinations of activities, such as attending youth clubs and sports/community centres, which was associated with reducing the impact that youth club attendance had on adult forms of social exclusion and socio-economic disadvantage (Robson and Feinstein, 2007). The overall findings of the 1970 birth cohort studies suggest, therefore, that although the social context of youth club participation was not 'objectively harmful' (Robson and Feinstein, 2007: 38) to young people's later life experiences, it was nevertheless clear that the provision of different leisure activities in varying social contexts during the teenage years did come to impact differentially on future behaviour. In this regard, it might be concluded that the extent to which participation in youth-focused social inclusion schemes can be effective in bringing about desired change among young people depends, to a significant degree, upon the contexts within which those schemes are provided and the particular network of relationships that characterize the delivery of them. It is also important to remind ourselves that

> we cannot take for granted that well-intentioned public funds to provide youth with meaningful leisure experiences will inevitably be beneficial ... [It is important] to specify what aspects of leisure activities are beneficial, the conditions under which leisure activities may be problematic, and the ways in which peer groups can be effectively organised during leisure time to facilitate positive social adjustment.
>
> (Mahoney *et al.*, 2001: 519)

The extent to which SDOs and other practitioners are able and/or willing to engage in project evaluations that focus on issues of context and process may, of course, be particularly limited and perhaps altogether neglected because of the perceived accountability culture this fosters and because of the perceived impact this will have on valuable resources (see Chapter 1). Collins *et al.* arrived at a similar conclusion following their review of sport-based social inclusion schemes, where the evaluation of the schemes they reviewed was often said to be 'tentative, indicative and anecdotal, because insufficient (human and financial) resources are given to it, and insufficient intellectual attention in most cases is expended to identify outcomes and gather the necessary evidence to demonstrate them' (Collins *et al.* 1999: 26). They also noted that these problems are frequently compounded by several other things, including: the short-term nature and changing political priorities of government; a lack of sustained funding from sponsors; and since many social inclusion projects typically last just three years, project staff are often more concerned with looking for another job or securing additional funding than they are with monitoring and evaluating the project they are working on (Collins *et al.*, 1999; see also Audit Commission, 2009).

Despite these constraints, it is clear that, as we have noted elsewhere in this book (see Chapters 1 and 3), insofar as few sport-based schemes include built-in processes for systematically monitoring and evaluating their effectiveness and outcomes, the efficacy of those programmes becomes increasingly difficult to determine. It is also clear that, in policy terms, the failure to monitor and evaluate adequately the effectiveness of such schemes is a matter of serious concern. Without such in-built processes it becomes increasingly difficult to monitor the intended and unintended outcomes of those policies and, most importantly, whether they have any medium- to long-term impact on the problems they are intended to address. As we noted in Chapter 1, such problems are not exclusive to evaluations of the effectiveness of sports schemes, for without appropriate monitoring and evaluation measures it is incredibly difficult to identify the various outcomes that non-sport reforms (e.g. government training measures) have on the identified objectives of programmes.

Developing a theoretically and empirically grounded rationale

In addition to the lack of systematic monitoring, several researchers have identified a further problem with most sport-based programmes: the absence of a clearly developed rationale for these schemes. One consequence of this is that in many of these projects the scale and nature of the problem to be targeted – as well as the goals to be achieved – become more diffuse, complex and wide-ranging such that the achievement of one goal might undermine the achievement of other goals and thus the likely success of the programme itself. This notwithstanding, proposals for the establishment of schemes of this kind are frequently accompanied by a list of alleged benefits of participation in sport without any attempt to articulate either the relationships between these alleged benefits or the connections between these benefits and a reduction in crime and drug use. For example, the DIVERT Trust, in its booklet *Match of the Day* (described as a step-by-step guide to setting up football projects for young people at risk), draws upon the West Yorkshire sports counselling project to list five benefits of participation in sport. These benefits include: (1) improved self-esteem; (2) improved relationships with peers; (3) constructive use of spare time; (4) the opening of opportunities, for example in training and employment; and (5) the development of new relationships with adults (DIVERT Trust, 1996: 10–12). However, the DIVERT Trust does not specify precisely how these alleged benefits have an impact on levels of youth delinquency; indeed, the West Yorkshire project, which provides the basis for these claimed benefits, was itself careful about overemphasizing the link between sport and crime prevention (Davis and Dawson, 1996).

The difficulties associated with such rationales might be fruitfully illustrated by examining briefly the claim that participation in sport leads to improved self-esteem, a claim that has been made in a number of studies. There are several problems here. First, as Nichols (1997) has noted, the increased self-esteem that may be associated with excellence in sporting achievement is, by definition, only attainable by a few and there may be difficulties of readjustment when the individual loses the capacity to perform sport at an exceptional level. Second, it is in the nature of sport that there are winners and losers; if enhanced self-esteem is a consequence of winning, then what, we may ask, is the impact on the self-esteem of those who are losers? In addition, the nature of the alleged link between enhanced self-esteem and reduced levels of criminal behaviour is by no means clear. Indeed, as Crabbe (2000) has pointed out, in some situations the 'drug use–crime' relationship can itself provide meaning and purpose in the absence of legitimate structured opportunities and can generate status and identity in contexts of social and economic exclusion. It is also the case that whilst it is commonly assumed that those with low self-esteem are more likely to engage in anti-social behaviour such as crime and use drugs of various kinds, on the basis of current evidence and the methods employed in the design of most published research there is little evidence from the UK and US in support of the presumed causal relationship between sports participation and improvements in self-esteem (Coalter, 2007a; Emler, 2001). Indeed, where there is evidence in support of a relationship between self-esteem and sports participation it is often not those with low self-esteem, but those groups with higher levels of self-esteem, who are most at risk of engaging in anti-social behaviour (Coalter, 2007a; Emler, 2001).

Summary

As we noted in Chapter 2, there has been a strong degree of continuity in the sport policy priorities and goals of successive governments from different sides of the political spectrum in many countries, including Britain, since the 1990s. We also explained that one of the policies that is central to the current Labour government's policy agenda in Britain, and that distinguishes its priorities from those of previous governments, is the explicit emphasis that it has come to place on social inclusion and particularly how activities such as sport can achieve broader welfare policy goals. In this chapter we have sought to examine some of the policy issues surrounding the use of sporting schemes as vehicles of social policy in which the intention is to contribute to the achievement of greater social inclusion by reducing levels of crime, delinquency and drug use, particularly among young people. In doing so, we have attempted to show that, perhaps with the exception of some Positive Futures projects and despite the strong and increasing political policy commitment to the social inclusion agenda, there is currently little evidence of the effectiveness of sport-based schemes in reducing crime, drug use or anti-social behaviour among identified target groups. This would appear to be for a variety of complex reasons. One major problem in this regard is that relatively few schemes have built-in techniques for monitoring and evaluating their impact on levels of crime, drug use or anti-social behaviour; as a result, it is difficult to be sure what impact, if any, they have on such behaviours. Moreover, the absence of any clearly articulated theoretical rationale for these schemes means that, even where success is claimed, it is often unclear what specific aspects of the schemes account for that claimed success. Of equal, if not greater, significance is that, contrary to the prevailing and largely uncritically accepted view of 'sport as good' (Coalter, 2007a) as a rationale for many social inclusion schemes, 'sport in any simple sense rarely achieves the variety of desired outcomes attributed to it and that issues of process and context ... are key to understanding its developmental potential' (Coalter, 2008: 48). More particularly, it is clear that if we are to enhance the effectiveness of such schemes there is a clear need to think far more clearly and analytically about the potential of 'sport' in helping to achieve desired social outcomes.

In addition, we have suggested that when considering the design of sport-based social inclusion schemes there is greater need to recognize the differential contribution that different kinds of sports and physical activities can make to different kinds of participants in particular contexts, and to consider the importance of fostering a greater understanding of the extent to which the wider social contexts in which programmes exist can impact on the effectiveness of those programmes. The latter consideration is of particular importance since one the major weaknesses of many sport-based social inclusion schemes has been the failure to change the habitus, that is, the deeply seated values and beliefs, of participants towards their propensity for engaging in what are regarded as undesirable behaviours (e.g. crime and drug use). Indeed, the expectation that one-off initiatives, shorter-term programmes or schemes that are delivered consistently over longer periods of time can, of themselves, begin to reverse the roots of complex social processes associated with social exclusion is, to put it at its most charitable, a rather unrealistic one. Such schemes are also particularly limited in their effectiveness because they cannot, on their own, reasonably be expected to bring about substantial change either in the wider contexts of people's lives or in their communities, where the complex causes of social disadvantage continue to exist relatively independently of the very schemes that are designed to tackle them. Finally, as Gratton and Taylor have noted in relation to crime reduction schemes – though the point would apply equally well to anti-drugs schemes and other social inclusion schemes – even if it is accepted that crime may be reduced by sport-based programmes, 'the evidence does not extend ... to proving that the value of the crime reduction is greater than either the costs of providing the programmes or the costs of dealing with crime after it has taken place, and more work is needed on these cost–benefit questions' (Gratton and Taylor 2000: 111).

Revision questions

1 Examine the various contributions that sport and physical activities are thought to make to the achievement of greater social inclusion.
2 Examine the evidence for the effectiveness of sports development programmes in which the intention is to prevent crime and drug use among young people.
3 To what extent is the social inclusion agenda coming to impact on the day-to-day activities of SDOs?

Key readings

Collins, M. and Kay, T. (2003) *Sport and Social Exclusion*, London: Routledge.
Nichols, G. (2007) *Sport and Crime Reduction*, London: Routledge.
Nicholson, M. and Hoye, R. (2008) *Sport and Social Capital*, Oxford: Butterworth-Heinemann.

Recommended websites

Centre for Economic and Social Inclusion: www.cesi.org.uk
Communities and Local Government: www.communities.gov.uk/communities
Crime Concern: www.crimeconcern.org.uk/home.asp

5 Community sports development
Promoting health

Objectives

This chapter will:

- examine the relationships between sport, physical activity and health;
- analyze the ways in which policies use sport and physical activity to combat obesity; and
- assess the impact that health policy has on sports development officers.

Introduction

The health benefits of physical activity have been extolled in many societies over many centuries. It was not until the second half of the twentieth century, however, that scientific evidence supporting such beliefs began to grow. Morris and colleagues' classic study examined the incidence of coronary heart disease (CHD) among postal workers delivering mail on foot or bicycle compared to that of their less physically active colleagues working in the sorting rooms (Morris et al., 1953a; 1953b) led to a raft of publications documenting the benefits of physical activity and the problems associated with physical inactivity. Nowadays, there are numerous scientific studies demonstrating the impact that physical exercise has on reducing the risk of non-communicable or lifestyle diseases (Barengo et al., 2006; Conroy et al., 2005; Dugdill et al., 2005; Hardman and Stensel, 2009; Haskell et al., 2007; Lee et al., 2003; Paffenbarger, 2000; Schnor et al., 2006; Sui et al., 2007; Vuori, 2001). Indeed, there is now considerable consensus among physiologists and epidemiologists that physical activity does have beneficial consequences for both physical and mental health even though there is some dispute over the intensity and frequency of physical activity required to generate substantial health benefits.

Set in this context, the objective of this chapter is to outline the scale and nature of the problems associated with overweight and obesity and physical inactivity globally, before assessing the policy responses to this perceived problem. Initially, we will examine the development of policy across the world before providing an in-depth case study of the way in which policies towards health in general, and physical activity and sport in particular, have developed in the UK. In doing so, it will become evident that there has been something of a blurring of what is deemed to constitute sport and physical activity, and that perhaps the general policy response has been couched in terms of an agenda characterized by moral panic over obesity levels. That is to say, although there are strong epidemiological data regarding obesity levels to show the social and economic problems associated with overweight and obesity, to some extent policy-makers and the media, especially, frequently overreact and sensationalize scientific evidence cited in support of the levels of overweight and obesity and their impact. Furthermore, a characteristic of policy developments in many countries has been to see physical activity and sport as some kind of 'quick fix' for the problems said to be caused by overweight and obesity. Consequently, many policies have tended to contain short-term goals. Even where they have set longer, arguably more realistic targets, these are frequently replaced by other policies that all but ignore the targets established previously. In addition, it is noteworthy that the health costs of sports injuries are frequently ignored by policy-makers and sports promoters alike. We conclude the chapter by focusing on the socio-economic and environmental issues related to health that have often been examined in a rather vague manner by policy-makers hitherto, but are arguably at the heart of developing a more reality-congruent understanding of health and health inequalities. In doing so, we will also examine the supposed role of physical activity and sport within these policies, and the impact that this has had on SDOs and others promoting sport.

Global concerns regarding physical activity, sport and health

According to the World Health Organization (WHO) (2000: 1), 'obesity is a chronic disease, prevalent in both developed and developing countries, and affecting children as well as adults'. The increase in levels of obesity around the world is said to be significantly linked to high, and increasing, levels of physical inactivity and poor diet. As such, the WHO (2004: 2) claims that 'unhealthy diets and physical inactivity are thus among the leading causes of the major noncommunicable diseases, including cardiovascular disease, type 2 diabetes and certain types of cancer, and contribute substantially to the global burden of disease, death and disability'. This has contributed to a 'profound shift in the balance of the major causes of death and disease', such that, 'globally, the burden of noncommunicable diseases has rapidly increased' (WHO, 2004: 2). This relates to the epidemiological transition that is associated with the fact that in most countries in the world the major causes of child mortality have been tackled but, as a consequence, an ageing population has developed and is now more susceptible to non-communicable diseases.

National data that also signal alarm regarding the high, and increasing, rates of non-communicable diseases and a lack of physical activity can be found across the industrialized world, including in Canada (Public Health Agency of Canada [PHAC], 2003a), the US (Centers for Disease Control and Prevention [CDC], 2008), the UK (Department for Culture Media and Sport [DCMS]/Strategy Unit, 2002; Department of Health [DH], 2004a), Australia (Australian Institute for Health and Welfare [AIHW], 2008; Stewart *et al.*, 2004) and now China (Wu, 2006) as well. The scale of the problem of obesity, in particular, is said to have reached epic proportions, such that Gard and Wright (2005: 6) point out that 'the idea that the world is in the grip of an "obesity epidemic" is currently ubiquitous'. For example, the US Surgeon General reported in 2001 that obesity had reached epidemic proportions in the US (US Department of Health and Human Services, 2001), and in England the House of Commons Health Committee (2004: 7) also claimed that 'an epidemic of obesity has swept over' the country. There is also much consensus on where the main causes of such widespread obesity lie. In Canada there is perceived to be an 'inactivity crisis' (ParticipACTION, n.d.), while the Chief Medical Officer for England also noted that 'physical inactivity, along with unhealthy diets, has contributed to the growth of obesity in England' (DH/DCMS, 2004: 4). At one level, of course, the cause of weight gain and obesity is simple: it relates to the tendency for people to consume too much energy and calories and not expend enough so that consumption outweighs expenditure. The issue is more complex in children, and 'there is a scarcity of truly longitudinal studies in contemporary children reporting on the impact of early weight gain on metabolic health' (Gardner *et al.*, 2009: e67), although the latest data from the Early Bird study indicate that most weight gain has occurred before they start school (Gardner *et al.*, 2009).

In addition to the health implications of being overweight or obese, as briefly outlined above, there are a number of economic impacts related to increasing obesity levels in the population that are related to complicated assessments regarding days lost by the workforce and to the cost of medical treatment of the problems associated with obesity. In light of these impacts, promoting physical activity and sport is seen as an important aspect of addressing such problems. Allender *et al.* (2007: 347), for example, argue that 'there is an economic case for developing policies and interventions that promote physical activity'. Furthermore, the WHO (2003: 1) state that 'physical activity and healthy sports are essential for our health and well being'. Garman (2007: 29) argues that because 'in all of the six World Health Organization (WHO) regions except the African region, non-communicable diseases are more frequent as causes of death than communicable diseases ... the primary causes of death and disability are now a factor of social and political agency within the control of societies, with effective civil and public health action'. Indeed, as Waddington (2000: 17) argues, 'there is now a substantial body of data from both epidemiological and clinical studies which indicates that moderate, rhythmic and regular exercise has a significant and beneficial impact on health'. There is no need to rehearse here what these specific studies have found, since the link between health and physical activity is extensively documented. What is rather less understood, and far less frequently examined in the literature, is the effectiveness of promoting sport and/or physical activity as vehicles of social policy designed to promote health.

The development of policies around the world

In most industrialized, Western countries, concern has been growing about the physical health of the population since the mid-twentieth century. As we saw in Chapter 2, in the UK, for example, the Central Council for Recreative and Physical Training (CCRPT) was established in 1935 amid concerns about the health of the nation, and especially of young people. Two decades later, in July 1956, President Eisenhower established the President's Council on Youth Fitness, which was later renamed the President's Council on Physical Fitness and Sports (PCPFS, 2008). Within this there was a 'strong emphasis' on the alleged role that team sports could play in the promotion of physical activity (Shalala; cited in US Department of Health and Human Services, 1996: i). With increasing evidence of the benefits of physical activity for health, by the 1970s 'the American College of Sports Medicine (ACSM), the American Heart Association (AHA), and other national organizations began issuing physical activity recommendations to the public' (US Department of Health and Human Services, 1996: 4).

More recently, the Canadian government is widely regarded as a model of best practice regarding its position on health promotion. In this respect, the Lalonde Report, published by the Canadian government in 1974, was arguably the first government publication that looked beyond the simple biological determinants of health, focusing as it did on the environment, individual lifestyles and access to healthcare, as well as biology. Since then, most governments around the world, but particularly in the West, have published policies concerned with broader notions of health promotion, even though there is still a tendency to focus primarily on healthcare services rather than the preventative measures that might be pursued (Hunter, 2007). Over the last thirty years or so, international organizations such as the WHO have developed 'international declarations and charters, through which the need for healthy public policies was identified and disseminated' (Scriven, 2007: 120). The Ottawa Charter for Health Promotion, for example, was launched by the WHO at the first international conference for health promotion, held in Ottawa, Canada, in 1986. Since the Charter was published, much health promotion activity has taken place by governments in more developed countries, in particular. This has frequently taken the form of focusing on the physical activity levels of the population. Such developments have been noticeable in the US (Kim *et al.*, 2006; Lightsey *et al.*, 2005), Canada (Katzmarzyk and Janssen, 2004; Pederson *et al.*, 2005; Warburton *et al.*, 2006), Australia and New Zealand (Chau *et al.*, 2008; Duncan *et al.*, 2006; Hearn *et al.*, 2005; Spinks *et al.*, 2007), China (Chen, 2008; Ji and Working Group on Obesity in China [WCOG], 2008; Wang *et al.*, 2007), Russia (Godinho, 2005) and most countries in Western Europe (Astrup, 2001; Cavill *et al.*, 2006; Fussenegger *et al.*, 2007; Moreno *et al.*, 2007; Ziglio *et al.*, 2005). In much of Eastern Europe, and in many developing countries, however, there has been 'a dearth of modern concepts of health promotion, as well as negligible resources, little public policy development and numerous one-off, discontinuous project activities' (Ziglio *et al.*, 2005: 234).

In 1988, the Australian government, through the AIHW, published its first 'Australia's Health' Report, which focused renewed effort on developing physical activity. Since then, every two years the AIHW has published the Report for the Australian government. Similarly, in the US in 1996, physical activity, generally, was made a more prominent feature of the health targets set by the federal government. It was announced in the first ever US Surgeon General's Report on physical activity, for example, that

> increasing physical activity is a formidable public health challenge that we must hasten to meet … Physical activity thus joins the front ranks of essential health objectives, such as sound nutrition, the use of seat belts, and the prevention of adverse health effects of tobacco.
>
> (US Department of Health and Human Services, 1996: iv)

The Report was declared 'a national call to action' (US Department of Health and Human Services, 1996: v). It included a specific focus on more traditional sports as a way of being physically active, but also emphasized the benefits from a broader range of activities, such as gardening and walking. In this respect, the Surgeon General announced that 'it is hoped that this different emphasis on moderate amounts of activity, and the flexibility to vary activities according to personal preference and life circumstances, will encourage more people to make physical activity a regular and sustainable part of their lives' (US Department of Health and Human Services, 1996: 3). *Healthy People 2010* (US Department of Health and Human Services, 2000) builds on the earlier *Healthy People 2000* in setting out an overarching national vision for health, with a clear focus on promoting physical activity. In addition, the PHAC's Healthy Living Unit has a mission statement 'to improve the health and well-being of Canadians through regular physical activity' (PHAC, 2003b).

It is evident, then, that there has been an increasing focus on physical activity in national and international policies around an emerging consensus that physical inactivity is a significant contributing factor to the growth in non-communicable diseases around the world. Policies have been, and continue to be, developed that focus on the amount and type of physical activity people should be doing in order to gain health benefits. According to the WHO (2003: 9), there is 'a new challenge and at the same time a tremendous opportunity for the sports movement as a whole, and sport for all in particular'. In this respect, it is argued that in taking a more 'active role' in reducing the 'global burden of non-communicable diseases', the 'sports community' could 'contribute uniquely and importantly to the promotion of public health and at the same time strengthen the social credibility and accountability of sport' (WHO, 2003: 9). This is a particularly interesting area of analysis since the contribution of sport to such physical activity targets has frequently been the source of much debate. Indeed, there are few ideas that are as uncritically accepted as those assumptions linking sports participation with good health (K. Green, 2008; Waddington, 2000). On the whole, as indicated by the WHO (2003) quotation above, sport is seen as making a positive contribution to health. However, as we will see in the case study below, increasingly sport is being defined so broadly in policy documents that the definition includes physical activities like walking. The impact this has on those promoting sport is of particular interest to us, because as policy on sport has broadened many are now finding that they are having to promote healthy lifestyle activities as part of their 'sport' promotion (Bloyce et al., 2008). We will examine the differential impact of policies focused on sport and broader notions of physical activity within our case study of the UK.

The development of health, sport and physical activity policies in the UK

As we have already seen, the CCRPT raised concerns about the health of the nation in 1935 and again in the Wolfenden Report in 1960. The assumed relationship between sports participation and health was one of the justifications for the publication in 1975 of *Sport and Recreation*. This was the first UK government White Paper on sport, and increased government concern relating to sports participation and physical activity followed it. The White Paper outlined the need to increase physical activity because of the desire to 'reduce the incidence of coronary heart disease' (Department of the Environment, 1975: 3). Sport and physical activity were promoted for good health and the Sports Council worked for the best part of a decade in the 1980s 'to improve the data on the links with health' (Collins, 2008: 65). However, Ian Sproat, in his short term in office as Sports Minister, devolved all responsibility for health targets to the Department of Health. With this, and the fact that local authority sports provision was not mentioned in *Raising the Game*, SDOs within local authorities arguably began to appreciate the precarious nature of their jobs. In doing so, many SDOs began to identify the links between sports participation and the assumed contribution this makes to good health as a way of seeking their own salvation in the sense that they perceived that they could make a significant contribution to health targets for their local health authorities (Ireland, 2001). This, according to Robson and McKenna (2008: 172), combined with the 'post-Thatcherite endorsements of active living' exemplified in the White Paper *The Health of the Nation* (DH, 1992), helped contribute to a growing perspective amongst SDOs that they, along with 'health promoters and medical practitioners were able to envisage a range of joint undertakings' related to sport and health. However, this is to rather overstate the position of local authority SDOs in this relationship at this time, and even the desire of medical practitioners and health promoters to focus on sport or even physical activity. Nonetheless, many of those people responsible for promoting sport in the UK have recognized 'that health provides an essential bargaining tool in winning support for local authority leisure development, from cardiovascular based health and fitness suites to new swimming pools' (Ireland, 2001: 106). Indeed, Ireland (2001: 105) argues that since the mid-1990s the emphasis in UK policy 'has moved firmly away from sport towards encouraging physical activity as part of our daily lifestyle', in large measure because of the funding available for using physical activity in general to promote health.

The Health of the Nation was widely criticized for not focusing on health inequalities and the cause of such inequalities (Adams, 2001). Such a stance was not unique to the UK at this time, and many academics have criticized public health policies for being too focused on the individual in taking control of their own health. Crawford (1980: 365) coined the term 'healthism' to refer to the process whereby 'the problem of health and disease' was situated 'at the level of the individual'. 'Solutions', he argues, have been 'formulated at that level as well' (Crawford, 1980: 365). In light of this, a key criticism of such policies is that they are reductionist and, in essence, ignore social, economic, cultural and environmental impacts on health. The notion that the individual can, therefore, choose to lead a healthy lifestyle, or not, ignores the enabling and constraining aspects of their socio-economic status and the environment around them.

Public health policy under New Labour, 1997–2000

The Active for Life campaign established under the Conservative government in 1995 was 'an important stepping stone towards the greater prevalence of physical activity on the contemporary agenda' (Robson and McKenna, 2008: 173). This has been reinforced under the New Labour government, along with a renewed, government-sanctioned focus on the contribution that sport, as well as physical activity, could make to help combat a number of social problems (see Chapter 4). Promoting physical activity and sport for health benefits was viewed by Labour as a cross-departmental issue, and part of the joined-up thinking philosophy of the third way politics that is permeating much Labour government policy (see Chapter 2). This is a clear demonstration of the broader ideologies within the government coming to bear on sport policy and sports development. Under New Labour, 'health was no longer seen as a private domain where individuals were free to make lifestyle choices, but rather as a collective issue where citizens had rights to health care, guaranteed by strong government action and funding' (Robson and McKenna, 2008: 173). Whilst this is certainly true of the rhetoric within much public health policy produced under the Labour government, some may argue that elements of the ideology of healthism can still be found in those policies.

Sport England positioned itself as an organization that could help in combating ill health under the new Labour government. As Trevor Brooking, the Chair of Sport England at the time, quite openly admitted in the foreword of a publication entitled *Best Value Through Sport: The Value of Sport to the Health of the Nation*, 'this document is aimed at those who hold the purse-strings in health' (Sport England, 1999: 1). To this end, the apparently positive contribution sport could make was promulgated throughout the document. Sport, we were told, 'in combination with other lifestyle interventions, can prove to be one of the "best buys" in preventive and rehabilitative health care' (Sport England, 1999: 3). This was a clear attempt to realign sport policy goals with the goals associated with the more well-established and better-funded goals of public health that had been partially severed under the previous Conservative administration. Interestingly, despite Robson and McKenna's (2008) claim regarding the alleged 'joint undertakings' for the promotion of physical activity shared by health promoters and SDOs, Sport England (1999: 5) noted that 'many health care professionals do not view "sport" as an effective way of promoting physical activity among the least active in the population as they associate sport with team games and competitive activity'. This prompted them to highlight what they perceived to be, 'for public policy purposes, a broad definition of sport' (Sport England, 1999: 5). The preferred definition was that offered six years earlier by the Council of Europe:

> Sport means all forms of physical activity which, through casual or organised participation, aim at expressing or improving physical fitness and mental well-being, forming social relationships or obtaining results in competition at all levels.
>
> (Council of Europe; cited in Sport England, 1999: 5)

Sport England (1999: 5) stated that 'this wide and inclusive definition of sport extends its relevance to the whole population and its value as a significant player in promoting the health of the nation'. However, as Coalter (2007a) rightly points out, it also confuses and fudges the issues concerned, because, he argues, there is a need to distinguish sport from more general physical activity since the former may not always have a positive impact on health, about which more later. Clearly recognition of the financial benefits of being considered a major player in helping to combat perceived health problems in the nation was a major driver in this broad definition of sport favoured by Sport England.

Saving Lives: Our Healthier Nation (DH, 1999) was the Labour government's successor to the previous administration's *Health of the Nation* White Paper. *Saving Lives* made a small reference to physical activity directly, although this was in reference to the perceived positives associated with a 'physically active lifestyle', and stated that the importance of this would be borne out in a sports strategy to be published later that year. Numerous goals were set to be achieved by 2010, and were related, among other things, to cancer, CHD and strokes. *Saving Lives* was, according to Scriven and Orme (2001: xix), a further reflection of the 'third way' approach of New Labour 'by putting on to the new public health agenda the objective of redressing inequalities'. Furthermore, they argued that 'to counter the possibility of being accused of political rhetoric, a range of strategies, such as Health Action Zones [established in 1997], have been put in place that are intended to achieve this objective' (Scriven and Orme, 2001: xix). Twelve Sport Action Zones were also established four years later. The Health Action Zones and Sport Action Zones were specifically located in areas of social and economic deprivation and went someway to recognizing that there was an impact on health of the socio-economic conditions in these areas. *Saving Lives* also stressed the importance of joined-up thinking, a key philosophy of the New Labour government, and focused on the range of organizations and agencies that might contribute to the goals therein. However, once again, the role of sports organizations in achieving such goals was barely mentioned. Even leaving aside sports organizations, 'a key issue', according to Scriven and Orme (2001: xx), 'is undoubtedly the different interpretations and ideological understanding of health promotion that the various agencies and their respective professional representatives espouse'. As Scriven and Orme (2001) imply, the different 'agencies' with an interest in the health agenda no doubt bring to the table a number of different preconceived ideological standpoints that often make it quite problematic to assume that they will each pull in the same direction. That is to say, it is highly unlikely that joined-up thinking will necessarily mean that organizations, whose main roles and responsibilities may be at distinct variance with those of other organizations, will be able to move towards commonly agreed goals and objectives. Indeed, for reasons we make clear in Chapter 1, it is often the case that the relational networks of which such organizations are a part are characterized by greater degrees of internal and external conflict than of cooperation and consensus. This becomes all the more complex by virtue of the network of interdependencies associated with health promotion becoming ever denser and more populated with different organizations, all vying for different positions of prominence and available funding streams.

Sport and physical activity for health policy under New Labour, 2000–04

Although numerous statements had been released regarding football, in particular, the new Labour government's first sport policy, *A Sporting Future for All*, was published in May 2000 (DCMS, 2000). Within the document, the DCMS (2000: 39) argued, amongst other things, that 'the strategy provides the context for local authorities to link the value of sport to the wider benefits of health'. On the whole, however, the document made little explicit mention of the contribution that sport might make to the health agenda. However, it is not only the case that sports development work has diversified to include broader notions of what such work should entail because the government seems to be encouraging this broadening of horizons. The important issue here, however, is that this diversification is seen to be worthwhile financially (Bloyce *et al.*, 2008). For example, according to the CCPR (2002: 5), 'the Government currently spends 800 times more on health than it does on sport and recreation'. As such, they argued at the time that, for sports organizations and the government at large, 'greater emphasis is required on pre-ventative health programmes' (CCPR, 2002: 5). The specific contribution that sports organizations could make to these 'programmes' was positively argued.

The focus on physical activity was extended quite explicitly as an aspect of NHS provision in the *National Service Framework for Coronary Heart Disease* (DH, 2000), insofar as all NHS bodies were required to have 'agreed to and be contributing to an increasing physical activity policy' (Ireland, 2001: 109). In this regard, it is important to note that emphasis came increasingly to be placed on the contribution that physical activity could make to public health strategies at this time. Perhaps almost inevitably this had implications for those promoting sport, and with the publication of *Game Plan* in 2002 the boundaries between the contribution to health by physical activity and by sport became even more blurred. As we noted earlier, Waddington (2000) had been rightly critical of what he perceived to be the blinkered focus of policy-makers on sport rather than physical activity and exercise in relation to health promotion within sport strategies.

Although Collins (2008: 70) argues that, with the publication of *Game Plan*, 'the link with health seemed to have run into the sand', this seems quite contrary to key themes within it. *Game Plan* makes very clear links between sport and physical activity strategy and health. Indeed, it is quite clearly stated within *Game Plan* that 'our primary aim is to develop a sport and physical activity culture to produce a fitter, more active population and realise the significant health benefits and savings available' (DCMS/Strategy Unit, 2002: 90). In fact, *Game Plan* places considerable emphasis on the role that participation in sport and physical activity can play in improving health and, in that respect, the prevailing policy commitments are but one further expression of Labour's attempt to enhance 'joined-up thinking' between disparate policy areas and of integrating policies across a range of government departments (such as the DCMS and the Department of Health).

An increasing feature of Labour policy that came to have a profound impact on sport policy and development was the establishment of performance indicators and targets (see Chapter 2). Thus a particular policy priority of *Game Plan* was that 'there should be a non-directive approach to local provision, with more use of performance framework tools such as public health focused targets and local PSAs [public service agreements]' (DCMS/Strategy Unit, 2002: 162). Such targets are now very much part of the day-to-day reality of the operations of sports development work in local authorities. As we have argued elsewhere,

> given the relatively powerful position of Sport England and their greater capacity to set the government's policy agenda for local authorities, it was not surprising that the current policy focus on health issues was also widely cited as a justification for re-orientating sports development activity away from the development of sport *per se*, towards using sport and physical activities as vehicles of social policy designed to achieve health outcomes.
>
> (Bloyce *et al.*, 2008: 369)

A quite specific target set out in *Game Plan* was to get at least 70 per cent of the target population sufficiently active for health benefits, with the recommended amount being 30 minutes of moderate-intensity exercise five times a week. This was, however, derided in some quarters for being overly ambitious given that the proportion of the population engaged in such health-enhancing physical activity (HEPA) was 32 per cent. As such, the target was soon modified to a 1 per cent increase annually until 2020. In order that it might achieve this annual increase, Sport England 'refocused its work and in doing so recast itself as the *de facto* national physical activity agency' (Robson and McKenna, 2008: 174). This is an interesting observation, for two reasons: first, the idea that Sport England recast itself, once again, downplays significantly the substantial constraints imposed upon it by the government; and, second, it highlights the increasingly blurred boundaries between sport and physical activity promotion. We shall discuss this in greater detail later, as these boundaries have become even more blurred in the period since then.

Derek Wanless published two government-commissioned reports into health promotion and policy in 2002 and 2004. These highlighted the need for the government to evaluate the provision of health care, and to focus more on prevention, especially in terms of the projected costs of not investing in a long-term public health strategy. Wanless also acknowledged the impact that a person's socio-economic status had on health, and prompted the government to publish a new paper on health at the end of 2004. *Choosing Health* (DH, 2004a), whilst clearly placing an emphasis on individual lifestyle choices (Hunter, 2007), does acknowledge the contributions that can be made by the broader community and government. There is also an explicit focus on 'joined-up thinking' that highlights the need to establish the idea that the health agenda has important implications for all departments within the government. Some mention is also made of the social inequalities in health, although much less attention is paid to this than to other perceived areas of importance. *Choosing Health* (DH, 2004a: 16) indicates, with no apparent sense of irony, that this is 'the start, not the end, of a journey'. This is despite the fact that *Saving Lives*, the Labour government's health action plan published just five years earlier, is mentioned just once. None of the targets set in *Saving Lives* to be achieved by 2010 were mentioned. As we have already noted, this is hardly untypical of government policy in sport, health or in any other policy area. Indeed, as Coalter (2007a) has rightly argued, it would appear that governments tend to be more interested in 'take-offs' than 'landings', insofar as they often release policies but rarely see them through until their scheduled 'landing', the date for which the original targets were set.

Choosing Health highlights the need to work 'with the sports and recreational activity sectors to deliver positive, innovative messages about healthy lifestyles through, for example, football, walking, cycling and fitness centres' (DH, 2004a: 24). Interestingly, within the White Paper there is a small section titled 'Sport's Unique Contribution', in which it is stated that 'sport in the broadest sense, which includes everyday activity, is attractive to many and offers people the kind of social networks [that are seen as desirable elsewhere in the White Paper]. And there is evidence that the right kind of investment can generate very significant increases in participation' (DH, 2004a: 91). None of this 'evidence' is cited to support this claim, and there is no elaboration on what sport 'in the broadest sense' means. This can be seen as a further illustration of the way in which sport is being used as a term to include a broad range of activities that do not necessarily involve more conventional competitive sports. This is something that was becoming an increasing part of sports strategies released under the Labour government, but it is perhaps even more significant since this is a public health strategy referring to 'sport' in this generic sense. Furthermore, *Choosing Health* also paid attention to a broader approach to health promotion, and focused on the possible benefits that could be accrued from promoting physical activity within people's everyday lives. A key development from this has been social marketing and the 'personalizing' of services. In linking this with motivation, it was suggested that pedometers would be a good motivational tool in 'marketing health' (DH, 2004a: 90). Evidently this proposal had an impact on Sport England. In its resource for Strategic Health Authorities (SHAs) and Primary Care Trusts (PCTs), it sets priority activities for children, adults and 'older people'. All of them included a key focus on walking as an everyday activity – to school, to work and whilst shopping – and encouraged 'the use of pedometers as a motivational tool' for all age groups (Sport England, 2006e: 20). Thus, it would seem that as part of the joined-up thinking approach within the government, public health policy is increasingly encroaching into sport, and sport policy encroaching into physical activity. This is a further blurring of the boundaries between sport and physical activity. However, notwithstanding the fact that this can be seen as part of government's broader philosophy of joined-up thinking, there would seem to be increasing tension for those charged with promoting sport because of the fact that they have had to broaden their remit regarding what, precisely, this is (Bloyce *et al.*, 2008; Houlihan and White, 2002).

The increased focus on sport and physical activity was further underlined in the Chief Medical Officer's Report *At Least Five a Week: Evidence on the Impact of Physical Activity and Its Relationship to Health*, published in 2004, in which it was stated that 'the health importance of physical activity, exercise and sport, is recognised in the *NHS Plan* and in the National Service Frameworks for the NHS' (DH, 2004b: iv). As noted earlier, Waddington (2000) pointed out that policies that have focused on sport as an activity that would be beneficial for health have tended to ignore the obvious health risks associated with competitive sport. However, in line with the WHO's (2003: 3) stated recognition that there are 'risks and harm' associated with sport, the Department of Health (2004b: 29) recognized that 'very high levels of fitness training or engagement in vigorous and contact sports also carries higher risk of sports/exercise-related injury'. The Department of Health (2004b: 92) also stated that 'we are currently consulting the medical profession on the recognition of sport and exercise medicine as a specialty within the NHS'. According to Verow (2006: 225), with '10% of attendances at accident and emergency departments being for sport-related injuries' the new specialism was to be welcomed. Furthermore, this 'new NHS medical speciality' was also 'to underpin the drive across the NHS to promote increased physical activity' (DH, 2005: 29). Although one might say that this is yet further evidence of joined-up thinking, it could also be argued that this is another area in which the traditional approach to sports development work is coming under threat because the proposal indicates that 'the NHS is responsible for taking forward the health improvement agenda and this will include promoting physical activity' (DH, 2005: 27). This, by implication, meant that because it was to include physical activity an increasing area of the work that many sports bodies had become 'responsible' for was now no longer seen to be under their jurisdiction.

In a series of papers put together by Sport England entitled *Driving Up Participation: The Challenge for Sport*, Rowe *et al.* (2004) provided an assessment for Sport England following the publication of government targets to increase the physical activity of the nation set out originally in *Game Plan*:

> Sport England has to determine within its own business planning process how it will position itself in relation to this overarching aim to increase physical activity levels in England. It is important for Sport England to keep its unique identity as the leading sports development agency whilst still being seen to be a key player in the physical activity and health agenda. In order to achieve this positioning it is proposed that Sport England within its business plan (and as part of its Funding Agreement with DCMS) set a target based on 'sports contribution to overall physical activity levels required for health'.
>
> (Rowe *et al.*, 2004: 19)

Following this, Sport England declared that it would be responsible for meeting three out of the proposed five bouts of thirty minutes physical activity per week required for HEPA. This was despite the fact that Rowe *et al.* (2004: 18) acknowledged the fact that in the most recent Health Survey for England available at the time 'sport' made up only 8 per cent of the total 'physical activity levels' of those currently meeting the target hours a week 'for health benefits'. Even combined with walking the total was just 20 per cent – in effect, only one of the five bouts on average. Clearly, this was a rather ambitious target for Sport England, the SDOs and other people involved in the delivery of community sport to achieve. It is hardly surprising, then, that many SDOs became increasingly involved in schemes associated with occupationally related physical activity, such as walking to work or school schemes.

The continued blurring of sport and physical activity 2004–2008

Sport England also became a key sponsor, together with the Department for Health and the Countryside Agency, in the delivery of ten Local Exercise Action Pilots (LEAPs) that were developed early in 2004 to 'assess a range of community approaches that aim to increase levels of activity across the community as a whole but also with targeted work with specific groups such as older people and children' (DH, 2005: 19). Furthermore, in

March 2005 Sport England announced that the Everyday Sport campaign was to be rolled out nationally after what it considered was a successful pilot in the North East of England. The campaign was seen, again, as more of a 'physical activity', rather than 'necessarily a sport campaign' (Sport England, 2005a) and was 'reminiscent of the Active for Life campaign of the previous decade' (Robson and McKenna, 2008: 174). With this, and its involvement in LEAPs, it was clear that the notion of 'sport' was being considered in a very broad manner within specific strategies and campaigns. This was further reinforced from the government's perspective when the policy statement on increasing physical activity that emanated from *Choosing Health* was called *Choosing Activity*, and focused attention much more on the broader dimension of physical activity rather than competitive sports (Allender *et al.*, 2007). Within this, it is recognized that 'the proportion of people who choose to be active in their leisure time show an upward trend' within certain socio-economic groups (DH, 2005: 5). However, at the same time it is also recognized that as the amount of manual work people are required to do decreases and reliance on the car increases, the overall physical activity people get in their daily lives is decreasing (DH, 2005). In particular, the Department of Health argued:

> We need a culture shift if we are to increase physical activity levels in England. This will only be achieved if people are aware of, understand and want the benefits of being active. Opportunities will be created by changing the physical and cultural landscape – and building an environment that supports people in more active lifestyles.
>
> (DH, 2005: 6)

This can be seen as a recognition that sedentariness cannot be explained by a rather simplistic focus on leisure-time physical activity promotion, or that the related health problems could be solved by only promoting leisure-time physical activity. A lack of such recognition by previous governments has been the source of much debate (Riddoch and McKenna, 2005; Waddington, 2000). What an SDO might be able to do in connection with this, however, is an interesting area of study. It is likely that few would have gone into the job specifically to become involved in walking or cycling to work/school schemes. This is likely to be an increasing aspect of their day-to-day jobs, as the boundaries between sport and physical activity become increasingly blurred (Bloyce *et al.*, 2008). It was proposed that

> Sport England is developing this new approach, which is based on the development of community 'hubs' with new management partnerships that link sport and physical activity with health, education, lifelong learning and social welfare.
>
> (DH, 2005: 20)

Interestingly, despite the obvious areas where *Choosing Activity* focused on the wider issues of physical activity relating to the environment, and to a lesser degree regarding the health inequalities related to socio-economic status, 'the individual' remained the key area of focus: 'the national engine for health improvement is to be found in the ambition of people themselves to live healthier lives' (DH, 2005: 37). It could be argued, therefore, that the ideology of healthism that underpins this approach is rarely far away from such policies.

Sport England's response to *Choosing Health* and *Choosing Activity* was encapsulated in the publication of *Sport Playing Its Part: The Contribution of Sport to Healthier Communities* (Sport England, 2006a), which was one in a series of publications entitled

Sport Playing Its Part. The then Chair of Sport England, in the foreword to *Healthier Communities*, claimed that 'the role of sport in promoting physical and mental health and in particular, its contribution to reducing obesity and chronic heart disease is being increasingly recognised' (Sport England, 2006a: 2). As has become the norm when Sport England focuses on 'health', 'sport' and 'physical activity' are terms used interchangeably throughout the document. This is a further illustration of how increasingly public health and sports development policy are converging, with greater focus on more generic definitions of sport and a greater focus on wider physical activity. As we have argued above, this has as much to do with vying for the larger pots of money available in 'health' as it has with the 'joined-up thinking' promulgated by the Labour government. Indeed, Sport England (2006a) admits quite openly that a key driver for focusing on health is the funding available. In other words, Sport England is more likely to be better funded, as are many of its partners, if it explicitly has objectives and targets linked to physical activity and health. This has led Robson and McKenna (2008: 171) to conclude that 'there has been an emerging trend of "healthy alliances" or health partnerships between sports development professionals and health practitioners to promote physical activity. In many instances past mutual suspicion has been supplanted by strategic partnerships, and debates about joint working have largely been won'. However, the idea that such 'healthy alliances' have come about due to an increasing mutual respect, or even a conscious synergy of aims, is to thoroughly downplay the constraints imposed, by and large by the government, on professionals working within sports development, health promotion and the NHS.

The 2007 Foresight Report, titled *Tackling Obesities: Future Choices* (Foresight, 2007), was commissioned by the government through its Office for Science in order to produce a long-term vision for dealing with the potential problems of rising overweight and obesity over the next forty years. The Report's conclusions suggest that obesity is a complex problem related to biological and social factors and warn that policies aimed only at individuals in tackling the so-called obesity crisis are destined to fail. Amongst the key stakeholders identified are the DCMS and Sport England, although sport is barely mentioned in the Report. The focus is very much more on generic physical activity, and building physical activity into people's everyday lives through commuting and changing the environmental setting. The Report suggested that the scale and complexity of the problem associated with obesity is comparable to climate change and should receive as great a focus. Indeed, the focus on broader concerns about the working and living environment are outlined in the Report, which stated:

> Provision of facilities for sport and formal exercise is an important part of a strategy to counter obesity. However, their lower usage by people of lower socioeconomic status, combined with the need to increase total activity levels across society, not merely among those motivated to engage in sports, suggests additional action needs to be taken. There are other ways to increase physical activity through designing opportunities for health and activity into architecture and urban design ... Promotion of 'active transport' (e.g. walking and cycling) is one way of increasing activity.
>
> (Foresight, 2007: 66)

In the same year, Sport England (2007) funded the Active Design project and published a report that went largely unnoticed by the press. The Report, and the project as a whole, was regarded by Derek Mapp, Chair of Sport England at the time, in the foreword as 'a fresh approach to urban planning and design funded by Sport England to help get local communities active and more involved in sport' (Sport England, 2007: i). It was also endorsed by the then Sports Minister, Richard Caborn. The central theme of the strategy is to attempt to promote physical activity through making physical environments more conducive to 'active travel' (Sport England, 2007: 2), by encouraging town planners to plan for more people to be able to walk and cycle around their towns and city centres. This was most important in terms of a focus on 'everyday activity destinations', but the strategy also focuses on more 'informal activity and recreation' that might be facilitated more through better planning of open spaces like parks, and a better focus on more amenable planning for 'formal sports and leisure activities' (Sport England, 2007: 10). It is far too early to assess the impact of the strategy, but this is a further illustration of the ways in which Sport England, prominent amongst many organizations whose primary focus, in theory, is on the promotion of sport, has had to increasingly diversify its activities. On the surface, town planning to encourage greater 'active travel' is not something one might expect as the remit of a sports organization. Although, of course, it can be seen, again, as part of the joined-up thinking of the Labour government, and the perspective of public health, focusing on promoting physical activity through 'active travel' is entirely consistent with the epidemiological data that indicate the important contribution that travel-related physical activity plays in promoting overall levels of daily physical activity.

A 'new' distinction between sport and physical activity for health policy?

In March 2008, the first major policy statement regarding health under the new Gordon Brown administration was published, entitled *Healthy Weight, Healthy Lives: A Cross-Government Strategy for England*. Gordon Brown in his foreword to the strategy announced that it 'marks an important shift in our focus to support everyone in making the healthy choices which will reduce obesity, especially among children' (DH/DCSF, 2008: iii). However, the extent to which this really does mark a shift is debatable. It is yet more evidence of the prevailing tendency for governments to produce new policies for 'old' problems, but, in doing so, to ignore all previous policy statements, and to offer only very limited difference from them. For example, *Healthy Weight, Healthy Lives* makes no mention of *Choosing Health, Choosing Activity* or *Game Plan*, the three existing policies associated with health and physical activity. It is difficult, therefore, to conclude anything other than that, once again, the targets set in each of these documents, associated with reducing levels of obesity, are ignored, to be superseded by yet more 'new' targets. The specific aim of this strategy is 'to be the first major nation to reverse the rising tide of obesity and overweight in the population by ensuring that everyone is able to achieve and maintain a healthy weight' (DH/DCSF, 2008: v).

Healthy Weight, Healthy Lives promises a multifaceted approach to dealing with the issue of obesity and the health-related problems associated with it. This includes promoting good health through promoting healthy foods, physical activity as part of our daily lives, promoting health at work, whilst also concentrating on treatment and support for people already overweight or obese. Sport and physical activity are both mentioned in terms of their contributions to arresting the rising levels of obesity amongst the population. However, some interesting distinctions are drawn. In this respect, this does represent something of a shift, since it redefines the boundaries between sport and physical activity. A quite specific focus on community sport is promoted, with £392 million promised from the government, and 'an estimated £324 million from Lottery funding over the period 2008–11, to deliver community sport' (DH/DCSF, 2008: 19). In relation to this, it is claimed that 'Sport England is developing a new strategy to build a world class community sport infrastructure to sustain and increase participation in sport and allow everyone the chance to develop their sporting talents' (DH/DCSF, 2008: 19). It also proposed that the government would review its overall strategy for physical activity. The new strategy would be 'clearly aligned to the new ambition on healthy weight' and would give consideration to 'establishing a potential new body, "Active England", to drive forward the Government's commitments relating to wider physical activity, complementing Sport England's work. The review will consider the scope and funding of any such body before reaching a final decision' (DH/DCSF, 2008: 20). As yet, no such decision has been made, though these developments are interesting in light of our earlier discussion regarding the blurring of the boundaries between those promoting physical activity for health and those promoting sport.

It is no surprise, given the aforementioned developments, that the most recent policy statements from the DCMS and Sport England suggest that the boundaries between sport, health and physical activity need to be made more distinct. As such, the DCMS in its new strategy statement, *Playing to Win*, comments that 'sports bodies will focus their efforts and investment on sport, while other bodies will lead on the delivery of physical activity' (DCMS, 2008a: 18). This, no doubt, further contributed to Sport England's refocusing on 'community sport', which in its latest annual report enabled Sport England to provide 'a clear distinction with the physical activity agenda being driven by a number of departments, including the Department of Health and Department of Transport' (Sport England, 2008a: 1). It is clear, as we will see in Chapter 7, that the Olympic Games to be held in London in 2012 have already started to impact on this decision to redefine the remit of organizations whose primary aim, on the surface, is the promotion of sport, rather than general physical activity. However, how long such a distinction will last, given the differential funding available to the 'sport' and 'health' agendas, remains to be seen. In fact, before the year was out, in November 2008 Sport England updated its *Sport Playing Its Part* series, and it was replaced by *Shaping Places through Sport*. One of five key areas of focus was on *Healthier Communities* (Sport England, 2008c). Within this document, Sport England (2008c: 4) outlines how the 'power of sport' can be used 'to develop healthier communities'. Once again the boundaries between sport and physical activity are completely blurred in this document. It is impossible to gauge at this early stage what these recent developments will mean for the working lives of SDOs. Suffice to say, however, that when the 2012 Games are over, and if 'Active England' is established as a non-departmental public body that, in essence, rivals Sport England for government funding, it is likely that Sport England will keep pressing the case that sport does have a role to play in achieving health-related outcomes, especially when one considers that the funding available to health is likely to continue to dwarf that available to sport. We now want to discuss the implications and issues associated with the emergence of policy aimed at health, from sport and public health strategies.

Moral panics and health

It might be argued that 'the past decade or so has witnessed a growing moral panic surrounding the alleged "ill-health" of people generally, and young people in particular' (Smith and Green, 2005: 241), not just in the UK, but throughout much of the developed world. It is actually quite difficult to assess the degree to which we really are witnessing a profound growth in obesity-related illness, brought on by apparently increasing levels of physical inactivity. Statistics are, of course, 'products of social activity [and yet] ... we sometimes talk about statistics as though they are facts that simply exist, like rocks, completely independent of people' (Best, 2001: 27). It is, therefore, extremely difficult to measure with any degree of object-adequacy levels of obesity, for example, across whole nations. On the basis of various government studies, however, we have access to data that have been produced regarding obesity, levels of physical activity and projections of future costs to the health service. In measuring certain perceived problems, as Best (2001: 44) points out, 'the broader the definition the bigger the statistic'. The use of the body mass index (BMI) to measure population levels of overweight and obesity is a particularly good example of this. The problems of using the BMI in such measurements have been acknowledged by the WHO (2000: 31) in recognizing that there is a 'lack of consistency and agreement' due to different interpretations of the measurements over time and between different countries. What is regarded as 'overweight' and 'obese' has also chan-ged over time and is interpreted differently in different countries, making 'trends' difficult to identify. This is something that is also recognized by the DH/DCSF (2008: 35), who acknowledge that the BMI

> can be less accurate for assessing healthy weight in individuals, especially for certain groups (e.g. athletes, the elderly) where a slightly higher BMI is not necessarily unhealthy ... For children the situation is more complicated. There is no fixed BMI to define being obese or overweight since this varies with gender and with growth and development.
>
> (DH/DCSF, 2008: 35)

However, in the main, Best (2001: 44) argues that 'because people promoting social problems favor big numbers (because they make the problem seem bigger and more important), we can expect that they will favor broad definitions'. It is perhaps unsurprising, therefore, that the DH/DCSF (2008: 35) consider BMI to be an 'effective measure of weight status at a population level', although they do not emphasize why this might be the case. Fur-thermore, the WHO continue to use it as a baseline measurement of increasing levels of obesity across the world. It might reasonably be argued, then, that 'the statistics do not measure changes in the incidence of the problem so much as changes in social attitudes toward that problem and the organizational practices of the agencies that keep track of it' (Best, 2001: 101–2). In other words, the greater the concern that has come to be expressed over physical inactivity and obesity in the recent past, particularly in the media, but also within government policy, the greater the level of attention that has been given to how we might measure the problem in this regard. Karpf (1988: 27) has referred to a process whereby media sources and, indeed, government departments, NDPBs and non-government organizations use 'graphs, maps and percentages' to 'give an aura of "facti-city"' to certain health issues. In other words, a degree of caution needs to be applied with regard to how such data are used. The problem with gathering population-level data on overweight and obesity is compounded further when one considers how difficult it is, also, to adequately measure levels of physical activity across populations. Indeed, Livingstone *et al.* (2003: 681) point out that 'the accurate measurement of physical activ-ity is fraught with problems'. Boreham and Riddoch's (2003: 17) review of the health benefits of physical activity for children and youth concludes that 'there is surprisingly little empirical evidence to support this notion'. Furthermore, as Coalter argues, although most authors accept the overall analysis that physical activity has health, and therefore economic, benefits, they admit that some of the estimates (taken from routine data sources) are somewhat crude. Inevitably such calculations are imprecise, contain substantial margins of error and are based on theoretically informed judgements.

(Coalter, 2007a: 154)

Indeed, one might say that the judgements are based on a high degree of involvement. As Smith and Green argue, 'claims regarding young people's involvement in sport and physical activity, and the relationship of these to their supposed "ill-health", have tended to be driven by "ideological rather than scientific concerns" (Dunning 1986, p. 2) and, as a consequence, have lacked "the degree of detachment necessary for fruitful sociological analysis"' (Smith and Green, 2005: 249). It is, after all, extremely difficult to get population data for appropriate levels of HEPA. Measuring the number of bouts of exercise individuals might do in a given week (as in the Active People Survey in England) is, of course, extremely time consuming and expensive (Rowe, 2009). However, it is almost impossible to draw from this the extent to which the people surveyed are actually engaged in levels of activity that are sufficient to derive health benefits. Nonetheless, it is a common assumption that the populations in most nations across the world are not engaged in enough exercise and, as such, the promotion of physical activity and/or sport is seen as a way to address this. Although, as we noted earlier, a concern over levels of sport and physical activity participation in England has long been expressed, it is only in more recent years that has this come to be most strongly associated with the levels of concern, perhaps even panic, over rising levels of overweight and obesity.

As Gard and Wright (2005: 5) state, 'what is interesting ... is the way people who talk and write about obesity and its causes [such as increasing levels of physical inactivity], in fields such as medicine, exercise science and public health, in the midst of great uncertainty, manage to speak with such unified certainty about the obesity crisis'. Certainly this is reflected in much of the policy covered within this chapter. The networks of interdependencies that have developed in health and physical activity promotion, including sport promotion, contain numerous people who have a vested interest in demonstrating that we are witnessing decreasing levels of physical activity and increasing levels of obesity. These interrelated processes are said to be having deleterious effects on the health of populations throughout the world. However, it could be argued that, as McDermott (2007: 313) points out, there is something of a 'circuitry of research funding'. In trying to exemplify this she argues that

when the public is potentially unable to separate fact from judgment, due to scientific experts being given the task of speaking to the implications of morally charged issues such as obesity and inactivity, the grounds for funding become questionable. Scientific journalism thus functions as an apparatus of governance as it acts as a conduit through which an epidemic vocabulary not only comes to be cemented to particular conditions (e.g., inactivity, obesity) in the public imagination but also facilitates a health issue being identified as of great consequence to population welfare, and thus requiring intervention and funding.

(McDermott, 2007: 313)

We might argue that groups of people in more established positions, within academia, within the government and within large organizations, have a greater control over the flows of communication (Elias and Scotson, 1994). Such a condition serves to perpetuate the idea that we are in the grip of a physical inactivity crisis and, unsurprisingly, those people employed to promote sport have, consciously or otherwise, taken the opportunities afforded by such developments. As Coalter (2007a: 153) argues in relation to the conclusive style in which organizations like Sport England report levels of obesity and physical activities, 'such calculations perform a dual purpose: they dramatize the nature of the issues and their broader, collective, consequences and also act as part of the lobbying process for greater public investment in sport'. This might be explained, in part, because Sport England, amongst others, remains ideologically committed to sport and not health.

It is important to recognize that, as Cohen (2002: viii), who first developed the concept 'moral panic' in his seminal work *Folk Devils and Moral Panics*, indicates, 'calling something a "moral panic" does not imply that this something does not exist or happened at all and that reaction is based on fantasy, hysteria, delusion and illusion or being duped by the powerful'. Instead, he argues, 'it has been exaggerated in itself and/or compared to other, more serious problems' (Cohen, 2002: viii). In fact, the anecdotal evidence is overwhelming insofar as in virtually all attempts to measure population obesity levels the fact that levels of obesity are increasing substantially is difficult to ignore, and, thus, this is difficult to deny. We do not subscribe, therefore, to Gard and Wright's (2005) suggestion that the obesity crisis is, to all intents and purposes, a myth. We also do not claim that there is no problem, but if we are to develop a more adequate appreciation of the levels of overweight and obesity within populations it is important that we seek to develop explanations of these issues that are based on a relatively detached view of the available data, and that take into account something about the complex ways in which the social patterning of overweight and obesity has developed over time. Only then are we in a position to provide more reality-congruent assessments that would contribute to more effective policy. Instead, we have a situation where, as McDermott (2007: 316) points out, 'physical activity is positioned as the modern preventative panacea'. However, problems arise with such a position, not least because of the potential health costs that stem from the promotion of sport and the potential injuries that might be incurred.

The promotion of sport or physical activity?

As we move further away from individualized, moderate and rhythmical physical activities (such as aerobics) towards more complex, physically vigorous activities (such as 'traditional' team games) the likely health 'costs' of involvement in these activities increase correlatively. From a sociological perspective, this can best be explained, at least in part, by reference to the rather different pattern of social relationships involved in these types of activities (Coalter, 2007a; K. Green, 2008; Waddington, 2000). Perhaps one of the most important differences between physical activities and team sports is that the former involves a rather different pattern of social relations from the latter – there are greater constraints when participating in team sports, and, of course, the potential for greater levels of explosive body contact. In relation to this, physical activities are more likely than are team sports to involve physical movements of a rhythmic nature that, in addition to the intensity and duration of the activity, can be controlled to a much higher degree by the individual participant (Waddington, 2000; Waddington *et al.*, 1997). So, perhaps the most important difference between sport and physical activity is that, whereas the competitive element is not central to most forms of physical activity, sport, by contrast, is inherently competitive.

Moreover, sport is arguably becoming increasingly competitive not just at the elite level but at lower levels too (Waddington, 2000). In this connection, Waddington (2000) has noted that the increased competitiveness of modern sport – one aspect of which is the increased emphasis that has come to be placed on winning – means that, unlike most people who take part in non-competitive physical activities, those who play sport are, particularly at the higher levels, frequently subject to strong constraints to 'play hurt', that is, to continue playing while injured or to play with painkilling injections 'for the good of the team', with all the associated health risks these behaviours entail (Liston *et al.*, 2006; Roderick *et al.*, 2000; Young *et al.*, 1994). However, as we have seen, sport is frequently promoted unproblematically alongside physical activity as a means of coping with the apparent health problems that are experienced by people in modern societies, whilst the physical risks to health that active participation in sport may entail are simultaneously ignored.

In this respect, as Coalter (2001: 5) argues, 'among many of the least active and least healthy groups, the promotion of a more active lifestyle may be a more useful strategy than offering only traditional sports'. To this end, he suggests that 'the traditional product-led [target group] "sports development" approach needs [to be] reviewed, with a more needs-based approach based on an understanding of personal and social circumstances' (Coalter, 2001: 5). In this respect, the Department of Health and DCMS in the UK recognized that 'people currently have limited and often conflicting information on healthy lifestyle choices' (DH/DCMS, 2004: 8). One might argue that this 'limited' information is borne out by a view that 'healthy' and 'physically active' are terms that many people associate with sport and that some react negatively to the idea of 'physical activity' as a result. For example, Sport England quotes one SHA report that stated:

> in a way Sport as an umbrella term can appear to be exclusive, signifying elite athletes, footballers who are frequently young and male. To succeed with the Public Health agenda of the delivery of increased physical activity this needs to be inclusive, so that women, the elderly, (those on) incapacity benefit or unemployment benefit and the frail can also participate.
>
> (Sport England, 2005b: 16)

In *Game Plan*, the government cited Finland as the main benchmark for success in relation to sports participation, claiming that here, as in Sweden, 'participation in organised and competitive sport actually increases amongst older people, due to the focus placed on this group in these countries' (DCMS/Strategy Unit, 2002: 23). However, Gratton (2004) suggests that this is incorrect. He argues that competitive sport decreases significantly with age throughout the whole of Europe, including Sweden and Finland. What does increase in Sweden and Finland, in stark contrast to the rest of Europe, is 'participants taking part with a high frequency (intensive) but not in a competitive and organised situation. Rather it is informal and non-competitive' (Gratton, 2004: 93). As a result, Gratton (2004: 94) argues that 'policy intervention to increase participation needs to be concentrated in the non-competitive, informal area of sport participation since this is where it is most likely to attract the groups that will yield the highest health benefits from participation, older age groups and the lower socio-economic groups'.

Waddington (2000) argues that it is not uncommon to find government policies where the concepts of sport, physical activity and exercise are frequently conflated. Indeed, as Coalter has noted:

Part of the reason for [largely] ignoring the negative consequences of sports participation is the consistent failure to distinguish systematically between physical activity
and *sport* ... [The] all-encompassing definition serves to fudge important distinctions
between physical activity, physical recreation, recreational and competitive sport. It
thereby permits the sports lobby to claim to be a major contributor to the fitness and
health agenda (although the concern with the costs of sports injuries would imply
that we require more precise definitions in this area).

(Coalter 2007a: 156; original emphasis)

It is clear, then, that in response to the apparently increasing levels of obesity and
decreasing levels of physical activity, we have seen a blurring of sport and physical
activity in policies and strategies in recent times. In some respects, this has resulted in
something of a tension between those promoting physical activity and the wider health
agenda, and those promoting community sport. This is not unlike the longer-standing
tension between elite sports promotion and mass participation sport. In other words,
tensions have now emerged regarding the kinds of activities to be promoted in the name
of 'mass participation' or 'Sport For All'. This blurring of the distinctions between sport
and physical activity has permeated down to SDOs on the ground (Bloyce *et al.*, 2008).
Indeed, as Robson and McKenna (2008: 175) argue, 'in many areas the traditional sports
development plan has been supplanted or augmented by a holistic physical activity strategy'.

The apparent willingness of Sport England and SDOs on the ground to embrace the
broader health agenda can be explained in relation to the enabling and constraining
aspects of their relational networks. As the government, in particular, placed an increasing emphasis on the health agenda, and identified sport, in its 'broadest' sense, as a key
contributing factor, it is not surprising that those involved in sports promotion became
embroiled in the promotion of HEPA. There are undoubtedly opportunities enabled by
the links with health, not least to do with the increased financial implications for those
promoting sport, but also to do with the legitimization and professionalization of the
vocation of sports development (Bloyce *et al.*, 2008; Coalter, 2007a; Houlihan and White,
2002). In this sense, it is perhaps unsurprising 'given the increasingly interventionist role
of government in sport policy over the last decade' that many SDOs 'are increasingly and
enthusiastically championing the perceived role of sport in contributing positively to the
achievement of broader social objectives' (Bloyce *et al.*, 2008: 368). However, their
involvement must always be explained in terms of the habitus of those employed in such
positions and strongly related to the fact they are likely to be sports enthusiasts and
believe that 'sports development work should be about the promotion of sport' (Bloyce *et
al.*, 2008: 367). A large part of the reason they sought employment in 'sport' in the first
place is because of their involved passion for sports. It would not be surprising, therefore,
if the SDOs on the ground broadly welcomed the apparent repositioning of community
sport so prominently on their agenda, in the UK at least, in 2008. However, as noted earlier,
this has not prevented Sport England from publishing its new policy outlines, *Shaping
Places through Sport*, in which the commitment to 'healthier communities' through the
'power of sport' very much remains high on the ideological agenda of Sport England.

Short-termism and healthism

The idea that we are witnessing a physical inactivity crisis is certainly not new. As Karpf
(1988: 32) pointed out over twenty years ago, 'leotarded health zealots, anxiously

charting their daily fibre intake, seem the very epitome of modernity – the result of recent knowledge about health and illness. So, it's chastening to cast back to the 1920s, 1930s, and 1940s and see a fitness craze and a preoccupation with nutrition almost identical'. Indeed, often the apparent '"modern" or "present day" problem represents ... [something of a] re-surfacing of a longstanding moral panic' (Smith and Green, 2005: 242). It is perhaps unsurprising, then, that, as is evident from the discussion above, often policies and strategies developed to deal with this apparently 'new' and 'worrying' problem can be considered as 'old wine in a new bottle'. Over the past decade or so of Labour governments in the UK, for example, there have been several different strategies that have the promotion of sport and/or physical activity for health outcomes at their heart, or at least as one of their central objectives. Frequently, however, despite setting sometimes reasonably long-term goals and targets, these are rarely commented upon in policies that succeed them. In other words, as we explained earlier and for reasons we outlined in Chapter 1, it seems that in the area of health, as elsewhere, governments are more interested in 'take-offs' than 'landings' (Coalter, 2007a). As such, Coalter (2001: 50) is critical of the 'short-term' nature of many government and local government sports development policies. He argues as follows:

> Many sports projects are subject to both short-term funding and unrealistic expectations for quick results (in part based on their own theoretical claims). Many practitioners, although wholly committed to their work, acknowledge that short-term projects have very limited impacts on deep-rooted fitness and health problems [and] attitudes to physical activity.
>
> (Coalter, 2001: 50)

In essence, those promoting sport have been persuaded that sports participation is good for health; it has become part of their habitus. One might argue that there has been a process of occupational socialization through the constraining and enabling aspects of increasing government involvement in, and development of, performance indicators for sport that have goals beyond sport, such as health. This, combined with the greater budgets available for health objectives and an apparently related 'status anxiety' amongst SDOs and others promoting sport, contributes to an increasing desire to claim more for the benefits that can be achieved from promoting sport (Bloyce *et al.*, 2008; Coalter, 2007a; Houlihan and White, 2002). An impact of this is that there would seem to be 'a widespread absence of robust monitoring information on the health benefits of provision. Much of the rationale for this has rested on assumed beneficial outcomes of any increased activity' (Coalter *et al.*, 2000: 28). In addition to this, Coalter *et al.* (2000: 28) argue that there is a lack of long-term monitoring of such programmes and 'this reflects the short-term nature of most initiatives, the lack of funding for such monitoring and the lack of expertise to undertake such work'.

It might be argued that such short-termism and the associated moral panics about health have been a part of the broader processes of medicalization and healthism of physical inactivity and the corresponding levels of obesity. As McDermott (2007: 312) argues, categorizing obesity as a disease, 'in the way this term is traditionally understood within epidemiology, signals ... [its] medicalization (Conrad, 1992; Gard and Wright, 2005), a representation that is increasingly critiqued'. A related development is that, as we noted earlier, this contributes to a process whereby attention is focused almost exclusively on the individual as being ultimately responsible for controlling his or her own health. At the same time, this serves to divert 'attention away from wider social processes – for example, poverty, unemployment, industrial pollution, or the poor quality or lack of accessibility to health services – which may be associated with high levels of illness' (Waddington, 2000: 15). In Western Europe, although there has been an evident substantial increase in focus by the various national governments on health promotion, for the most part there has been a 'continuing preoccupation with individual risk behaviours and the promotion of healthy lifestyles … and little evidence of the creation of the institutions and systems necessary to sustain the development of effective population health promotion' (Ziglio *et al.*, 2005: 234). Much the same criticism is made of the current focus on health promotion in Canada (Pederson *et al.*, 2005) and the US too (Lightsey *et al.*, 2005). However, in the twenty-first century several policies have emerged, in the UK at least, that pay attention to some of the wider issues that are likely to impact on health, like socio-economic status and the broader physical environment (Foresight, 2007; Sport England, 2007). The extent to which they have an impact on the ground, however, cannot yet be determined. It is to this concern with the wider contributing factors to health that we now turn.

Socio-economic and environmental factors

There are two main areas of criticism that can be levelled at many of the health policies promoted by governments around the world. These centre around the wider, but nevertheless central, contributing factors of the impact of socio-economic status and the broader environment in which people live their everyday lives. Roberts and Brodie's (1992: 141) seminal study of sport and physical activity participation in inner-cities in the UK concluded that there is a 'niche rather than a foundation role for sport within health policy and promotion'. These niche benefits, they add, offer 'no solutions to socio-economic health inequalities' (Roberts and Brodie, 1992: 142), for relying on sport as a vehicle for the promotion of public health has always been a problematic policy strategy for the government (Roberts and Brodie, 1992). That such sports promotion does not appear to offer a 'solution' to such socio-economic inequalities is neatly captured by Snape (2005: 146), who argues that, 'despite a plethora of government-sponsored initiatives to encourage and enable more people of Black ethnic minority status to engage in exercise and sport … participation within these ethnic minority groups continues to remain low and to exhibit substantial differences to that of the majority White community'. Clearly, it is not just ethnic minority groups that have been the target of several sports and physical activity campaigns (and neither are these trends limited to the UK) but also people from socio-economically disadvantaged groups, and yet most data reveal that their participation rates remain low in comparison to people from higher socio-economic groups. In addition, Gratton (2004: 87) points out that 'overall inequalities by socioeconomic group can be demonstrated across a wide range of measures of health and the determinants of health'. For these and many other reasons, it is clear that physical activity promotion can only have a marginal impact until the broader inequalities and social divisions in health within society are addressed, which is something that is beyond the remit of those promoting sports, including, of course, SDOs.

The socio-economic factors contributing to health are arguably exacerbated in certain areas by physical environments that are 'toxic to physical activity' (Riddoch and McKenna, 2005: 193). In this respect, Riddoch and McKenna argue that

> if population-level change is desired, as opposed to just a few individuals changing
> for the better … communities must address the issue of exactly why the members of

those communities are inactive. In the UK, and probably in the rest of the western world, the reasons almost certainly lie within the types of environment in which most people live.

(Riddoch and McKenna 2005: 192)

Summary

We noted earlier that in order make more adequate sense of the complex relationships that exist between participation in sport, physical activity and health we need to pay particular attention to the ways in which health inequalities are socially patterned and to the differential health outcomes that are to be found amongst various social groups. As Riddoch and McKenna (2005: 194) argue, 'there has been no communal, nationwide population decision to take less exercise. Rather, it has happened surreptitiously, stealthily, without most even noticing'. The significance of broader long-term changes associated with aspects of commercialization, urbanization, globalization, medicalization, automation and mechanization processes, in addition to the growing affluence – both relatively and absolutely – of particular social groups has contributed to changes in most people's lifestyles. Such changes, we would argue, have contributed to people becoming less physically active in their day-to-day lives. There are a number of key developments that need to be considered in this regard. These include the kinds of jobs in which people are employed, and especially the long-term tendency for many occupations to shift away from being characterized by manual, physically demanding activity towards those jobs that promote sedentariness to a greater degree. Developments in travel, and particularly the growth in the number of cars purchased and the extension of bus services, has also meant that more people, including schoolchildren of course, than formerly use a car in their daily lives. In addition, the increasing variety of media technologies and commercial leisure opportunities available to people in their leisure time have also contributed to rising levels of sedentariness, overweight and obesity. Indeed, these are just some among many other unintended consequences emanating from the intended actions of people developing technologies that are increasingly designed to meet evident demand to make it easier to be sedentary, whether it be time-saving devices in the home or at work, or in terms of the number of people relying on automated transport. Notwithstanding the recent attempts to address 'active travel' in promoting health in the UK, for example, the House of Commons Health Committee was critical of its own government's position on this, and it provides a particularly apposite way to conclude this chapter. The Committee suggested that, 'given the profound impact increased levels of activity would have on the nation's health, quite aside from the obvious environmental benefits, it seems to us entirely unacceptable that successive governments have been so remiss in effectively promoting active travel' (House of Commons Health Committee, 2004: 77).

Revision questions

1 Provide a sociological examination of the increasing concern that is coming to be expressed over the state of the nation's health.
2 Reflect on how effective the public health and sport policy response has been in impacting on existing health inequalities.
3 Discuss the interrelationships between sport, health and physical activity.

Key readings

Gard, M. and Wright, J. (2005) *The Obesity Epidemic: Science, Morality and Ideology*, London: Routledge.

Hardman, A. and Stensel, D. (2009) *Physical Activity and Health: The Evidence Explained*, 2nd edn, London: Routledge.

Waddington, I. (2000) *Sport, Health and Drugs: A Critical Sociological Perspective*, London: Routledge.

Recommended websites

British Heart Foundation: www.bhfactive.org.uk

Foresight: Tackling Obesities: Future Choices: www.foresight.gov.uk/OurWork/ActiveProjects/Obesity/Obesity.asp

World Health Organization: www.who.int/en

6 Elite sports development
Promoting international success

Objectives

This chapter will:

- examine the increasing spread of elite sports development systems around the world;
- explore the key characteristics of elite sports development systems; and
- examine the inter-state rivalry contributing to the increasing seriousness with which sport is competed at the international level.

Introduction

The emergence of state-sponsored, elite sports development (ESD) 'systems' has become an increasingly prominent feature of sport policy in numerous countries throughout the world, most especially since the 1960s and 1970s. It should be noted that when we refer to systems in this chapter we are aware, of course, that they do not exist independently of human interaction. Indeed, the ESD systems to which we will refer are, in fact, the figurations of interdependent groups of people that have developed quite specifically with the aim of developing elite-level sport. With the growing social significance of sport internationally, governments have sought to invest in promoting international sporting success, most particularly, though not exclusively, in Olympic sports. The global dissemination of achievement sport, and the subsequent desire to succeed on the global media stage, has seen a dynamic interchange of ideas regarding ESD systems. This growing interdependency of sporting systems, and the people comprising them, has contributed to a diminution in the disparity between the approaches taken by people to develop elite sports structures in the major sporting nations in the world. The central objective of this chapter is to examine the emergence of the increasing willingness of governments to intervene in setting the ESD policy process and the organization of ESD systems. This has contributed to more systematic talent identification and development (TID) programmes being implemented in several countries. We will also examine the growing emphasis that is being placed upon sports science support and the provision of 'modern' sporting facilities for the exclusive use of elite sports performers. These developments cannot be understood adequately unless they are conceptualized as elements in the increasing professionalization of coaching systems. They have involved governments in devising more specific strategies for the prioritization and targeting of funding. These are the key characteristics of the modern ESD system that will be discussed within this chapter. However, in many countries the extent to which governments facilitate the implementation of ESD over and above their contribution to mass sport promotion has been prominent in the debate. In several countries this has resulted in considerable tension between the prevailing focus on elite sports and the development of mass sports. There have also been various other domestic issues that have impacted on the development of elite sport systems that have contributed simultaneously to the emergence of subtle variations in the ESD systems that are currently in operation in many countries. The chapter will conclude with a discussion of the 'diminishing contrasts and increasing varieties' (Elias, 2000) that are, it will be argued, characteristic of the global spread of ESD policies.

The increasing social significance of sport and growing government involvement in elite sports development

In the physical sciences a substantial body of literature has been produced focusing on factors that are 'trainable (physiology, psychology and biomechanics)', 'teachable (tactics)', and other factors 'outside the control of the athlete and coach (genetics and age)' (Smith, 2003: 1105). There is little doubt, however, that the physical dimensions of sport would be enhanced still further by a greater understanding of the ways in which policies are implemented. In pursuit of this end we will begin with an analysis of the emergence of ESD systems, and how the prevailing characteristics of such systems became more widespread.

The global spread of modern achievement sport, largely from the West, has been strongly associated with the increasing social significance of sporting performance in very many countries and has contributed to the spread of particular kinds of elite sports (e.g. soccer) and global sporting competitions (e.g. the Olympic Games). Waddington and Smith (2009) have identified some of the processes that have contributed to the growing social significance of sport on an international scale. The processes include the medicalization of life and sport, the growing commercialization and politicization of sport and, of particular significance, here, the de-amateurization of sport (Waddington and Smith, 2009). The general de-amateurization of sport involved performers moving away from seeing sport as primarily a source of intrinsic pleasure towards placing a greater emphasis on winning, as they were having to play for broader social and sometimes political units (e.g. city, region, nation-states). In addition to this, Beamish and Ritchie (2006) have observed that there has been a growing tendency, since the inauguration of the Olympic Games, for media corporations, the sporting goods industries and other commercial interest groups to become influential in the organization of the Games. They argue that such developments have 'played significant roles in shaping contemporary world-class, high-performance sport and created the enormous impetus behind the quest for pushing human athletic performance to increasingly rarefied heights' (Beamish and Ritchie, 2006: 67). The commercialization of sport developed substantially from 1945 onwards and this has increased pressure on athletes to perform for the increasing financial rewards on offer. This process is linked to a growing politicization of sport (Waddington and Smith, 2009), whereby governments seeking to bask in the potential reflected glory of sporting success have invested more in terms of providing the best sporting infrastructure possible to generate and support world-class athletes. Indeed, according to Houlihan and Green (2008: 3), governments have increasingly used 'sport as a policy instrument' and most governments now 'espouse a commitment to elite sport and competition', and for those

that can afford to make this commitment it is frequently backed by large public investment. Governments increasingly take this position for a variety of reasons, among them
the promotion of their political system, the generation of national pride and the associated 'feel good' factor, in search of economic advantage and diplomatic objectives (De
Bosscher *et al.*, 2008; Green and Houlihan, 2005; Hoberman, 1993). In order to increase
the possibility of obtaining some of the perceived rewards of achieving some success at
the level of elite sport, since the Second World War many governments have developed
quite explicit ESD objectives.

In relation to the development of ESD objectives, several authors have argued that
there is an increasing tendency for a homogenous 'model' of ESD systems to be adopted
and pursued in a growing number of countries (De Bosscher *et al.*, 2008; Oakley and
Green, 2001a; 2001b; Green and Houlihan, 2005; 2008; Houlihan and Green, 2008). In
this respect, within this chapter when we refer to ESD systems we are specifically meaning
state-sponsored systems. There is some evidence, as will become clear below, that there
was an ESD system in place in the US even before this time, based on the college system for
sport. However, this was not state funded and was rather more ad hoc within the
American colleges. State-sponsored ESD systems have emerged as part of the overall
development of elite sport, especially in conjunction with the increasing economic, political and cultural significance of sport. These developments were part of a wider process
towards using scientific and technologically assisted pursuits for enhanced athletic performance that have accompanied, as we noted earlier, the de-amateurization, commercialization and politicization of sport (Waddington and Smith, 2009). More specifically,
Beamish and Ritchie (2006: 92) argue that there was a political commitment by the East
Germans, as well as the Soviet Union, to 'keep ahead of the competition [the West in
general, and the US and West Germany in particular] in all aspects of the scientific preparation of world-class, high-performance athletes' (Beamish and Ritchie, 2006: 92). In
this respect, they claimed that the desire to succeed in sport on an international scale can
only be adequately understood when located within the context of the Cold War rivalry,
the development of high-performance sport systems in East Germany (German Democratic Republic [GDR]) and West Germany (Federal Republic of Germany [FRG]), and
East–West relations more generally from the 1950s through to the 1980s (Beamish and
Ritchie, 2006), although it might be appropriately argued that this desire is far more widespread than the context in which they try to place it. As Waddington and Smith (2009) and
Oakley and Green (2001a; 2001b) argue, one must also consider the emergent nation-states
from Africa following the Second World War, and, more recently, following the break-up of
the Soviet Union, the emerging nation-states in the Balkan and Baltic regions, that have given
a fresh impetus to the quest for international sporting success. In order to make more sense
of these developments, we will briefly survey the emergence of ESD policies in various
countries that, we will argue, are crucial to an understanding of their subsequent diffusion.
We will begin with an overview of the systems developed in the former communist countries
of the Eastern bloc, before examining how these impacted on selected countries in the West.
Finally, we will present a case study of the development of ESD systems in the UK.

The significance of the Eastern bloc: ESD systems in the Soviet Union and the GDR

The first consistent and systematic approach to ESD was developed in the 1950s in the
Soviet Union and the GDR. The emergence of several communist states, most notably in
Eastern Europe, prior to and immediately after the Second World War, provided the

context within which many 'loose confederations of diverse ethnic groups: different races, languages, traditions, religions, stages of economic growth, prejudices' (Riordan and Cantelon, 2003: 91) converged. Sport was increasingly seen by the communist leaders in many of these emerging states as a useful tool with which to promote national cohesion and identity, and to project this image to the outside world. Hoberman (1993: 18) argues that 'in the Soviet Union, the official promotion of competitive sport began in the 1930s'; however, a Soviet team did not compete in the Olympic Games until 1952 in Helsinki, by which time international sports competitions (particularly the Olympics) were coming to be seen as a useful means by which the superiority of communism over capitalism could be demonstrated.

Sport has provided a particularly apposite, albeit potentially risky, arena in which to demonstrate the superiority of one nation, or one political system, over another. It is an arena that very many people across a range of societies follow through the media; and which provides outcomes that, on paper at least, no one can dispute; and therein lies the risk. That is to say, the promotion of propaganda and ideology within capitalist and communist countries meant that sport, with clear result-based outcomes, became increasingly viewed as a very effective barometer by which objective measurements could supposedly be made. Within the GDR and the Soviet Union, in particular, considerable attention was paid to developing systems of ESD that could produce gold medal-winning athletes and teams, with the Olympic Games being regarded as the key arena for the demonstration of sporting superiority. Indeed, according to van Bottenburg (2001: 141), in 1948 Soviet officials declared that their 'leading athletes had the task of "securing first place in the world in the most important sports over the next few years"'. Furthermore, the newly emerged GDR government became a significant geographical and symbolic aspect of the East–West political divide. This arguably contributed to the high priority given by the GDR government to establishing an effective ESD system. It was a priority driven by the desire of the GDR's Communist Party to build national pride not only in competition with West Germany but also in relation to the Soviet Union. The fact that much of the Western world did not recognize the GDR as a political entity no doubt fuelled this desire further. In fact, the International Olympic Committee (IOC) only recognized the GDR in 1965 and it competed in its first Games in Mexico in 1968.

Riordan and Cantelon (2003: 100) argue that 'policies of pervasive social welfare in which sport was an essential feature in constructing the infrastructure of socialist society provided conditions that were more conducive to discovering, organising and developing talent in specific sports than those of the more disparate and private Western systems'. In this respect, the totalitarian regimes in office helped create an atmosphere where there was little, if any, public accountability for the relatively huge sums of money that were made available to fund elite sport policies in the Soviet Union and the GDR (Grix, 2008; Hoberman, 1993; Riordan and Cantelon, 2003). The ESD systems established in East Germany, in particular, soon came to be regarded with admiration, fear and a large degree of scepticism from many outside of the country. The scepticism related to the belief of some in the West that there was also a systematic doping programme in the GDR – something, of course, that was proved after the break-up of the communist regimes. Nonetheless, other parts of the system came to be seen as 'the vanguard of developing sporting excellence' (Green and Oakley, 2001: 247). The GDR team only finished outside the top three of the medals table once in all the Summer and Winter Games it entered from 1968 to 1988. The Soviet Union was even more successful, albeit with much greater resources, and its athletes finished in the top two of the medals table for every Summer and Winter Games it entered, coming first in 13 out of 18 of those Games. The GDR, in particular, 'developed and applied a highly sophisticated system to produce top-level athletes and became renowned for its international sporting accomplishments' (Merkel, 1995: 100). This system, according to some, was 'unparalleled' across the world (Hoberman, 1993: 18). It was characterized by a range of key developments: the increasing use of scientific methods, utilizing anthropometric and physiological measurements, to identify athletic talent; systematic selection of potentially gifted children based on scientific profiling and the establishment of sport schools; professional development of high-quality coaches; scientific focus on training regimes; and a highly centralized, state-funded system of coordinated groups responsible for developing athletes at national training centres (Beamish and Ritchie, 2006; Hoberman, 1992). Notwithstanding the suspicion at the time that many of the results achieved by the GDR (and Soviet Union) were affected by a systematic doping programme, many of the characteristics of the systems in place, as we will see later, became key features of ESD outside the GDR in later years.

The system for funding elite sport in the GDR 'was characterised by a strict and clear decision-making and competency hierarchy' (Petry *et al.*, 2008: 117). The East Germans, with a comparatively small population (circa 17 million), developed a quite systematic targeting of medals at the Olympic Games. The targeting focused on those areas where medal aspirations were more realistic. They analyzed sports performances in the 1950s, for example, and ascertained that women's field events at the Summer Games were not nearly as keenly contested as the more blue-riband events such as the men's, and to a lesser degree women's, 100 metre sprints. Given the increasing propensity of the world's media to focus on overall medal tables, the East Germans targeted areas where numerous medals could be won relatively easily. This is not to deny the success achieved by the GDR in some of the more 'popular' events, but simply to recognize that the country enjoyed unprecedented success in men's and women's field events and some other more 'minor' sports, such as long-distance walking, shooting and, at the time, gymnastics. These helped boost its overall medal tally.

Funds were almost exclusively devoted to ESD, and this policy was rarely, if ever, challenged (Grix, 2008). As Merkel (1995: 102) points out, 'Sport For All' was never 'a major issue on the political agenda of the East German government, since from the beginning of the 1960s onwards the emphasis was almost exclusively on the production of top-level athletes'. Significant financial assistance from the state was provided for state of the art facilities and scientific and coaching support to the elite athletes in the Soviet Union and East Germany. Moreover, notwithstanding the communist sporting ideology of these countries, elite athletes received substantial rewards, partly to ensure that those athletes involved in the more commercially lucrative sports remained in the country, rather than absconding to the West. Of course, it also meant that these so-called amateur athletes were able to train and prepare for competition on a full-time basis.

The vast population of the Soviet Union meant that the need to identify 'talent' early was less acute than was the case in the GDR. Although there was some talent identification in place within the ESD system of the Soviet Union, 'the system lacked rigour and was not based on a nationwide programme of strictly uniform tests and norms' (Green and Houlihan, 2005: 22). Nonetheless, the Soviets were amongst the first to endeavour to identify talent on the basis of scientific measurements related to physiological performances at various ages. In essence, this represents the first stage of what Green and Houlihan (2005) identify as a three-stage approach to TID. The second stage involved matching the physical attributes of those children identified at stage one as having 'potential' to the ideal physical profile required for specific sporting events. The third stage involved the selected individuals in programmes of participation in sporting competition, and the necessary coaching to develop their skills (Green and Houlihan, 2005).

Given the success and the relatively small population in the GDR, it is no surprise that the East German system involved considerable attention being given to identifying talent. The GDR 'implemented state run, systematic talent identification programs as early as the 1960s and 70s' (Abbott and Collins, 2002: 158). It seems that the talent selection and identification techniques employed built on the 'same anthropometric procedures developed by the racial scientists [in Germany] prior to 1945' (Krüger, 1999: 44). Much of the testing occurred in sport-specific boarding schools and, as in the Soviet system, involved matching the physiological profile of children as young as four to particular sports. All children within the GDR were subject to a variety of physical and physiological measurements, and those who matched certain criteria were to attend the sports boarding schools. The system was based on the same three-stage approach for identifying talent developed in the Soviet Union (Green and Houlihan, 2005), but conducted with more scientific rigour.

An important aspect of the ESD system developed in the GDR was the establishment of the Deutsche Hochschule für Körperkultur (German University for Physical Culture [DHfK]), founded in Leipzig in 1950. The complex included a 100,000 seater stadium and numerous training facilities. It housed both more established and developing athletes, and was also a site for the development of elite-level coaches. This establishment was complimented by two other organizations, the Forschungsinstitut für Körperkultur und Sport (Research Institute for Physical Culture and Sport [FKS]), which was the venue for top-secret sports science research, and the Gessellschaft für Sportmedizin der DDR (GDR Society for Sports Medicine), established in 1956. The FKS was at the heart of the East German experimentation with performance enhancing drugs. There is not the time, or the scope, within this chapter to discuss the development of performance-enhancing drugs (PEDs) and the impact that such developments had on elite sports. For an overview of the development of PEDs, which is, of course, not unrelated to the development of ESD systems, see Waddington and Smith (2009).

Alongside the research into PEDs, other research was conducted that has now become commonplace in sports science support in other ESD systems, such as nutritional and medicinal support. Together, these institutes were the first centrally administered and funded centres for the development of elite sports performance and sports science research in the world. In addition to the development of state of the art facilities, there was a focus on the development of coaching techniques (Merkel, 1995), such that the coaching system in many Eastern bloc countries was, in large measure, fully professionalized, with dedicated career structures for full-time coaches and a wide network of support from semi-professional coaching staff. In many non-communist bloc countries at this time the prevailing pattern was for coaching to be ad hoc, based largely on a system of volunteering. However, as we will see, specialist institutions, with an increased emphasis on sports science and 'professional' coaching, soon spread to the West. In fact, the systems developed in the Eastern bloc countries for promoting elite sport 'provided a "template" for the subsequent development of elite sport models in Western nations' (Green and Houlihan, 2005: 19).

Learning lessons from the 'enemy': ESD systems in West Germany, Canada, the United States and Australia

The disproportionate success the GDR enjoyed at the Olympics heightened the desire amongst national sports organizations (NSOs) from other countries to learn more about the systems in place there. It is likely that these NSOs then brought it to the attention of governments that were receptive to greater or lesser degrees to the idea of establishing similar systems. As Green and Oakley (2001: 252) argue, 'in their relatively recent drive for (global) elite sporting excellence, many Western nation-states have embraced elements of the Eastern Bloc's managed approach to sporting supremacy'. In West Germany, where the political leaders were most acutely aware of the Olympic successes of their East German neighbours, there was increased pressure to perform at least as well on the international stage. The West German government embarked on a process of developing an elite sports system of its own, a commitment given further impetus by Munich winning the right to host the 1972 Olympic Games. Those people attempting to develop elite sport in West Germany 'began to coordinate their first High-Performance Sport Plan in 1965. Not surprisingly, the main reference point was East Germany' (Beamish and Ritchie, 2006: 94). With the success of the GDR at its first Olympic Games in 1968 and with the Munich Games in prospect, the West German government was under particular pressure to establish 'nationwide structures for supporting top level sport' and to pursue its elite sport priorities (Petry *et al.*, 2008: 118). The allocation of substantial funding allowed national team coaches to be appointed for various sports and the establishment of high-performance training centres along the lines of those in the GDR. In addition, there was an increasing focus on talent identification and the development of sport boarding schools, as well as a greater focus on sport science support, with the establishment, in 1970, of the Bundesinstitut für Sportwissenschaft (Federal Institute of Sports Science [BISp]) and then the Deutsche Vereinigung für Sportwissenschaft (German Union of Sport Science [DVS]). The apparent similarities to the ESD system in the GDR are quite striking. However, a significant difference was that although the West German government provided large sums of money for the programmes, it 'did not become directly involved in sport development, nor did it directly fund the high-performance system' (Beamish and Ritchie, 2006: 95). Instead, the system of financing continued to be a complex mix of public funds, private funds and a system based on volunteering. The funding was not, therefore, as acutely focused on elite sport as was the case in East Germany, and 'the degree of direct control exercised over sport was slight by comparison to that found in the GDR where sport remained tightly under state management' (Bergsgard *et al.*, 2007: 57). In West Germany there was more apparent accountability of government funding, and greater pressure to maintain a focus on the promotion of mass participation and physical activity more generally. In contrast, in their pursuit of sporting success many of the governments in Eastern bloc countries spared no expense.

With the Montreal Games (1976) in prospect, the Canadian government's reaction to Canadian athletes' relatively poor performances on the international stage was to venture down the same path as West Germany. It too established an ESD strategy not unlike those that had been developed in the communist world. In West Germany and Canada the contexts within which the desired ESD system emerged were in some ways similar. The governments in both countries had concerns over internal cohesion. In some respects West Germany was a 'new' nation, while Canada wrestled with the problem of the French-Quebec separatist movement. Playing host to the Olympic Games made both governments conscious of the expectations of their citizens, the fact that national pride was at stake and, therefore, the need to ensure a respectable performance. These pressures were compounded by the success enjoyed in international competition by their respective immediate neighbours, the GDR and the US.

The Canadian government implemented a sport policy designed to produce elite performers in 1970, and during the 1970s the Canadian government provided substantial funds to develop elite sport, and especially Olympic events. Indeed, such was the desire to pursue Olympic success that during the 1970s and 1980s 'there was a steady centralization of state control over elite sport underpinned by increasing public subsidy. Mass participation was largely pushed to the margin of political debate at the federal level and was increasingly left to the provinces and municipalities to administer and finance as they saw fit' (Bergsgard *et al.*, 2007: 49–50). There was a growing professionalization of sporting structures, and a move away from the volunteerism that had characterized the organization of sport in Canada up until this point (Macintosh and Whitson, 1990). In 1970, the Canadian Academy of Sport Medicine (CASM) and a number of centres of excellence were established. Performance targets for priority sports were established. The 'professionalization' of the 'management' of sports structures and a more direct input from the 'sports sciences' were key characteristics of the new ESD systems in place in Canada (Macintosh and Whitson, 1990: 41). Such was the perceived success of these ESD systems that 'for years after its triumph at the 1978 Edmonton Commonwealth Games, Canada was frequently referred to as "the East Germany of the Commonwealth"' (Hoberman, 1993: 19). Following the scandal surrounding Ben Johnson's positive drugs test at the Seoul Games of 1988, and the Dubin Inquiry that followed it, elite sport policy in Canada was pared back somewhat, and a greater focus was given, once again, to mass participation (Green and Houlihan, 2005). It is likely, however, that the cutbacks had rather more complex roots and that the Johnson case and the subsequent enquiry may have been a useful rationalization.

Successive American governments have resisted (on occasions, resolutely opposed) any movement in the direction of such a centralized system (Sparvero *et al.*, 2008). However, it is the case that by American Olympic standards their performance at the Munich Games in 1972 had been poor and this was made all the more difficult to accept by the continuing success of the Soviet teams. In combination these elements engendered a short period in which there was a federal focus on elite sport policy. For example, in 1975 President Ford established the President's Commission on Olympic Sports (Chalip, 1995; Galemore, 2003; Hunt, 2007). The 'commission was asked to study the way in which amateur sports were organized in the United States, to determine whether and how federal subsidies should be given to amateur sports and to make recommendations about how best to develop all Olympic sports' (Wakefield, 2007: 778). Obviously, a strong motivation behind this was an increasing concern about the fact that the Soviet Union and the Eastern bloc countries were making effective use of their success in the Olympics as a propaganda tool in the Cold War. President Ford himself commented that 'the Communists "do things we would never find acceptable in a free society. Completely regimented, state-supported, state-manipulated athletic programs are not for us". However, he believed that "the Government does have a role in helping to promote United States competition in international sporting events"' (Hunt, 2007: 805). However, it might be argued that there was then, and still is today, a ruthless pursuit of athletic success in the American collegiate system. But on this occasion it was clear that key politicians in the US were looking for a way to defeat the Soviets, 'but to do so without resorting to government control' (Chalip, 1995: 7). The President's Commission on Olympic Sports published numerous reports over the next two years. The final one, published in January 1977, recommended that

> the United States rationalize its Olympic sport governance by establishing the USOC [United States Olympic Committee] as a 'central sports organization' with a 'vertical

structure' for governance of all Olympic sports. The report argued that administrative rationalization was a panacea for the ills plaguing American Olympic
sport ... This recommendation became the basis for the Amateur Sports Act.

(Chalip, 1995: 8)

The Act was a response to the problems created by the ongoing power struggles between
two of the most prominent national sports organizations (the National Collegiate Athletic Association [NCAA] and the Amateur Athletics Union [AAU]) within the US at that
time (Wakefield, 2007). It could be argued, though, that the limitations of the internal
organization only became a pressing concern in response to performances in comparison
to the Soviet Union, in particular, in the international arena. This was a time when more
serious thought than ever before had been given to direct federal involvement in establishing some kind of coordinated sports development approach, and the idea that the
ongoing conflict between the NCAA and AAU 'was detrimental to American Olympic
efforts' (Galemore, 2003: 2). As Hunt (2007: 797) points out, as the sporting 'rivalry developed,
it became increasingly apparent that the American sport system was ill-equipped to keep pace
with the Soviet Union'.

Despite resisting any kind of federal government involvement in sport, several of the
President's advisers were by now focusing their attention on developing 'an athletic framework oriented around "elite" sport' (Hunt, 2007: 801). The Amateur Sports Act, after
various deliberations, was eventually published in 1978 and it established the USOC as a
privately operated, not-for-profit organization to be responsible for all 'rights and
responsibilities associated with elite sport development', at least in terms of international
competitions (Sparvero *et al.*, 2008: 244). That is to say, 'it was agreed that the government should facilitate the reorganization of sport into a more efficient system, but government should not run sport' (Chalip, 1995: 7). The USOC was to provide a more
coordinated approach to the development of elite sport, but was to do so 'without
recourse to federal [financial] assistance' (Sparvero *et al.*, 2008: 244). Thus, while the
federal government took the unusual step of giving a direct steer to the processes that
were to underpin future American involvement in the Olympics, it stopped short of
offering any financial assistance or intervening in strategy. That having been said, many
features of ESD systems can now be identified within the US' approach to elite sport. For
example, 'in 1989, the USOC created an athlete identification and development committee' (Chalip, 1995: 9), and with numerous established centres of excellence (or 'Training
Sites') and 'a strong provision of science/medical backup' for American athletes (Oakley
and Green, 2001b: 99), the provisions for elite sports people are clearly a significant
aspect of the American sports structure. However, this approach has developed far less
systematically and without federal, and with only a modicum of state, involvement.
Moreover, it is on nothing like the scale seen elsewhere (USOC, 2008). Indeed, notwithstanding this brief period of governmental concern, it could be argued that the success
achieved by American athletes in the Olympic Games over the years has been attained
despite a lack of federal involvement. Today there is still 'no federal agency with any
responsibility for elite sport development, and there is no government level official whose
portfolio encompasses sport' (Sparvero *et al.*, 2008: 245). On the whole, then, the Americans have relied on a very competitive and well-established system in relation to high
school and college sporting competition, and with the vast comparative wealth and size
of the US this has been sufficient to sustain success at the Olympics (Oakley and Green,
2001b; Sparvero *et al.*, 2008). There is a need to distinguish between, on one hand, state

and private involvement in sport and, on the other, more or less systematic approaches to the development of athletes and the organization of sport. It could be argued that the American college system from the end of the nineteenth century has been in the vanguard of this approach. In effect America had the first professional athletes. Whether the recent emergence of the Chinese as a dominant force in Olympic sports will prove to be another watershed or, in Chalip's (1995) words, a 'focussing event' that triggers a further bout of American federal introspection, similar to the one produced by Soviet dominance in the 1970s, remains to be seen.

A similar pattern of events to those that encouraged the Canadian government's involvement in ESD and the American government's discussions about ESD influenced the Australian government's decision to establish ESD systems that have arguably become the most lauded in the non-communist world. The poor performance of the Australians at the Montreal Games of 1976 is considered to have been the central driving force behind the government's decision to establish a systematic sports development pro-gramme. They failed to win a single gold medal and came thirty-second in the overall medals table, having finished in the top ten in each of the previous six Summer Games. The change in policy involved a shift of emphasis away from a concern with the provision of mass participation towards a more explicit emphasis on elite development (Green and Houlihan, 2005; Stewart *et al.*, 2004). The Australian government learned from the Eastern bloc systems, and also, arguably, from their commonwealth partner Canada. The focus turned to a 'systematic sifting of school-age children as a means of identifying the potential elite, the development of specialist training academies, the subordination of domestic governing bodies to government policy and the use of public money to support elite athletes' (Houlihan, 1997: 6). To this end, a more formalized education and training programme of coaches was established that contributed to the establishment of the Australian Coaching Council in 1978 (Stewart *et al.*, 2004). Many sports promoters in Australia complained that there was a stark shortage of 'international' sports facilities in their country, a shortage brought into sharper relief following the Montreal Games. These concerns sparked a significant investment in sports facilities aided by the development of the Australian Institute of Sport (AIS) in Canberra in 1981. It became part of 'a more concerted approach to facility development for elite level training in many sports' (Green and Houlihan, 2005: 67). The development of the AIS was part of a wider recognition by the Australian government and NSOs of what was needed if they were to compete at the highest levels in Olympic competition. They needed to put in place 'organisational stra-tegies and the more professional and scientific approach to "producing" athletes that had underscored the success of the Eastern Bloc athletes' (Magdalinski, 2000: 317). The AIS was initially based on the centralized institute established within the GDR. However, in a country the size of Australia a centralized system soon proved to be impractical. There-fore, while it still operated as the AIS, under pressure from state governments and national sporting bodies it quickly devolved into regional centres of sporting excellence (Stewart *et al.*, 2004).

The Australian government justified this diversion of public money away from the development of grassroots sport, or 'Sport For All', to elite sport on the grounds that success at the highest level would stimulate mass participation (McKay, 1991). In the wake of Australia's performance in Montreal, this change in policy received public backing (Stewart *et al.*, 2004). According to Oakley and Green (2001b: 93), not only did the new focus on ESD stimulate the building of the AIS, much as in the GDR before it, there was a direct campaign to target '"softer" medals, particularly in some women's disciplines at which Australia [now] leads the way. Women's Rowing, Judo and Weight-lifting have been targeted by Australia in this way'. Much as in the GDR, the relatively small Australian population (circa 20 million) limited 'the pool from which talented athletes can be secured and developed' (Stewart *et al.*, 2004: 100). It is not surprising, then, that in Australia talent identification also became a central feature of the system. To this end the National Talent Search Program (NTSP) was established. This is a national programme implemented by the AIS that was based on a highly successful rowing talent search programme already in place (Stewart *et al.*, 2004). It could be argued that the NTSP is a rather more sophisticated, computerized 'stages approach', based on that first developed in the Soviet Union and the GDR (Green and Houlihan, 2005). According to Green and Houlihan (2005: 38), 'the primacy of sports science and sports medicine expertise is also a key principle underlying the contemporary development of Australia's elite sport model'. They liken it to the research developments that took place in East Germany under the auspices of the DHfK and FKS. When, in 1993, Australia was awarded the right to host the 2000 Olympic Games, the funding and provision for elite sport increased yet more (Cashman, 2006). Australia's sustained success in international sports encouraged other Western nations, the UK in particular, to view its system as a model of good practice.

The development of ESD systems in the United Kingdom

Green and Houlihan (2005: 63) state that the UK is 'a "late adopter" of many of the principles of organisation and administration developed by former Eastern bloc countries'. As we explained in Chapter 2, up until the 1960s successive British governments considered sport policy as something largely beyond government remit. However, since the 1960s there has been a growing propensity for British governments to intervene in sport policy and to utilize sport policy to achieve a wide range of goals. In the last decade or so, this has seen the development of many of the structures that were commonplace in the former Eastern bloc countries and later came to be adopted in modified forms by West Germany, Canada and Australia. However, no systematic attempt was made to enhance ESD until the election of John Major's government in the 1990s. As Green (2006: 226) argues, 'before the mid-1990s, support for elite sport development was uncoordinated and fragmented, with little sustained support from government and its sporting agencies'. Even after the publication of *Raising the Game* in 1995, a document that signalled the determination of the Major government to concentrate resources on elite sport, there was continued debate over exactly how this might be achieved. Nonetheless, since 1995, and following what was the worst performance, in terms of their overall place in the Summer Olympics medal table, by the Great Britain and Northern Ireland Olympic team at the 1996 Olympic Games, 'both Conservative and Labour governments have promoted, legitimised, and funded a system for supporting elite athlete development that bears little resemblance to the fragmented, makeshift and unplanned state of affairs of just 10 years ago' (Green, 2006: 218). A significant dimension of this approach has been the greater willingness of UK Sport to allow athletes to be funded by their NGBs. This broad shift in emphasis and resources to elite sport has in large measure been driven by the fact that such policies are also being increasingly pursued by the governments of other nations. This international competition is the principal driving force behind the adoption of these policies for all the countries involved. There would be little incentive for British governments to pursue new policies if their athletes had been holding their own in international sports competitions. In fact they have been playing catch-up. In this regard, there is little doubt that the success achieved by Australian athletes, in particular, made a significant contribution to this sea-change in British government policy.

As we saw in Chapter 2, the establishment of the National Lottery in 1994, and the increased money available for expenditure on sport that it has generated, changed the working environment for many of those promoting sport. This new source of funding gave the declared commitment to pursue an ESD approach a substantial kick-start. For example, the lottery-funded 'World Class Performance Programme', set up in 1996, was specifically geared to elite athletes, with the intention of targeting the winning of medals at major international competitions. In the past, many NGBs in the UK have had to rely heavily on government funding, and with the emergence of a commitment to an ESD approach this dependency has grown. The Labour government commissioned a review of elite sports funding, led by Jack Cunningham. It was published by the DCMS in 2001. The Cunningham Review argued that 'radical steps need to be taken if we are to create a world class system capable of producing consistent success in the international arena' (DCMS, 2001: 5). It was also acknowledged that 'decisive leadership and a strong commitment from UK Government' was a requirement if such a system was to work (DCMS, 2001: 7). It proposed that UK Sport should become the lead body responsible for overseeing the World Class Programme. Moreover, in an attempt to ensure that it was clearly understood which bodies were responsible for elite sport funding and grassroots funding, respectively, it recommended that 'home nation' sports councils concentrate on the latter. The following year these proposals were endorsed by the publication of *Game Plan*. Since then the British government, largely through UK Sport, has adopted a more ruthless approach that has been based on a strategy of stringent accountability by those NGBs in receipt of government funding. These NGBs are required to set quite specific targets related to world rankings and the number of medals they aim to win. As Green (2007a: 938) argues, 'any resistance to the drive for Olympic medals is somewhat [futile] as NGBs become ever more dependent on government resources, which are linked inextricably to Olympic medal targets'. The government stipulated four key areas: 'medal potential; evidence of a performance system able to produce a high number of talented athletes; track record; and significance of the sport in the eyes of the public' (UK Sport, 2001: 6). These criteria have, by and large, remained consistently in place since then, although M. Green argues that the last criterion has, to all intents and purposes, been ignored by UK Sport and the British government (M. Green, personal communication, 2009). In pursuit of these goals, 'UK Sport has put together what is termed a "no compromise" strategy in its aim to be placed fourth in the Olympic medals table in 2012 ... which targets resources solely at those athletes capable of delivering medal winning performances' (Green, 2007b: 940). In theory, and this has often happened in practice, sports that do not meet their stated targets have their funding cut or, sometimes, withdrawn completely (National Audit Office [NAO], 2008).

The Cunningham Review proposed that 'there is a need to focus more resources on talent and club development similar to many of our successful international competitors' (DCMS, 2001: 28). Such a view also found expression in *Game Plan* (DCMS/Strategy Unit, 2002: 9); however, concern was also raised about the 'damaging effects of over-specialisation', and the promotion of the Long-Term Athlete Development (LTAD) model was encouraged. LTAD is a periodization model, first developed by Istvan Balyi. It sets out 'a framework for structuring young athletes' development through a number of stages, from the "FUNdamental" through to the "Training to Win" stage' (Green, 2007b: 437). The LTAD model was a central feature of *Game Plan*, despite the fact that it has been criticized for being more participation related, as opposed to being a performance-based model (Earle, 2004), is not based on rigorous scientific examination or testing, and is not particularly 'grounded in the reality of young people's sport socialisation experiences' (MacPhail and Kirk, 2006: 73). In this respect, it could be argued that 'the promotion and indeed legitimation, of the LTAD model is a pertinent example of the ways in which dominant policy ideas and discourses generated at central government level ... become embedded as "common sense" ways of working for sport organisations and practitioners' (Green, 2007b: 437). Notwithstanding the promotion of LTAD, talent identification has become 'a further important element of the recent support for the elite level that closely parallels Australia's "Talent Search" programme' (Green, 2004: 374).

Funding that is made available to the NGBs through the World Class Programme requires that they also have in place a TID strategy, which involves providing pathways to elite levels of performance between sports clubs and schools. There has not quite been the level of focus on TID as there was in the former communist countries, or as there is in Australia. However, since London won the right to host the 2012 Olympics, it is arguably the case that TID has become a more obvious and central feature of the ESD policy in the UK. A number of recent programmes focus quite specifically on identifying potentially talented performers on the basis of their physiological profile and their sporting aptitudes, particularly in time for the 2012 London Olympics. The 'Sporting Giants' campaign was launched in February 2007, and is aimed at getting those people who are of a certain height to consider becoming involved in rowing, handball or volleyball. Having gone through a process of selection, a number of applicants have been identified and are now included in Olympic development programmes. The Talent Transfer scheme currently specifically focuses on gymnasts who, by virtue of their age, are in effect too old to be considered as having medal potential in that sport, who might consider diving, with its related, 'transferable' skills, as a sport for competition in 2012. Similar to Talent Transfer, Pitch2Podium is a scheme aimed at young footballers who were not able to secure a professional football contract to see if they can transfer their sporting ability and assesses their talents in relation to a number of potential sports (including cycling, hockey, athletics, canoeing, bob skeleton and the modern pentathlon). The Girls4Gold scheme is a TID strategy that is also aimed at identifying and developing talented female athletes in a number of prioritized sports (cycling, bob skeleton, canoeing, modern pentathlon, rowing, sailing and windsurfing). Phase One of this programme involves a number of physiological and psychological tests, in order to identify successful candidates for Phase Two. This involves more sports-specific assessment on an intensive Talent Confirmation Training Programme lasting between three and six months (UK Sport, 2008a). This is not unlike the three-stage approach first developed in the Soviet Union and the GDR. The PESSCL strategy (now PESSYP), discussed in Chapter 3, set out to achieve, amongst various other things, 'success in international competition by ensuring talented young sports people have a clear pathway to elite sport and competition whatever their circumstances' (DfES/DCMS, 2003: 1).

Such strategies have been put in place because there is an increasing recognition that, contrary to the traditional concept of sports development in the UK being based on the 'pyramid structure', a wide participation base does not necessarily contribute to greater numbers of elite performers. In 2000, Sport England produced a consultancy document in which various key personnel were asked to comment on the structure and organization of sport in the country following the publication of *A Sporting Future for All*. In it, a 'performance consultant', David Whitaker (cited in Sport England, 2000: 41), noted that 'a broad base does not guarantee excellence, a narrow one does not preclude it ... Numbers are not the answer, pathways are'. Many NGBs have been, until quite recently, run on very traditional lines, so much so that the Labour government has made a process of modernization a key aspect of its sport policy agenda (see Chapter 2). Part of this reform process is that not only should they have talent identification strategies in place, but NGBs must have development strategies, 'part of which involves the construction of "performance pathways" to higher levels of competition especially between school and clubs' (Green, 2007a: 940). The attempt to establish SSCs is a major part of this process, and it was considered necessary 'to incorporate such schools into a planned, co-ordinated and integrated organizational and administrative model of elite sport development' (Green, 2004: 374). A major aspect of the PESSCL strategy is the Gifted and Talented strand, launched in September 2003. The Ofsted (2004) report into gifted and talented young people in several SSCs argued that more needed to be done to identify and work with talented children. To this end, a proposal within the Gifted and Talented strand of the PESSCL strategy is to provide 'a school-based profiling and tracking system' (Ofsted, 2004: 4). The system is run under the auspices of the YST under the banner 'Talent Matters' and the development of on-line resources through the Talent Ladder scheme. Both schemes are voluntary for schools. The websites include suggestions for potential policy implementation (YST, 2008). The Talented Athlete Scholarship Scheme (TASS) is, to all intents and purposes, an extension of this, and provides a range of support services to young sports people attending further and higher educational establishments.

After several years of wrangling over the details, it was eventually decided to establish the United Kingdom Sports Institute (UKSI) and various 'home nation' institutes in 2000. In essence, the UKSI is 'based on the Australian decentralized institute network' (Green, 2004: 374), although the government had initially favoured a centralized system. However, De Bosscher *et al.* (2008: 131) argue that 'sports administrators in the UK learnt from the Australian model and implemented a regional model from the outset rather than the originally planned centralised "flagship" approach'. This rather oversimplifies the processes involved. The discussions that took place in the UK occurred over a period of several years. They were as much about internal politics as about 'learning' from the newly revised decentralized system in place in Australia. If anything, it is illustrative of the ways in which it is common for the British government to look briefly at other policies and development models. It then selects the 'best bits', and expects them to work in a different social context. Nonetheless, since its establishment, the UKSI has provided 'much needed world class facilities and a higher standard of co-ordinated support services than the UK has ever had before' (DCMS, 2006). Today, the UKSI exists as a network of often sport-specific centres of excellence, comprising the four Home Country Sports Institutes (the English Institute for Sport [EIS], for example, was established in 2002), with a central services team based at UK Sport.

Although Baker *et al.* (2003: 4) appear to be stating the obvious when they point out that 'research is starting to show the distinct advantages of having access to an expert coach', little focus was placed on elite-level coaching in the UK until quite recently. Arguably, the roots of this neglect of quality coaching can be traced to the commitment to an amateur ethos and a concept of volunteering that have traditionally been at the heart of sport in England, if not the UK. As we have already briefly noted, this was not uncommon in other countries, but it could be argued with justification that such an embracing of the 'volunteer coach' was especially embedded within British sporting culture (McDonald, 2005). The National Coaching Foundation (NCF) had been established in the UK in 1983 as a sub-committee of the Sports Council. It was formed to establish a comprehensive coach education programme throughout the UK. It is fair to say, then, that concerns had been expressed in numerous circles regarding the lack of direction and education for coaches within numerous sports in the UK prior to this more recent focus on ESD (Green and Houlihan, 2005). Even so the Cunningham Review noted that

> the UK is a long way behind other countries in the licensing and employment of sports coaches. The vast majority of sports coaches are still volunteers despite the increased amount of time and expertise required in the rapidly changing world of sports performance. This is an area which requires a radical new approach – a step change in how we recruit, train, employ and deploy sports coaches.
>
> (DCMS, 2001: 5–6)

Not long after the Cunningham Review was published a specific programme for 'the professionalization of coaching (from "The Coaching Task Force") was launched in 2002' (Bergsgard *et al.*, 2007: 167). The establishment of various 'Performance Director' posts within NGBs in the UK has created 'clearly identified, limited and specialist responsibilities' (Green and Houlihan, 2005: 180), and the performance directors, amongst several other duties, were charged with developing more professional approaches to coaching within their sport.

The Cunningham Review also outlined a need to develop sports science and sports medicine and look to develop and nurture young sports scientists emerging from British universities. However, Green and Houlihan (2005: 177) argue that, 'in the case of the UK, the effective utilisation of sports science and medicine is clearly some way off'. However, following the unprecedented successes at the Beijing Olympics of 2008, many people beyond the UK are looking enviously at the advances made in sports science support and ESD provision more generally, largely enabled through the substantial sums of money given to NGBs for this, especially in light of the successful bid to host the 2012 Games. The process of 'modernization' that NGBs in receipt of government funding have been subjected to, it might be argued, has impacted upon the ESD provision and a growing receptiveness to sports science support. It is now routinely provided by many of the more prominent NGBs of Olympic sports in the UK.

In relation to the global flow of such multi-sport, multi-site institute facilities, and the increased organization and administration of coaching and sport science within them, Oakley and Green (2001b: 95) argue that 'it is difficult to replicate exactly what other countries do and, therefore, programmes have to be developed in sympathy with each country's own environment and circumstances'. This is not just the case with the establishment of institutes, but across the board of ESD policy. There are increasing similarities in the way in which the broad objectives and structural arrangements of ESD systems and policy more generally have been adopted in numerous countries around the world. Simultaneously, the 'local' situation, in terms of geographical, demographical, cultural and political constraints, has contributed to an increasing variety in approaches to ESD in terms of the detail of the content. It is to a discussion of the diminishing contrasts and increasing varieties in ESD systems that we now wish to turn.

The global flow of ESD systems: a case of diminishing contrasts and increasing varieties

The spread of ESD systems is part of a long-term process of lengthening interdependency chains known as globalization. As Elias (2001: 163) argues, 'the network has become visibly more dense in the course of the twentieth century'. Elias argued that the civilizing process is part of a broader trend of global diffusion (Elias, 2000). In the course of developing his theory of civilizing processes (first published in 1939) he made reference to the diminishing contrasts between different cultures and growing Western influence long before the current spate of publications concerning globalization. In respect of 'diminishing contrasts', Elias argued that

> the course taken by all these expansions is determined only to a small degree by the plans or desires of those whose patterns of conduct were taken over. The classes supplying the models are even today not simply the free creators or originators of the expansion … We find in the relation of the West [for example] to other parts of the world the beginnings of the reduction of contrasts which is peculiar to every major wave of the civilizing movement.
>
> (Elias, 2000: 384)

The spread of achievement sport around the world, and the increasing social significance of such sporting competition, is a good example of diminishing contrasts in the cultural wares across the globe, as other (perhaps equivalent) activities such as folk forms of sport are disappearing or have disappeared. Several authors go so far as to argue that across the world elite sport policy is becoming more uniform. For example, De Bosscher *et al.* (2008: 13) write: 'In their quest for international success in a globalizing world, the elite sports systems of leading nations have become increasingly homogenous'. There seems to be a widely held perception, then, that a 'formula' exists for the production of elite athletes. The major driving force behind the establishment of ESD systems has been a combination of some or all of the following elements: a perceived desire to demonstrate an internally cohesive nation-state; the forthcoming hosting of major international sports events; and a perception of poor sports performance on the international stage. All of these developments have to be understood in the context of the development of nation-states and this cannot be understood adequately unless one locates it within inter-state rivalries.

Globalization processes are an aspect of greater interdependence. The initial spread of ESD is the unintended consequence of intentional actions. Whilst the development of ESD systems in the Soviet Union and the GDR was intentional, it was not their intention to see these systems replicated, in one form or another, by their major competitors in other parts of the world, much as when American scientists developed the atomic bomb it was not their intention for the Soviet Union to develop its own soon afterwards. Of course, the Americans made strenuous, albeit unsuccessful, efforts to try to ensure that the Soviets did not develop the atomic bomb. Whilst such strenuous efforts might not have been made by the Soviet Union and the GDR to 'protect' their ESD systems, they certainly remained guarded about their precise make-up – a point reinforced with the break-up of the communist bloc, when in the new, united Germany, specific research was carried out by West German sports scientists to discover what, specifically, was involved in the former East German system. The increasingly high levels of global interdependency and the associated competition make it very difficult for any group to monopolize knowledge for any length of time. As part of this inter-state rivalry the social significance of sport has grown. As Oakley and Green (2001a: 89) put it, there has been a widespread 'recognition by politicians of the (symbolic) public value of sporting success'. It is the increasing prioritization given to sport that has found expression in both state-sponsored and state-run ESD systems. The former British Minister for Sport, Tony Banks, argued that 'in a world where sport seems to be replacing war as a measure of national ascendancy, the pressure on governments to promote sporting success is irresistible' (Banks; cited in Theodoraki, 1999: 187). This is obviously something of an exaggeration, and somewhat premature, given the wars in Iraq and Afghanistan that Banks's own government became heavily involved in. Nonetheless, the argument that inter-state rivalry is a significant process in the proliferation of state-funded and state-led ESD systems is the centrepiece of the argument here. These processes have contributed to what some have referred to as a 'global sporting arms race' (De Bosscher *et al.*, 2008; Oakley and Green, 2001a, 2001b). In other words, a global sport figuration has emerged in which various governments, with significant influence from various commercial enterprises, have become increasingly interdependent in the provision of sporting competition. At the same time they are each trying to be more successful than one another at international sports events. As the various nations become increasingly interdependent within the context of elite sport, this has a constraining impact on all nations competing, making them measure their performance in relation to one another. This process is not unlike the global spread of weapons of mass destruction. In this respect, as Elias points out,

> the most powerful state-societies are no less constrained than the smaller, less powerful state-societies which have been drawn into their orbit. Together they form a common figuration – a structural 'clinch'. The balance of power between inter-dependent states is such that each is so dependent on the others that it sees in every opposing state a threat to its own internal distribution of power, independence and even physical existence. The result of the 'clinch' is that each side constantly tries to improve its power potential and strategic chances in any warlike encounter [and, arguably, international sports competitions]. Every increase in the power chances of one side, however slight, will be perceived by the other side as a weakening and a setback in its own position. Within the framework of this figuration it *will* constitute a setback. So countermoves will be set in motion as the weakened side attempts to improve its chances; and these in turn will provoke the first side to make its own countermoves.
>
> (Elias, 1978: 169–70; emphasis in the original)

One can make direct application of this passage to the development of ESD systems. In relation to the global sports figuration, the development of ESD systems within various countries around the world, particularly in light of perceived 'failures' in international competitions and perceived advancements in such systems in other competitor nation-states, has helped increase the interdependencies and global flows of ESD systems. For example, with the collapse of communism in Eastern Europe in the 1990s, several key individuals employed as coaches and sports scientists within the Soviet Union, and more particularly the GDR, were soon being employed within various Western countries. In addition, over the longer term, fluctuations in power differentials will occur. As we have seen, the first countries where ESD systems were clearly articulated and implemented were the former Eastern bloc countries of East Germany and the Soviet Union, and the systems put in place undoubtedly contributed to athletes from these countries achieving significant success, most notably at the Olympics. Since then other nations have enjoyed greater success at international sporting events. Systems first developed in the Soviet Union and the GDR have diffused to other countries, where they have been subsequently modified. It is important to take into account, therefore, a wide range of interrelated processes when examining the emergence of ESD systems around the world. We need to consider the development of such systems not in isolation, but as the outcome of differential power struggles between groups that comprise the dynamic figurations of interdependent and competing nation-states. It is not possible to understand adequately the emergence and development of the AIS or the UKSI, for example, by looking solely at the political and social conditions within Australia and the UK, respectively. Furthermore, a good example of the inter-state rivalry and success of others contributing further to 'countermoves' being made is the ongoing 'reaction' of Australian sports administrators and politicians to Team GB's success at the Beijing 2008 Olympics (Australian Sports Commission [ASC], 2008; M. Green, personal communication, 2009).

Hoberman (1993: 29) argued that 'the only major difference between these two worlds [the capitalist and communist countries of the world] was state-sponsored doping in East Germany and the USSR', although it should be recognized that doping was present in the West as a form of private enterprise. He also recognizes, however, that, amongst other things, the success of the Soviet and GDR elite sports systems cannot be reduced to a simple understanding that they involved a systematic performance enhancing drugs programme. As noted above, following the reunification of Germany in 1990, several West German sports science scholars examined the former East German system, and identified four principle characteristics of the system, apart from the systematic doping, that many had already tried to emulate in one form or another beyond these communist countries anyway (Beamish and Ritchie, 2006; Merkel, 1995). The key characteristics identified were:

> The systematic and scientifically organized selection of boys and girls, in their early childhood, for particular sport activities; immersion of those young athletes in the best possible facilities where a methodical, developmental approach to training and conditioning was followed; the development of extensive networks of support by well-qualified scientists from all areas of research relevant to the enhancement of human physical performance; and the concentration of their efforts into a very restricted range of sports (usually individual sports as well as those with some Germanic tradition).
>
> (Beamish and Ritchie, 2006: 100)

Many of these characteristics were emulated in the ESD systems that emerged in several capitalist countries over the decades following their emergence in the Soviet Union and East Germany in the 1950s and 1960s. As such, it is our intention now to briefly discuss in turn what we perceive to be the main characteristics of these so-called 'homogenous' ESD systems. With this in mind, we will examine the following characteristics associated with ESD:

- the extent to which funding was provided and prioritized;
- the extent to which emphasis was placed on the identification of talent and its subsequent development; and
- the extent to which facilities were provided, including the provision of both sports science support and professional sports coaches.

Diminishing contrasts: prioritization of funding, talent identification and development and the professionalization of support structures and personnel

The sports organizations of nations that have achieved international sporting success, particularly in the context of the Olympic Games, have been the recipients of substantial central government assistance in the form of funding and policy direction. The only exception to this rule is the US. We have already seen how central governments in the Soviet Union and the GDR provided substantial funds to the centralized ESD systems established in these countries. A number of Western countries developed systems that placed a similar emphasis on funding. In this respect, 'the targeting of resources' has been a major 'strategic issue' (Oakley and Green, 2001b: 93). A common feature of the ESD systems discussed here is that the strong political support created by ESD has contributed to sport policy interventions across the elite–mass spectrum that have been framed in such a way that elite success is the 'ultimate' goal that all within these systems work towards (M. Green, 2008). Following the success achieved by the East German system in particular, Beamish and Ritchie (2006: 23) noted that 'government planning and coordination … [became] increasingly significant in shaping the world of high-performance sport'. The other key feature is the targeting of funding for particular sports, and particularly in terms of providing money directly to the athletes themselves. Given the substantial sums of money various governments continue to invest in their respective ESDs, it is perhaps not surprising that 'governments have become more willing to intervene directly in the elite development process requiring substantial changes … as a condition of grant aid' (Green and Houlihan, 2005: 2).

Undoubtedly the perceived success of the three-pronged TID system in the GDR, discussed above, contributed 'to the increased deployment of systematic TI [talent identification] processes worldwide' (Abbott and Collins, 2002: 158). This process was, of course, primarily driven by inter-state rivalry. The adoption of aspects of the East German system was a means to this overarching end. The growing commitment toward the development of ESD involved, among other things, the increasing use of scientific knowledge generated by state-funded, systematically developed research. This was all geared to ensure substantial increases in the frequency and intensity of training regimes. The emphasis on the need to be seriously competitive on the international stage also meant that 'a trend towards initiating serious, systematic training at earlier and earlier ages … [and] increased specialization at younger and younger ages' (Beamish and Ritchie, 2006: 27) became increasingly commonplace. In fact a more 'scientific' approach to identifying talent has become a key characteristic of virtually all national ESD systems. According to Martindale *et al.* (2007: 187), 'first-class TID systems capable of delivering highly able and prepared athletes to the senior level are particularly important against the backdrop of ever-increasing professionalism and standard of world-class performance in the modern era'.

Whilst most sports scientists agree that an effective TID system is essential for sustained success in international sports competitions (Abbott and Collins, 2002), there is less agreement on precisely what this should entail. Most of the ideas behind TID have stemmed from the Soviet Union, although some of the Soviet methods of talent identification involved tests that 'would seem relatively primitive to Western coaches' (Riordan, 1986: 228). Several sports scientists argue that many of the celebrated Western ESD systems for identifying talent also remain fairly rudimentary. A number of academics argue that there is a lack of clarity regarding the theoretical underpinnings of the approaches that typify talent identification strategies. For example, Abbott and Collins (2002: 158) note in their review of the 'typical procedures adopted' within talent identification schemes that, 'although objective and systematic, the theoretical principles that underpin this traditional approach to TI remain unclear'. Talent identification is problematic insofar as simply choosing children on the basis of their height/weight/upper body strength/hand–eye coordination at a young age does not take into account the dramatic changes that occur in adolescence, or those who might be considered as 'late-developers'. In this respect, many academics advise caution when estimating the predictive powers of such physiological factors at a young age (Abbott and Collins, 2002; Bailey and Morley, 2006; Bompa, 1994). Consequently it is argued that 'talent detection and early development processes are complex and lack clear-cut theoretical-based knowledge. Therefore, they are difficult to evaluate' (Falk *et al.*, 2004: 354). As we have seen elsewhere in this book, this shortcoming tends to be typical of sport policy and sports development more generally (see Chapter 1). It is, therefore, unsurprising that, not just the specific talent identification strategies, but ESD systems in general exhibit the same characteristic.

Perhaps because the 'science' behind the identification of talent is complex, there appears to be no consensus within the scientific community regarding how best to go about identifying talent. Clearly, the development of talented athletes requires considerable scientific support. The most obvious way in which this support has been developed is through national centres of excellence, in which facility provision, coaching and scientific support are provided and coordinated. As with the other key characteristics of ESD systems, the development of a specific central institute of elite sport was first established in the Eastern bloc countries.

Green and Houlihan (2005: 175) argue that in many Western nations where ESD systems are in place funding has been initially established for facilities and the athletes themselves, with funding for 'the supporting services of coaching, sports science and medicine [being] generally an afterthought'. They also argue that in the early phases of 'engagement with sports science [the tendency was to] focus on equipment rather than the athlete, primarily because the application of science to equipment and apparel design has greater potential to generate profits than research into nutrition, psychological preparation and training regimes' (Houlihan and Green, 2008: 8). Sports science support has, therefore, become a significant area of commercial investment which, of course, transcends the boundaries of national ESD policy. Nonetheless, following the successes of the GDR athletes, in particular, sport science support has become an increasingly important area of national government funding in other countries. It is a development that has been associated with the development of 'an elite level organisational focus', such as by the AIS and UKSI, that has given some 'direction to sports science research' (Green and Houlihan, 2005: 177). It has also contributed to a more coordinated approach to coaching. The success of the AIS approach to ESD has seen 'multi-sport academies or institute facilities' become 'a common feature within elite sport strategies' (Oakley and Green, 2001b: 83) in many nations competing at the top end of international sports competitions.

Green and Houlihan (2008: 291) argue that 'it is clear that increasing global competition is encouraging a growing number of nations to adopt a more strategic approach to the development of elite athletes in order to differentiate themselves from "rival" countries'. In order to sustain, improve upon or surpass their previous achievements, they are constrained to respond to developments in rival countries and in doing so they are often prone to pursuing similar approaches. As Green and Houlihan (2008: 291) observe, there is 'strong evidence of strategic approaches based increasingly around a homogenous model of elite sport development but with subtle domestic variations'. Thus Elias (2000: 385) argues that as the diminution of 'the contrasts in conduct between the upper and lower groups are reduced with the spread of civilization … the varieties or nuances of civilized conduct are increased'. Consistent with this thesis, while the spread of ESD around the world seems to have resulted in 'diminishing contrasts' in the way in which governments, NGBs and NSOs, and even the athletes themselves, prepare for international sporting competitions, there emerge subtle differences in the approaches pursued. Any examination of globalization processes must also deal with 'local' cultures and knowledgeability (Bloyce, 2008; Bloyce and Murphy, 2008; Houlihan, 2008; Maguire, 1999). That is to say, if we are to understand the global spread of ESD systems it is not sufficient to take account of the similarities that characterize their diffusion; we must also be cognizant of how indigenous populations adapt these systems in light of their own perceived needs, experiences and traditions.

Increasing varieties: the emergence of subtle local nuances in elite sports development

It is important to remember that although reference is often made to the 'Eastern bloc' countries as if they are homogenous, the respective countries exhibited noticeable differences in the approaches taken to ESD. When the Soviet Union and the GDR were developing their ESD systems they were responding to different domestic pressures. For example, as was pointed out above, the ESD system of the Soviet Union was not nearly as sophisticated as that of the GDR. The vast population of the Soviet Union meant that it could rely on elite performers emerging from vast pools of competitors, and so less emphasis was placed on talent identification. The comparatively small population of East Germany and the pre-war German focus on scientific analysis of human performance led the GDR to place a more sophisticated emphasis on TID.

Green and Houlihan (2005) observe that the systems of Australia, Canada and the UK generated a similar axis of tensions. They all experienced an 'apparent incompatibility between the needs of the elite athlete' and 'the needs of the club infrastructure and the grass roots participant' (Green and Houlihan, 2005: 169). Green and Houlihan (2005: 169) also note that this has found expression in a parallel 'tension between an aspiration towards a professionalized rational-bureaucratic model of management and the voluntaristic and more sectional/political model of decision-making found in many sports'. Predictably, the governing bodies of sport in many Western countries have struggled to appease all the stakeholders in sports development. This has resulted in considerable tensions, and has also placed NGBs in the difficult position of trying to square the circle. In the totalitarian states of the former communist bloc countries such tension was never expressed, at least not in a sustained and public fashion. As Green (2007a: 922) points out, 'scant regard [was given] by the governing regimes in these Eastern bloc countries and others ... to balanc[ing] support for elite sport success with sporting opportunities and provision for the generality of the population'. One major difference between these ESD systems and those in the West is that in the latter there has been greater pressure for public accountability in terms of policy, expenditure and general well-being. However, the extent to which grassroots opinion has made itself felt has varied from country to country. In some instances this pressure has helped to bring about modifications in sport policy and even in the way in which ESD systems have been implemented. In doing so it has helped to bring about variations that mediate and mitigate the push towards uniformity. As Green has noted,

> on one level, Houlihan may be correct that the former Eastern bloc model of elite sport development bears several similarities to elite sport systems in Australia, Canada and, indeed, now the UK. However, on another level, a deeper analysis

reveals some stark discontinuities ... Australian talent identification systems bear little resemblance to what many have claimed about the Soviet Union and GDR ... [In Australia] there remains a strong reliance on club-based development and social systems of recruitment, rather than formal talent identification programmes.

(Green, 2007b: 433)

One might argue that such 'club-based development' also remains a feature of UK sports provision. Hence, as De Bosscher *et al.* (2008) recognize, there have actually been quite different approaches taken to TID in a range of countries. Of course, even in cases where an attempt was made to replicate the system of another country, its implementation would be bound to give rise to differences. Contrasts are likely to have arisen, for example, out of a failure to adequately comprehend the 'model' in place. Another might stem from a rigidity of thought. Even though it is not uncommon to have talent identification as part of the wider ESD system, in numerous countries national strategies ensure that approaches take idiosyncratic forms. For example, in the GDR athletes were subjected to intense measurement and testing protocols that were not regarded as ethical in many democratic countries, not to mention the drug regimes to which athletes were subjected, knowingly or otherwise. In Australia the system is more sophisticated, but still involves some considerable analysis and measurement of individuals. In the UK, the system employed to identify talent is more rudimentary and, to a certain extent, 'voluntary'. Collins (2008) makes a similar point with regard to the attempt to professionalize coaching in the UK. He argues that while higher-level coaching has received some funding, 'much training is left for individuals to fund themselves' (Collins, 2008: 75).

While Australia is still wrestling with problems emanating from friction between the regional provision of mass sport and the federal support for elite sport, this falls short of the tensions generated in this regard by the efforts to establish ESD systems in the UK (Green and Oakley, 2001). Green and Oakley (2001: 255) argue that developing effective ESD systems 'becomes a real challenge when faced with the political and sporting autonomy of the UK with four international sporting nations and one Olympic team. This mosaic of different interests is likely to hinder the development of a truly Olympic-focused national elite sport system'. For example, the UKSI is now an establishment that relies essentially on the home nation institutes. The EIS, for instance, 'is a wholly owned subsidiary of UK Sport, having been funded by Sport England until March 2006 ... Each of the sports councils for Northern Ireland, Scotland and Wales also fund similar institutes to service athletes throughout the rest of the UK' (NAO, 2008: 14). The Great Britain cycling team is but one example of this geographical diversity, being based in Manchester and working on the whole with the EIS quite specifically.

As we saw in Chapter 2, the Conservative governments of the 1990s tried to distinguish quite specifically between what they regarded as the appropriate focus for central government, namely elite sport, and mass sports participation, which they held to fall within the brief of local authorities. Under the Labour governments of the last decade or so ESD has remained a very live concern, especially in light of the London Olympics of 2012. At the same time, grassroots participation has been placed firmly back on the agenda. This, together with the traditional reliance on volunteer coaches and administrators, contributed to the distinctive form taken by elite sport policy in the UK.

Oakley and Green (2001b) highlight the minimal involvement of the US federal government compared with the higher levels of government involvement in other countries. They point out that 'it is the traditions and patterns of government involvement in sport that [have in large measure] shape[d] the sports system in each country' (Oakley and Green, 2001b: 101). While the establishment of ESD systems in the Eastern bloc countries was largely an outgrowth of rivalries with the US, in the US itself the federal government's involvement in elite sport has been negligible. As Sparvero *et al.* (2008: 247) observe, 'the federal government's refusal to become a sport policymaker is consistent with the ideological foundations of American governance. The traditional American political philosophy is that the powers and intervention of government must be limited in order for individual liberties to be protected'. The dominance of commercial team sports, coupled with the comparative lack of federal or even state funding, means that the facilities and associated support for many Olympic sports in the US are relatively scarce. This severely reduces the ability of American teams to make a sustained impact at the Olympics across a range of events. Thus again we see how the broader traditions of a country can mediate the prevailing approach to sport and, in the process, extend still further the range of global variation. As noted earlier, many of the characteristics of ESD systems have been a longstanding feature in the US in the form of centres of excellence and sports science support, but these have emerged under the auspices of a commercially funded USOC and the prominence of the NCAA collegiate sports system. They are not state-funded or state-supported systems. In this respect, it is difficult not to agree with the view of Sparvero *et al.* (2008: 251) that 'there is no "system" for elite sport development' in the US.

This chapter has afforded insufficient space to present a more comprehensive account of the myriad ways in which governmental and sporting cultures have shaped their ESD systems. A further layer of complexity should be added to this already complex mix, namely, the influence that multinational companies have had upon the trajectory of ESD policies. For example, in the case of commercially advanced sports like soccer, basketball and baseball there has been considerable difficulty in establishing government-led ESD systems because in many countries professional clubs have greater control over the development of players than the national federations. They are also not restricted nearly as much by TID based on national boundaries. For example, much has been written about the inability of domestic NGBs of soccer in African countries to establish and control ESD systems for soccer without interference from wealthy European clubs (Darby *et al.*, 2007). Green and Houlihan (2005) have raised another issue that relates to the commercial influences with which some national federations of athletics have to contend. Some individual athletes have refused to compete in their own national trials, preferring to secure the lucrative individual sponsorships on offer by competing at other global events. These contingencies make it difficult to establish criteria for funding athletes and for ensuring that they conform to certain training and competition regimes. This has led Slack (1998: 3) to argue that athletes 'no longer represent their club, their country, or themselves, they represent the corporations who provide the money for their sport'. This is something of an oversimplification because many athletes represent themselves, their clubs and their countries, in the course of which tensions and conflicting loyalties are bound to arise.

The Eliasian concepts of diminishing contrasts and increasing varieties also sensitize us to the need to address the differential popularity of different sports in different countries. This has meant that specific ESD systems have had to adjust to and accommodate certain sports. Baker *et al.* (2003: 6) recognize that 'the importance that a country or society places on a particular sport can have a dramatic influence on any success achieved' and on the level of funding provided by the government. The fact that British governments were relatively slow off the mark in developing ESD systems can be strongly related to Britain's gentlemanly amateur traditions. This may also go some way towards explaining the apparent reluctance of British governments, at least publicly, to target the 'soft' medal sports that have been a focus in other countries. Although, as indicated above, in reality the 'no compromise' approach taken by UK Sport has meant that, despite it outlining this as a priority (DCMS/Strategy Unit, 2002), the reality, as was evident in the successes at the 2008 Beijing Games, is quite different. There are clear signs that in the wake of the 2012 Games being awarded to London in 2005 (see Chapter 7) ESD policy in the UK is embracing a broader focus on identifying talent in so-called 'minor' sports, where medals may not be as keenly contested. This is a good example of the way in which the hosting of a mega-event is a significant 'focusing event' (Chalip, 1995) on the strategies and policies adopted for ESD, an issue that will be discussed in greater detail in Chapter 7.

Summary

In concluding this chapter, it is worth reflecting upon Green and Oakley's (2001: 250) question, in relation to the global flow of ESD systems, namely 'whether we are witnessing a trend towards uniformity in elite sport development systems – diminishing contrasts – or whether there is room for diversity – increasing varieties – within such systems'. However, this formulation falsely dichotomizes the processes involved. Elias argued that these figurations involve a blend of diminishing contrasts and increasing varieties. Therefore, we would argue that over the past fifty or so years the emergence of ESD systems has been characterized by processes of diminishing contrasts *and* increasing varieties. While more and more countries are looking to develop ever more sophisticated ESD systems, the chances of some of them gaining a competitive edge may be enhanced by a conscious appreciation of the need to take account of the distinctive features of their sporting environment. Of course, such is the nature of global sport that no sooner will one country develop an approach that proves successful than other countries will seek to emulate it. But in the process they are bound to modify it.

In our view, the way in which ESD systems have undergone global diffusion needs to be understood in the context of deeply rooted dynamic human figurations. This framework helps to sensitize us not only to the increasing uniformity that characterizes processes of globalization, but also to the inevitable variations that arise. Such a perspective also sensitizes us to limitations of viewing the present structure and organization of elite sport in the world as somehow the consequence of processes of Westernization or even Americanization. As Maguire (1999: 93) circumspectly observes, 'it is possible ... to overstate the extent to which the West has triumphed in terms of global sport structures, organizations, ideologies and performances'.

Revision questions

1 Examine the way in which elite sports development policy is implemented in a national governing body of your choice.
2 Compare and contrast elite sports development systems in the UK and the US.
3 Examine the impact that elite sports development policy has had on 'Sport For All' in a country of your choice.

Key readings

De Bosscher, V., Bingham, J. Shibli, S., van Bottenburg, M. and De Knop, P. (2008) *The Global Sporting Arms Race: An International Comparative Study on Sports Policy Factors Leading to International Sporting Success*, Oxford: Meyer and Meyer.

Green, M. and Houlihan, B. (2005) *Elite Sport Development: Policy Learning and Political Priorities*, London: Routledge.

Houlihan, B. and Green, M. (eds) (2008) *Comparative Elite Sport Development: Systems, Structures and Public Policy*, Oxford: Butterworth-Heinemann.

Recommended websites

Australian Institute of Sport: www.ausport.gov.au/ais
English Institute of Sport: www.eis2win.co.uk/pages/
UK Sport: www.uksport.gov.uk/

7 The politics and policy of mega-events
A case study of London 2012

Objectives

This chapter will:

- discuss how sports mega-events impact upon existing sport policy;
- examine various legacies from recent Olympic Games; and
- examine the bid and build-up to the London 2012 Olympic Games.

Introduction

There is a small, but growing, literature on so-called sporting 'mega-events', such as the Olympic Games, and their impact on the political, economic and cultural landscape of the hosting country and city. Much of this existing literature has examined the economic impact of such events. Rather less has been written, however, about the policy processes associated with hosting mega-events and the impact they have on broader aspects of sport policy and other associated legacies alleged to emerge from hosting them. Roche (2000: 1) defines mega-events as 'large-scale cultural (including commercial and sporting) events which have a dramatic character, mass popular appeal and international significance. They are typically organised by variable combinations of national governmental and international non-governmental organisations'. The Olympic Games have, arguably, become the biggest global event known to humankind and it is hardly surprising that, given their huge global appeal, politicians are often very keen to host them in their country. In this respect, they 'have been important points of reference for processes of change' (Roche, 2000: 7) and recently governments have made significant policy changes and promises having secured the right to host the Olympics. Whilst, for brevity's sake, we will discuss the London 2012 bid, and the organizations behind it, from the point of view of a 'single' bidding party, it is important to note that bidding cities comprise complex networks of interdependent groups that are constituted by some who are advocates of the Games, some who are prepared to go along with the proposals of the bid, others who are against the proposed reforms and others who might be completely against hosting the Games in 'their' city.

In this chapter we will seek to examine the reasons why cities and governments bid for mega-events. The optimism that goes, sometimes wildly so, with the apparent benefits of staging such events is of particular interest to us here because it is frequently the apparent, additional benefits of hosting an event such as the Olympics that tend to be among the major justifications provided by bidding cities and/or governments for doing so. We will then examine the benefits that are often widely extolled for the impact of mega-events by examining the various 'legacies' said to have been provided by previous Olympic Games. The chapter will draw on a case study of the successful London bid to host the 2012 Summer Olympics in order to analyze some of the policy issues and processes associated with the bid, in particular the ways and extent to which the bid, and the subsequent build-up to hosting the Games, has come to impact on sport policy in the UK. We reflect upon the IOC's response to criticisms that the number of events in which athletes compete at the Summer Games, in particular, have meant that the Games have become too large – a process widely referred to as 'gigantism' – and that there is a need to restrict the number of sports that are part of the Games. We conclude by examining the fact that at the same time that the IOC is attempting to manage the size of the Games as a sporting contest it is complicit in a process whereby bidding cities, at least in countries with democratically elected politicians, are increasingly constrained to promise more and more long-lasting benefits in order to host the Games, a process which has contributed to what one might refer to as 'legacy gigantism'. Let us first examine the reasons why so many politicians are keen to pursue the Games.

In pursuit of the Olympic Games

Bidding to host the Summer Olympic Games has not, generally, been as fiercely competitive as the last four or five bid processes have been. After the infamous Montreal Games of 1976, which were so poorly managed that the people of Montreal were still paying for them through their taxes thirty years later, only one city, Los Angeles, bid to host the 1984 Games (Whitson and Horne, 2006). The Los Angeles 1984 bid helped change the process to make it more appealing to major international cities to host the Games. The perceived commercial success of the Los Angeles Games coincided with Juan Antonio Samaranch's presidency of the IOC, which was the start of a very prosperous era for the Olympics. Since 1984, bidding has become so intense, and investment in the Games so expensive, that it is difficult to generate sufficient income for hosting the Games from commercial sources alone. Indeed, the 1996 Atlanta Games are the only Games since 1984 to have been almost entirely funded by commercial sources. This may be explained, in part, by the reluctance of the federal or even state governments to be involved in such projects, which has been a consistent theme over the years (Sparvero *et al.* 2008).

The public funding for the bid and subsequent hosting of the Games by the successful city is often justified on the basis of the numerous associated benefits said to accrue from doing so. In this regard, those hoping to win the right to host the Games expect, amongst other things, that doing so will result in them being able to develop new and existing physical infrastructure within and around the host city, and to regenerate urban areas through fast-tracking developments in transportation and buildings (Chalkley and Essex, 1999; Digby, 2008; Essex and Chalkley, 2004; Evans, 2007; Gold and Gold, 2007a; Malfas *et al.*, 2004; Preuss, 2004; 2008). As Evans (2007: 305) has noted, the Olympic Games provide those attempting to develop urban areas with 'sources of finance and political opportunities for fast-tracking projects not feasible under "normal" conditions'. The immoveable deadline of hosting the Games themselves means that the planning process is often accelerated, even though at some point in the past applications for planning approval may have proved to be difficult. This has become particularly important, for among many of the other numerous additional claimed benefits of hosting the Games has been the need to boost the 'image' of a city to attract tourists and international business clients – before, during and after the Games (Gold and Gold, 2007a; Preuss, 2004; 2008; Wang and Theodoraki, 2007). In this respect, it is clear that 'the Olympic Games have emerged as an important tool of urban and regional renewal through their ability to justify redevelopment and enhancement' (Wang and Theodoraki, 2007: 125) of the host city and the immediate surrounding locations in which they take place.

The concerns that came to be expressed over the need to provide the host city with a variety of 'legacies' from hosting the Games can be traced back to the mid-1950s (Gold and Gold, 2007a). Despite this, legacy concerns were really crystallized after the perceived success of the Barcelona Games in 1992, which were widely heralded with having a regenerative impact on the city (Coaffee, 2007; Gold and Gold, 2007a; Monclús, 2007). Indeed, as Coaffee (2007: 155) argues, in part 'the "Barcelona Model" for regenerating the urban environment through staging the Olympics now provides the blueprint for other cities bidding for Summer Games'. The Olympic Games were used for 'public policy objectives' (Preuss, 2008: 420), as a catalyst to stimulate the local economy by attempting to rival Madrid as a centre for the development of international investment and tourism. In this regard, the Games were 'used to justify the substantial public investment during the Olympiad and to create within the city and the province of Catalonia the desired impetus to make good the long-term underinvestment in leisure, culture, sport and transportation during previous decades' (Preuss, 2008: 420). As noted above, with the exception of the Atlanta Games, held on the centenary of the first modern Games, in 1996, and heavily funded by private, commercially generated sources, all of the Games since Barcelona 1992 have justified large sums of public expenditure in pursuit of stimulating the local and even national economy. After the Atlanta Games had been widely criticized for being over-commercialized the IOC welcomed the blend of public – from the federal government and New South Wales state funds – and private enterprise investment that was the hallmark of funding for the Sydney Games (Preuss, 2004). Indeed, so successful was this perceived model of funding that it is a model that came to be used by the bidding committees for the following three Games: Athens 2004, Beijing 2008 and London 2012. Indeed, in relation to these latter three bids, 'the overwhelming majority of the costs have been financed by the public purse, [and] this also appears to reflect the growing importance governments have attached to the notion of Olympic legacy' (Kasimati and Dawson, 2009: 140). This is, of course, an expression of the growing cultural and economic significance of sport, with the Games seen as the epitome of elite-level sport.

Between 1980 and 2000 the Olympic Games grew significantly in terms of the number of sports and events that were included within the Olympic programme, a process that has been widely referred to as the 'gigantism' of the Games (Essex and Chalkley, 2004; Preuss, 2004). This expansion of the Games has come to substantially increase the burden on host cities, by increasing numbers of athletes, their respective aides and the huge number of media personnel in attendance at the Games, whose needs must all be catered for. One unintended consequence of this growth of the Games has meant that only 'larger urban centres in the developed world' can realistically hope to bid for the Games, because 'these places have both the financial capacities to stage the event and established tourism industries that can be enhanced' (Essex and Chalkley, 2004: 201). In addition, it is no coincidence that as the logistics of hosting the Games entails huge sums of public expenditure there are growing pressures on democratically elected governments to be seen to demonstrate that hosting the Games should yield significant exogenous developments.

Perhaps unsurprisingly, it is now increasingly the case that 'in order to justify the large public subsidies required to host such an event, advocates have tended to argue that there are significant economic benefits both directly and indirectly attributable to hosting these events' (Atkinson *et al.*, 2008: 420). In other words, the increasingly expensive nature of the Games has had the effect of constraining those cities and governments bidding to host them to make wider and wider claims, and inflated unrealistic promises, about the benefits that may be accrued from doing so. In this regard, the concept of 'legacy' has increasingly 'become an essential part of the IOC and the Organizing Committee of the Olympic Games (OCOG) vocabulary' (Girginov and Hills, 2008: 2092). Indeed, one of the identified 'roles' of the IOC now enshrined in the Olympic Charter is 'to promote a positive legacy from the Olympic Games to the host cities and host countries' (IOC, 2007: 15). The various alleged legacies for host cities and countries are worth considering in more detail.

The exogenous legacies of the Games

Prominent amongst the desired legacies for the bidding committees is that by hosting the Games a positive economic legacy will be generated. In particular, it is frequently claimed that hosting the Games will attract significant investment from international commercial enterprise as well as significant income from large numbers of international tourists (Baade and Matheson, 2002; Cashman, 2006; Preuss, 2004, Roche, 2000). As we noted earlier, far from stimulating the local economy the costs of the Montreal Games were eventually assumed by the Montreal taxpayer for over a generation – although the world economic situation at the time was not exactly conducive to hosting an event of this magnitude, since the Games 'took place against a backdrop of severe world recession and inflation that profoundly affected costings' (Gold and Gold, 2007b: 36). However, the claimed economic success of the Los Angeles Games just eight years later has often been cited by bidding city organizations ever since as a reason for attempting to win the right to host the Games (Preuss, 2004). Kasimati (2003), amongst others, has suggested that there are a number of long-term economic benefits to a city hosting the Summer Olympics. These include, as we suggested above, newly constructed sporting facilities and related infrastructure, such as the athletes' village, hotel and transport development. The hoped-for urban revival is said to bring with it investment and an enhanced international reputation, which in turn may generate increased tourism, additional employment opportunities and increased inward investment (Kasimati, 2003).

Despite the claimed economic benefits of hosting the Olympic Games, many economists 'have consistently found no evidence of positive economic impacts from mega-sporting events' (Owen, 2008: 3), and, as Gratton *et al.* (2006: 43) have argued, 'the economic benefit of the Games ... is often overestimated in both publications and economic analyses produced by or for the OCOG'. Indeed, even where some studies have provided some evidence of the positive economic impact of the Olympics, 'what is clear is that the estimated net economic impact of the Olympic Games is relatively small in terms of the host city's annual GDP' (Vigor *et al.*, 2004: 18). Thus, although enhancing the local economy is widely seen by bidding parties as a key justification for hosting the Games, it is very difficult to establish the extent to which previous Games can, indeed, be regarded as having had a measurable and valid positive impact on the local economy (Atkinson *et al.*, 2008; Crookston, 2004; Gold and Gold, 2008; Gratton *et al.*, 2005; 2006; Owen, 2008; Preuss, 2004; Vigor *et al.*, 2004). But what about the impact that the Games have on generating a strong tourist economy?

As Preuss (2004: 46) has noted, 'the Olympics especially are seen as catalysts for driving tourism, but not just for the time of the Olympics itself … [but] for attracting future tourists long after the event has been staged'. However, evidence in support of the extent to which hosting the Olympic Games can have a positive impact on increasing tourism is sketchy at best, for, as Preuss (2004: 59) himself points out, 'there is a risk of over-estimating the numbers for post-Olympic tourism'. In a not dissimilar way, Cashman (2006: 107) has argued in relation to the Sydney Games in 2000 that there had been 'excessive optimism' regarding the potential benefits that the Games would bring to tourism, and many involved had been guilty of 'overstating the importance of Olympic tourism' (Cashman, 2006: 107). In addition, evidence from various Games suggests that even where tourism may have matched anticipated levels 'the flow of new tourists tends to dry up fast' (Vigor *et al.*, 2004: 3) once the Games have ended. Furthermore, as we will examine in our case study of London 2012, it can properly be said that many of the bigger cities that are, in the main, the cities most likely to host the Games in the first place already enjoy sizeable international tourist economies and the Games may well put off some tourists (Gratton *et al.*, 2006). Despite some of these concerns raised by several academics about the presumed positive impact of hosting the Games on the local economy, many of these concerns relate to specific operational costs related to hosting the Games. It is arguably through the capital infrastructure investments that most potential gains could be made, where investment is more long-term, relating to the sporting venues, the new and upgraded transport and housing infrastructure. It is not altogether surprising, therefore, that many of the main legacy outcomes that are frequently cited in support of hosting the Games are related to the broader infrastructural, social, sporting and ecological benefits (Gratton *et al.*, 2006; Hall, 2006; Preuss, 2004; Whitson and Horne, 2006). Let us briefly examine some of the claims that are made in relation to the regeneration benefits that cities may derive from holding the Games.

The Olympics and urban regeneration

An increasingly prominent dimension of the motivations for bidding committees to host mega-events has been the apparent associated regeneration of the host city or cities, especially in terms of the built environment, housing development and employment in the local regions (Raco, 2004). This strategy has been used in mega-events beyond the Olympics. For example, some grounds built and redeveloped for the Soccer World Cup held in Germany were developed on so-called 'brownfield' sites (Digby, 2008). Brownfield sites are on the whole previously used sites that now lie abandoned or, sometimes, underused industrial sites, as opposed to 'greenfield' sites, which would require uprooting living flora. Furthermore, the main stadia that were developed for the Manchester 2002 (Digby, 2008; Gratton *et al.* 2005) and Melbourne 2006 (Digby, 2008) Commonwealth Games were both developed on 'brownfield' sites as part of a broader regeneration strategy. The North West Development Agency (NWDA) (2004) heralded the regenerative effects of the Manchester Commonwealth Games. However, although the Manchester region undoubtedly benefited from substantial investment as a direct result of the Games, and some areas of east Manchester, where the main stadia and other sports complexes were built, did, in fact, benefit from some initial regeneration, it is not yet possible – indeed, it is almost impossible – to determine the likelihood of longer-term impacts on the region (Gratton *et al.*, 2005). Roche (2000: 140) has also noted that the 'long-term impacts are always difficult to establish given the relative infrequency of and lack of funding for, systematic longitudinal studies' of the legacy benefits that are believed to accrue from hosting mega-events. The further away one moves from an event the more difficult it becomes to establish that any changes that have occurred are a direct result of hosting a mega-event. Indeed, even though there were measurable short-term benefits in terms of the construction industry in the build-up to the Montreal Games, and increased tourism during the Games, the post-Games 'legacy', as is well documented, never really materialized (Whitson and Horne, 2006). On the contrary, as we noted above, the citizens of Montreal were left with a 'debt' that was only paid off in 2006.

Despite the difficulty faced when trying to establish evidence for a regenerative effect, the Munich Games of 1972, although synonymous with the terrorist attack and subsequent murder of several Israeli Olympic team members, have been well regarded by some for having 'become a showcase of regeneration' (Raco, 2004: 41). Furthermore, numerous Games have sparked massive investment in transport infrastructure improvements. As Roche (2000: 139) points out, the new 'bullet train' was 'inaugurated in the Tokyo Games in 1964; new metro systems introduced or extended for the Games of Rome, Tokyo, Montreal, Seoul, Barcelona and Athens (2004); major new urban road systems for Barcelona; and the creation of new international airports for the Barcelona and Athens Games'. However, as we discussed earlier, in many respects it was the perceived success of the so-called regeneration of Barcelona in 1992 that heralded a new era of utilizing the Olympics as a tool for the promotion of urban development. It was suggested, for example, that 'massive new infrastructural investments were made in the city which were connected with the Olympics. These included a new waterfront and residential area (which continues to be called "the Olympic village"), a new international airport' (Roche, 2000: 143), as well as the construction of six new sports stadia and the upgrading of the main Olympic stadium.

In relation to the 'legacy' of such developments that accompanied the hosting of the Barcelona Games, Raco (2004: 41) argued that the 'Olympic Village development has been a commercial success story', although a related development has seen house prices and rental inflation well above the national average in Spain. In this regard, it was pointed out in a recent report by the London East Research Institute, commissioned for and published by the Greater London Authority (GLA), that the local populations in and around the Olympic Village area of Barcelona 'have not [had] significantly improved ... access to housing and jobs' (GLA, 2007a: 9). In relation to this, many have questioned, more generally, the idea that Barcelona can be considered a regeneration success story (GLA, 2007a; Raco, 2004; Roche, 2000). Similar reservations might be expressed about the alleged regenerative effects of Sydney and Athens. In Sydney, for example, 'rates of evictions and homelessness increased markedly in the neighbourhoods alongside the Olympic development' and, according to Raco (2004: 37), it could be argued from this and other case studies that 'although development takes place in such cities it does not always lead to the development of its poorer urban neighbourhoods and communities. In fact, it can make things worse by creating blight, congestion and community displacement'. Indeed, in relation to the regeneration of the local economy, through employment opportunities, during and after the Games in Barcelona, Atlanta, Sydney and Athens, the evidence is also far from clear cut, and, if anything, suggests that the 'long-term unemployed and "workless" communities were largely unaffected by the staging of the Games in each of the four previous host cities' (GLA, 2007a: 9). For all the stated benefits associated with the regeneration that hosting the Olympics will bring, 'there is a need for research to concentrate on the longer-term urban regeneration benefits that sport has the potential to deliver' (Gratton *et al.*, 2005: 998). It is, however, very difficult to establish a direct cause and effect relationship between investment in the infrastructure and tangible benefits associated with that investment. In this regard, Essex and Chalkley (2004: 201) have noted that 'the precise effectiveness of this form [hosting the Olympics] of urban renewal policy is contested and difficult to measure', especially because not only is it impossible to isolate the impact of hosting the Games from other events or programmes that may be running simultaneously, but it is also especially difficult for policy-makers to control the outcomes of wider social processes that can both enable and constrain, to a greater or lesser degree, their ability to achieve the desired objectives. As we explain in more detail below, of particular significance at the moment is, of course, the wider global economic downturn that is being experienced in many countries and that appears to be strongly associated with the escalating costs of hosting the London 2012 Games. At the time when the London bidding committee was preparing the Candidate File to host the 2012 Games, it was clearly very difficult to not only anticipate the emergence of the global economic downturn, but also to foresee the extent to which this may come to impact the economic implications of hosting the Games. As we noted in Chapter 1, this reminds us of a point of fundamental importance: that there are many processes – especially those that result from the interweaving of the more or less goal-directed actions of large numbers of people on a global scale, as is the case here – that are beyond the direct control of policy-makers and that come to limit the extent to which they can achieve their formally stated goals.

The Olympics and sustainability

More recently, the idea that the Olympics should have a sustainable, 'green' legacy has come increasingly to dominate aspects of the ideological agenda for the IOC and the bidding committees for cities hoping to host the Games. The Sydney bid had focused on the growing international sensitivity toward environmental concerns, and, as Cashman (2006: 191) argues, 'the idea of the Green Games was an important selling point of the Sydney 2000 Olympic bid because it coincided with a move by the IOC to recognise the environment as a core principle of Olympism in the 1990s'. The growing sensitivity concerning the environmental impact of hosting the Games helps explain the series of critical headlines (at least in the Western press as far as Beijing was concerned) that accompanied the Athens and Beijing Games. In this regard, in Athens 'environmentalists ... were particularly critical that the rules laid down in the tender for the Olympic Village were largely ignored when reducing construction costs became the priority' (Gold, 2007: 279), and much was made of the prevalence of smog in Beijing. Sustainable living had become a significant feature for the IOC and this, of course, cannot be divorced from the increasing concern over the environment that has been a feature of the politics of most industrialized nations around the world in the twenty-first century.

The Sydney bid included several prominent references to sustainable living, and the regeneration of parts of Sydney for the hosting of the Games required a significant environmental transformation as part of the alleged regeneration that would result from hosting the Games. Much of the existing site was polluted with toxic waste and the Olympic Park and stadium were built on disused chemical sites, landfill sites and an armaments dumping ground. The ecological regeneration of the area was heralded as a success by many, and the Sydney Organizing Committee of the Olympic Games (SOCOG) invited Greenpeace to provide a 'green score' for the Games. However, despite the rhetoric behind the view that the environment was a strong feature of the successful Olympic bid, in the build-up to the Games there was something of a 'retreat' from the tag of the Green Games. Cashman (2006: 193) argues that, in part, this was because 'SOCOG realised that the idea of the Green Games was open-ended, leading to unrealistic green expectations'. This is another example of making inflated promises that appeal to the prevailing ideological agenda at the time in order to increase the chances of winning the right to host the Games. Indeed, 'in retrospect, those who promoted such an idealistic environmental platform in 1993 [when the bid was won] may have been naïve to talk up the environment, thereby raising expectations about the delivery of such a wide range of environmental promises' (Cashman, 2006: 195). Cashman (2006: 213) goes on to argue that 'the Green Games were imperfectly realised in Sydney and attracted much criticism', especially as Greenpeace, contrary to prevailing expectations, actually scored the whole operation relating to the Games as 5 out of 10 for the 'sustainable principles' employed. However, it is undoubtedly the case that the Sydney Games did raise the issue of sustainable living and energy sources, and kept it on the agenda, ensuring that it was a topic of considerable discussion amongst Australians, and especially those who may not have been interested, at least publicly, in the environment beforehand (Cashman, 2006). It might be argued, therefore, that this aspect of the exogenous 'legacy' that was seen as a potentially desirable impact of the Games is, at best, difficult to measure, and at worst hosting the Olympic Games may actually have the opposite impact of what was intended. More specifically, it may be suggested that hosting the Games may potentially do more harm than good to the environment, with the global travelling encouraged by hosting the Games and the sheer industrial work required in order to develop the infrastructure to host them. Certainly, once again, any perceived 'positive' legacy impact on the environment is extremely difficult to measure. It is one of the many 'known unknowns' of the Games, as Horne (2007: 85) refers to the rather intangible legacy impacts associated with such mega-events. What, then, of the direct 'sporting legacy' of the Olympics? After all, for all that the Games are a celebration of culture and have recently become synonymous with generating a variety of exogenous developments, they are recognized and celebrated by many across the world, first and foremost, as a global sporting event. What impact do the Olympics have, then, on the sporting landscape of the host city and country?

A lasting sporting legacy

There is little doubt that the sporting infrastructure of a host city is improved in the aftermath of hosting the Olympics. On occasions this will entail upgrading existing facilities (like the Olympic stadium at Barcelona) but it also often involves the development of substantial new sporting facilities, such as those that were developed as a consequence of hosting the Games in Sydney, Athens and Beijing. In addition, it is frequently expected that several related sporting impacts will be generated from hosting the Games. A more tangible 'benefit' is that frequently host nations perform much better in terms of medal acquisition at 'their' Games. Of course, it would be unrealistic to suggest that this, alone, is a reason for bidding to host the Games. Some have argued that there is a 'trickle-down effect', whereby the intensity of the build-up and hosting of the Games will have a necessary and positive impact on sports participation rates within the host city and country at large (GLA, 2007a; Murphy and Bauman, 2007). Once again, however, it is hard to identify the tangible benefits for a positive 'sporting legacy'. In fact, there has been little research into the impact that the hosting of such mega-events has on mass sport participation rates (Hamlyn and Hudson, 2005; Wang and Theodoraki, 2007), and what evidence does exist tends to be anecdotal and inconclusive (GLA, 2007a). Research into the impact that the Sydney Games had on mass participation rates, for example, suggested that if there was any impact at all it was extremely short lived and fleeting (Cashman, 2006; GLA, 2007a; Murphy and Bauman, 2007). In addition, although the NWDA (2004) argues that the Manchester Commonwealth Games in 2002 had a positive impact on participation levels, most academics agree that they had no measurable impact (Coalter, 2004; Murphy and Bauman, 2007). Once again, it is difficult to draw any firm conclusions regarding the legacy impact of increasing sports participation because of the difficulty of establishing a simple cause and effect impact of hosting the Games on participation (Coalter, 2004; 2007b). What, then, of the potential impact of the new sporting infrastructure?

There have been widely reported problems in terms of the extent to which many of the facilities that are built for the purpose of the Olympic Games remain underused in the post-Games era. This was certainly the case after both the Sydney and Athens Games (Gold and Gold, 2007a). In relation to Sydney the main Olympic stadia 'have experienced major revenue shortfalls which threaten their viability' (Searle, 2002: 845) and the Sydney Olympic Park has been described by some as a 'white elephant' (Cashman, 2006: 153). The Sydney Games were also criticized in this regard because new, permanent facilities were built, despite the additional cost that they involved. Such has been the concern over the lack of participation and facility use that it is now 'current IOC policy that if there is no identified post-Games community use for sports facilities temporary facilities are preferable' (Cashman, 2006: 181). However, since 2003 more events have been held within the stadium, including Australian Rules Football matches and inter-state cricket matches. A 'master plan' for Sydney Olympic Park was 'finally adopted in May 2002' in which it was recognized that the park 'could not survive on sport and recreation alone and proposed greater residential and commercial development' (Cashman, 2006: 161). In the case of the main facilities developed for the Athens Games, the Athens OCOG 'made much of the idea that it was creating permanent facilities that would have post-Olympic use' (Gold, 2007: 278), but the reality is that, in part due to much internal political wrangling after the Olympics, 'progress towards realizing a new life for the venues has been patchy' (Gold, 2007: 282). The main Olympic stadium is now used by the city's two main professional football teams, but the surrounding landscaped spaces of the Olympic Park area 'are not part of the local amenities or accessible to visitors' (Gold, 2007: 282).

Notwithstanding the difficulty of generating relatively object-adequate evidence for most, if not all, of the claimed legacies of hosting the Olympics, and the potential spiralling costs involved, there remains, for many politicians and sports organizations, 'an unquestioning belief in the ... benefits of hosting such large scale events' (Hall, 2006: 66). In this respect, 'the sheer size and scope of the Olympics may well blind suitors for the Games to the substantial financial risks' (Baade and Matheson, 2002: 127–28). As we explain later, these issues can also be related to the London 2012 Games. In the rest of this chapter, we will examine the extent to which those behind the London 2012 bid are blinded by the supposed benefits of hosting the Olympics and examine whether lessons have been learned from the experiences of previous Games.

London 2012: the bid

Coalter (2004: 96) argues that the lack of research and tenuous evidence related to the various supposed positive impacts from hosting the Olympics raises 'critical questions about some of the assumptions underpinning the London 2012 claims about its potential impact on sports participation'. It would seem that, initially at least, the British government was also being told by its own advisors that 'the benefits of hosting mega sporting events, whether economic, social or cultural are difficult to measure and the available evidence is limited' (DCMS/Strategy Unit, 2002: 149). This quotation, it should be noted, is taken from the Labour government's own sport policy, *Game Plan*, published in December 2002. Whilst recognizing the limited evidence to support hosting such a 'mega-event', the DCMS and Strategy Unit (2002: 151) also recommended that although it tends to be local authorities that bid for the Games, 'due to the sensitivity of bidding for and hosting events, central government will be under great pressure to step in with additional funding if required'. It was recommended, therefore, that instead of viewing the hosting of mega-events with scepticism 'central government should always be involved from the earliest stages' (DCMS/Strategy Unit, 2002: 148) in order to influence policy from the start of any such bid. Despite the lack of available evidence for the legacy benefits of hosting the Games, just four months later the same government backed the London bid to bring the Olympics to the UK in 2012. The government's ideological commitment to sport, and the perceived benefits of hosting the Games, not least the potential positive political impact that winning the right to host the Games might bring in the immediate short term to the government, meant, it would seem, that it ignored the evidence in blind faith. As Gratton *et al.* (2005: 996) have noted, this underlines the point that despite the underwhelming evidence in favour of hosting such Games for their exogenous or even sports development legacies, 'in the end such decisions are political rather than part of a rational planning process'. Politicians frequently consider there to be kudos in being associated with sport, and especially the Olympic Games, which is frequently seen as the biggest prize of all. In much the same way that we argued in Chapter 6 that there is a global sporting arms race, one might include the securing of the rights to host the Olympics as something that is regularly considered as being worth virtually any cost. This tendency to make a variety of ideological claims on behalf of the alleged benefits that hosting a global event such as the Olympic Games is thought to bring is not altogether surprising, such is the growing cultural, economic and political significance of sport which has been accelerating during the post-1945 period.

Nine cities, including London, eventually submitted bids to host the 2012 Games. These included the early favourites Paris and Madrid, as well as Havana, Istanbul, Leipzig, Moscow, New York and Rio de Janeiro. Those responsible had to submit bids to the IOC by the summer of 2003, and the next summer the IOC reduced the number of bid cities to five (London, Madrid, Moscow, New York and Paris). The bid files for each of these city's bids were to be submitted by November 2004, and the IOC Evaluation Commission sent inspection teams to visit each of the five cities early in 2005. Following the bribery scandals that emerged in the international media associated with the Winter Games in Salt Lake City in 2002, this bidding process was the first under the new, more tightly scrutinized process implemented by the IOC. Initially, Barbara Cassani, an American businesswoman, who was largely based in the UK, was appointed as Chair of the London bid. This was considered by many as an appointment based on concerns about the organizational problems following the initially successful bid to host the World Athletics Championships in London in 2005. Poor management and organization after winning the bid meant that London had to withdraw from hosting them because it was clear that the required developments were not going to be delivered on time. That is to say, the appointment of someone with a good reputation in business to lead a very technical bid was initially seen as a way of ensuring a more professional approach, given that organizing large sports events in the UK had only recently been tarnished by the London World Athletics bid. This coincided with a deliberate process of the 'modernization' of many British sports organizations that was brought about by increasing government involvement in the running of sport in the UK in the recent past (see Chapter 2). There is little doubt that the failure to meet the requirements for hosting the 2005 World Athletics Championships contributed to the fact that most commentators considered that London was not a particularly serious contender because Paris and Madrid were still considered very strong favourites.

Throughout the bidding process, the London bid was highly ambitious in the variety of 'sustainable legacies' that were being promised for after the Games. Indeed, some might say that, given the apparent outside chance of winning the bid, rather like a party in opposition that is extremely unlikely to win the next general election, London could 'afford' to make a series of inflated promises about the alleged benefits that hosting the Games would have for London and the UK (Evans, 2007). Ironically, given the desire for Cassani to lead the original bid, because London was still believed to be trailing behind Paris and probably Madrid it was decided that her deputy, Lord Sebastian Coe, a former Olympic champion and politician, would be a better figurehead due to his standing in the Olympic Movement. Accordingly, Coe replaced Cassani as Chair of the Bid Committee for a final push in the summer of 2004. The London bid was still seen as having only an outside chance of winning even on the day of the final vote and it was seen as something of an upset when London was awarded the Olympic Games on 6 July 2005.

The various documents that were submitted on behalf of the London bid, most notably one of the preliminary reports, *London 2012: A Vision for the Olympic Games and Paralympic Games* (London 2012, 2004a) and the actual Candidate File (London 2012, 2004b), made a range of inflated promises for the proposed London Games. To achieve the various policy goals for the set budget, those responsible for the bid considered that the Games would represent considerable value for money: 'When all the sums have been done we would be better off than before. £2.375bn has been earmarked to stage the Games, but they bring in benefits and rewards to match' (London 2012, 2004a: 25). The alleged benefits and rewards were similar to many of those that had been legacy promises at previous Olympic Games. However, the London bid also consistently focused on the diversity of the city of London and in the Candidate File it was stated that, 'for the city, hosting the Games would leave an enduring sporting, social and economic legacy' (London 2012, 2004b: 1). More specifically there were four main themes proposed for the 'vision' of the London 2012 bid. These were:

- delivering the experience of a lifetime for athletes;
- leaving a legacy for sport in Britain;
- benefiting the community through regeneration;
- supporting the IOC and the Olympic Movement.

(London 2012, 2004b: 17)

Sport was declared to be 'at the heart' of the bid (London 2012, 2004b: 1). At the same time, Sebastian Coe declared that the Olympic and Paralympic Games, whilst they were the 'biggest sporting event in the world', also provided the opportunity for 'economic benefits and long-term legacies from which the whole country can benefit' (cited in London 2012 Nations and Regions Group, 2004: 18). The legacies, as set out in the Candidate File, were supposed to be achieved for sport, for the community, for the environment and for the economy (London 2012, 2004b). In a similar vein to the various claims made by bidding committees of previous host cities, the legacy for sport, it was proposed, was to see 'the Olympic ideals ... flourish at all levels. Grassroots sport would boom in our schools and local communities. Our most talented youngsters would be supported, offering them every chance to fulfil their promise and their dreams' (London 2012, 2004a: 12). Furthermore, given that the bid proposed the development of a range of new facilities for the Olympic Park at Lea Valley, including a new Olympic stadium, a velodrome and Olympic swimming and diving pools, it was declared that, 'after the Games are over, London will possess some of the finest sports facilities for hosting national and international events' (London 2012, 2004b: 19). To this end it was proposed that the London Olympic Institute would be created and would be 'a world-class institution for sport, culture and the environment, which will provide facilities and services for elite athletes as well as encouraging participation in sport' (London 2012, 2004b: 19). One might argue that such a proposal had its origins in the fact that the stadia in Sydney were, by this time, being criticized for being underutilized.

In addition to the development of a sporting legacy, it was proposed that an economic legacy would result from hosting the Games, with 'the creation of wider employment opportunities and improvements in the education, skills and knowledge of the local labour force in an area of very high unemployment' (London 2012, 2004b: 25) said to be among the major economic benefits of hosting the Games. This would, it was claimed, 'enable residents of the Lower Lea Valley to have a stake in the economic growth of their region and begin to break the cycle of deprivation in the area' (London 2012, 2004b: 25). It was claimed that local residents would gain not only from the creation of new jobs, but also from the new 'sustainable' sporting, housing and transport infrastructure that was being proposed. In this regard, it was claimed that

> the Olympic Park will create a high quality environment for the neighbouring mixed-use communities. It will enhance the amount and quality of greenspace, promote sustainable travel, conserve local biodiversity and wetlands, and improve air, soil and water quality. Its design will take account of the potential impacts of climate change and will set new standards for sustainable production, consumption and recycling of natural resources.
>
> (London 2012, 2004b: 23)

A further alleged benefit thought to be an important legacy of the Olympics would be the promotion of greater social inclusion (Chapter 4). The Candidate File ambitiously set out to use the Olympic Park as 'a hub for east London, bringing communities together and acting as a catalyst for profound social and economic change' (London 2012, 2004b: 19). In this respect, it was proposed that the Olympic Park area 'will become a model of social inclusion, opening up opportunities for education, cultural and skills development and jobs for people across the UK and London, but especially in the Lea Valley and surrounding areas' (London 2012, 2004b: 19). In the process, it was proposed that since the new facilities would be available for use by the broader community, as well as elite athletes, 'this will create a more inclusive, more active community, leading to a fitter society and reducing health inequalities' (London 2012, 2004b: 19). The tendency for such largely uncritical acceptance of non-evidence-based, exaggerated promises can be related to the fact that those involved in the London bid had been constrained to set out a wider array of ambitions because of the considerable external constraints that they were experiencing from the IOC and in competition with other bidding cities, to ensure that, like many other Games, the London Games would be seen to be 'bigger and better' than preceding ones. Thus it could be argued that the London bid is based on a 'best of the rest' strategy that is likely to prove far too ambitious, especially given the difficulties that were associated with the various legacies expected to have been generated by previous Games.

Before we begin to examine the claims for the proposed legacies expected to result from the London 2012 Games, and the progress made in preparing for the Games over the last four years, it is important to briefly outline the organizational structure that has been implemented in order to support the hosting of the Olympic and Paralympic Games in London.

London 2012: structure and organization in preparation for the Games

Once London was announced as the host of the 2012 Olympic and Paralympic Games, the London Organizing Committee of the Olympic and Paralympic Games (LOCOG) was established with Lord Coe as its Chair. The LOCOG, as is the case in all recent Olympic Games, is responsible for the staging of the Games, and is largely financed by raising money from the private sector, through sponsorship, broadcasting rights and selling merchandise. Under IOC guidelines, the government is not allowed to take any part in 'running' the Games (IOC, 2007). This is rather spurious, however, since the government does play an important part in ensuring the Games can take place by providing the majority of the funds to ensure that the infrastructure, including the sporting venues, is delivered on time. To this end, the British government passed the London 2012 Olympic Games and Paralympic Games Act in March 2006. One of the motions passed in the Act was the creation of the Olympic Delivery Authority (ODA) as a non-departmental public body (NDPB), and, like other NDPBs, such as UK Sport and Sport England, the ODA is accountable to the DCMS. The ODA is responsible for the delivery of the infrastructure for the Olympic Park and it reports to the Olympic Board, which is made up of representatives from the LOCOG, the BOA, the GLA and the government. The Olympic Board is chaired jointly by the Mayor of London (currently Boris Johnson) and the Minister for the Olympics, a newly created ministerial position that was taken up by Tessa Jowell, who had been an integral part of the bid process in her previous role as Secretary of State for Culture, Media and Sport. The Olympic Board 'is the strategic decision making body with responsibility for the whole Olympic programme' (HMSO, 2007: 7). Finally, the Government Olympic Executive (GOE) provides support to the Minister for the Olympics, with the specific role of 'maintain[ing] oversight of the entire programme on behalf of Government' (HMSO, 2007: 7). In this respect, the GOE is accountable for the national expenditure of public funds and the GLA is accountable for the distribution of public funds regionally (CSL 2012, 2007). In addition, in an attempt to secure UK-wide legacies, the LOCOG has established a Nations and Regions Group (NRG), in which each of the home nations (Northern Ireland, Scotland and Wales) and the nine various regions of England have boards that are represented. Each sets in place its own vision for 2012.

Since the winning of the bid and the implementation of the organizational structure to set about working towards hosting the Games in 2012, a flurry of official publications have been produced that will form the basis for our analysis here. Many of these policy documents set out in greater detail the 'legacy commitments' for the Games and a more specific (and much larger) budget. Perhaps, given the broader goals established by some of the key parties involved in producing the Olympics, it is no surprise that the budget for the Games has risen substantially. Before we examine some of the legacy commitments in more detail, let us briefly consider more specific details of the budget that has been set aside for hosting the Games.

The London 2012 budget

When the bid to host the Games was originally submitted, it was claimed that 'the estimated cost to the public sector was approximately £3.4 billion' (House of Commons Culture, Media and Sport Committee, 2008: 8). Approximately £2.375 billion was the capital budget from the public sector funding package for the ODA to build the permanent sports venues and broader infrastructure required for the Games mentioned in the original bid documentation (London 2012, 2004a), and approximately £1.044 billion was the operating budget to be spent by the Exchequer on the 'wider regeneration in the Lower Lea Valley' (House of Commons Culture, Media and Sport Committee, 2008: 8). A further £738 million, it was suggested, 'would be forthcoming from the private sector, as a contribution to the costs of facilities and infrastructure' (House of Commons Culture, Media and Sport Committee, 2008: 8). In total, the proposed original budget stood at over £4 billion. The budget for the Games is focused on 'those costs that are to be publicly funded and therefore exclude the staging costs to be incurred by the London Organising Committee of the Olympic Games and Paralympic Games (LOCOG), which is intended to be self-financing' (NAO, 2007: 4–5). This is a requirement of the IOC, although 'the Government is the ultimate guarantor of funding for the Games, including LOCOG's staging costs' (NAO, 2007: 5).

It was announced in March 2007, however, that the proposed costs of the Games had increased considerably, to £9.325 billion. Many media sources reported that the new budget announced by the Minister for the Olympics, Tessa Jowell, was 'nearly four times' the originally proposed budget (e.g. BBC, 2007). This is because many within the media considered the original budget to be around £2.4 billion, a fact never openly disputed by the government or others involved in the bid at the time, of course, since the much larger sum would, no doubt, have contributed to a significant amount of bad press at the time. This could have detracted substantially from the likely success of the bid given that one of the IOC's concerns in awarding the Games is that the host city can demonstrate that the public are in favour of the Games being staged in their city and country. The £2.4 billion sum did not include the operating costs required for the development of the Lower Lea Valley or, of course, the money that it was hoped would be generated from the private sector. Nonetheless, as has been the case in most Olympic Games where the budget has been examined, the budget that is currently being proposed for hosting the London Games is substantially higher than at the time of the bid. The failure, at least publicly, to anticipate budgetary rises is not surprising given the limited perspective that the government adopted at the outset – and still does – largely, it might be argued, because of the prevailing tendency to claim for sport benefits for which there is little evidence.

A good illustration of the government's failure to anticipate appropriately the budget requirements of hosting the Games is that in the original bid there appears to have been no specific budget set aside for security at the Games, which was, of course a significant oversight, made to look especially ill-judged when on 7 July 2005, the day after London won the right to host the Games, several coordinated terrorist attacks took place in the capital, resulting in the deaths of fifty-six people. Thus '£0.6 billion for policing and wider security … in the wake of the events of 7 July 2005' was but one addition to the original budget (House of Commons Culture, Media and Sport Committee, 2008: 9). However, it is not our intention here to offer a detailed, economic evaluation of the budget, but it is clear that the current budget for the Games has attracted particular criticism, including from the government's own House of Commons Committee of Public Accounts (2008) and House of Commons Culture, Media and Sport Committee (2007; 2008). Such criticism is neatly captured in the following quotations:

> We are not particularly surprised at the increase in costs, and it should not be forgotten that substantial savings are being made in certain areas. But we are very disappointed that the cost estimates have been found to be faulty so early in the process.
>
> (House of Commons Culture, Media and Sport Committee, 2007: 3)

> Although it is not surprising that early assessments underestimated the final costs, such a radical revision of cost estimates has been damaging to confidence in the management of the overall programme. It has also exposed the Government and Games organisers to the charge that the initial bid was kept artificially low in order to win public support.
>
> (House of Commons Culture, Media and Sport Committee, 2008: 3)

Irrespective of the criticisms regarding the budgeting for the Games, there is widespread belief, at least publicly, within the government and those responsible for delivering the Games that a number of legacy outcomes will emerge following the hosting of the Games in 2012.

The legacy promises for London 2012

The original London 2012 Candidate File, as we have already seen, set out four general 'vision' themes. Two years after the Games were awarded to London, these vision statements were developed further in specific statements that outlined numerous legacy promises, which came from the DCMS, the GLA and a new public service agreement (PSA 22), which was to 'Deliver a successful Olympic Games and Paralympic Games with a sustainable legacy and get more children and young people taking part in high quality PE and sport' (HMSO, 2007: 5). The various stated legacy aims are given in Table 7.1.

Despite the variety of legacy aims that have been proposed by the DCMS, the GLA and in PSA 22, these might be summarized as being about regeneration, social inclusion, sustainability and a sporting legacy for elite sport and mass participation, which is expected to have health benefits. One might argue that for a Labour government keen to focus on what it perceived to be the importance of joined-up thinking, hosting the Games would be seen as a perfect opportunity to exhibit such an approach because of the myriad interrelated legacies alleged to emerge from hosting them. However, this fails to appreciate the relational complexities involved, as in many cases the achievement of one aim may have unintended consequences that help to undermine others.

The various DCMS and LOCOG publications that have been produced thus far in the build-up to the Games refer to the idea that the 'Plans' are 'live documents', suggesting that they are regularly updated and monitored, at least on an annual basis, and there is a

Table 7.1 Legacy visions for London 2012

Our Promise for 2012: How the UK will Benefit from the Olympic Games and Paralympic Games (DCMS, 2007: 4)	PSA Delivery Agreement 22 (HMSO, 2007: 5–6)	Five Legacy Commitments (GLA, 2007b: 3)
1 Make the UK a world-leading sporting nation	1 Construction of the Olympic Park and other Olympic venues	1 Increasing opportunities for Londoners to become involved in sport
2 Transform the heart of East London	2 Maximising the regeneration benefits of the 2012 Games	2 Ensuring Londoners benefit from new jobs, business and volunteering opportunities
3 Inspire a generation of young people to take part in local volunteering, cultural and physical activity	3 The Olympic Park and venues are designed and built according to sustainable principles	3 Transforming the heart of East London
4 Make the Olympic Park a blueprint for sustainable living	4 Public participation in cultural and community activities across the UK and participation in sporting activities both in the UK and in other countries, particularly those in development	4 Delivering a sustainable Games and developing sustainable communities
5 Demonstrate the UK is a creative, inclusive and welcoming place to live in, visit, and for business	5 Creation of a world-class system for Physical Education (PE) and sport	5 Showcasing London as a diverse, creative and welcoming city

promise to develop 'Legacy Action Plans' annually. In the 'second Legacy Action Plan' report Tessa Jowell claimed that 'too often in the past, governments have expected major events to bring automatic windfall benefits. But we know now that nothing is guaranteed without careful planning and initiative from the outset', and here was a 'chance to turn the rhetoric of legacy into fact' (DCMS, 2008b: 2). In the next section, we will analyze aspects of the planning and the policy process using the various documents' focussing on each defined legacy area. In the process, it will become evident just how significantly the 2012 Games is coming to impact on the broader direction of sport policy in the UK.

London 2012: regeneration legacy?

Although some sports are due to take place beyond the Olympic Park area in 2012, including sailing events at Weymouth, football matches at various stadia around the UK, and tennis, archery, beach volleyball, shooting and riding events at other venues in and around London, on the whole the main focus of the Olympics will, of course, be at the main Olympic Park. The area where this is being developed, in the Lower Lea Valley, and the surrounding boroughs are some of the most deprived areas in the country. In England a measurement of deprivation based on economic, environmental and social (which includes measurements of educational attainment) factors produces a score for comparison within the Index of Multiple Deprivation (IMD). Based on this, '62 per cent of the Olympic zone neighbourhoods … are ranked in the top ten most income-deprived areas in England, and 48 per cent in the worst five' (Evans, 2007: 312). In addition, the site identified for the Olympic Park was a brownfield site. In this regard, it is clear that regeneration of the area is high on the political agenda, for it led Ken Livingstone, the former Mayor of London and one of the key figures behind the bid, to claim that 'regeneration was the main reason why I backed the bid' (GLA, 2007b: 3). Regeneration is also one of the key features of PSA 22, in which it is stated:

> Regenerating the heart of East London is central to the commitment to provide a lasting and sustainable legacy long after 2012. This will be driven by the development of a Legacy Masterplan Framework (LMF), an overarching plan which will govern delivery of the regeneration agenda. It is also vital that a sustainable legacy for the Games's venues is effectively incorporated into this planning and successfully delivered when the Games finish in 2012.
>
> (HMSO, 2007: 5)

Even before the Games were awarded to London, proposals were introduced to develop the area as part of the wider plans to attempt to regenerate the Thames Gateway. The immutable deadline for when the facilities must be transferred to the IOC in order to hold the Games has contributed to significant progress being made in relation to receiving planning permission. The fast injections of cash that substantial regeneration projects of the kind being proposed here are rarely able to enjoy, and without which they might never be completed, have also helped in this respect (House of Commons Culture, Media and Sport Committee, 2007). However, at the same time, 'by linking capital projects to an unalterable Olympic timetable, costs may end up higher than they otherwise would have been' (House of Commons Culture, Media and Sport Committee, 2007: 10). This is a particularly good illustration of the constraining and enabling aspects of the development associated with the building work currently taking place in preparation for the 2012 Games. In other words, by winning the right to host the Games, and with an immoveable timetable for the completion of the projects, development work has been able to proceed more swiftly than may have been the case otherwise and planning permission appears to have been easier to come by. Simultaneously, however, the constraints associated with the additional pressures to ensure that the build is finished to someone else's timetable have meant that some contractors have been able to negotiate higher than normal prices. An additional unintended consequence, some would argue, of the need to complete the project by a deadline set by the IOC means that other projects for the region and beyond may be adversely affected. For example, a planned project to link East and West London by extending the rail network has been postponed until at least after the Games have taken place 'because it would have been impossible to complete in time for 2012' (Atkinson *et al.*, 2008: 426). In this respect, Raco argues that in previous Games

> the failure to build on the existing strengths and continuities of regeneration areas has resulted in many flagship projects and spectacle-based forms of development failing to engage with local communities' needs and aspirations. Indeed, often implicit in such programmes is the need to change 'problem' communities entirely through processes of gentrification and displacement.
>
> (Raco, 2004: 35)

It is clear that some local groups have been deeply resistant to the changes brought about to the Lower Lea Valley already in preparation for the Games, and some small local businesses have been forcibly moved on. For example, the Lee Valley Regional Park Authority (2008: 14) 'identified the 2012 Olympics as a major risk that could affect all our key business objectives into the future. The award of the Olympics to London will affect our land, business, financial and human resources'. Nonetheless, those groups who have developed the Legacy Action Plans still claim that the regeneration of the area will emerge from the 'hard' infrastructural development, especially from building the Olympic Village and the sports venues, as well as extending and updating the transport links to and from the region. Furthermore, it is claimed that new jobs and provision for skills training for much of the local population will be amongst the other developments that the lead-up to the Games will generate. Similar claims were made, in the early 1980s, about the 'Docklands development', which saw the building of Canary Wharf and the establishment of a large financial services sector and housing developments in close proximity to the Olympic Park. However, this did not produce any noticeable regenerative effects in terms of sustained employment for the local population (Evans, 2007; Macrury and Poynter, 2008). Indeed, 'critics have rightly argued that the Docklands development has served to reinforce the polarization between rich and poor communities in East London' (Macrury and Poynter, 2008: 2077), with the new housing in and around Canary Wharf becoming rather exclusive and beyond the means of most of the existing local population. Furthermore, in the 1990s the development of the Millennium Dome (the venue for the gymnastics competitions in 2012), also in close proximity to the Olympic Park, contributed to 'limited' regeneration of the region (Evans, 2007: 300). So what, if anything, will the infrastructural changes brought about by hosting the Olympics do differently? Of course, investment and, to a certain degree, infrastructural development are on a much greater scale. It is argued that after 2012 there will be '9,000 high-quality homes on the Olympic Park site, many of which will be affordable to Londoners on low incomes. A further 30,000 homes will be built in the surrounding area providing more affordable accommodation' (GLA, 2007b: 3). Whilst there is significant potential for affordable new housing, we have already seen in the case of Barcelona's Olympic Village how this, subsequently, served to exacerbate existing social divisions, with many local residents being unable to afford many of the flats in the Village. It is not clear at this stage either quite what controls, if any, the GLA has put in place to ensure that what happened after Barcelona is avoided on this occasion.

A further argument put forward by those hoping that a lasting legacy will emerge from London 2012 is the new and improved transport links being developed to and from the main Olympic Park. The ODA (2008: 2) has published an accessible transport strategy and considers that the Olympics in 2012 'will be a catalyst to improve the accessibility of transport networks across London and the UK'. New underground stations are part of the transport plan, as well as 'active transport', such as walking and cycling, through the Active Spectator Programme, which 'is designed to ensure that public transport, walking and cycling displace all nonessential car use at the Games completely, promoting healthier lifestyles as well as reduced social and environmental impact' (GLA, 2007c: 9). The cycle and walkways will remain in and around the Olympic Park once the Games have finished, with the intention, as with Sport England's (2007) policy agenda on 'active design' (Chapter 5), of promoting physical activity in the day-to-day lives of local residents.

Finally, the development of employment opportunities that is expected to result from, in the first instance, the building work carried out on the Olympic Park, and thereafter from the new businesses that it is hoped will be attracted to the region, forms part of the rationale for the proposed regeneration legacy, and it is hoped that this will 'create local jobs, improve skills and help to get thousands of people into work' (GLA, 2007b: 3). As noted earlier, however, despite the claimed impact few previous Olympic Games have generated sustained local employment once the Games have ended. Perhaps in light of this, the GLA established the London 2012 Employment and Skills Task Force in 2006 and is attempting to use its 'Olympic' leverage to ensure that businesses in the area commit to providing low-level entry jobs for the large number of the adult population in the Thames Gateway that have no formal qualifications (Evans, 2007). Together with this comes the establishment of the Personal Best programme (formerly known as the Pre-Volunteering Programme [PVP]), designed to 'help Londoners who are not already in training or work to learn about volunteering and to improve their employment prospects – and their chance to become a London 2012 volunteer – by developing new skills' (GLA, 2007c: 5).

London 2012: social inclusion legacy?

We saw in Chapter 4 that the social inclusion agenda is a significant feature of the current Labour government's political philosophy and has come to impact significantly on its sport policy priorities and goals. Perhaps unsurprisingly, then, and especially given the ethnic diversity and socio-economic deprivation that characterize the regions surrounding the Olympic Park, social inclusion is a key feature of the legacy plans for London 2012. Indeed, particular emphasis is given in many of the Olympic policy statements of the population diversity of London as a whole, which is said to be the most diverse city in the world, where over 300 languages are spoken every day. The legacy plans suggest that Londoners should embrace the cultural celebrations around the Olympics and demonstrate a united, inclusive but ethnically diverse city (GLA, 2007b). In doing so, it is intended that a diverse range of volunteers will be recruited who would be able to ensure that 'all competing teams and spectators will be made welcome by Londoners who speak their language or who share their culture' (GLA, 2007c: 5). Whilst London is, indeed, an extremely ethnically diverse city, it is difficult to see how hosting the Olympic Games, like many other sporting events and programmes (see Chapter 4), will help promote community integration by bringing people from a variety of socio-economic and ethnic backgrounds 'together' in anything other than an ephemeral way.

Volunteering is central to the broader aims associated with social inclusion. Getting volunteers involved, as was the case with the Manchester Commonwealth Games, is frequently cited as making a significant contribution to widening sports participation, generating 'active citizenship' and promoting social inclusion (NWDA, 2004). However, the GLA (2007a: 9) points out that at previous Olympics 'many volunteers were trained for specific low-skilled, customer-focused service tasks. There is little evidence of volunteer skills transferring to the post-Games economy'. Furthermore, the very people who volunteer in sport are often those people who are already disproportionately involved in sport, and, in that respect, volunteer recruitment for sports events 'seems a case of preaching to the converted and may have had limited impact on sports development' (Coalter, 2004: 103). The aim of Personal Best, however, following eleven pilot schemes that took place, 'engaging over 500 people across London in basic volunteer-related training' (LOCOG, 2007a: 8), is to roll the programme out across London, specifically targeting 'unemployed people from hard to reach groups' (HMSO, 2007: 22). It is recognized that 'the attraction of the course is likely to be its Olympic hook' (HMSO, 2007: 22). As Coalter (2007b) has noted, however, it is difficult to see how sporting events, even a global event such as the Olympics, can engage people who are typically considered 'hard to reach' in terms of sports participation. Amongst those groups identified as 'heard to reach' are those who are eligible for, or are in receipt of, incapacity benefits, including disabled people, people aged over 50, ex-offenders, homeless people in sheltered accommodation, refugees, asylum seekers eligible to work in the UK and migrants (LDA, n.d.). Many of these groups are not traditionally already involved in sport. It is hoped that by 2012 some 20,000 people will have engaged with Personal Best, and then those who have completed the programme will be given an interview to become a volunteer at the Games (GLA, 2007b). According to the London Development Agency (LDA), who, in partnership with the Learning and Skills Council (LSC) and JobCentre Plus, run Personal Best, 875 people eventually took part in the eleven pilot schemes. Of these 'so far 14.5% have already moved onto either full or part time employment and 23.5% into further learning. Their achievements were celebrated alongside Olympians and Paralympians at a ceremony in Wembley Stadium' (LDA, n.d.). However, given, as is the case with many of the legacies proposed, that no obvious targets were set, it is not clear whether these figures are regarded as having matched expectation or desires. As we will discuss later, the lack of stated distinct performance indicators (PIs) for the number of legacies being proposed seems at variance with a Labour government which, for reasons we explain in Chapter 1, has placed increasing emphasis on accountability, measurement and evaluation, and evidence-based policy-making.

As well as these tangible attempts to encourage more people to become involved in community developments and focusing on developing new skills to promote employment opportunities, it is recognized that there is a need to tackle the health inequalities that 'profoundly affect east London's communities' (LOCOG, 2007b: 48). It is hoped that by getting more people involved in volunteering, but also by providing more employment opportunities and altering the environmental landscape of the area, these measures will go some way to helping improve the health of people across the region.

Another area where the promotion of social inclusion is emphasized is through the development of sustainable ways of living (e.g. developing a cleaner environment in which to live) and it is hoped that hosting the Olympics will help to generate and promote such sustainability. Indeed, according to the LOCOG,

> inclusion underpins all other sustainability themes – poorer people and minority groups are the first to feel the effects of climate change and declining biodiversity – and has a particularly close link to health. Deprivation also remains a strong determinant of ill-health.
>
> (LOCOG, 2007b: 40)

As we have seen already, the idea that the Olympics can be a catalyst for sustainable, 'green' living first really came to the fore in the legacy statements of the Sydney Games. It is also an important aspect of the message about legacy that those behind London 2012 want to promote.

London 2012: sustainability legacy?

According to some, 'the commitments [to sustainable development] contained in the Candidate File were key to London winning its bid to host the 2012 Games' (CSL 2012,

2007: 8). In one of its Legacy Action Plans, the LOCOG (2007b: 5) declared that the sustainability legacy is 'framed by the concept of "Towards a One Planet Olympics"'. This was specifically developed from the BioRegional and World Wide Fund for Nature's (WWF) 'One Planet Living' concept, which sets out various principles required for sustainable living. According to the LOCOG (2007b: 5), 'as the most high-profile event in the world, the Games give us the chance to show how changes to the way we build, live, work, do business and travel could help us to live happy and healthy lives, within the resources available to us'. With this in mind, the LOCOG (2007b: 9) has set out to promote education about climate change. It also sets out to manage waste in and around the Olympic sites more efficiently, promoting biodiversity by leaving a 'legacy of enhanced habitats within the Olympic Park' and attempting to 'foster an understanding of the importance of biodiversity in supporting healthy lifestyles' (LOCOG, 2007b: 9), and promoting healthy, sustainable ways of living. Furthermore, the building projects associated with the Games, it is suggested, will be carried out to the highest, most efficient environmentally aware specifications (CSL 2012, 2007). In their assessment of the potential impact of hosting the Games in London, Mean *et al.* (2004: 131) declared that 'if a London 2012 Olympics is to deliver a sustainable legacy, it will be vital to embed the Olympics within broader programmes and policy agendas that start well before 2012 and continue well afterwards'. The fact that the four key stakeholders in London 2012, the DCMS, the GLA, the ODA and, of course, the LOCOG, were all involved in setting up the Commission for a Sustainable London 2012 (CSL 2012) in January 2007 seems to go some way towards addressing these concerns. The CSL 2012 is responsible for regularly reviewing the sustainability process leading up to the 2012 Games, and is to publish regular reports on progress being made on the legacy commitments for the Games. One of its earliest reports made the following claim:

> Two years since winning the bid, London is further advanced than any other host city in establishing structures, objectives and policies to implement these [sustainable development, SD] commitments. In addition, London's integrated concept of SD, incorporating social, economic and environmental considerations puts it at the forefront of sustainability thinking worldwide.
>
> (CSL 2012, 2007: 8)

However, at this time there are concerns expressed by the CSL 2012 about the failure of some contracts for building work to meet the required standards for the development of 'excellent', sustainable building development as set out in the Building Research Establishment Environmental Assessment Method (BREEAM) (CSL 2012, 2009). As with any assessments of the action plans in place for all 'legacies' associated with the Games, it is clearly too early to make some kind of assessment of the 'green' credentials of the London 2012 Games here, but it is likely that the ambitions surrounding the ability to generate a 'green' Games are, perhaps inevitably, hampered by major building work. The sustainable agenda permeating the bid may be explained, in part, by the more ideologically led dimensions of the bid. As we noted in relation to the bidding process surrounding the Sydney Games, 'green politics' has been very much on the international political agenda in the twenty-first century. Consequently, it is not altogether surprising to find that the LOCOG, ODA and others appear to have felt constrained to be 'seen to be doing' something in this regard. A key element of the sustainable living approach in general, however, is the promotion of active transport and healthy living. Both of these policy aims are related to the particular focus on the sporting legacy that the 2012 Games are expected to leave.

London 2012: sporting legacy?

Perhaps the most obvious claim by various governments for a legacy of hosting the Olympic Games is the impact that it has on the numbers of people participating in sport at the grassroots level, but also the focus it can bring to bear on elite-level sport. As we explained earlier, within the Candidate File a sporting legacy was seen to be 'at the heart' of the London bid (London 2012, 2004b: 1), with particular emphasis being placed on the fact that the population had a great deal of 'passion' for sport and that people in the UK demonstrate that they are keen sports spectators on a regular basis (London 2012, 2004b: 11). This is a rather ambiguous claim that is a rather one-sided, idealistic view of sport based on an emotional generalization from the few to the whole (Elias and Scotson, 1994). In addition to these claims, it is also expected, somewhat uncritically, that the Games will help contribute to a central directive of the government's sport policy: to increase sports participation by '1% year-on-year by 2012' (DCMS, 2007: 7). Part of this concern with raising participation generally is the specific focus that has come to be placed on young people (see Chapter 3). The preoccupation with raising participation levels among young people found further expression in the 2012 Legacy Action Plan of the DCMS, in which it was stated that 2008 was 'to mark the beginning of a golden decade of sport – raising participation, especially among young people and those who are least active and to stem the tide of young people dropping out of sport' (DCMS, 2007: 19). This was even though it was reported by the Culture Select Committee that 'no host country has yet been able to demonstrate a direct benefit from the Olympic Games in the form of a lasting increase in participation' (House of Commons Culture, Media and Sport Committee, 2007: 37).

The uncritically accepted view that the Games will have a sporting legacy was also prominent in the LOCOG's (2007b: 48) strategy, in which it was stated that, 'as the world's pre-eminent festival of sporting excellence, the Olympic and Paralympic Games offer huge opportunities to inspire and promote sports participation, play and other forms of physical activity, and other elements of healthy living'. Such a desire also found expression in the PSA 22, where it is stated that 'the hosting of the 2012 Games is expected to increase public participation in cultural and community activities across the UK' (HMSO, 2007: 6). At the time of writing, it was interesting to note that there is no explicit mention made of the part played by SDOs in helping to achieve these aims in the legacy action plans of the DCMS, LOCOG or the PSA 22. It is, however, likely that there 'will be community activities and educational programmes throughout the country' (DCMS, 2007: 4) and that SDOs will, indeed, be expected to make some contribution to these aspects of community activity.

In addition to the sporting legacy aims of increasing participation, mostly of young people, considerable attention is also focused in many of the policy statements related to London 2012 on enhancing elite success as a significant target for the Games. Even before the unprecedented modern-day success of Team GB at the Beijing Games, targets for performance in 2012 were being set and it was hoped that, given the unprecedented successes that 'home' athletes had enjoyed at previous Olympic Games, 'home advantage' would be an important factor in London too. Of course, it is rather naïve to assume that the better than normal performances by athletes in front of their own crowds at previous

Olympics are somehow related to 'home advantage' alone, if at all. Without fail in the recent past, the financial support in place for elite athletes in the host nation has always exceeded proportionately that available before. In this sense, the home advantage might be more reasonably assumed to come from the increased funding offered to the athletes. Nevertheless, the DCMS (2007: 7) announced that 'our ultimate goal is to finish fourth in the Olympic medal table and first in the Paralympic medal table', goals which, at the time of publication, were widely regarded as being far too optimistic. However, given the unprecedented modern-day success of British athletes in Beijing, where fourth and second place were achieved at the Beijing Olympics and Paralympics, respectively, this overall target actually remains the same for London 2012.

All of these policy statements are characteristic of the many kinds of legacy promises being made in a variety of policy publications leading up to the Games. This is not uncommon, for, as Murphy and Bauman (2007: 199) rightly point out, 'considerable and extravagant claims continue to be made by hosts of some major events regarding their impact on PA [physical activity], sports participation, or the social-change agenda'. They are made, in the case of those writing policies and legacy action plans for London 2012, contrary to the government's rhetoric of evidence-based policy, as they are made without the support of much, if any, evidence at all. But are the requisite resources being provided to help ensure the desired ends are achieved?

The London Summer of Sport scheme that started in 2006, and is scheduled to go beyond 2012, 'offers free sporting activities for people of all ages across London' (GLA, 2007b: 6). Numerous clubs have been invited to take part to ensure that this offer is realized, and, according to the GLA (2007b), several of those clubs taking part have enjoyed increased numbers of paying members as a direct result of their involvement in the scheme. The apparent success of the scheme is said to be a significant factor in extending it over the winter months as well, in the London Winter of Sport programme, which is more narrowly focused on 5–16-year-olds and is linked to the government's desire to offer young people the opportunity to take part in a minimum of five hours of sport every week (see Chapter 3). It is also related to the London Youth Offer, which is a programme funded by the LDA and the DCSF aimed at giving young people, particularly those deemed to be 'at risk of missing out', the opportunity to develop new skills and to 'raise their aspirations' (GLA, 2007b: 6). In addition, numerous roadshows have been implemented, in London and elsewhere, in an attempt to showcase the London 2012 Games and provide people, particularly young people, with opportunities to participate in sport and community activities. Taster sessions in various Olympic and Paralympic sports like rowing, tennis and boccia are available, with the provision of information about how and where they can join in beyond the roadshow also being one of the main priorities of the scheme. To help reinforce the alleged relationship between expected rising levels of participation and the benefits of this to health, the GLA (2007c: 17) claimed that the Games represent the chance to 'showcase … fitness, healthy living, willpower and self-improvement'. To help achieve this the GLA (2007c: 17) is said to be working with various partners and, 'with critical support from the NHS, will use the inspiration and excitement generated by the Games to improve physical and mental wellbeing in London'. But to what extent can these aspirations be achieved in practice? Can increasing participation among the general population be expected to emerge out of hosting the Olympics?

In assessing the potential for a sporting legacy to be left from hosting the Olympics in 2012, Coalter (2004: 98) argued that 'if a London 2012 Games is to make any contribution to a sustained increase in sports participation, it must be as a partner in a much broader development strategy, with a wide range of organisations seeking to build on the heightened profile of sport'. To some degree the kind of partnership working suggested by Coalter is beginning to take place in London, with the GLA working with the LDA, the NHS and others to promote sport and physical activity to the population of London. There is evidence that such strategies are in operation beyond London as well. For example, to coincide with the build-up to 2012, the DCMS, in partnership with Communities and Local Government, the Department of Health, the Department for Work and Pensions and the DCSF, has introduced a scheme whereby local authorities can 'offer free swimming to the over 60s' (DCMS, 2008b: 18). It is also proposed that this scheme be rolled out to include children, with aspirations 'to move towards universal free swimming' (DCMS, 2008b: 18). However, offering free swimming, or free use of leisure centres, does not have particularly good success rates (Coalter, 2007a; Roberts and Brodie, 1992). Just because such sessions are free does not mean that people will participate, especially those traditional non-participants who are the focus of many of the schemes. Additionally, this provides a further opportunity for those already participating to do so more frequently and in more cost-effective ways.

Nonetheless, it is expected that the introduction of these kinds of schemes to encourage more people to participate in sport and physical activity will help contribute to improving health among the participating groups. These schemes are said to be complemented by a range of other health-based policy initiatives. In December 2008, for example, the LOCOG announced that 'we will soon launch "Healthy Active Lifestyles" which will promote the right balance between healthy eating, physical activity and emotional well-being, helping children and young people to take small steps to living a more healthy lifestyle' (LOCOG, 2008: 23). In addition to these proposals, the government's latest strategy on health, *Healthy Weight, Healthy Lives* (see Chapter 5), sets numerous targets that coincide with, and are related to, the policy aims of the 2012 Games. Various national walking campaigns, including the Schools Walking Challenge for 2012, and other campaigns that are said to be 'harnessing the inspirational power of the Games' (LOCOG, 2008: 24) are also being introduced across the country. These include schemes such as the '£140m invested in Cycling England for improved cycling infrastructure and training, to demonstrate visible change in cycling provision', and the 'Healthy Community Challenge Fund, which will support new approaches to promoting physical activity, such [as] increasing the number of cycle lanes, initiating walking promotion schemes, or referring patients to a gym for a programme of exercise' (LOCOG, 2008: 24).

In some respects, it might be argued that the build-up to the 2012 Games are having a direct impact on the declared policy aims and directives of much sport and physical activity policy in Britain. In the case of those schemes where the promotion of health-enhancing physical activity (HEPA) is a central objective, especially in more public health-oriented policy, these schemes tend to be broadly complementary to other existing policies that are in place already. In relation to sport and elite sports provision, however, the 2012 Games have come to impact significantly on the policy priorities and objectives of sport policy more generally. The funding that has been made available to UK Sport from the government in the run-up to 2012, for example, has nearly doubled with 2012 in mind, although it was also proposed that UK Sport attempt to raise £100 million from the private sector (NAO, 2008). In light of the increased funding that has become available from the government and the National Lottery funding streams, in May 2007 UK Sport launched its Mission 2012 evaluation programme for NGBs as a 'response to those demanding high levels of accountability for the significantly increased level of investment [from the government] in our high-performance system' (UK Sport, 2007a: 20). Through Mission 2012, UK Sport will assess each Olympic and Paralympic governing body in relation to three broad areas: (1) the systems in place for the governance, organization, coaching and other support systems, and facilities; (2) the athletes' performance, development and general well-being; and (3) the perceived climate within the sport, related to the experiences of athletes and staff (DCMS, 2008b; NAO, 2008; UK Sport 2007b). However unrealistic it might be, NGBs will 'be expected to deliver and operate at high standards of internal organisation and democracy, ensuring that the voices of all levels and participant groups are heard' (Sport England, 2008a: 2), and, in this respect, athletes' opinions are sought. Mission 2012 uses a traffic light system in the build-up to the Games to benchmark NGBs against agreed goals set for 2012, and this means that, according to UK Sport (2007b), NGBs 'will be more effectively monitored and evaluated than ever before'. Results are published for UK Sport quarterly, and green indicates that the progress is on track for 2012, amber means that there are areas that have been identified that need closer examination and red means that the UK Sport panel considers that immediate intervention is required (UK Sport, 2007b).

These developments are clear examples of the way in which hosting the Games in 2012 is both constraining and enabling those in the UK sport policy figurations. No doubt such developments will enable those NGBs that can demonstrate that they are achieving targets, and which can therefore potentially obtain greater levels of funding, to develop the ESD systems in place in their sport even further. However, they do place a further constraint on NGBs already subjected to monitoring and evaluation procedures because Mission 2012, it seems, is being used alongside these. According to the NAO (2008: 7), 'some governing bodies were unclear how UK Sport would use the information from Mission 2012, alongside other performance information, to make funding decisions or how it would intervene if sports identified significant risks to achieving their goals'. Furthermore, as we saw in Chapter 6, having won the right to host the 2012 Games, UK Sport broadened its funding, moving from a 'no compromise' approach that concentrated funding primarily on those sports and athletes most likely to achieve medal success, to 'all Olympic and Paralympic sports to achieve creditable performances at the Games, even if these will not lead to winning medals, to further their aims to deliver an elite sporting legacy from the Games' (NAO, 2008: 6). The NAO (2008: 5) considered that this 'new' policy approach, combined with the required focus on generating the £100 million that had not yet been secured from the private sector, 'may distract UK Sport's focus and funding from its primary goal of winning medals ... and on the longer term legacy for elite sport in the United Kingdom'. UK Sport has, however, since argued that it has not abandoned its 'no compromise' strategy, but that the extra money available had meant that it was now able to fund sports that could perform 'creditably' at home (House of Commons Committee of Public Accounts, 2008: 9). However, there are no clear performance indicators for what a 'creditable' performance means. Nonetheless, the first Mission 2012 report indicated prior to the Beijing Games that two sports, shooting and the Paralympic sport of goalball, had received the only overall 'red' lights. The Team GB shooting team failed to win any medals at Beijing, and after their funding was cut by some 78 per cent shooting could no longer afford to employ a Performance Director (*The Times*, 12 February 2009). Although several sports were provided with considerable increases in funding, the reduction in funding for shooting was also compounded by virtue of the fact that, in part due to the global economic downturn experienced in 2008 and 2009, UK Sport was not able to raise the hoped-for £100 million from the private sector. This was a risk reported by the House of Commons Public Accounts Committee even before the global financial downturn began to accelerate because it claimed that UK Sport did not have the 'skills or capacity to raise the £100 million from the private sector' (NAO, 2008: 6). The media reaction to the apparent shortfall in funding available to 'our Olympians' was considered by many to be a grave situation when 'we' are hosting the Games (e.g. *The Independent*, 2 December 2008). In view of the concerns expressed by many within the media and within sports organizations, the government has pledged to make up some of the shortfall to minimize the impact of this on other NGBs. The irony here is that the same British media that were initially scathing of the fact that costs for the Olympics were running so high were now demanding that the government act in light of this shortfall. It could be argued that an unintended consequence of hosting the Games is the higher level of scrutiny given by the media, amongst others, to sport policies in the build-up to them, which can further constrain the government, and NGBs, to be 'seen' to be doing something about a perceived problem relating to the Games. Furthermore, in light of the increased public funding that has become available to the various NDPBs with a sporting interest, the Sports Minister, James Purnell, called on Sport England to be more clearly focused on 'sport development and sports participation' (cited in House of Commons Culture, Media and Sport Committee, 2008: 49). The Culture Select Committee expressed disappointment that

> fifteen months after publication of our initial Report on preparations for the Games, no comprehensive plan for maximising participation in sport has been published. A draft strategy was drawn up and was subject to consultation; but the Central Council for Physical Recreation told us that it was 'simply a repackaging of existing Sport England commitments, within existing spending plans' and that it was in any case withdrawn ... There appears to be no shortage of activity in developing plans for participation. In fact, the profusion of commitments, promises and plans for using the potential of the Games to increase participation in sport being developed, whether real or rumoured, is bewildering; but none of what is proposed amounts to a single, comprehensive, nationwide strategy.
> (House of Commons Culture, Media and Sport Committee, 2008: 53–54)

When Sport England (2008a) eventually did publish its 'new' strategy in June 2008, which focused, in particular, on community sport, the strategy and goals for sport were strikingly similar to what preceded it, which amounted, in many respects, to little more than a restatement of previous policy statements. Nonetheless, the fact that the London Olympics were 'little over four years from now' was regarded as being 'an appropriate time [for the government] to take a clear look at the sport development system and its fitness for purpose' (Sport England, 2008a: 1). The proliferation of plans and policy statements that have been produced, most especially since the bid to host the Games was won, provide us with plentiful examples that the government, and related organizations, seems to suffer from what has been referred to as 'intiative-itis' regarding sport. That is to say, it is further illustration that the government seems to be more interested in take-offs and not landings (Coalter, 2007a).

Summary

There is much to be commended in some of the preparations taking place for London 2012, and especially the attempts being made to integrate into existing policy some of the new policy directives that are emerging as a direct result of the Games. This, together with the development of partnerships working with a variety of sports and non-sports organizations already involved in the delivery of similar policy goals and initiatives, is essential if progress towards the legacy ambitions is to be realized to any degree (Coalter, 2004). This is also a conclusion that was drawn by EdComs, a company commissioned by the DCMS in 2007 to assess the legacy potential for mega-events, who also argued that 'legacy strategies will need to be embedded in existing programmes and policy areas to achieve success in the long term and real benefits to participation provided' (EdComs, 2007: 9). In addition to these potential strengths, there are also tentative signs that those responsible for writing and implementing the London bid are learning from some of the mistakes made in the build-up to, and hosting of, previous Olympic Games. Cashman (2006: 165), for example, argued that 'the history of Sydney Olympic Park suggests the need for future Olympic cities to plan carefully beforehand for the post-Olympic outcomes of venues and precincts'. That there are already plans in place for a London Olympic Institute, utilizing most of the permanent facilities, suggests that some things have been learned from the Sydney Games. At the time of writing, however, debate regarding the post-Games use of the main Olympic Stadium is ongoing, and at present there is little concrete evidence to suggest that much thought has been given to ensuring that the stadium does not become a 'white elephant'. Although there are still plans to ensure that an athletics track remains at the venue and that its capacity will, in all likelihood, be downgraded from an 85,000 to a 25,000 capacity stadium, it is hoped that a professional football or rugby union club may use the venue, as was the case following the Manchester Commonwealth Games, when Manchester City Football Club took up residence. However, so far no sports club has pledged to do this.

Notwithstanding the attempts to integrate the Olympic-specific policy priorities into other existing policy, it is also clear from our above analysis that the general consensus amongst academics, at least, is that recent bids for the Olympic Games have been rather ambitious and unrealistic considering the lack of prevailing evidence and, as such, it is important that more 'caution needs to be exercised in accepting all that is claimed' (Vigor *et al.*, 2004: 3). As we noted earlier, the legacies that are expected to follow the Summer Olympic Games are very difficult to measure, and, if anything, the evidence suggests that these impacts 'are fleeting, at best, and as the years pass it becomes difficult to isolate the impacts of the mega-event on the fortunes and stature of a city from those of other economic triggers or from larger cycles of growth and recession' (Whitson and Horne, 2006: 86). On the basis of the available evidence, it is extremely unlikely that the London Games will be any different, especially because the legacy action plans that have been developed, and, in some cases, are now being implemented, are 'trying to achieve change that no other Olympic and Paralympic Games have delivered' (EdComs, 2007: 50). Indeed, even one of the government's own Select Committees, for example, has noted that 'doubts have already emerged, both about the cost of staging the Games and about whether a lasting benefit can be achieved' (House of Commons Culture, Media and Sport Committee, 2007: 3).

Not only can the potential benefits derived from the hosting of the Olympics be excessively exaggerated and risk huge cost overruns, it is inevitable that several unintended consequences will emerge from hosting the Games that may not always be seen as desirable by several of the groups involved (Gold and Gold, 2007a; Gratton *et al.*, 2006). As Gratton *et al.* point out, amongst the most obvious unintended consequences that frequently result from the hosting of mega-events such as the Olympic Games are:

high construction costs of sporting venues and related other investments, in particular in transport infrastructure; temporary congestion problems; displacement of other tourists due to the event; and underutilized elite sporting facilities after the event which are of little use to the local population.

(Gratton *et al.*, 2006: 42)

In addition to these issues, it is clear that, given the sheer size of the Games and the vast sums of money required to support their delivery, the government funds (especially National Lottery monies) allocated to other organizations, including charities and those responsible for sport, have already been reduced in some cases, as the cost of the Games continues to escalate (Coalter, 2007b). The House of Commons Culture, Media and Sport Committee has noted in this regard that

National Lottery distributors for the main 'good causes' – arts, charities, heritage and sport ... are already suffering a decrease in income because a significant part of Lottery funds are going towards financing the Games. A further call on the Lottery would deprive existing good causes of even more resources and threaten severe delay or damage to existing programmes.

(House of Commons Culture, Media and Sport Committee, 2007: 3)

The direct impact that this diversion of funds has had already on grassroots sport is made clear by Girginov and Hills (2008: 2096–97), who point out that, 'at the national level, the lottery funding was raided to help pay rising games costs to the tune of £65m, reducing funds for sports development. The diversion represented an 8% cut of Sport England's budget'. Sport England, of course, now has a specific responsibility for the development of community sport, and its ability to realize its community-sport objectives might be further compromised as growing emphasis comes to be placed on the need for UK Sport to sustain its funding of NGBs in the build-up to the Games. This, in turn, will inevitably come to impact on the capacity of NGBs, and especially those whose funding may be reduced by UK Sport's 'no compromise' strategy, to balance and support both their grassroots and elite sport priorities.

In relation to the expected regeneration benefits thought to be derived by those living in the Lower Lea Valley area, as Raco (2004: 37) argues, 'if the Olympic Games is to be judged as "successful" then the quality of life in such neighbourhoods needs to be significantly improved. In short, it needs to generate development of, not just development in, local areas'. At the moment, it is difficult to establish the extent to which hosting the Games may bring about these benefits for local residents. In this respect, it is not at all clear what, if any, plans are in place to ensure that the very people whom the regeneration of the area is supposed to benefit will not be adversely affected and what, for example, is in place to ensure that the area does not experience a process of gentrification that would make the new housing unaffordable for most of the current residents. As Preuss (2004: 80) argues, 'the people who are often seriously impacted by Olympic Games are those who are least able to form community groups and protect their own interests'. It is difficult to see, apart from the volunteer programmes in place to try and engage the current local community, how simply developing the area will actually 'address the causes of multiple deprivation in the area' (Vigor *et al.*, 2004: 28).

It is also not at all likely that the hoped-for economic gains through hosting the Games will be matched. There are certainly no guarantees that the money generated through tourism will yield significant gains, if any. Indeed, it is highly likely that, as Newman (2007: 256) argues, 'London is already the most visited city globally ... [and] the large numbers of visitors expected to attend the 2012 Games will replace other tourists who will avoid London during this period' (Newman, 2007: 256). It is also a distinct possibility that, as we explained earlier, various construction firms will increase the costs involved in constructing the infrastructure given the time constraints under which the ODA and the LOCOG are placed by virtue of the immoveable Games deadline. This is further compounded by the fact that hosts of the Games frequently try to ensure their events are more 'spectacular' than previous Games. As part of these broader constraints, it is not uncommon for commissioned designs for buildings to be overly ambitious, and that can contribute to already escalating costs. This has been a point of criticism regarding the design of the proposed Aquatics Centre for London, for example, which has already been scaled back from the original proposal, and even at the time of writing the final architectural design specification is sufficiently ambitious that only one firm bidder for the project was secured. The failure to develop a competitive and cost-effective design was criticized by the Culture Select Committee, who stated that 'the history of the Aquatics Centre shows a risible approach to cost control and that the Games organisers seem to be willing to spend money like water' (House of Commons Culture, Media and Sport Committee, 2008: 4). Such a criticism must, of course, be seen in the climate of rising costs generally, and in light of the current global economic climate. We have already mentioned how the Montreal Games took place against the backdrop of a global recession, and clearly the current economic situation is already having a significant impact on London. The potential threat of the organizers going beyond the already revised £9.325 billion budget will severely hamper them from sustaining their claim that the London 2012 Games will be an 'economic success story'. At the time of writing, it is clearly impossible to know when there will be an upturn in the global economic situation and when the current financial pressures that are being experienced will be relieved to some extent. However, what this serves to demonstrate is that, even with careful planning – although we are not saying that this bid has been carefully planned in this sense – it is impossible for policy-makers to control broader social processes that have contributed to the global recession.

Notwithstanding all of this, 'the reproach of Olympic opponents that funds could be used for more "sensible" projects than for the Games is not correct since the largest part of the funds would not come into the host city without the Games' (Preuss, 2004: 292). Therefore, it might be argued that the temptation to bid for the Games in view of the potential economic and cultural gains to be made is something of a double-bind for the local and national governments involved. The likely investment makes it, in some cases, the only realistic prospect for large-scale development to take place. On the other hand, however, as costs escalate, often simply to cover the logistical requirements of hosting such mega-events as the Olympic Games, the desired legacy outcomes tend to become more ambitious. We have already seen that the sheer logistical task of hosting the Games has contributed to increasing costs that, when heavily subsidized by public monies, need to be presented by the government to the voting public as contributing to the achievement of broader social, economic and even ecological goals. This situation is compounded by the growing relational complexity of an increasingly globalized economy, where international competition for jobs and capital investment has contributed further to seeing the Olympic Games as a potential 'panacea' for meeting the 'social and economic' priorities of government (Horne, 2007: 92).

As Andranovich *et al.* (2001: 113) argue, in the global competition for urban invest-ment 'a new and potentially high-risk strategy for stimulating local economic growth has emerged. This strategy, called the mega-event strategy, entails the quest for a high-profile event to serve as a stimulus to, and justification for, local development'. The measure-ment of Olympic legacies is, therefore, susceptible to 'political interpretation' (Malfas *et al.*, 2004: 209). In this respect, the phrase 'sustainable legacy' has become part of the Olympic discourse, but, as Vigor *et al.* (2004: 8) argue, '"sustainable legacy" is a slippery term subject to different interpretations and diverse perspectives as to what type of legacy is desirable or achievable'. In the case of London 2012 we have seen that, whilst several specific 'performance indicators' have been included in legacy plans relating to increasing participation in sport, for example, most aims are so general as to represent what, in the event, amounts to little more than a 'wish list' of outcomes from hosting the Games. As Gold and Gold (2007b: 46) have noted in relation to analyses of previous bids, there is 'a strong dose of wish fulfilment' in the projected legacy outcomes. The people writing the bids are, to put it bluntly, too involved to be able to see the wood for the trees. In other words, wishful thinking can be traced back to the individual and group ideological lean-ings of those involved. Of course, they are constrained, as the competition to host the Games becomes stronger, to offer more and more goals that are, in fact, likely to prove unattainable and may result in outcomes that no one has intended. To this end, it is clear that 'the winning of the competition is a distinct exercise from the actual budgeting for the event' (GLA, 2007a: 8), and those involved in bidding for cities often, perhaps quite deliberately, underestimate the cost whilst overestimating the potential achievement of the Games in bringing about desired social outcomes. The GLA (2007b: 15–16) has noted in a similar manner that 'enthusiasm, perhaps inspired by the powerful affective charge associated with the Olympic brand, can encourage an overestimation and presumption, in terms of specific socio-cultural outcomes ushered in by the "magic" of the Olympics'. The extent to which these outcomes can be achieved will, of course, be a matter of empirical investigation. But whether they are, in fact, achieved and the processes through which they are delivered will, at the very least, result from the intended and unintended out-comes of the differential power relationships that characterize the networks of inter-dependencies that constitute the global Olympic figuration. We consider, in fact, that a broad unintended consequence of the increasing competition to host the Games between cities and governments is a process of 'legacy gigantism', where each bidding city com-petes with the others to host an Olympic Games with the 'best legacies ever'.

Revision questions

1   Analyze the Olympic legacies that have emerged from previous Olympic Games.
2   Provide a sociological assessment of the developments that have been implemented so far to help deliver the legacy outcomes of the London 2012 Games.
3   Examine the impact that hosting the Games has had on domestic sport policy in a country of your choice.

Key readings

Preuss, H. (2004) *The Economics of Staging the Olympics: A Comparison of the Games 1972–2008*, Cheltenham: Edward Elgar.

Roche, M. (2000) *Mega-Events and Modernity: Olympics and Expos in the Growth of Global Culture*, London: Routledge.

Vigor, A., Mean, M. and Tims, C. (2004) (eds) *After the Gold Rush: A Sustainable Olympics for London*, London: IPPR and Demos.

Recommended websites

Games Monitor: Debunking Olympic Myths: www.gamesmonitor.org.uk
International Olympic Committee: www.olympic.org
Olympic Games and Paralympic Games: London 2012: www.london-2012.co.uk

References

Abbott, A. and Collins, D. (2002) 'A theoretical and empirical analysis of a "state of the art" talent identification model', *High Ability Studies*, 13: 157–78.

Adams, L. (2001) 'The role of health authorities in the promotion of health', in A. Scriven and J. Orme (eds) *Health Promotion: Professional Perspectives*, Basingstoke: Palgrave Macmillan.

Advisory Sports Council (ASC) (1965) *Terms of Reference of the Sports Council and Its Committees*, London: Advisory Sports Council.

Allender, S., Foster, C., Scarborough, P. and Rayner, M. (2007) 'The burden of physical activity-related ill health in the UK', *Journal of Epidemiology and Community Health*, 61: 344–48.

Andranovich, G., Burbank, M. and Heying, C. (2001) 'Olympic cities: lessons learned from mega-events politics', *Journal of Urban Affairs*, 23: 113–31.

Aranut, J. (2006) *Independent European Sport Review*, Nyon: UEFA.

Astrup, A. (2001) 'Healthy lifestyles in Europe: prevention of obesity and type II diabetes by diet and physical activity', *Public Health Nutrition*, 4: 499–515.

Atkinson, G., Mourato, S., Szymanski, S. and Ozdemiroglu, E. (2008) 'Are we willing to pay enough to "back the bid"? Valuing the intangible impacts of London's bid to host the 2012 summer Olympic Games', *Urban Studies*, 45: 419–44.

Audit Commission (1989) *Sport for Whom? Clarifying the Local Authority Role in Sport and Recreation*, London: HMSO.

—— (2009) *Tired of Hanging Around: Using Sport and Leisure Activities to Prevent Anti-Social Behaviour by Young People*, London: Audit Commission.

Australian Institute for Health and Welfare (AIHW) (2008) *Australia's Health 2008*, Canberra: AIHW.

Australian Sports Commission (ASC) (2008) 'ASC welcomes $12.6 million boost for high performance sport'. Available at: http://www.ausport.gov.au/supporting/news/funding_boost_for_high_performance_sport (accessed 13 December 2008).

Baade, R. and Matheson, V. (2002) 'Bidding for the Olympics: fool's gold', in C. Baros, M. Ibrahimo and S. Szymanski (eds) *Transatlantic Sport: The Comparative Economics of North America and European Sports*, Cheltenham: Edward Elgar.

Bailey, R. and Morley, D. (2006) 'Towards a model of talent development in physical education', *Sport, Education and Society*, 11: 211–30.

Bailey, R., Armour, K., Kirk, D., Jess, M., Pickup, I. and Sandford, R. (2009) 'The educational benefits claimed for physical education and school sport: an academic review', *Research Papers in Education*, 24: 1–27.

Baker, J., Horton, S., Robertson-Wilson, J. and Wall, M. (2003) 'Nurturing sports expertise: factors influencing the development of elite athlete [sic]', *Journal of Sports Science and Medicine*, 2: 1–9.

Barengo, N.C., Kastarinen, M., Lakka, T., Nissinen, A. and Tuomilehto, J. (2006) 'Different forms of physical activity and cardiovascular risk factors among 24–64-year-old men and women in Finland', *European Journal of Cardiovascular Prevention and Rehabilitation*, 13: 51–59.

BBC (2007) 'Olympic budget rises to £9.3 bn'. Available at: http://news.bbc.co.uk/1/hi/uk_politics/6453575.stm (accessed 21 September 2008).

Beamish, R. and Ritchie, I. (2006) *Fastest, Highest, Strongest: A Critique of High-Performance Sport*, London: Routledge.

Bergsgard, N., Houlihan, B., Mangset, P., Nødland, S. and Rommetvedt, H. (2007) *Sport Policy: A Comparative Analysis of Stability and Change*, Oxford: Elsevier.

Best, J. (2001) *Damned Lies and Statistics: Untangling Numbers from the Media, Politicians, and Activists*, Berkeley, CA: University of California Press.

Bloyce, D. (2004) 'Research is a messy process: a case-study of a figurational sociology approach to conventional issues in social science research methods', *Graduate Journal of Social Science*, 1: 144–76.

— (2008) '"Glorious rounders": the American baseball invasion of England in two world wars – unappealing American exceptionalism', *International Journal of the History of Sport*, 25: 387–405.

Bloyce, D. and Murphy, P. (2008) 'Baseball in England: a case of prolonged cultural resistance', *Journal of Historical Sociology*, 21: 120–42.

Bloyce, D., Smith, A., Mead, R. and Morris, J. (2008) '"Playing the game (plan)": a figurational analysis of organizational change in sports development in England', *European Sport Management Quarterly*, 8: 359–78.

Bompa, T.O. (1994) *Theory and Methodology of Training: The Key to Athletic Training*, Champaign, IL: Human Kinetics.

Boreham, C. and Riddoch, C. (2003) 'Physical activity through the lifespan', in J. McKenna and C. Riddoch (eds) *Perspectives on Health and Exercise*, Basingstoke: Palgrave Macmillan.

Bramham, P. (2008) 'Sports policy', in K. Hylton and P. Bramham (eds) *Sports Development: Policy, Process and Practice*, 2nd edn, London: Routledge.

Bramham, P. and Hylton, K. (2008) 'Introduction', in K. Hylton and P. Bramham (eds) *Sports Development: Policy, Process and Practice*, 2nd edn, London: Routledge.

British Medical Association (BMA) (2002) *Drugs in Sport: The Pressure to Perform*, London: BMJ Books.

Cabinet Office (2006) *Public Bodies: A Guide for Departments*, London: Cabinet Office. Available at: http://www.civilservice.gov.uk/about/public/bodies.asp (accessed 18 December 2008).

Carlisle City Council (2002) 'Draft community sports development strategy, LCD 3/02' Carlisle: Carlisle City Council

Cashman, R. (2006) *The Bitter-Sweet Awakening: The Legacy of the Sydney 2000 Olympic Games*, Sydney: Walla Walla Press.

Cavill, N., Foster, C., Oja, P. and Martin, B.W. (2006) 'An evidence-based approach to physical activity promotion and policy development in Europe: contrasting case studies', *Promotion and Education*, 13: 104–11.

Centers for Disease Control and Prevention (CDC) (2008) 'US physical activity statistics'. Available at: http://www.cdc.gov/nccdphp/dnpa/physical/stats/index.htm (accessed 17 July 2008).

Central Council for Physical Recreation (CCPR) (1960) *Sport and the Community*, London: CCPR.

— (2002) *Saving Lives, Saving Money: Physical Activity – the Best Buy in Public Health*, London: CCPR.

Chalip, L. (1995) 'Policy analysis in sport management', *Journal of Sport Management*, 9: 1–13.

Chalkley, B. and Essex, S. (1999) 'Urban development through hosting international events: a history of the Olympic Games', *Planning Perspectives*, 14: 369–94.

Chau, J., Smith, B., Bauman, A., Meron, D., Eyeson-Annan, M., Chey, T. and Farrell, L. (2008) 'Recent trends in physical activity in New South Wales: is the tide of physical inactivity turning?', *Australian and New Zealand Journal of Public Health*, 32: 82–85.

Chen, C.M. (2008) 'Overview of obesity in mainland China', *Obesity Reviews*, 9: 14–21.

Coaffee, J. (2007) 'Urban regeneration and renewal', in J. Gold and M. Gold (eds) *Olympic Cities. City Agendas, Planning and the World's Games, 1896–2012*, London: Routledge.

Coalter, F. (1989) *Sport and Anti-Social Behaviour: A Literature Review*, Edinburgh: Scottish Sports Council.

— (1999) 'Sport and recreation in the United Kingdom: flow with the flow or buck the trends?', *Managing Leisure*, 4: 24–39.

— (2001) *Realising the Potential of Cultural Services: The Case for Sport* London: Local Government Association.

— (2002) *Sport and Community Development: A Manual*, Edinburgh: Sportscotland.

— (2004) 'Stuck in the blocks? A sustainable sporting legacy', in A. Vigor, M. Mean and C. Tims (eds) *After the Gold Rush: A Sustainable Olympics for London*, London: IPPR and Demos.

— (2006) *Sport-in-Development: A Monitoring and Evaluation Manual*, London: UK Sport.

— (2007a) *A Wider Social Role for Sport: Who's Keeping the Score?*, London: Routledge.

— (2007b) 'London Olympics 2012: "the catalyst that inspires people to lead more active lives"?', *Perspectives in Public Health*, 127: 109–10.

— (2008) 'Sport-in-development: development for and through sport?', in M. Nicholson and R. Hoye (eds) *Sport and Social Capital*, Oxford: Butterworth-Heinemann.

Coalter, F., Allison, M. and Taylor, J. (2000) *The Role of Sport in Regenerating Deprived Urban Areas*, Edinburgh: Scottish Office Central Research Unit.

Coalter, F., Dowers, S. and Baxter, M. (1995) 'The impact of social class and education on sports participation: some evidence from the General Household Survey', in K. Roberts (ed.) *Leisure and Social Stratification*, Publication No. 53, Eastbourne: Leisure Studies Association.

Coghlan, J. (1990) *Sport and British Politics since 1960*, London: Falmer Press.

Cohen, S. (2002) *Folk Devils and Moral Panics*, 2nd edn, London: Routledge.

Collins, M. (2008) 'Public policies on sports development: can mass and elite sport hold together?', in V. Girginov (ed.) *Management of Sports Development*, Oxford: Butterworth-Heinemann.

Collins, M. and Kay, T. (2003) *Sport and Social Exclusion*, London: Routledge.

Collins, M., Henry, I., Houlihan, B. and Buller, J. (1999) *Sport and Social Inclusion: A Report to the Department of Culture, Media and Sport*, Loughborough: Loughborough University.

Commission for a Sustainable London 2012 (CSL 2012) (2007) *On Track for a Sustainable Legacy? Review of Governance Arrangements for the London 2012 Olympic Games and Paralympic Games Programme*, London: CSL.

— (2009) *Procuring a Legacy: A Review of the Olympic Delivery Authority's Procurement Specification, Management and Contract Administration: Delivery of Sustainability Objectives*, London: CSL.

Conrad, P. (1992) 'Medicalization and social control', *Annual Review of Sociology*, 18: 209–32.

Conroy, M., Cook, N., Manson, J., Buring, J. and Lee, I. (2005) 'Past physical activity, current physical activity, and risk of coronary heart disease', *Medicine and Science in Sports and Exercise*, 37: 1,251–56.

Crabbe, T. (2000) 'A sporting chance? Using sport to tackle drug use and crime', *Drugs: Education, Prevention and Policy*, 7: 381–91.

— (2008) 'Avoiding the numbers game: social theory, policy and sport's role in the art of relationship building', in M. Nicholson and R. Hoye (eds) *Sport and Social Capital*, Oxford: Butterworth-Heinemann.

Crawford, R. (1980) 'Healthism and the medicalization of everyday life', *International Journal of Health Services*, 10: 365–88.

Crookston, M. (2004) 'Making the Games work: a sustainable games for London', in A. Vigor, M. Mean and C. Tims (eds) *After the Gold Rush: A Sustainable Olympics for London*, London: IPPR and Demos.

Daly, M. (2007) 'EU social policy after Lisbon', *Journal of Common Market Studies*, 44: 461–81.

Darby, P., Akindes, G. and Kirwin, M. (2007) 'Football academies and the migration of African football labor to Europe', *Journal of Sport and Social Issues*, 31: 143–61.

Davis, G. and Dawson, N. (1996) *Using Diversion to Communicate Drugs Prevention Messages to Young People: An Examination of Six Projects*, Home Office Paper 12, London: Home Office.

De Bosscher, V., Bingham, J. Shibli, S., van Bottenburg, M. and De Knop, P. (2008) *The Global Sporting Arms Race. An International Comparative Study on Sports Policy Factors Leading to International Sporting Success*, Oxford: Meyer and Meyer.

De Knop, P. and De Martelaer, K. (2001) 'Quantitative and qualitative evaluation of youth sport in Flanders and the Netherlands', *Sport, Education and Society*, 6: 35–52.

De Knop, P., Wylleman, P., Theeboom, M., De Martelaer, K. and van Hoecke, J. (1998) 'Youth and organized sport in Flanders: past and future developments', *International Review for the Sociology of Sport*, 33: 299–304.

Department for Culture, Media and Sport (DCMS) (2000) *A Sporting Future for All*, London: DCMS.

— (2001) *Elite Sports Funding Review* (report of the Review Group, chaired by the Rt Hon. Dr Jack Cunningham MP), London: DCMS.

— (2006) 'United Kingdom Sports Institute'. Available at: http://www.culture.gov.uk/sport/uk_sports_institute/ (accessed 24 January 2006).

— (2007) *Our Promise for 2012: How the UK Will Benefit from the Olympic Games and Paralympic Games*, London: DCMS.

— (2008a) *Playing to Win: A New Era for Sport*, London: DCMS.

— (2008b) *Before, During and After: Making the Most of the London 2012 Games*, London: DCMS.

Department for Culture, Media and Sport (DCMS)/Strategy Unit (2002) *Game Plan: A Strategy for Delivering Government's Sport and Physical Activity Objectives*, London: DCMS/Strategy Unit.

Department for Education and Skills (DfES)/Department for Culture, Media and Sport (DCMS) (2003) *Learning through PE and Sport*, London: DfES/DCMS.

Department of the Environment (DoE) (1975) *Sport and Recreation*, London: HMSO.

Department of the Environment, Transport and the Regions (DETR) (1999) *Best Value and Audit Commission Performance Indicators for 2000/2001. Volume One: The Performance Indicators Including the Publication of Information Direction 1999 (England)*, London: DETR.

Department of Health (DH) (1992) *The Health of the Nation*, London: HMSO.

— (1999) *Saving Lives: Our Healthier Nation*, London: HMSO.

— (2000) *National Service Framework for Coronary Heart Disease*, London: DH.

— (2004a) *Choosing Health. Making Healthier Choices Easier*, London: HMSO.

— (2004b) *At Least Five a Week: Evidence on the Impact of Physical Activity and Its Relationship to Health. A Report from the Chief Medical Officer*, London: DH.

— (2005) *Choosing Activity: A Physical Activity Action Plan*, London: DH.

Department of Health (DH)/Department of Children, Schools and Families (DCSF) (2008) *Healthy Weight, Healthy Lives: A Cross-Governmental Strategy for England*, London: DH.

Department of Health (DH)/Department for Culture, Media and Sport (DCMS) (2004) *Choosing Health? Choosing Activity: A Consultation on How to Increase Physical Activity*, London: DH.

Department of National Heritage (DNH) (1995) *Sport: Raising the Game*, London: DNH.

Digby, B. (2008) 'This changing world: the London 2012 Olympics', *Geography*, 93: 41–47.

DIVERT Trust (1996) *Match of the Day*, London: The DIVERT Trust.

Dollman, J., Boshoff, K. and Dodd, G. (2006) 'The relationship between curriculum time for physical education and literacy and numeracy standards in South Australian primary schools', *European Physical Education Review*, 12: 151–63.

Dopson, S. (2005) The diffusion of medical innovations: can figurational sociology contribute?', *Organization Studies*, 26: 1125–44.

Dopson, S. and Waddington, I. (1996) 'Managing social change: a process-sociological approach to understanding change within the National Health Service', *Sociology of Health and Illness*, 18: 525–50.

Driver, S. and Martell, L. (2002) *Blair's Britain*, Cambridge: Polity Press.

Dugdill, L., Graham, R. and McNair, F. (2005) 'Exercise referral: the public health panacea for physical activity promotion? A critical perspective of exercise referral schemes; their development and evaluation', *Ergonomics*, 48: 1390–410.

Duncan, J., Schofield, G. and Duncan, E. (2006) 'Pedometer-determined physical activity and body composition in New Zealand children', *Medicine and Science in Sports and Exercise*, 38: 1,402–09.

Dunning, E. (1992) 'Figurational sociology and the sociology of sport: some concluding remarks', in E. Dunning and C. Rojek (eds) *Sport and Leisure in the Civilizing Process*, London: Macmillan.

— (1999) *Sport Matters: Sociological Studies of Sport, Violence and Civilization*, London: Routledge.

Dunning, E. and Waddington, I. (2003) 'Sport as a drug and drugs in sport: some exploratory comments', *International Review for the Sociology of Sport*, 38: 351–68.

Dunning, E., Malcolm, D. and Waddington, I. (eds) (2004) *Sport Histories: Figurational Studies in the Development of Modern Sports*, London: Routledge.

Eady, J. (1993) *Practical Sports Development*, London: Longman.

Earle, C. (2004) 'You've got me, now keep me! An introduction to the principles and practice of long term athlete development'. Available at: http://www.sportdevelopment.org.uk/earleltad.pdf (accessed 19 June 2008).

EdComs (2007) *London 2012 Legacy Research: Final Report*, London: DCMS.

Eiðsdóttir, S., Kristjánsson, Á., Sigfúsdóttir, I. and Allegrante, P. (2008) 'Trends in physical activity and participation in sports clubs among Icelandic adolescents', *European Journal of Public Health*, 18:289–93.

Elias, N. (1956) 'Problems of involvement and detachment', *British Journal of Sociology*, 7: 226–52.

— (1978) *What is Sociology?*, London: Hutchinson.

— (1987) *Involvement and Detachment*, Oxford: Blackwell.

— (2000) *The Civilizing Process*, Oxford: Blackwell.

— (2001) *The Society of Individuals*, New York: Continuum.

Elias, N. and Dunning, E. (1986) *Quest for Excitement*, Oxford: Blackwell.

Elias, N. and Scotson, J. (1994) *The Established and the Outsiders*, London: Sage.

Emler, N. (2001) *Self-Esteem: The Costs and Causes of Low Self-Worth*, York: Joseph Rowntree Foundation.

English Sports Council (ESC) (1996) *England: The Sporting Nation*, London: ESC.

— (1999) *Sports Development Planning*, London: ESC.

Essex, S. and Chalkley, B. (2004) 'Mega-sporting events in urban and regional policy: a history of the Winter Olympics', *Planning Perspectives*, 19: 201–32.

European Commission (EC) (2007) *White Paper on Sport*, Brussels: European Commission.

Evans, G. (2007) 'London 2012', in J. Gold and M. Gold (eds) *Olympic Cities: City Agendas, Planning and the World's Games, 1896–2012*, London: Routledge.

Evans, H. (1974) *Service to Sport: The Story of the CCPR: 1935–1972*, London: Pelham Books.

Falk, B., Lindor, R., Lander, Y. and Lang, B. (2004) 'Talent identification and early development of elite water-polo players: a 2-year follow-up study', *Journal of Sports Sciences*, 22: 347–55.

Feinstein, L., Bynner, J. and Duckworh, K. (2005) *Leisure Contexts in Adolescence and Their Effects on Adult Outcomes*, London: Centre for Research on the Wider Benefits of Learning.

Flintoff, A. (2003) 'The School Sport Co-ordinator Programme: changing the role of the physical education teacher?', *Sport, Education and Society*, 8: 231–50.

— (2007) 'Physical education and school sport', in K. Hylton and P. Bramham (eds) *Sports Development: Policy, Process and Practice*, 2nd edn, London: Routledge.

— (2008) 'Targeting Mr Average: participation, gender equity, and school sport partnerships', *Sport, Education and Society*, 13: 393–412.

Football Foundation (2008) *Kickz – Goals Thru Football. First Season Progress Report*, London: Football Foundation.

Foresight (2007) *Tackling Obesities: Future Choices – Project Report*, 2nd edn, London: The Stationery Office.

Fussenegger, D., Pietrobelli, A. and Widhalm, K. (2007) 'Childhood obesity: political developments in Europe and related perspectives for future action on prevention', *Obesity Reviews*, 9: 76–82.

Galemore, G.L. (2003) 'Sports legislation in the 108th Congress. CRS report for Congress. order code RS21479'. Available at: https://www.policyarchive.org/bitstream/handle/10207/3715/RS21479_20031208.pdf?sequence = 1 (accessed 23 July 2008).

Gard, M. and Wright, J. (2005) *The Obesity Epidemic: Science, Morality and Ideology*, London: Routledge.

Gardner, D., Hosking, J., Metcalf, B., Jeffery, A., Voss, L. and Wilkin, T. (2009) 'Contribution of early weight gain to childhood overweight and metabolic health: a longitudinal study (EarlyBird 36)', *Pediatrics*, 123: e67–e73.

Garman, S. (2007) 'Trends and transitions: the socio-political context of public health', in A. Scriven and S. Garman (eds) *Public Health: Social Context and Action*, Maidenhead: Open University Press/McGraw Hill Education.

Girginov, V. and Hills, L. (2008) 'A sustainable sports legacy: creating a link between the London Olympics and sports participation', *International Journal of the History of Sport*, 25: 2,091–116.

Godinho, J. (2005) 'Public health in the former Soviet Union', in A. Scriven and S. Garman (eds) *Promoting Health. Global Perspectives*, Basingstoke: Palgrave Macmillan.

Gold, J. and Gold, M. (2007a) 'Introduction', in J. Gold and M. Gold (eds) *Olympic Cities: City Agendas, Planning and the World's Games, 1896–2012*, London: Routledge.

— (2007b) 'Athens to Athens: the Summer Olympics, 1896–2004', in J. Gold and M. Gold (eds) *Olympic Cities: City Agendas, Planning and the World's Games, 1896–2012*, London: Routledge.

— (2008) 'Olympic cities: regeneration, city rebranding and changing urban agendas', *Geography Compass*, 2: 300–18.

Gold, M. (2007) 'Athens', in J. Gold and M. Gold (eds) *Olympic Cities: City Agendas, Planning and the World's Games, 1896–2012*, London: Routledge.

Goudsblom, J. (1977) *Sociology in the Balance*, Oxford: Blackwell.

Goudsblom, J. and Mennell, S. (1998) *The Norbert Elias Reader*, Oxford: Blackwell.

Gratton, C. (2004) 'Sport, health and economic benefit', in Sport England (ed.) *Driving up Participation: The Challenge for Sport*, London: Sport England.

Gratton, C. and Taylor, P. (2000) *Economics of Sport and Recreation*, London: Routledge.

Gratton, C., Shibli, S. and Coleman, R. (2005) 'Sport and economic regeneration in cities', *Urban Studies*, 42: 985–99.

— (2006) 'The economic impact of major sports events: a review of ten events in the UK', in J. Horne and W. Manzenreiter (eds) *Sports Mega-Events: Social Scientific Analyses of a Global Phenomenon*, Oxford: Blackwell.

Greater London Authority (GLA) (2007a) *A Lasting Legacy for London? Assessing the Legacy of the Olympic Games and Paralympic Games*, London: GLA.

— (2007b) *Five Legacy Commitments*, London: GLA.

— (2007c) *Your 2012*, London: GLA.

Green, C. (2008) 'Sport as an agent for social and personal change', in V. Girginov (ed.) *Management of Sports Development*, Oxford: Butterworth-Heinemann.

Green, K. (2008) *Understanding Physical Education*, London: Sage.

Green, K., Smith, A. and Roberts, K. (2005a) 'Young people and lifelong participation in sport and physical activity: a sociological perspective on contemporary physical education programmes in England and Wales', *Leisure Studies*, 24: 27–43.

— (2005b) 'Social class, sport, physical education and young people', in K. Green and K. Hardman (eds) *Physical Education: Essential Issues*, London: Sage.

Green, M. (2004) 'Changing policy priorities for sport in England: the emergence of elite sport development as a key policy concern', *Leisure Studies*, 23: 365–85.

— (2006) 'From "sport for all" to not about "sport" at all? Interrogating sport policy interventions in the United Kingdom', *European Sport Management Quarterly*, 6: 217–38.

— (2007a) 'Olympic glory or grassroots development? Sport policy priorities in Australia, Canada and the United Kingdom, 1960–2006', *International Journal of the History of Sport*, 24: 921–53.

— (2007b) 'Policy transfer, lesson drawing and perspectives on elite sport development systems', *International Journal of Sport Management and Marketing*, 2: 426–41.

— (2008) 'Non-governmental organisations in sports development', in V. Girginov (ed.) *Management of Sports Development*, Oxford: Butterworth-Heinemann.

Green, M. and Houlihan, B. (2004) 'Advocacy coalitions and elite sport policy change in Canada and the United Kingdom', *International Review of the Sociology of Sport*, 39: 387–403.

— (2005) *Elite Sport Development: Policy Learning and Political Priorities*, London: Routledge.

— (2006) 'Governmentality, modernisation and the "disciplining" of national sporting organisations: athletics in Australia and the United Kingdom', *Sociology of Sport Journal*, 23: 47–71.

— (2008) 'Conclusion', in B. Houlihan and M. Green (eds) *Comparative Elite Sport Development: Systems, Structures and Public Policy*, Oxford: Butterworth-Heinemann.

Green, M. and Oakley, B. (2001) 'Elite sport development systems and playing to win: uniformity and diversity in international approaches', *Leisure Studies*, 20: 247–67.

Grix, J. (2008) 'The decline of mass sport provision in the German Democratic Republic', *International Journal of the History of Sport*, 25: 406–20.

Hall, C.M. (2006) 'Urban entrepreneurship, corporate interests and sports mega-events: the thin policies of competitiveness within the hard outcomes of neoliberalism', in J. Horne and W. Manzenreiter (eds) *Sports Mega-Events: Social Scientific Analyses of a Global Phenomenon*, Oxford: Blackwell.

Hamlyn, P. and Hudson, Z. (2005) '2012 Olympics: who will survive?', *British Journal of Sports Medicine*, 39: 882–83.

Hanstad, D., Smith, A. and Waddington, I. (2008) 'The establishment of the World Anti-Doping Agency: a study of the management of organizational change and unplanned outcomes', *International Review for the Sociology of Sport*, 43: 249–71.

Hardman, A. and Stensel, D. (2009) *Physical Activity and Health: The Evidence Explained*, 2nd edn, London: Routledge.

Hartmann, D. (2001) 'Notes on midnight basketball and the cultural politics of recreation, race, and at-risk urban youth', *Journal of Sport and Social Issues*, 25: 39–71.

Hartmann, D. and Depro, B. (2006) 'Rethinking sports-based community crime prevention: a preliminary analysis of the relationship between midnight basketball and urban crime rates', *Journal of Sport and Social Issues*, 30: 180–96.

Haskell, W., Lee, I., Pate, R., Powell, K., Blair, S., Franklin, B., Macera, B., Heath, G., Thompson, P. and Bauman, A. (2007) 'Physical activity and public health: updated recommendation for adults from the American College of Sports Medicine and the American Heart Association', *Medicine and Science in Sports and Exercise*, 39: 1,423–34.

Haywood, L., Kew, F., Bramham, P., Spink, J., Capenhurst, J. and Henry, I. (1995) *Understanding Leisure*, 2nd edn, Cheltenham: Stanley Thornes.

Hearn, S., Martin, H., Signal, L. and Wise, M. (2005) 'Health promotion in Australia and New Zealand: the struggle for equity', in A. Scriven and S. Garman (eds) *Promoting Health. Global Perspectives*, Basingstoke: Palgrave Macmillan.

Henry, I. (2001) *The Politics of Leisure Policy*, 2nd edn, Basingstoke: Palgrave Macmillan.

Henry, I. and Bramham, P. (1993) 'Leisure policy in Britain', in P. Bramham, I. Henry, H. Mommaas and H. van der Poel (eds) *Leisure Policies in Europe*, Oxford: CAB International.

HMSO (2007) *PSA Delivery Agreement 22: Deliver a Successful Olympic Games and Paralympic Games with a Sustainable Legacy and Get More Children and Young People Taking Part in High Quality PE and Sport*, London: HMSO.

Hoberman, J. (1992) *Mortal Engines: The Science of Performance and the Dehumanization of Sport*, New York: The Free Press.

— (1993) 'Sport and ideology in the post-communist age', in L. Allison (ed.) *The Changing Politics of Sport*, Manchester: Manchester University Press.

Holt, R. (1989) *Sport and the British: A Modern History*, Oxford: Oxford University Press.

— (2005) 'Sport and recreation', in P. Addison and H. Jones (eds) *A Companion to Contemporary Britain: 1939–2000*, London: Blackwell.

Home Office (2003) *Cul-de-sacs and Gateways: Understanding the Positive Futures Approach*, London: Home Office.

Horne, J. (2007) 'The four "knowns" of sports mega-events', *Leisure Studies*, 26: 81–96.

Houlihan, B. (1991) *The Government and Politics of Sport*, London: Routledge.

— (1997) *Sport, Policy and Politics: A Comparative Analysis*, London: Routledge.

— (2000) 'Sporting excellence, schools and sports development: the politics of crowded policy spaces', *European Physical Education Review*, 6: 171–93.

— (2002) 'Political involvement in sport, physical education and recreation', in A. Laker (ed.) *The Sociology of Sport and Physical Education: An Introductory Reader*, London: Routledge Falmer.

— (2005) 'Theorising public sector sport policy-making', *International Review of the Sociology of Sport*, 40: 163–85.

— (2008) 'Sport and globalisation', in B. Houlihan (ed.) *Sport and Society: A Student Introduction*, 2nd edn, London: Sage.

Houlihan, B. and Green, M. (2006) 'The changing status of school sport and physical education: explaining policy change', *Sport, Education and Society*, 11: 73–92.

— (2008) 'Comparative elite sport development', in B. Houlihan and M. Green (eds) *Comparative Elite Sport Development: Systems, Structures and Public Policy*, Oxford: Butterworth-Heinemann.

Houlihan, B. and Lindsey, I. (2008) 'Networks and partnerships in sports development', in V. Girginov (ed.) *Management of Sports Development*, Oxford: Butterworth-Heinemann.

Houlihan, B. and White, A. (2002) *The Politics of Sports Development: Development of Sport or Development through Sport?*, London: Routledge.

Houlihan, B., Bloyce, D. and Smith, A. (2009) 'Editorial. Developing the research agenda in sport policy', *International Journal of Sport Policy*, 1: 1–12.

House of Commons Committee of Public Accounts (2008) *Preparing for Sporting Success at the London 2012 Olympic and Paralympic Games and Beyond: Forty-Second Report of Session 2007–08*, London: The Stationery Office.

House of Commons Culture, Media and Sport Committee (2007) *London 2012 Olympic Games and Paralympic Games: Funding and Legacy. Second Report of Session 2006–07*, London: The Stationery Office.

— (2008) *London 2012 Games: The Next Lap. Sixth Report of Session 2006–07*, London: The Stationery Office.

House of Commons Health Committee (2004) *Obesity: Third Report of Session 2003–04*, London: The Stationery Office.

Hoye, R. and Nicholson, M. (2008) 'Locating social capital in sport policy', in M. Nicholson and R. Hoye (eds) *Sport and Social Capital*, Oxford: Butterworth-Heinemann.

Hunt, T. (2007) 'Countering the Soviet threat in the Olympic medals race: the Amateur Sports Act of 1978 and American athletics policy reform', *International Journal of the History of Sport*, 24: 796–818.

Hunter, D. (2007) 'Public health: historical context and current agenda', in A. Scriven and S. Garman (eds) *Public Health: Social Context and Action*, Maidenhead: Open University Press/McGraw Hill Education.

Hylton, K. and Bramham, P. (eds) (2008) *Sports Developments: Policy, Process and Practice*, 2nd edn, London: Routledge.

Hylton, K. and Totten, M. (2008) 'Developing "sport for all"? Addressing inequality in sport', in K. Hylton and P. Bramham (eds) *Sports Development: Policy, Process and Practice*, 2nd edn, London: Routledge.

Institute of Youth Sport (IYS) (2008a) *The Impact of School Sport Partnerships on Pupil Attendance*, Loughborough: Institute of Youth Sport/Loughborough University.

— (2008b) *The Impact of School Sport Partnerships on Pupil Attainment*, Loughborough: Institute of Youth Sport/Loughborough University.

— (2008c) *The Impact of School Sport Partnerships on Pupil Behaviour*, Loughborough: Institute of Youth Sport/Loughborough University.

— (2008d) *School Sport Partnerships. Annual Monitoring and Evaluation Report for 2007: Partnership Development Manager Survey*, Loughborough: Institute of Youth Sport/Loughborough University.

— (2008e) *School Sport Partnerships. Annual Monitoring and Evaluation Report for 2007: School Sport Coordinator Survey*, Loughborough: Institute of Youth Sport/Loughborough University.

— (2008f) *School Sport Partnerships. Annual Monitoring and Evaluation Report for 2007: Primary Link Teacher Survey*, Loughborough: Institute of Youth Sport/Loughborough University.

International Olympic Committee (IOC) (2007) *Olympic Charter*, Lausanne: IOC.

Ireland, R. (2001) 'Promoting physical activity with local authorities', in A. Scriven and J. Orme (eds) *Health Promotion: Professional Perspectives*, 2nd edn, Basingstoke: Palgrave Macmillan.

Jackson, D. (2008) 'Developing sports practice', in K. Hylton and P. Bramham (eds) *Sports Development: Policy, Process and Practice*, 2nd edn, London: Routledge.

Ji, C. and Working Group on Obesity in China (WCOG) (2008) 'The prevalence of childhood overweight/obesity and the epidemic changes in 1985–2000 for Chinese school-age children and adolescents', *Obesity Reviews*, 9: 78–81.

Karpf, A. (1988) *Doctoring the Media: The Reporting of Health and Medicine*, London: Routledge.

Kasimati, E. (2003) 'Economic aspects and the Summer Olympics: a review of related research', *International Journal of Tourism Research*, 5: 433–44.

Kasimati, E. and Dawson, P. (2009) 'Assessing the impact of the 2004 Olympic Games on the Greek economy: a small macroeconometric model', *Economic Modelling*, 26: 139–46.

Katzmarzyk, P.T. and Janssen, I. (2004) 'The economic costs associated with physical inactivity and obesity in Canada: an update', *Canadian Journal of Applied Physiology*, 29: 90–115.

Keech, M. (2003) 'England and Wales', in J. Riordan and A. Kruger (eds) *European Cultures in Sport: Examining the Nations and Regions*, Bristol: Intellect.

Kim, D., Subramanian, S., Gortmaker, S. and Kawachi, I. (2006) 'US state- and county-level social capital in relation to obesity and physical inactivity: a multilevel, multivariable analysis', *Social Science and Medicine*, 63: 1,045–59.

Kirk, D. (1992) *Defining Physical Education: The Social Construction of a Post-War Subject*, London: Falmer Press.

— (2004) 'Framing quality physical education: the elite sport model or sport education?', *Physical Education and Sport Pedagogy*, 9: 185–95.

Kristèn, L., Patriksson, G. and Fridlund, B. (2003) 'Parents' conceptions of the influences of participation in a sports programme on their children and adolescents with physical disabilities', *European Physical Education Review*, 9: 23–41.

Krüger, A. (1999) 'Breeding, rearing and preparing the Aryan body: creating superman the Nazi way', in J.A. Mangan (ed.), *Shaping the Superman: Fascist Body as Political Icon – Aryan Fascism*, London: Frank Cass.

Laakso, L., Telama, R., Nupponen, H. and Pere, L. (2008) 'Trends in leisure time physical activity among young people in Finland, 1977–2007', *European Physical Education Review*, 14: 139–55.

Lee, I., Sesso, H., Oguma, Y. and Paffenbarger, R. (2003) 'Relative intensity of physical activity and risk of coronary heart disease', *Circulation: Journal of the American Heart Association*, 107: 1,110–16.

Lee Valley Regional Park Authority (2008) *Statement of Accounts for the Year Ended 31 March 2008*, London: Lee Valley Regional Park Authority.

Levitas, R. (2004) 'Let's hear it for humpty: social exclusion, the third way and cultural capital', *Cultural Trends*, 13: 41–56.

Lightsey, D., McQueen, D. and Anderson, L. (2005) 'Health promotion in the USA: building a science-based health promotion policy', in A. Scriven and S. Garman (eds) *Promoting Health: Global Perspectives*, Basingstoke: Palgrave Macmillan.

Liston, K., Reacher, D., Smith, A. and Waddington, I. (2006) 'Managing pain and injury in non-elite Rugby Union and Rugby League: a case study of players at a British university', *Sport in Society*, 9: 388–402.

Livingstone, M., Robson, P., Wallace, J. and McKinley, M. (2003) 'How active are we? Levels of routine physical activity in children and adults', *Proceedings of the Nutrition Society*, 62: 681–701.

LOCOG (2007a) *Everyone: London 2012 Annual Update*, London: LOCOG.

— (2007b) *Towards a One Planet 2012*, London: LOCOG.

— (2008) *Towards a One Planet 2012 Sustainability Plan Update*, London: LOCOG.

London 2012 (2004a) *London 2012: A Vision for the Olympic Games and Paralympic Games*, London: London 2012. Available at: http://www.london2012.com/documents/bid-publications/vision-for-olympic-games-and-paralympic-games.pdf (accessed 15 September 2008).

— (2004b) *London 2012 Candidate File*, London: London 2012. Available at: http://www.london2012.com/news/publications/candidate-file.php (accessed 12 September 2008).

London 2012 Nations and Regions Group (2004) *Backing the Bid: The UK's Games*, London: London 2012.

London Development Agency (LDA) (n.d.) 'Personal best programme'. Available at: http://www.lda.gov.uk/server/show/ConWebDoc.1954 (accessed on 13 January 2009)

Long, J. and Sanderson, I. (2001) 'The social benefits of sport: where's the proof?', in C. Gratton and I. Henry (eds) *Sport in the City*, London: Routledge.

Long, J., Welch, M., Bramham, P., Hylton, K., Butterfield, J. and Lloyd, E. (2002) *Count Me In: The Dimensions of Social Inclusion through Culture and Sport*, London: Department of Culture, Media and Sport.

McDermott, L. (2007) 'A governmental analysis of children "at risk" in a world of physical inactivity and obesity epidemics', *Sociology of Sport Journal*, 24: 302–24.

McDonald, I. (2005) 'Theorising partnerships: governance, communicative action and sport policy', *Journal of Social Policy*, 34: 579–600.

Macintosh, D. and Whitson, D. (1990) *The Game Planners: Transforming Canada's Sport System*, Montreal: McGill-Queen's University Press.

McKay, J. (1991) *No Pain, No Gain: Sport and Australian Culture*, Victoria: Prentice Hall.

MacPhail, A. and Kirk, D. (2006) 'Young people's socialisation into sport: experiencing the specialising phase', *Leisure Studies*, 25: 57–74.

Macrury, I. and Poynter, G. (2008) 'The regeneration Games: commodities, gifts and the economics of London 2012,' *International Journal of the History of Sport*, 25: 2,072–90.

Magdalinski, T. (2000) 'The reinvention of Australia for the Sydney 2000 Olympic Games', in J.A. Mangan and J. Nauright (eds) *Sport in Australasian Society: Past and Present*, London: Frank Cass.

Maguire, J. (1999) *Global Sport*, Cambridge: Polity Press.

Mahoney, J., Stattin, H. and Magnusson, D. (2001) 'Youth leisure activity participation and individual adjustment: the Swedish youth recreation center', *International Journal of Behavioral Development*, 25: 509–20.

Malcolm, D. (2008) 'A response to Vamplew and some comments on the relationship between sports historians and sociologists of sport', *Sport in History*, 28: 259–79.

Malfas, M., Theodoraki, E. and Houlihan, B. (2004) 'Impacts of the Olympic Games as mega-events', *Municipal Engineer*, 157: 209–20.

Mamen, A. and Aaberge, K. (2006) 'Leisure time physical activity among Norwegian youth', abstract presented at the 11th Annual Congress of the European College of Sport Science, 5–8 July, Lausanne: European College of Sport Science.

Martindale, R.J.J., Collins, D. and Abraham, A. (2007) 'Effective talent development: the elite coach perspective in UK sport', *Journal of Applied Sport Psychology*, 19: 187–206.

Mean, M., Vigor, A. and Tims, C. (2004) 'Conclusion: minding the gap', in A. Vigor, M. Mean and C. Tims (eds) *After the Gold Rush: A Sustainable Olympics for London*, London: IPPR and Demos.

Mennell, S. (1992) *Norbert Elias: An Introduction*, Oxford: Blackwell.

Merkel, U. (1995) 'The German government and the politics of sport and leisure in the 1990s: an interim report', in S. Fleming, M. Talbot and A. Tomlinson (eds) *Policy and Politics in Sport, Physical Education and Leisure*, Brighton: LSA.

Miettinen, S. (2006) 'The Independent European Sport Review: a critical overview', *International Sports Law Journal*, 3–4: 57–62.

Monclús, F.-J. (2007) 'Barcelona 1992', in J. Gold and M. Gold (eds) *Olympic Cities: City Agendas, Planning and the World's Games, 1896–2012*, London: Routledge.

Moreno, L., González-Gross, M., Kersting, M., Molnár, D., de Henauw, S., Beghin, L., Sjöström, M., Hagströmer, M., Manios, Y., Gilbert, C., Ortegall, F., Dallongeville, J., Arcella, D., Wärnberg, J., Hallberg, M., Fredriksson, H., Maes, L., Widhalm, K., Kafatos, A. and Marcos, A. (2007) 'Assessing, understanding and modifying nutritional status, eating habits and physical activity in European adolescents: the HELENA (Healthy Lifestyle in Europe by Nutrition in Adolescence) Study', *Public Health Nutrition*, 11: 288–99.

Morris, J., Heady, J., Raffle, P., Roberts, C. and Parks, J. (1953a) 'Coronary heart disease and physical activity of work', *The Lancet*, ii: 1,053–57.

— (1953b) 'Coronary heart disease and physical activity of work', *The Lancet*, ii: 1,111–20.

Morris, L., Sallybanks, J., Willis, K. and Makkai, T. (2003) *Sport, Physical Activity and Anti-Social Behaviour*, Research and Public Policy Series, 49, Canberra: Australian Institute of Criminology.

Murphy, N. and Bauman, A. (2007) 'Mass sporting and physical activity events: are they "bread and circuses" or public health interventions to increase population levels of physical activity?', *Journal of Physical Activity and Health*, 4: 193–202.

Murphy, P. (1998) 'Reflections on the policy process', MSc in the Sociology of Sport, Module 4, Unit 7, Part 15. Leicester: Centre for Research into Sport and Society.

Murphy, P. and Sheard, K. (2006) 'Boxing blind: unplanned processes in the development of modern boxing', *Sport in Society*, 9: 542–58.

Murphy, P., Sheard, K. and Waddington, I. (2000) 'Figurational sociology and its application to sport', in J. Coakley and E. Dunning (eds) *Handbook of Sports Studies*, London: Sage.

Murphy, P., Williams, J. and Dunning, E. (1990) *Football on Trial: Spectator Violence and Development in the Football World*, London: Routledge.

National Audit Office (NAO) (2007) *The Budget for the London 2012 Olympic and Paralympic Games*, London: HMSO.

— (2008) *Preparing for Sporting Success at the London 2012 Olympic and Paralympic Games and Beyond*, London: HMSO.

Nesti, M. (2001) 'Working in sports development', in K. Hylton, P. Bramham, D. Jackson and M. Nesti (eds) *Sports Development: Policy, Process and Practice*, London: Routledge.

Newman, P. (2007) '"Back the bid": the 2012 Summer Olympics and the governance of London', *Journal of Urban Affairs*, 29: 255–67.

Nichols, G. (1997) 'A consideration of why active participation in sport and leisure might reduce criminal behaviours', *Sport, Education and Society*, 2: 181–90.

— (2004) 'Crime and punishment and sports development', *Leisure Studies*, 23: 177–94.

— (2007) *Sport and Crime Reduction*, London: Routledge.

Nichols, G. and Taylor, P. (1996) *West Yorkshire Probation Service Sports Counselling Project Final Evaluation Report*, Sheffield: Sheffield University.

Nicholson, M. and Hoye, R. (eds) (2008) *Sport and Social Capital*, Oxford: Butterworth-Heinemann.

North West Development Agency (NWDA) (2004) *Commonwealth Games Benefits Study: Final Report*, Warrington: NWDA.

Oakley, B. and Green, M. (2001a) 'Still playing the game at arm's length? The selective re-investment in British sport, 1995–2000', *Managing Leisure*, 6: 74–94.

— (2001b) 'The production of Olympic champions: international perspectives on elite sport development system', *European Journal for Sport Management*, 8: 83–106.

Office for Standards in Education (Ofsted) (2004) *Provision for Gifted and Talented Pupils in Physical Education*, London: HMSO.

— (2005) *Specialist Schools: A Second Evaluation*. London: HMSO.

— (2006) *School Sport Partnerships: A Survey of Good Practice*, London: HMSO.

Olympic Delivery Authority (ODA) (2008) *All Change: London 2012 Accessible Transport Strategy for the London 2012 Olympic and Paralympic Games*, London: ODA.

Owen, J. (2008) 'Estimating the cost and benefit of hosting Olympic Games: what can Beijing expect from its 2008 Games', *Industrial Geographer*, 3: 1–18.

Paffenbarger, R. (2000) 'Physical exercise to reduce cardiovascular disease risk', *Proceedings of the Nutrition Society*, 59: 421–22.

ParticipACTION (n.d.) 'The inactivity crisis: facts and stats'. Available at: http://www.participaction. com/en-us/TheInactivityCrisis/FactsAndStats.aspx (accessed 12 January 2009).

Pawson, R. (2006) *Evidence-Based Policy: A Realist Perspective*, London: Sage.

Pederson, A., Rootman, I. and O'Neill, M. (2005) 'Health promotion in Canada: back to the past or towards a promising future?', in A. Scriven and S. Garman (eds) *Promoting Health: Global Perspectives*, Basingstoke: Palgrave Macmillan.

Penney, D. and Chandler, T. (2000) 'Physical education: what future(s)?', *Sport, Education and Society*, 5: 71–87.

Penney, D. and Evans, J. (1999) *Politics, Policy and Practice in Physical Education*, London: E & FN Spon.

Petry, K., Steinbach, D. and Burk, V. (2008) 'Germany', in B. Houlihan and M. Green (eds) *Comparative Elite Sport Development. Systems, Structures and Public Policy*, Oxford: Butterworth-Heinemann.

Pickup, D. (1996) *Not Another Messiah: An Account of the Sports Council 1988–93*, Durham: The Pentland Press.

Polley, M. (1998) *Moving the Goalposts: A History of Sport and Society since 1945*, London: Routledge.

Pollitt, C. (2003) 'Joined-up government: a survey', *Political Studies Review*, 1: 34–49.

President's Council on Physical Fitness and Sports (PCPFS) (2008) 'About the council'. Available at: http://www.fitness.gov/about/index.html (accessed 17 June 2008).

Preuss, H. (2004) *The Economics of Staging the Olympics: A Comparison of the Games 1972–2008*, Cheltenham: Edward Elgar.

— (2008) 'The Olympic Games: winners and losers', in B. Houlihan (ed.) *Sport and Society: A Student Introduction*, 2nd edn, London: Sage.

Public Health Agency of Canada (PHAC) (2003a) 'Our mission'. Available at: http://www.phac-aspc.gc. ca/pau-uap/fitness/about.html (accessed 21 June 2008).

— (2003b) 'Physical activity for health: the evidence'. Available at: http://www.phac-aspc.gc.ca/pau-uap/ fitness/evidence.html (accessed 21 July 2008).

Raco, M. (2004) 'Whose gold rush? The social legacy of a London Olympics', in A. Vigor, M. Mean and C. Tims (eds) *After the Gold Rush: A Sustainable Olympics for London*, London: IPPR and Demos.

Ramwell, A., Schostak, J., Pearce, C. and Brown, A. (2008) *Barclays Spaces for Sports: Developing People and Places through Sport*, Manchester: Manchester Metropolitan University.

Riddoch, C. and McKenna, J. (2005) 'Promoting physical activity within the community', in L. Cale and J. Harris (eds) *Exercise and Young People: Issues, Implications and Initiatives*, Basingstoke: Palgrave Macmillan.

Rigg, M. (1986) *Action Sport: An Evaluation*, London: Sports Council.

Riordan, J. (1986) 'The selection of top performers in East European sport', in G. Gleeson (ed.) *The Growing Child in Competitive Sport*, London: Hodder and Stoughton.

Riordan, J. and Cantelon, H. (2003) 'The Soviet Union and Eastern Europe', in J. Riordan and A. Kruger (eds) *European Cultures in Sport: Examining the Nations and Regions*, Intellect: Bristol.

Roberts, K. (1996a) 'Young people, schools, sport and government policy', *Sport, Education and Society*, 1: 47–57.

— (1996b) 'Youth cultures and sport: the success of school and community sport provisions in Britain', *European Physical Education Review*, 2: 105–15.

— (2004) *The Leisure Industries*, Basingstoke: Palgrave Macmillan.

— (2009) *Key Concepts in Sociology*, Basingstoke: Palgrave Macmillan.

Roberts, K. and Brodie, D. (1992) *Inner-City Sport: Who Plays and What Are the Benefits?*, Culemborg: Giordano Bruno.

Robins, D. (1990) *Sport as Prevention: The Role of Sport in Crime Prevention Programmes Aimed at Young People*, Occasional Paper Number 12, Centre for Criminological Research, Oxford: University of Oxford.

Robinson, L. (2004) *Managing Public Sport and Leisure Services*, London: Routledge.

Robson, K. and Feinstein, L. (2007) *Leisure Contexts in Adolescence and Their Associations with Adult Outcomes: A More Complete Picture*, London: Centre for Research on the Wider Benefits of Learning.

Robson, S. and McKenna, J. (2008) 'Sport and health', in K. Hylton and P. Bramham (eds) *Sports Development: Policy, Process and Practice*, 2nd edn, London: Routledge.

Roche, M. (2000) *Mega-Events and Modernity: Olympics and Expos in the Growth of Global Culture*, London: Routledge.

Roderick, M., Waddington, I. and Parker, G. (2000) 'Playing hurt: managing injuries in English professional football', *International Review for Sociology of Sport*, 35: 165–80.

Rowe, N. (2009) 'The Active People Survey: a catalyst for transforming evidence based decision-making in sports policy in England', *International Journal of Sport Policy*, 1: 89–98.

Rowe, N., Beasley, N. and Adams, R. (2004) 'Sport, physical activity and health: future prospects for improving the health of the nation', in Sport England (ed.) *Driving up Participation: The Challenge for Sport*, London: Sport England.

Samdal, O., Tynjälä, J., Roberts, C., Sallis, J., Villberg, J. and Wold, B. (2006) 'Trends in vigorous physical activity and TV watching of adolescents from 1986 to 2002 in seven European countries', *European Journal of Public Health*, 17: 242–48.

Sandford, R., Armour, K. and Warmington, P. (2006) 'Re-engaging disaffected youth through physical activity programmes', *British Educational Research Journal*, 32: 251–71.

Scheerder, J., Vanreusel, B., Taks, M. and Renson, R. (2005) 'Social stratification patterns in adolescents' active sports participation: a time trend analysis 1969–99', *European Physical Education Review*, 11, 5–28.

Schnor, P., Lange, P., Scharling, H. and Jensen, J.S. (2006) 'Long-term physical activity in leisure time and mortality from coronary heart disease, stroke, respiratory diseases, and cancer: the Copenhagen City Heart Study', *European Journal of Cardiovascular Prevention and Rehabilitation*, 13: 173–79.

Scriven, A. (2007) 'Healthy public policies: rhetoric or reality?', in A Scriven and S. Garman (eds) *Public Health: Social Context and Action*, Maidenhead: Open University Press/McGraw Hill Education.

Scriven, A. and Orme, J. (2001) 'Introduction', in A. Scriven and J. Orme (eds) *Health Promotion: Professional Perspectives*, Basingstoke: Palgrave Macmillan.

Seabra, A., Mendonça, D., Thomis, M., Malina, R. and Maia, J. (2007) 'Sports participation among Portuguese youth 10 to 18 years', *Journal of Physical Activity and Health*, 4: 370–80.

Searle, G. (2002) 'Uncertain legacy: Sydney's Olympic stadiums', *European Planning Studies*, 10: 845–60.

Sisjord, M.-L. and Skirstad, B. (1996) 'Norway', in P. De Knop, L.-M. Engstrom, B. Skirstad and M. Weiss (eds) *Worldwide Trends in Youth Sport*, Champaign, IL: Human Kinetics.

Skille, E. and Waddington, I. (2006) 'Alternative sport programmes and social inclusion in Norway', *European Physical Education Review*, 12: 251–71.

Slack, T. (1998) 'Studying the commercialization of sport: the need for critical analysis', *Sociology of Sport Online*, 1(1). Available at: http://www.physed.otago.ac.nz/sosol/v1i1/v1i1a6.htm (accessed 12 January 2008).

Smith, A. (2006) 'Young people, sport and leisure: a sociological study of youth lifestyles', unpublished PhD thesis, Liverpool, University of Liverpool.

Smith, A. and Green, K. (2005) 'The place of sport and physical activity in young people's lives and its implications for health: some sociological comments', *Journal of Youth Studies*, 8: 241–53.

Smith, A. and Platts, C. (2008) 'The Independent European Sport Review: some policy issues and problems', *Sport in Society*, 9, 583–97.

Smith, A. and Waddington, I. (2004) 'Using "sport in the community schemes" to tackle crime and drug use among young people: some policy issues and problems', *European Physical Education Review*, 10: 279–97.

Smith, A., Green, K. and Roberts, K. (2004) 'Sports participation and the "obesity/health crisis": reflections on the case of young people in England', *International Review for the Sociology of Sport*, 39: 457–64.

Smith, A., Leech, R. and Green, K. (2009) 'Evidence. What evidence? A study of the management of school sport partnerships in North-West England', unpublished paper, University of Chester.

Smith, A., Odhams, H., Platts, C. and Green, K. (2009) 'School sport partnerships in North-West England: a sociological study', unpublished paper, University of Chester.

Smith, D. (2003) 'A framework for understanding the training process leading to elite performance', *Sports Medicine*, 33: 1,103–26.

Snape, R. (2005) 'Steps to Health: an evaluation of a project to promote exercise and physical activity amongst Asian women in a post-industrial town in England', *Managing Leisure*, 10: 145–55.

Social Exclusion Unit (1998) *Bringing Britain Together*, London: Cabinet Office.

Sparvero, E., Chalip, L. and Green, B.C. (2008) 'United States', in B. Houlihan and M. Green (eds) *Comparative Elite Sport Development: Systems, Structures and Public Policy*, Oxford: Butterworth-Heinemann.

Spinks, A., Macpherson, A., Bain, C. and McClure, R. (2007) 'Compliance with the Australian national physical activity guidelines for children: relationship to overweight status', *Journal of Science and Medicine in Sport*, 10: 156–63.

Sport England (1999) *Best Value through Sport: Case Studies*, London: Sport England.

— (2000) *English Sports Summit*, London: Sport England.

— (2001) *Performance Measurement for the Development of Sport: A Good Practice Guide for Local Authorities*, London: Sport England.

— (2002) *Positive Futures: A Review of Impact and Good Practice*, London: Sport England.

— (2003) *Young People and Sport in England 1994–2002*, London: Sport England.

— (2005a) 'Everyday sport campaign goes national'. Available at: http://www.sportengland.org/ news/press_releases/everyday_sport_campaign_goes_national.htm (accessed 21 May 2008).

— (2005b) *Choosing Health: Physical Activity and Sport Playing Its Part in Delivering on the Health Agenda. A Resource for Strategic Health Authorities and Primary Care Trusts* (draft 4 discussion document), London: Sport England.

— (2006a) *Sport Playing Its Part: The Contribution of Sport to Healthier Communities*, London: Sport England.

— (2006b) *Sport Playing Its Part: Sport's Contribution to Building Strong, Safe and Sustainable Communities*, London: Sport England.

— (2006c) *Sport Playing Its Part: The Contribution of Sport to Meeting the Needs of Young People*, London: Sport England.

— (2006d) *Sport Playing Its Part. The Contribution of Sport to Economic Vitality and Workforce Development*, London: Sport England

— (2006e) *Physical Activity and Sport Playing Its Part in Choosing Health: A Resource Strategy for Strategic Health Authorities and Primary Care Trusts*, London: Sport England.

— (2007) *Active Design: Promoting Opportunities for Sport and Physical Activity Through Good Design*, London: Sport England.

— (2008a) *Sport England Strategy 2008–2011*, London: Sport England.

— (2008b) *Shaping Places through Sport: Building Communities. Developing Strong, Sustainable and Cohesive Communities through Sport*, London: Sport England.

— (2008c) *Shaping Places through Sport: Healthier Communities. Improving Health and Reducing Health Inequalities through Sport*, London: Sport England.

— (2008d) *Shaping Places through Sport: Transforming Lives. Improving the Life Chances and Focusing the Energies of Children and Young People through Sport*, London: Sport England.

— (2008e) *Shaping Places through Sport: Creating Safer Communities. Reducing Anti-Social Behaviour and Fear of Crime through Sport*, London: Sport England.

— (2008f) *Shaping Places through Sport: Increased Prosperity. Increasing Skills, Employment and Economic Prosperity through Sport*, London: Sport England.

Sports Council (1982) *Sport in the Community: The Next Ten Years*, London: Sports Council.
— (1988) *Sport in the Community. Into the 90's*, London: Sports Council.
— (1993) *Sport in the Nineties: New Horizons. Part 2: The Context*, London: Sports Council.
Sports Council for Wales (SCW) (2003) *Secondary Aged Children's Participation in Sport 2001*, Cardiff: SCW.
Sports Council Research Unit (1991) *National Demonstration Projects: Major Lessons and Issues for Sports Development*, London: Sports Council.
The Stationery Office (TSO) (2003) *Every Child Matters*, London: The Stationery Office.
— (2007) *The Children's Plan: Building Brighter Futures*, London: The Stationery Office.
Stewart, B., Nicholson, M., Smith, A. and Westerbeek, H. (2004) *Australian Sport: Better by Design? The Evolution of Australian Sport Policy*, London: Routledge.
Sui, X., LaMonte, M. and Blair, S. (2007) 'Cardiorespiratory fitness and risk of nonfatal cardio-vascular disease in women and men with hypertension', *American Journal of Hypertension*, 20: 608–15.
Tacon, R. (2007) 'Football and social inclusion: evaluating social policy', *Managing Leisure*, 12: 1–23.
Taylor, P., Crow, I., Irvine, D. and Nichols, G. (1999) *Demanding Physical Programmes for Young Offenders under Probation Supervision: Research Findings 91*, London: Home Office.
Telama, R., Laakso, L. and Yang, X. (1994) 'Physical activity and participation in sports of young people in Finland', *Scandinavian Journal of Medicine and Science in Sports*, 4: 65–74.
Telama, R., Nupponen, H. and Piéron, M. (2005) 'Physical activity among young people in the context of lifestyle', *European Physical Education Review*, 11: 115–39.
Telama, R., Naul, R., Nupponen, H., Rychtecky, A. and Vuolle, P. (2002) *Physical Fitness, Sporting Lifestyles and Olympic Ideals: Cross-Cultural Studies on Youth Sport in Europe*, Schorndorf: Hoffman.
Theodoraki, E. (1999) 'The making of the UK Sports Institute', *Managing Leisure*, 4: 187–200.
TNS (2007) *School Sport Survey 2006/07*, London: TNS.
— (2008) *School Sport Survey 2007/08*, London: TNS.
Tsuchiya, M. (1996) 'Leisure recreation programmes for young delinquents: the non-custodial option', in M. Collins (ed.) *Leisure in Industrial and Post-Industrial Societies*, Eastbourne: Leisure Studies Association.
UK Sport (2001) *Road to Athens: Annual Review 2001–02*, London: UK Sport.
— (2007a) 'UK Sport launches "Mission 2012"'. Available at: http://www.uksport.gov.uk/news/uk_sport_launches_mission_2012_/ (accessed 12 January 2009).
— (2007b) *Annual Review 2007*, London: UK Sport.
— (2008) 'Girls4Gold'. Available at: http://www.uksport.gov.uk/pages/girls4goldhome/ (accessed 18 November 2008)
United States Olympic Committee (USOC) (2008) 'US Olympic training sites'. Available at: http://teamusa.org/content/index/1276 (accessed 23 October 2008).
US Department of Health and Human Services (1996) *Physical Activity and Health: A Report of the Surgeon General*, Atlanta, GA: US Department of Health and Human Services, Centers for Disease Control and Prevention, National Center for Chronic Disease Prevention and Health Promotion.
— (2000) *Healthy People 2010: Understanding and Improving Health*, 2nd edn, Washington, DC: US Government Printing Office.
— (2001) *The Surgeon General's Call to Action to Prevent and Decrease Overweight and Obesity*, Washington, DC: US Government Printing Office.
van Bottenburg, M. (2001) *Global Games*, Chicago: University of Illinois Press.
van Krieken, R. (1998) *Norbert Elias*, London: Routledge.
Verow, P. (2006) 'Sports and occupational medicine: two sides of the same coin?', *Occupational Medicine*, 56: 224–25.
Vigor, A., Mean, M. and Tims, C. (2004) 'Introduction', in A. Vigor, M. Mean and C. Tims (eds) *After the Gold Rush: A Sustainable Olympics for London*, London: IPPR and Demos.

Vuori, I.M. (2001) 'Health benefits of physical activity with special reference to interaction with diet', *Public Health Nutrition*, 4: 517–28.

Waddington, I. (2000) *Sport, Health and Drugs: A Critical Sociological Perspective*, London: Routledge.

Waddington, I. and Malcolm, D. (2008) 'Eric Dunning: this sporting life', in D. Malcolm and I. Waddington (eds) *Matters of Sport. Essays in Honour of Eric Dunning*, London: Routledge.

Waddington, I. and Smith, A. (2009) *An Introduction to Drugs in Sport: Addicted to Winning?*, London: Routledge.

Waddington, I., Malcolm, D. and Green, K. (1997) 'Sport, health and physical education: a reconsideration', *European Physical Education Review*, 3: 165–82.

Wakefield, W. (2007) 'Out in the cold: sliding sports and the Amateur Sports Act of 1978', *International Journal of the History of Sport*, 24: 776–95.

Wang, W. and Theodoraki, E. (2007) 'Mass sport policy development in the Olympic City: the case of Qingdao – host to the 2008 sailing regatta', *Perspectives in Public Health*, 127: 125–32.

Wang, Y., Mi, J., Shan, X., Wang, Q. and Ge, K. (2007) 'Is China facing an obesity epidemic and the consequences? The trends in obesity and chronic disease in China', *International Journal of Obesity*, 31: 177–88.

Warburton, D., Nicol, C. and Bredin, S. (2006) 'Health benefits of physical activity: the evidence', *Canadian Medical Association Journal*, 174: 801–9.

Whitson, D. and Horne, J. (2006) 'Underestimated costs and overestimated benefits? Comparing the outcomes of sports mega-events in Canada and Japan', in J. Horne and W. Manzenreiter (eds) *Sports Mega-Events: Social Scientific Analyses of a Global Phenomenon*, Oxford: Blackwell.

Williams, J., Dunning, E. and Murphy, P. (1984) *Hooligans Abroad*, London: Routledge.

Witt, P. and Crompton, J. (1996) *Recreation Programs that Work for At-Risk Youth*, State College, PA: Venture Publishing.

World Health Organization (WHO) (2000) *Obesity: Preventing and Managing the Global Epidemic*, Geneva: WHO.

— (2003) *Health and Development through Physical Activity and Sport*, Geneva: WHO.

— (2004) *Global Strategy on Diet, Physical Activity and Health*, Geneva: WHO.

Wu, Y. (2006) 'Editorial: overweight and obesity in China', *British Medical Journal*, 333: 362–63.

Young, K., McTeer, W. and White, P. (1994) 'Body talk: male athletes reflect on sport, injury and pain', *Sociology of Sport Journal*, 11: 175–94.

Youth Sport Trust (YST) (2007) *Annual Report 2006/07*, Loughborough: Youth Sport Trust.

— (2008) 'Talent matters'. Available at: http://gifted.youthsporttrust.org/page/welcome/index.html (accessed 20 November 2008).

Ziglio, E., Hagard, S. and Brown, C. (2005) 'Health promotion development in Europe: barriers and new opportunities', in A. Scriven and S. Garman (eds) *Promoting Health: Global Perspectives*, Basingstoke: Palgrave Macmillan.

Index